What Readers Are Saying About *Windows Management Instrumentat*

"This book is *very* good. It's very practical, hands-on, and detail-oriented. The descriptions and hints are well written, and they flow well. System administrators and programmers will find this book invaluable. The chapter on security is a real gem—I've worked with WMI quite a bit, yet that chapter taught me things that I didn't even realize I didn't know. I definitely recommend this book."

–L.J. Johnson, Microsoft MVP (Visual Basic)

"WMI scripting is complex and the documentation from Microsoft has been scanty. Figuring out how to perform simple tasks can take hours of trial and error. I've been waiting for someone who is both a system administrator and a knowledgeable coder to put together a comprehensive reference. Matthew Lavy and Ashley Meggitt have done just that. The authors show over and over that they understand the kind of information administrators need from WMI. The examples are thoughtfully organized and clearly stated. Every major topic has a sample script and every sample script I tried worked. The book explains very clearly how event consumers work and how to set up scripts for both synchronous and asynchronous consumers. This is *must have* information. The coverage of CIM Studio and the Object Browser are excellent. WMI script syntax can be very tricky. The authors point out potential pitfalls and are careful to show how to avoid them. The writing style throughout the book sets it apart from other books in its class. This is not a developer's tone. It's a practical reference that I've already used in a dozen ways to improve my scripts. WMI is a critical feature in modern Windows. This book is the key to figuring out how to use WMI to deliver useful information and solve real-world problems. Highly recommended."

–Bill Boswell, best-selling author of Inside Windows 2000 Server

"WMI is the remote management facility of choice for Windows 2000/XP because of its power and vendor-neutrality. But the price of this power is the complexity of writing WMI code to exploit it. This book makes sense of WMI's unique syntax and object model in a liberating way: yYou realize, after reading it, that WMI is not so complex after all. The example scripts are useful from the get-go, and the authors don't gloss over details when the going gets tough. This book is definitely not just a repackaging of Microsoft MSDN articles."

–Jason Fossen, The SANS Institute (System Administration, Networking, and Security)

"This book really shows the potential scriptability of Windows 2000 and goes against the grain of more point-and-click types of books. Any competent NT administrator will be able to use the information in this book to develop home-grown tools for their day-to-day work. The book is also suited for programmers and utility developers looking for a great guide to WMI. The book is script-based and therefore entirely focused on solutions – not screen-shots. I would recommend that any administrator bringing up a Windows 2000 environment have a copy of this book. It helps to expose the underlying organization of Windows 2000 administration while providing the foundation for creating custom tools to streamline a network of windows machines."

–Tim Ritchey, Vice President of Product Development, Telena Communications

Windows Management Instrumentation (WMI)

Contents At A Glance

Windows Management Instrumentation (WMI)

Matthew M. Lavy, Ashley J. Meggitt

www.newriders.com

201 West 103rd Street, Indianapolis, Indiana 46290
An Imprint of Pearson Education
Boston • Indianapolis • London • Munich • New York • San Francisco

Windows Management Instrumentation (WMI)

FIRST EDITION: September, 2001

International Standard Book Number: 1-57870-260-7

Library of Congress Catalog Card Number: 00-110881

Printed in the United States of America

First Printing:

06 05 04 03 02 7 6 5 4 3 2 1

Interpretation of the printing code: The rightmost double-digit number is the year of the book's printing; the rightmost single-digit number is the number of the book's printing. For example, the printing code 02-1 shows that the first printing of the book occurred in 2002.

Printed in the United States of America

Trademarks

Warning and Disclaimer

Publisher
David Dwyer

Associate Publisher
Al Valvano

Executive Editor
Stephanie Wall

Managing Editor
Kristy Knoop

Acquisitions Editor
Jeff Riley

Development Editor
Grant Munroe

Product Marketing Manager
Stephanie Layton

Publicity Manager
Susan Nixon

Project Editor
Todd Zellers

Copy Editors
Keith Cline
Gayle Johnson

Indexer
Chris Morris

Manufacturing Coordinator
Jim Conway

Book Designer
Louisa Klucznik

Cover Designer
Aren Howell

Proofreader
Sossity Smith

Composition
Barb Kordesh

❖

From Matthew:
Toucani eisdemque

From Ashley:
To my family, friends, and L.K. Beaver

❖

Table of Contents

About the Authors

Matthew Lavy, MA MPhil ARCM LTCL, is the Technical Systems Developer at Jesus College, Cambridge University. His main responsibilities are developing solutions for UNIX/NT systems integration, running the email systems, and providing technical support to Windows 2000 system administrators. He has been both an author and technical reviewer for the O'Reilly Windows NT series, and is a member of the Cambridge University Windows 2000 Technical Strategy Group. Outside of working hours, his main interest is music psychology: He is in the process of completing a Ph.D. modeling emotional response to music. Matthew has been writing scripting solutions for system administration ever since he started working in IT and has been playing with WMI since he first set eyes on a Windows 2000 beta release.

Ashley Meggitt, MSc, is the IT Manager for Jesus College, Cambridge University, responsible for the management of the IT department and for formulating the college's long-term IT strategy. He is the co-author of two books on Windows NT system administration, both published by O'Reilly, for whom he has also acted as a technical reviewer. He sits on several Cambridge University technical committees, including the Windows 2000 Technical Strategy Group. He has always maintained an interest in the technical as well as managerial aspects of IT, having started off his working life as a database programmer.

About the Technical Editors

These reviewers contributed their considerable hands-on expertise to the entire development process for *Windows Management Instrumentation (WMI)*. As the book was being written, these dedicated professionals reviewed all the material for technical content, organization, and flow. Their feedback was critical to ensuring that *Windows Management Instrumentation (WMI)* fits our reader's need for the highest quality technical information.

Andrew Schafer is a solution development consultant for Avanade, Inc., based out of the New York development center. He has been programming for more than 14 years, if you include work done before being old enough to legally drive a car. Before working for Avanade, he served as a technical lead for a high-traffic Internet company, and before that as an independent consultant. He graduated with a degree in computer engineering from Purdue University in 1997.

David Sundberg earned his bachelor of science degree in computer science from Oregon State University in December 2000. He has worked in the computer industry for more than four years as a system administrator, network administrator, programmer, and support consultant. David has worked extensively with both Windows NT and Windows 2000.

Jon Boggs is an MCSE, MCSD, MCDBA, and CNE. He is a consultant in the Chicago area, and has provided consulting services to a number of nationally known corporations. He is an expert at automating administrative tasks and system deployments, typically employing a mix of Windows NT/2000, SMS, and Visual Basic/VBScript. Jon co-authored *Planning for Windows 2000* and *Windows 2000 Essential Reference*, and has served as a technical reviewer on several BackOffice-related books. He enjoys reading and biking in his spare time.

Acknowledgments

Writing this book has taken a significant amount of time, much of which we could not have devoted had it not been for the patience and tolerance of our respective families, friends, and colleagues. Together, we want to thank our colleagues at the Jesus College IT Department (Adrian Asher, Alison Campbell, Donato Colella, Robert Spragg, and Charlie Moore); and the staff at the Centre for Jewish-Christian Relations at the University of Cambridge (for whom we work on Wednesday mornings), who have kept their support queries to a minimum while we have been writing. We also want to thank the team at New Riders, particularly Jeff Riley and Grant Munroe, for their constant advice, support, and encouragement. We also are extremely grateful to our three technical editors, Andrew Schafer, Jon Boggs, and David Sundberg, for their thorough reading of the draft chapters and their helpful comments and suggestions that have made this a much better book than it would otherwise have been.

From Matthew: Matthew wants to thank his family for continued and quite undeserved support, particularly his sister Philippa who this year has had the dubious pleasure of sharing a house with him. He also wants to thank a number of friends who have not forgotten his existence despite his recent lack of social life caused by the combined effort of writing this book and a Ph.D. thesis. He also is grateful to his Ph.D. supervisor, Dr. Ian Cross, for being reasonably understanding at those few moments when book took priority over thesis!

From Ashley: Ashley wants to thank the following, mostly for their derision but also for their occasional encouragement: Nick Court, Sandra Last, Sue Lightfoot, Karen Roberts, Melissa Franklin, Kinky Friedman, Justin Meggitt, Melanie Wright, Deborah and Bruce Emerson, Paulette Catherwood, John Willis, Frank Zappa, and Brenda and Bernard Meggitt. Last but not least, he wants to thank his wife Jane, and children Ben and Lucie. The following deserves none of Ashley's thanks at all: John Darlington.

Tell Us What You Think

As the reader of this book, you are the most important critic and commentator. We value your opinion and want to know what we're doing right, what we could do better, what areas you would like to see us publish in, and any other words of wisdom you're willing to pass our way.

As Executive Editor for the Web Development team at New Riders Publishing, I welcome your comments. You can fax, email, or write me directly to let me know what you did or didn't like about this book[md]as well as what we can do to make our books stronger.

Please note that I cannot help you with technical problems related to the topic of this book, and that due to the high volume of mail I receive, I might not be able to reply to every message.

When you write, please be sure to include this book's title and author as well as your name and phone or fax number. I will carefully review your comments and share them with the author and editors who worked on t he book.

Fax: 317-581-4663

Email: stephanie.wall@newriders.com

Mail: Stephanie Wall
Executive Editor
New Riders Publishing
201 West 103rd Street
Indianapolis, IN 46290 USA

Introduction

A central component of Windows 2000 is Windows Management Instrumentation, a technology designed to provide a unified programming interface for querying and controlling the diverse range of devices and subsystems that constitute a Windows-based computer. Sitting somewhere between the complex web of APIs that programmers typically use to write Windows applications and the high-level graphical and command-line interfaces with which we are all familiar, *Windows Management Instrumentation (WMI)* provides a relatively simple and consistent "object-based" representation of a computer system that can be accessed easily from almost any modern programming language. Furthermore, the WMI "objects" exposed by a computer can be queried and controlled from a remote computer; a program that uses WMI can operate on a fleet of remote computers virtually as easily as on the machine on which it is running.

WMI is an exciting development for system administrators for two reasons. First, it makes life much easier for software developers writing management applications, which means that we should expect a range of excellent ones to arrive on the market very soon! Second, and more importantly for this book, virtually every facility that WMI makes available to programmers is directly accessible through a scripting interface. The significance of this is profound: The ability to achieve fine-grained control over a set of Windows-based computers, once the preserve of only experienced programmers, is now available to anyone who is prepared to learn a simple scripting language. In conjunction with a scripting language such as VBScript, WMI brings the efficiency and power of sophisticated automated management within the reach of everyone.

This book is a tutorial on WMI and its applications in Windows 2000 administration. It aims to arm the system administrators with all the knowledge they need to use the power of WMI, in conjunction with VBScript, to build sophisticated system administration solutions. WMI is a complex infrastructure whose applications in system management are almost limitless. Likewise, the management needs of a system administrator can vary radically from organization to organization. Therefore, the book tries to make as few assumptions as possible about the management problems that any particular system administrator might face. It avoids prescriptive solutions to particular problems. Instead, the focus is on imparting the general knowledge and understanding required to harness the power of WMI to solve specific problems as and when they occur. The book does provide fully working real-world scripting examples, and we hope that many of them prove useful in many situations. The real emphasis is not on the examples themselves, however, but on what they can tell us about the way WMI works. This book, like WMI itself, is about flexibility.

Who Should Read This Book

This book is primarily aimed at system administrators who are responsible for maintaining large numbers of Windows 2000 machines, who are frustrated with the limitations of the standard GUI tools, and who are tempted by the idea of overcoming these limitations with scripting and WMI. If your workday dream is to sit drinking coffee while all the routine workstation maintenance tasks are carried out automatically by a fleet of scripts, or to leave the server room sure in the knowledge that if ever a problem should occur on any critical server, you would be notified instantly by email, then this book is for you!

In terms of style and approach, this book is aimed at people who want to understand WMI to the extent that they can use it comfortably to write management scripts. Our ideal readers are people who want practical examples, but also want to know how things work under the hood, and who are sometimes happy using recipes but also like to understand enough to be able to make up new ones themselves. We make no assumptions about readers' prior knowledge of scripting.

Who This Book Is Not For

This book is not intended for people who are looking for just a quick theoretical overview of the topic. Such readers will probably be annoyed by the frequent practical script examples. Likewise, those who just wants a recipe book full of management scripts and who do not care how they work will be irritated by having to read the sometimes lengthy explanations about how and why scripts are written as they are.

This book assumes a good working knowledge of the Windows 2000 platform. Therefore, it is probably not the best starting point for someone looking for an introduction to Windows 2000 administration. Because it is aimed primarily at system administrators, it does not provide sufficient information for application developers or hardware-driver writers wanting to write C/C++ code that interacts with WMI. Such developers might find some parts of the book (notably Chapters 1, 5, 8, and 11) a useful starting point for introducing you to core WMI concepts and architecture, but will also need to look elsewhere.

Overview

The book is structured as a tutorial. It consists of 11 chapters, each of which focuses on a particular aspect of WMI or a supporting technology. Every time a new concept is introduced, it is accompanied both by a thorough theoretical discussion and by real-world practical usage suggestions. In addition, every chapter contains examples of fully fledged scripts that perform useful system administration functions. At the outset, the reader is assumed to have no prior knowledge of WMI. All concepts presented in the first few chapters are considered in detail, and every line of the script examples is fully explained. Later chapters assume familiarity with earlier material. Only new concepts are explained in detail, and script examples become increasingly sophisticated and more sparsely documented. Owing to the tutorial nature of the book, we recommend that chapters be read in the order in which they appear. However, it is only really necessary to read the first five chapters in this way; Chapters 6 to 11 are more independent of each other and can safely be read in any order.

Chapter 1, "Introduction to WMI," introduces the concepts and terminology required to understand and use WMI. It presents a brief history of the political and technical forces behind WMI's conception, a structural overview of the WMI architecture, and a discussion of the technologies upon which it is based.

A prerequisite for really making use of WMI in a system administration context is familiarity with a scripting language. Therefore, Chapter 2, "Using VBScript," provides a tutorial on VBScript, an easily learnable yet reasonably powerful language that comes as a standard part of Windows 2000. The chapter focuses on elements of VBScript that are needed to write effective system administration scripts. It assumes no prior knowledge of programming. If you are already a VBScript programmer, you can safely skip straight on to Chapter 3.

Our real WMI journey begins with Chapter 3, "Examining the Filesystem with WMI." On one level, this chapter is just a description of the Windows filesystem as seen from a WMI perspective. It shows how WMI represents files and directories, and demonstrates the writing of VBScript scripts that use WMI to manipulate and gather information about them. More importantly, however, the chapter is a practical introduction to the fundamentals of WMI's model of a computer system. It illustrates how WMI objects map on to underlying system components, and explains how to write scripts that can interrogate and command these objects to manipulate and gather information from the components that they represent. Finally, it explains how WMI objects are related to each other and shows how to write scripts that can navigate through parts of the WMI world.

Chapter 4, "Remote Administration," introduces one of the most exciting features of WMI from the perspective of a system administrator, namely the ability to interrogate and control Windows machines remotely. It explains how a script can connect to the WMI service of a remote computer and perform operations as if running locally. In addition, it suggests scripting techniques that enable batch operations to be carried out on an entire fleet of computers and introduces VBScript error handling.

The ability to control machines remotely brings with it a number of security concerns. These are addressed by WMI's three-layer security model, the subject of Chapter 5, "WMI Security." The chapter opens with a general overview of WMI security, covering everything that a system administrator needs to know to run management scripts securely and to overcome the limitations that WMI security imposes on their operation. Finally, the chapter turns to the representation of NTFS security within WMI. It presents sophisticated examples of scripts that manipulate security descriptors, units that lie at the very heart of Windows 2000 security.

The first five chapters introduce a large number of concepts, many of which are likely to be new to many readers. In Chapter 6, "Logs and Reports," and Chapter 7, "System Administration," therefore, we take a break from the onslaught and pause to explore how the knowledge gleaned from the previous chapters can be used to write scripts that carry out a range of system administration tasks. Chapter 6 concentrates on reporting, presenting scripts that search and archive Event Logs and interrogate the Windows Installer service for information about installed applications. In Chapter 7 the focus shifts to configuration, demonstrating how WMI and VBScript can be used to modify network settings, configure services, and write to the Registry.

WMI is more than an interface to machine management. Thanks to the WMI event model, it also can constantly monitor a system for signs of trouble and take automatic action when required. This sophisticated topic is covered in Chapter 8, "Proactive Troubleshooting with WMI Events," which explains how the various components of the event model fit together and demonstrates their use in proactive trouble-prevention scenarios.

No book on any aspect of Windows 2000 administration could possibly be complete without mentioning the Active Directory! Chapter 9, "WMI and Active Directory," explains the relationship between Active Directory and WMI. It shows how information stored within the Active Directory can be used to retrieve WMI objects representing computers on which a script should operate.

In Chapter 10, "Script Development and Deployment," the focus moves temporarily away from WMI itself and turns instead to scripting.

It suggests techniques for maintaining libraries of commonly used script functions, and introduces some tools that can help the process of debugging complex scripts. It also considers deployment, and illustrates various ways in which a set of disparate scripts can be consolidated into a coherent management environment.

Finally, in Chapter 11, "WMI Internals," we discuss some of the more technical aspects of WMI, such as some of the more obscure functions of the scripting interface, MOF (the language used to define new WMI classes), and the so-called WMI system properties. None of the material covered in this chapter is essential reading for a system administrator just wanting to write management scripts with WMI. Anyone who takes the time to learn a little more about these WMI internals, however, will find occasions when this knowledge will help solve certain problems or in writing slightly cleverer, more sophisticated scripts.

Although this book focuses exclusively on Windows 2000, WMI is available for other Microsoft platforms as well. Appendix A, "WMI on Other Microsoft Platforms," explains the installation and configuration process on non-Windows 2000 platforms and briefly discusses usage limitations.

Appendix B, "Accessing WMI from Other Languages," demonstrates the use of WMI from languages other than VBScript. It gives examples of two scripts translated into JScript, VB, and Perl. Finally, it provides brief notes for C/C++ programmers wanting to access WMI.

1

Introduction to WMI

Managing a Windows-based network should be a system administrator's dream: The Windows 2000 operating system is highly configurable; the domain-based security model, although it isn't exactly the most flexible in the world, is simple and ample for most environments; and the logging and auditing facilities provide a wealth of management data. Nothing should ever go wrong—or, if it does, at least it should be easy to diagnose and fix.

Unfortunately, anyone who has ever been responsible for a Windows-based network knows that the picture painted here is far from accurate: Far too often, administration can be a challenge; at its worst, it can be a dark, miserable nightmare. The problem is that information on configuration and management tends to hover strangely out of reach, first because data relating to different parts of a system is stored in disparate locations, and second because revealing each location's secrets requires the use of a different set of obtuse and proprietary tools. Here are a few examples: User information is stored in the SAM and is accessed with the User Manager program or by scripted access to the Network API. System policies are stored in .pol files and are accessed with the System Policy Editor. Logging information is stored in the Event Logs and is accessed using the Event Log API—either directly through a programming language or via a tool such as the Event Viewer. Additionally, information about any installed software and the operating system is stored in the Registry and is accessed through tools such as Regedit or Regedt32, or through a programming language using the Registry API.

With such a profusion of data repositories and tools for accessing them, it is remarkable that administrators ever manage to tame the gargantuan beast that is a Windows-based network! Even ignoring the difficulties associated with becoming an expert on so many systems and tools, this situation is ridiculous. Frequently, a domain-wide problem involves complex interactions between different components, such as a conflict between a workstation-based Registry and server-based policies. Yet no single tool can be used to observe a Registry and system policy together, let alone the effect of their interactions. This often makes finding a solution a time-consuming process that even the most patient of administrators find tedious.

With the advent of Windows 2000, much of this absurdity has vanished. It is now possible for a single tool, such as the Microsoft Management Console (which is included with the operating system), to provide access to virtually all aspects of configuration and management data on a Windows-based network. Underlying this possibility is an architecture that allows any type of information about a computer—whether its source is the Event Log, the Registry, a device driver, or even the core operating system itself—to be accessed, and any subsystem to be controlled in a consistent, detail-independent way. This architecture is the Windows Management Instrumentation (WMI).

WMI Functions

On a fundamental level, WMI fulfills three main roles:

- It defines a standard model for describing components of computer systems.
- It uses this model to describe components of the Windows 2000 operating system and a PC on which it runs.
- It provides tools that allow programs to read these descriptions and interact with the components they describe without having to know anything about the way the component itself works.

As this book progresses, you will see that these three roles together make WMI a powerful, unified interface to virtually every aspect of a Windows 2000 computer.

Standard Model

WMI provides a detail-independent standard model for specifying schemata that describe all facets of a device, system, or information provider's operation. This model is known as the *Common Information Model (CIM)*. A CIM-compliant schema can define types of objects that encapsulate information that a data source, device, or system can provide, the operational aspects that can be configured, and the actions it can perform.

Description of Windows 2000

The CIM specification is used to write a *CIM Schema* that describes virtually every aspect of a Windows 2000 system. For example, filesystems, Event Logs, devices, services, hardware controllers, processes, and memory are described, as are higher-level concepts such as users and domains. Some of these descriptions belong to the *CIMv2 Schema,* which describes objects common to all operating environments; equivalents of WMI on other platforms could use exactly the same schema to describe their systems. Others are specific to Microsoft operating systems. The distinction between these two types will emerge as this book progresses. Meanwhile, the important thing to note is that WMI describes everything that could conceivably be of interest to anyone running a Windows-based network or even a stand-alone workstation!

Tools

A model and set of specifications are not very helpful unless there is a way of making use of them. The final role of WMI, therefore, is to provide mechanisms that glue the whole system together. These mechanisms allow applications to find out what aspects of a system are defined by WMI object specifications and provide hooks to these objects that a management application can query and control. These hooks can be used by applications and scripts to transparently field requests for information or action, providing a layer of abstraction between systems and devices providing information and applications that want to make use of it.

Why Is This Relevant to the System Administrator?

From this description of WMI's three basic roles, you might be wondering why it is of any direct relevance to a system administrator. Of course, it is great news for programmers who are trying to write management applications, but surely the details are of no interest to someone at the management level. Wrong! It is certainly true that WMI is primarily a tool that makes it easier for programmers to write really good management applications. Ultimately, of course, system administrators will benefit from the new programs that are being written. But there is a more immediate benefit for system administrators too. One crucial aspect of the WMI implementation should be sending quivers of delight down the spine of anyone who has ever administered a Windows-based network: WMI objects can be accessed from scripts. Furthermore, the scripts can run on a remote computer.

Scripting has always had a strange status among NT system administrators. Although everyone uses a script somewhere (most typically, a login script), making large-scale use of scripting as a fundamental part of administration has tended to be the preserve of a relatively small number of administrators. These people often happen to also be UNIX administrators (a community among whom scripting is a ubiquitous pastime). Although everyone who uses scripts to administer Windows networks knows of the benefits—the most obvious being that repetitive, tedious management tasks can be carried out automatically—it is hardly surprising that scripting is not a mainstream activity among NT administrators. In fact, Microsoft has never really supported it as a means of accessing information and controlling the operating system. Scripts have always been a nightmare involving hacks and tricks that are different for almost every task. The difficulty of having to use a large number of separate management tools in the pre-2000 era was completely trivial in comparison with some of the problems facing administrators who made regular use of scripts!

WMI changes all of this. Now, any system administrator who is prepared to put a little effort into learning a scripting language suddenly has enormously powerful tool at his disposal. The flexibility of WMI allows the writing of scripts that can accomplish many previously manual tasks. WMI can create an inventory of hardware and software across a network, automate the execution of almost any management task, detect faults before they become troublesome, and even take corrective action without any administrative intervention. Most importantly, all such scripts can be written with ease by anyone who has some understanding of the WMI architecture and a scripting language. Imparting such an understanding is the subject of this book.

History

Windows is not the only operating system to suffer from a profusion of different management tools that do not interoperate well. Neither are servers and workstations the only devices for which central administration is desirable. Unsurprisingly, therefore, the concept of WMI is neither unique nor particularly new. This section puts WMI in context by considering briefly some of the motivational factors that led to its invention.

In May of 1990, RFC1157 was released. This RFC addressed the specification of a Simple Network Management Protocol (SNMP). In conjunction with several companion documents ("memos" in RFC-speak), RFC1157 laid the foundation for platform-independent remote management of network hubs and switches. SNMP performed three functions: It defined a system for describing the capabilities of a piece of network equipment (MIBs), it specified a standard mechanism for querying and controlling equipment based on the MIBs, and it suggested a standard set of parameters that certain generic types of equipment (such as network switches) should always support. The result of SNMP is that network switches and routers can be managed centrally by software that needs to know nothing about the workings of the managed equipment. The software only needs to know which of the standard MIBs the equipment supports, or, for nonstandard equipment, it needs a copy of the MIB table that describes the equipment's behavior. The fact that SNMP is now a ubiquitous standard whose usage spreads far beyond the management of simple network equipment is a testament to the cleverness of the design and the usefulness of the concept. Parallels with WMI should already be obvious!

In 1992, a consortium of large software companies, PC hardware manufacturers, and network equipment manufacturers founded an organization called the Distributed Management Task Force (DMTF). Their goal was to design and promote implementation-independent standards for remote computer management. Four years later, in 1996, the CIM was published. It specified an implementation-independent remote management framework for entire networks. Like SNMP, it consisted of both a language to describe a system's capabilities and a set of standard schemata to define generic capabilities of common components. Unlike SNMP, however, the object-oriented CIM framework provides a mechanism for defining relationships between managed objects. Furthermore, the standard schema encompasses not just network equipment, but almost every facet of a PC-based server or workstation. It even includes a mechanism for assimilating systems that would otherwise be managed by SNMP or DMI. At the time the DMTF was busy developing CIM, another initiative with similar goals was also being developed. This was Web-Based Enterprise Management (WBEM), whose purpose was to develop web-based standards for administering enterprise computing systems. In 1998, the DMTF took ownership of WBEM, and all the technologies were fused. The initiative now known as WBEM incorporates CIM, an XML specification for describing CIM objects, and a protocol for communicating with such objects using HTTP. The hope has been that all hardware and software vendors would provide CIM-compliant management interfaces, making it possible for entire networks and all the equipment connected to them to be controlled and monitored from a single point.

Note: DMI

DMI, or the Desktop Management Interface, was a 1993 DMTF initiative that specified a standard interface for remote administration of desktop computer systems. ◆

WMI is Microsoft's implementation of the CIM standard. In other words, WMI implements the CIM core components (it exposes the properties that all CIM-compliant systems must support). Additionally, it implements the common components relating to desktop computers (it supports the standard objects specified by the CIM schema for desktops). It also takes advantage of the extensibility of the CIM framework by providing CIM-compliant objects that describe concepts specific to the Windows-based networks. In other words, it is Microsoft's implementation of a system that allows every machine on a Windows-based network to be monitored and controlled from a single point.

WMI Technology

Before investigating the structure of WMI and thinking about how a system administrator can put it to use, it is worth spending a few moments considering some of the technologies that have led to the development of WMI and its scriptable interface.

Perhaps the single most important development has been the widespread adoption of the object-oriented programming model over the last decade. Before object orientation, a program consisted of two things: data and procedures. Data were inanimate blocks of information; procedures were blocks of code that read, wrote, and generally manipulated the data. Imagine, for example, a simple and completely useless program that lists several types of food and then outputs the phrase "this food is suitable for barbecuing" for every item whose name contains fewer than five letters. Such a program would consist of several pieces of data (the words corresponding to the food names and the words of the output phrase) and a procedure that looks at each food name, counts the number of letters contained in it, and displays the output phrase if necessary. The important thing to note about this structure is that all the data is "exposed" to procedures that manipulate it, but in no sense are the data and procedures fundamentally bound together. As far as the programming language is concerned, they are totally separate.

An object-oriented program has a very different structure. Rather than having data and then a set of separate procedures that operate on the data, such a program contains only one thing—an *object*. Objects encapsulate both data and procedures. An object-oriented food program would consist of a class that defines the properties of food (all food has a `name` property, for example) and the actions, or methods, that food objects can perform (for example, food can answer the question "Are you barbecueable?"). Having designed the food class and implemented the "Are you barbecueable?" method (presumably by specifying a calculation based on the `name` property), every type of food can be represented by its own instantiation of the food class. In other words, each food is represented by its own food object. Finally, you write a procedure that asks all pieces of food whether they are barbecueable. Rather than read the data and work out whether each piece of data corresponds to barbecueable food, all you do is ask each of the food objects to tell you. The data and the mechanism for calculating barbecueability are encapsulated in a single self-contained object.

The distinction between the two programming methods might not seem very large in this example, but it has drastic implications if you want to alter the program by adding several more types of food and complicating the rules. Suppose you specify that if the food is fruit, a different rule specifies its barbecueability (for example, it is barbecueable only if the second letter is "a," so that bananas could be barbecued whereas apples could not be). In writing a non-object-oriented program, you have to change your data structures so that each food word has another piece of data associated with it, indicating whether it represents a piece of fruit. In addition, you have to completely rewrite your main procedure. Instead of looking for the number of letters that the food name has, the procedure must be able to determine, based on the new data, whether each word corresponds to a fruit. All ensuing action depends on the outcome of this lookup. Add a few more different types of food, each of which has a different criterion for barbecueability, and the main procedure very quickly becomes exceedingly large and convoluted.

The object-oriented approach is quite different. First, you make a subclass of the food class to represent the new type of object, fruit. As a subclass of food, the fruit class automatically inherits all properties of food (such as the fact that food has a name). It also inherits all methods of food (for example, it can be queried about barbecueability). You want fruit to behave quite differently from other food when asked about its barbecueability, so you override the implementation of the "Are you barbecueable?" method to perform the new operation. Then you create new objects of the fruit class for each item of fruit you want to represent. In this scenario, you make no changes to the existing food class or to any existing food objects, and you make no changes to the main procedure that asks all food objects whether they can be barbecued. To the outside world, all fruit objects can be seen quite simply as "food." The fact that fruit calculates its barbecueability in a way that is totally different from other food is of no importance to anything but the fruit class itself. Just as before, the main procedure can run through the entire list of food objects, asking each one about its barbecueability.

Figure 1.1 illustrates the relationship between the food and fruit classes and adds a few more details to introduce more facets of the object-oriented model. In the figure, food objects have two methods: `barbecueable` and `tasty`. These report whether the food in question is barbecueable and whether it tastes good. Fruit *inherits* all of these methods, so all fruit also has `barbecueable` and `tasty` methods. In addition, fruit has a new `ripe` method, which reports whether the food is ripe. In other words, fruit can tell you something about itself that other food cannot. The code needed to work out whether fruit is tasty is exactly the same as that needed to work out whether any other type of food is tasty, so whenever this method is executed, the code specified by food is run. By contrast, as we have discussed, the rules for working out whether fruit is barbecueable are quite different from the rules for working out whether other food is barbecueable, so the subclass *overrides* the method, providing its own code to fulfill the task.

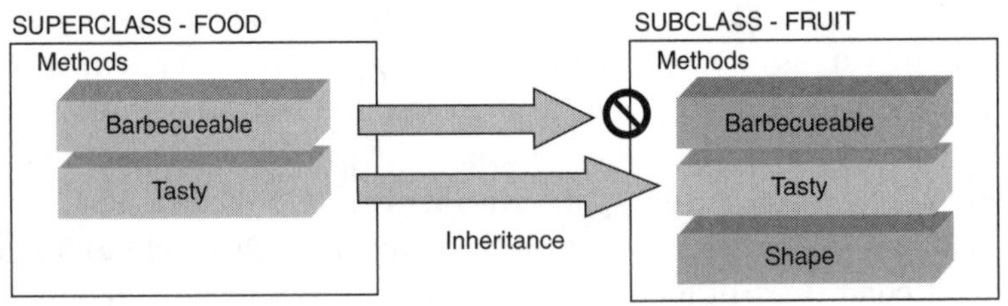

Figure 1.1 *Inheriting and overriding methods*

Note: Methods

Methods hide the implementation and all data from the outside world so that a program that wants to interact with an object only needs to know about the methods. However, sometimes objects actually want to expose some of their internal data. For example, in addition to using their names to work out barbecueability, food objects might want to expose their names to the outside world. This could, of course, be accomplished with a method called `PrintName` *or something similar; however, it would be far simpler just to expose the data. classes can allow objects of their type to expose some of their internal data to the outside world. Data exposed in this way is called a property.* ◆

This is not the place for an in-depth discussion of object-oriented programming, but one vital point to note is that in an object-oriented system, individual parts of a program never need to know how other parts operate. All they need to know about other parts is what methods they can perform and, sometimes, what properties they have. The result of this is that the underlying structure or mechanism part of a program can change completely. Provided that its external behavior remains the same, nothing else that relies on it ever has to be rewritten. The other important concept to consider is that of inheritance. With inheritance, new classes can be created that build upon, adapt, and extend existing ones. An object of any class can be addressed as though it were an object of a parent class.

Tip: Polymorphism

Strictly speaking, the reason that an object of any class can be addressed as though it were an object of a parent class is not directly due to inheritance but to the more general concept of polymorphism. Polymorphism is the mechanism that allows a program to call a method or access a property of an object without needing to know what specific class the object belongs to. All the caller needs to know is that the object is of a class that directly or indirectly implements the interface to which the method or property belongs. ◆

A natural extension of the object-oriented programming paradigm is Microsoft's Component Object Model (COM). Object orientation is a tool for the programmer that helps him build large applications out of small, self-contained components. The fact that a program has been written in an object-oriented style is normally of little interest to anyone but the programmer himself. COM, on the other hand, specifies a system for creating objects that are visible in their own right outside of the framework of a larger application. COM objects can interact with each other even if they do not belong to the same program. Furthermore, interacting COM objects do not both have to reside on the same computer, because facilities exist for these objects to talk to each other across networks. The benefit of COM is to allow large and complex systems to be built out of any number of distinct components that can be written by totally different people who do not need to use the same programming language to write their code. DCOM, the extension to COM that allows code to access objects residing on different computers, even has a built-in security model that restricts access to objects based on standard NT security. This allows large distributed webs of objects to interact safely and securely across networks. To return to barbecued food, a COM-based implementation might look something like this: You write a small program that initializes a number of COM objects, each of which represents a piece of food. You run a copy of this program on various computers across your network. You then write a barbecue-finder program whose task is to search each machine on the network, looking for food objects. Each time it finds some, it asks about barbecueability. Silly, perhaps, but very good fun!

Although it's potentially very powerful, COM as described so far has one serious limitation: Any object that wants to talk to any other object must have prior knowledge of that object's capabilities. In our example, the barbecue finder needs to know in advance that there is a type of object called food and that food objects can be queried about their barbecueability. A computer system might be brimming with useful COM objects, but someone who wants to take advantage of them might not be able to work out that they are there, let alone what any of them may do. To solve this problem, COM includes a technology for overcoming this limitation. Any application that exposes COM objects provides a system for telling other programs what objects are contained in it; in turn, the objects themselves can be asked, "What can you do?" COM makes it possible to write a generic program whose purpose is simply to manipulate objects, without any regard for the specific objects it will ultimately be used to manipulate.

If you are wondering why you would ever want to write such a program, think about scripting languages, whose job is usually to provide easy programmatic access to the scripted system. For example, most spreadsheet programs provide scripting facilities so that complex, repetitive numerical procedures can be carried out reliably and quickly. One obvious way that the designer of a spreadsheet program could provide such a facility would be to write a proprietary language that contains special syntax for accessing spreadsheet-specific features such as cells, rows, and columns. The advantage of this solution is that the language could be highly tuned and tailored to the job at hand. The downside is that users of the program have to learn how to use it, and it can be a tedious, long-term process to learn a scripting language from scratch. Another rather different approach might be to expose the components that make up a spreadsheet (rows, cells, columns, and so on) as COM objects. In doing so, users of the program could then control it using any language that supports COM. In this scenario, there is no need to learn new, proprietary languages; instead, you just use your favorite COM-compliant language, such as VBScript or Perl, and learn about the COM objects that the spreadsheet makes available. In fact, if you are prepared to take a few risks and indulge in some guesswork, you don't even have to find out in advance about the objects exposed by the spreadsheet. You can use the scripting language to ask the spreadsheet for a list of all the objects it exposes and then ask each one in turn what it can do. For a real-life example of this, look no further than Microsoft Office. From any of the applications, switch to the Visual Basic Editor, and then open the Object Browser to reveal a list of objects that the application exposes.

Finally, we are ready to consider what all this has to do with WMI. As you have probably figured out, the WMI architecture is highly object-oriented in its design. WMI consists of objects that represent facets of the Windows operating system and the computer on which it sits. The schemata are effectively class definitions; they define different types of things. For example, there is a class in the Win32 schema called Win32_UserAccount, which (unsurprisingly) defines attributes of user accounts. It specifies properties such as `FullName`, `Domain`, and `SID`. The `Win32_UserAccount` class itself is a subclass of `Win32_Account`, which means that it inherits properties such as `SID` and `Name`. On the computer we are using to write this chapter, there are four instances of `Win32_UserAccount`—four WMI objects of that type—representing the Guest user, the Administrator, someone called Matthew Lavy, and someone called Ashley Meggitt. Another example is the class `Win32_BIOS`, which defines properties such as `SerialNumber` and `Manufacturer`. A class such as this is likely to have only one instance on a single machine, referring to the computer's only BIOS.

As for the relationship between WMI and COM, all WMI objects are COM-compliant, and the scripting interface talks to the objects through COM interfaces. In other words, leaving aside the politics and the wider conceptual frame discussed earlier, WMI could be described as an attempt to expose the Windows platform as a set of COM objects. Given that both Microsoft Office and Internet Explorer have been COM-compliant and scriptable for several years, to extend this functionality to the core of Windows itself, far from being revolutionary, was surely in technological terms just the next logical step.

Note: Exposing the Windows API as COM Objects

It is worth noting that exposing large chunks of the Windows API as a set of COM objects is far from trivial. WMI effectively provides an object-oriented wrapper for large chunks of the Windows API. This C-based interface, in common with that of most operating systems, is not object-oriented in any respect! ◆

WMI Structure

Having considered both the conceptual and technological issues surrounding WMI, we are now in a position to be able to look in more detail at its structure and the components that comprise it.

The WMI implementation consists of a vast number of objects, some of which are persistent and some of which are created on demand. Each of these kinds of objects refers to some aspect of the operating system, hardware or network. Depending on the underlying system to which they refer, objects may remain static over their lifetimes, or they may contain properties that change constantly. Many WMI objects refer to other objects that might or might not share a similar life span. Two aspects of WMI help management applications or scripts make use of this seemingly miasmatic zoo: a rigid structure that decouples the management application from the machinations of managed objects, and a sophisticated mechanism for finding objects of interest.

Central to the physical structure of WMI are the CIM repository and the Object Manager. The Repository is a store containing lots of WMI objects, and the Object Manager is the store assistant. If an application or script needs a reference to a specific object, it simply asks the Object Manager, which retrieves it from the store and passes it over. If the object of interest resides on a machine other than the local computer, the Object Manager on the relevant remote machine must be asked instead. As soon as the object has been passed over, the management application or script can query it and control it. Life is not always so simple, because just like with a real store, it is possible to ask for an object that is not in stock! In this case, the Object Manager must order it on demand from a WMI provider. This process, however, is completely transparent to the customer. A script or application does not need to know whether an object has been retrieved from the Repository or ordered from a WMI provider, because the Object Manager handles everything. This relationship is illustrated in Figure 1.2.

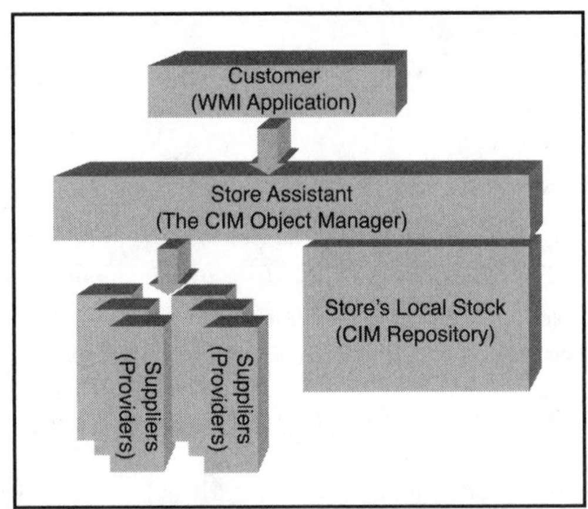

Figure 1.2 *Asking the Object Manager for objects.*

Two obvious questions emerge from this description:

- What determines whether an object is "in stock"?
- Does the Object Manager know which WMI provider to use?

A further question, "How does an application or script ask the Object Manager for an object?", will be dealt with later in this chapter and will be covered extensively throughout this book.

All WMI classes can be static or dynamic. A static class is one whose definition is fixed (for example, a class that is part of the CIM core model), whereas a dynamic one has a definition that can change. Further, some classes always have a fixed number of instances associated with them (for example, the `Win32_Bios` class has only one instance, referring to the computer's one and only BIOS), whereas others can have any number of instances that are regularly created and destroyed (classes associated with objects on the filesystem are good examples). Classes with a fixed number of instances are said to have *static instances*. Classes with a varying number of instances are said to have *dynamic instances*. A final complication is that even a static class with static instances might have properties that change dynamically.

Whether a WMI object is stored in the Repository depends on the persistence of the class and its instances. Static instances of static classes are stored in the Repository until they are explicitly deleted. If an instance happens to contain a dynamic property, it is retrieved as required from a provider. Dynamic instances of static classes must always be retrieved from a provider, but the class definitions themselves are stored in the Repository. Dynamic classes are never stored in the Repository; both their definitions and instances must always be retrieved on demand from a provider. When a requested instance or its class is not stored in the Repository, the Object Manager knows which provider to ask, because all providers register with WMI when they are initialized, providing details of all the objects they support.

Namespaces and Object Groupings

There are three ways to go shopping: If you know what you are looking for, you can just go to the store and ask for it; you can wander around the store and browse; or you can go to an online store and search using plausible keywords. Looking for a WMI object is no different: An object can be requested from the Object Manager by name, the list of all available objects or a specific subset can be browsed, or objects can be retrieved based on the results of a keyword search. These things are possible because WMI objects are not merely "stacked up" in the Repository in a jumbled mess; they all live within a specific namespace and can be referred to according to a defined naming convention. Furthermore, sets of objects are connected to each other in two ways. First, all objects are of a type—that is, they are all *instantiations* of a specific *class*. All objects of a particular class form a natural grouping. For example, all files or all processes make a natural grouping. Second, pairs of objects are linked with associations. Both class membership and associations can be used to browse for objects in the Repository.

Namespaces organize WMI objects into logical groupings. As such, they perform a function very similar to directories in a filesystem. Just as filesystem directories can be nested to form a conceptually logical structure, namespaces within WMI can also be nested. Despite the potential for nesting, the standard WMI installation uses namespaces for grouping only on a large scale. Almost all of the objects discussed in this book live within a single, unnested namespace.

Note: Hierarchical Organization

It is important to note that this hierarchical organization has nothing to do with the inheritance hierarchy of classes in the WMI schemata. ◆

The top level of the namespace hierarchy in any WMI installation is called the *root*. Every object in the system lies somewhere within its branches. A standard WMI installation has only two subnamespaces—default and CIMv2. The default namespace contains classes and objects relating to the operation of WMI itself. These objects are rarely of interest to a system administrator, because they are largely concerned with the inner workings of WMI. The CIMv2 namespace, on the other hand, is very interesting indeed in that all of the classes and associated objects conforming to the CIM reside there.

In addition to providing high-level structural organization, namespaces are central to security within WMI. This is because system administrators can specify access permissions on a per-namespace basis. When connecting to the WMI system on a local or remote machine, users log on and connect to a specific namespace. (WMI security is discussed in detail in Chapter 5, "WMI Security.")

An association is a special type of object that connects other objects within a namespace. Associations represent relationships in WMI by both connecting pairs of objects and encapsulating information about the nature of the relationship or the role that each object plays in the pairing. Whereas standard WMI objects represent individual components of a system, webs of associations represent the way in which these components interact to create a functioning whole. Several different types of associations are defined by the CIM, many of which have WMI-specific subclasses that describe a specific kind of relationship between WMI objects. For example, a `CIM_Dependency` defines a relationship in which one object (or the underlying system that the object represents) is dependent on another. An object participating in this type of association can perform the role of an antecedent or a dependent. An antecedent is an object whose presence is required for the dependent to function. Another common type of association is a `CIM_Component`, which relates a part to a group. `Win32_DependentService` is a subclass of `CIM_Dependency` that is used to map the interdependency of services. `Win32_SubDirectory` is an example of a `CIM_Component` that maps a subdirectory to its parent.

Note: Associations

Associations are themselves WMI objects; they are instances of associator classes. ◆

Associations relate the objects within a namespace in functional or structural terms. Another way in which objects are organized within a namespace is by type or class. Instead of finding an object and tracing the connections between it and other components, it is possible to look at a type of object (a class) and discover all the instances of that class. To understand the difference between these two approaches, consider two ways of finding information about every directory on the C: drive of a single-partioned workstation. One approach would be to retrieve a WMI object corresponding to the root directory of the C: drive and to map the structure of the filesystem by recursively following `Win32_Subdirectory` associations. This approach would be equivalent to looking at the drive in Explorer and clicking each subfolder in drive C:, and each of their subfolders, and so on, until you have opened every directory. The other approach would be to look at the class `Win32_Directory` and examine all local instances. This would be the equivalent of getting a list of every directory name on your C: drive, regardless of where it fits in the folder hierarchy. Although the result in both cases would be an exhaustive list of directories on the filesystem, there is a very important difference. Whereas following associations would give a list that mapped the logical structure of a filesystem, examining instantiations of the class would not. The second approach, however, is not without its advantages. Whereas following the associations requires a reference to an object that can be used as a starting point, here you need only know that objects of the type `Win32_Directory` have the potential to exist. In other words, if you have a known starting point, associations constitute the best way to follow relationships between WMI objects. Class groupings are invaluable, however, for fishing expeditions! Associations can be used to answer questions such as "Which user created this entry in the Event Log?". Class groupings, on the other hand, are perfect for questions such as "How many hard disks does this computer have?".

Referencing Objects

WMI objects sit within a namespace and are bound by associations and class groups, but this structure is of no use to a system administrator without a mechanism for referring to objects and following associations. To pose the problem in a slightly different way, a management application or script that needs to interact with a WMI object must have some way of explaining its requirements to the Object Manager. The details of the mechanism used for communication between a management application or script and the Object Manager are partly dependent on the programming language and WMI interface being used. The various components of a typical object path are illustrated in Figure 1.3. We will see how to accomplish this through VBScript in the next chapter. The fundamental principle is the same regardless of language, however. Retrieving an object reference from the Object Manager entails describing the object of interest in a way that identifies it uniquely. This is achieved by means of object paths, URL-like structures that take the following form:

```
\\ComputerName\Namespace:ClassName.KeyPropertyName="value"
```

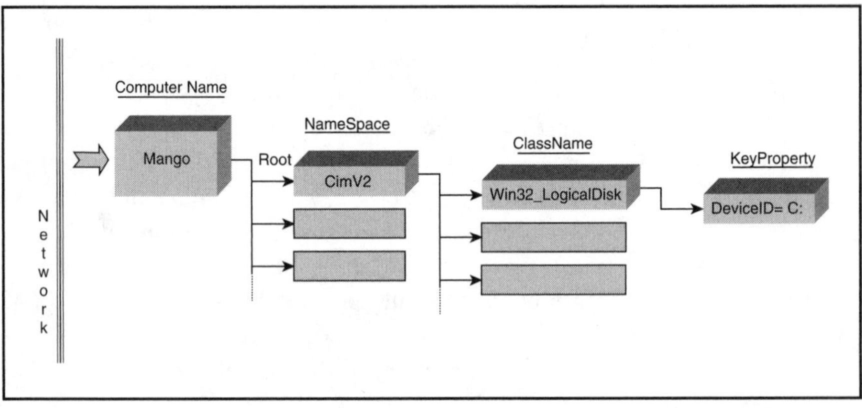

Figure 1.3 *Components of an object path.*

An object path consists, then, of four components: the name of the computer and the namespace in which the object resides, the name of the class that identifies the object type, and the name of a key property that uniquely identifies a specific instance of the class. For example, you could ask the Object Manager for a reference to the WMI object that represents the C: drive on a Windows 2000 workstation called Mango by specifying this object path:

```
\\MANGO\Root\CIMv2:Win32_LogicalDisk.DeviceID="C:"
```

This means "Look in the \Root\CIMv2 namespace on Mango for the object of type `Win32_LogicalDisk` whose property `DeviceID` has the value C:." Note that the namespace is hierarchical: CIMv2 is fully qualified as \Root\CIMv2. This arrangement is discussed further in Chapter 5.

You can be sure that this object path points to a unique object only if you are certain that there is only one type of object in the CIMv2 namespace called `Win32_LogicalDisk` and that there is only one instance of this type whose `DeviceID` has the value `"C:"`. Two features of WMI's design ensure that these are both safe assumptions:

- The types of objects that can exist within a namespace (that is, the classes) are defined in the WMI schema. Any attempt to add a new class definition to a namespace that already contains a class of the same name will fail. This ensures that class names within a namespace are always unique.
- The CIM specification dictates that all classes defined in the schema must possess at least one key property. Keys are no different from any other property that a class can define, except that the values of all the keys of a particular instantiation of a class taken together, in any permutation, must be unique. In other words, it is not possible to instantiate an object all of whose key values are identical to those of another existing object of the same class. This ensures that objects of a specific class can always be uniquely identified by the combined values of one or more keys.

You may have noticed that the generic form of an object path just shown does not allow for the specification of multiple key properties. In cases where unique identification of an object depends on more than one key, they are separated in a comma-separated list. For example, the following object path refers to a single Event Log entry, which is uniquely identified by two keys—`Logfile` and `RecordNumber`:

```
\\MANGO\Root\CIMv2:
Win32_NTLogEvent.Logfile="Security",RecordNumber=1
```

It might already be obvious that object paths have the potential to become rather long and cumbersome beasts. WMI offers three conventions designed to allow for more succinct specifications of object paths under the following circumstances:

- Certain classes, so-called singleton classes, are defined to allow the instantiation of only a single object. The concept of key is superfluous here; a reference to the one and only object of a singleton class can be specified by `ClassName=@`. The rationale for this notation is that an object path that ends with a class name alone refers to the class rather than to an actual object. Very few singleton classes exist, but one example is the `Win32_WMISetting` class, whose only instance represents information about the WMI system on a computer. This object can be retrieved with the object path `Win32_WMISetting=@`.

Object paths, then, provide a universally consistent means of referring unambiguously to a specific WMI object of any type, sitting within any namespace on any computer. They are used not only in dealings with the Object Manager, but also by associations, which can now be seen as special objects whose job is to store pairs of object paths. You will probably not be surprised to hear that object paths will appear regularly in various guises throughout this book, both in scripts and in the text. Use of the various conventions just outlined will also be exemplified throughout. By the time you have finished reading, they will all be extremely familiar!

Searching for Objects

Although object paths provide a convenient way of unambiguously identifying an object or class, their use is restricted to situations in which you know the name of the class and the key properties of the object you are looking for. Although many management tasks require nothing more, suppose, for example, that you have disk space problems on your file server, and you want to compress all files that are larger than approximately 10 MB. If you could get references to WMI objects representing each such uncompressed file, you could use the compress action defined by the `CIM_DataFile` class to perform the compression.

Asking the Object Manager to return references to all these objects would clearly require more than an object path. The solution is provided by the WMI Query Language (WQL), which, as the name suggests, is a special language designed to express queries about WMI objects and classes. A WQL query to retrieve objects according to the criteria just described would look something like this:

```
SELECT * FROM CIM_DataFile
WHERE FileSize > 10000000 AND Compressed=false
```

If you are familiar with SQL, a standard language for querying relational databases, this syntax will look comfortingly familiar. WQL is actually a subset of ANSI SQL, with a few syntactic differences designed to accommodate the special requirements of WMI.

WQL is typically used to search for specific objects or a set of objects (as in the preceding example). However, it can also be used to search for associations, making it a very powerful tool for browsing relationships between objects. For example, the WQL query `ASSOCIATORS OF {Win32_ParallelPort.DeviceID="LPT1"}` returns all the associations connected to a computer's parallel port. Typically, these include a `Win32_ComputerSystem` and a number of `Win32_PortResource` objects. Another use of WQL is to search the WMI schema. Suppose, for example, that you are unsure of what types of objects are available on a particular WMI system. The query `SELECT`

`* FROM meta_class WHERE __this ISA "CIM_ManagedSystemElement"` would return a list of all classes on the system that subclassed `CIM_ManagedSystemElement`. The result of this particular query would return a large chunk of the WMI schema that could be of great interest to a system administrator.

This introduction is no place for a detailed discussion of WQL syntax, which will be considered at several points later in this book (notably, in Chapter 5, Chapter 7, "System Configuration," and Chapter 9, "WMI and Active Directory"). For now, suffice it to say that WQL is an extremely powerful tool that allows an administrator using a management application or script to view and control aspects of a managed computer system in a flexible, dynamic way.

Accessing WMI from Scripts

Throughout this chapter, we have referred to "management applications or scripts" as potential users of WMI. In practice, however, this book is not about writing—or using—management applications but about scripting. The goal is to arm administrators of Windows-based networks with the knowledge required to automate management tasks by scripting WMI. It seems appropriate, therefore, to briefly consider how a script can interact with WMI.

WMI provides a *scripting API,* a small set of functions that can be accessed from a scripting language that can be used to find, create, and manipulate WMI objects and classes. These functions include facilities for obtaining object references using object paths or WQL and others for executing object methods and reading and writing object properties. There are also features for logging on to WMI and connecting to a namespace. In addition to the special functions through which WMI objects can be manipulated, it is sometimes possible to access such objects directly as though they are a seamless part of the scripting language. The extent to which this is possible depends on the way in which the scripting language integrates with COM. The implications for scripting languages, particularly for VBScript, will be demonstrated in the next chapter and throughout the rest of this book.

One service that makes scripting so convenient on Windows 2000 is the Windows Scripting Host (WSH). This allows scripts written in languages such as VBScript, JavaScript, or PerlScript to be run "natively" on the Windows platform, rather than having to be run in their own sealed environment. The current version of WSH (2.0) enables the integration of script components written in different languages, allowing administrators to take advantage of the powerful text manipulation facilities of Perl and the COM integration of VBScript. The advanced facilities of WSH, such as the ability to combine scripts written in different languages, and its place in WMI scripting are discussed in detail in Chapter 10, "Script Development and Deployment."

The WMI Event Model

So far, from the perspective of a systems administrator, it might seem as though WMI is a somewhat passive web of classes and objects that sit quietly in a repository, dormant until an administrator accesses them, or in some cases coming into being only when the Object Manager tells a provider to create them. Although it is certainly possible to think of WMI in those terms and to treat WMI objects merely as a convenient interface to Windows management, to do so is to ignore one of the most exciting aspects of the WMI system—event notification.

Far from being static, the web of associations and objects that make up WMI form a constantly changing flux: objects are constantly created and destroyed, their properties vary, and associations are formed and broken. The reason for this is that WMI objects represent a computer system consisting of subsystems such as filesystems, network connections, the Registry, and the Event Log, all of whose properties change dynamically. Many aspects of this dynamism are of potential interest to an administrator. For example, a WMI object representing a network printer (a `Win32_Printer`) has a number of properties whose values would change if the printer represented by the object developed a problem. The WMI Event Notification system makes it possible for a management application or script to subscribe to potential dynamic changes such as this. If the change occurs, WMI notifies the script concerned.

Note: Creation of Dynamic Instances

In practice, classes whose instantiations are very dynamic are created by providers on demand, rather than constantly appearing in and disappearing from the CIM Repository. However, this is an implementation issue dictated by efficiency considerations and is transparent to a WMI client. Therefore, the principle holds. ◆

The implications for an administrator are immense. It's not only possible, but also reasonably easy to write scripts that detect and automatically respond to a plethora of problems on a network or computer system. Event notification can be used to detect security breaches, monitor use of software or the health of a server, or even respond to a user's overenthusiastic use of a mouse! The possibilities are endless. Chapter 9 explains how event notification and the subset of WQL that supports it can be used to write event-driven scripts that preempt trouble, take corrective action, or, if they cannot, warn a human administrator.

Summary

The Windows Management Interface provides a consistent, unified object-oriented model of almost every facet of a computer system and Windows-based network. It is an implementation of the platform-independent Common Information Model standard designed by the Desktop Management Taskforce to facilitate the central management of large computer networks. Because they are based on COM and COM technology, WMI objects can be accessed from scripts running either on a local machine or, security permitting, across a network. Provision for the retrieval of WMI objects based on names or complex searches, together with the Event Notification system, makes WMI an extremely powerful tool for the system administrator who is prepared to learn a scripting language. Over the course of the next three chapters, you will see how to write WMI management scripts using VBScript running under the Windows Scripting Host.

2

Using VBScript

VBScript is a simple but still reasonably powerful programming language specifically designed for writing scripts on the Windows platform. Crucially for this book, such scripts can also access WMI objects and classes.

A simple script might be nothing more than a sequence of commands, each of which is executed in turn. More sophisticated ones, however, are much, much more: They are sets of building blocks that execute commands conditionally and modify their behavior according to complex patterns that can change each time they are run. This chapter introduces the basic building blocks of VBScript and teaches the aspects of the language that are required to start writing simple administration scripts. This chapter is categorically not a programmers' reference manual. It does not attempt to give a rigorous treatment of every subtle detail; neither does it discuss every feature of the language. Throughout this book, we will introduce novel language features and consider some of the subtleties of the simpler ones. In contrast, in this chapter, we aim to simply give you the basic toolkit required to understand the concepts and tools upon which the rest of this book is based.

We assume no prior knowledge of VBScript here; in fact, we assume no prior knowledge of programming at all. Therefore, if you are already a VBScript programmer, or if you have knowledge of a similar language, you might find much of the material rather tedious. If so, just skip straight to the section "Accessing WMI with VBScript," near the end of this chapter.

Programming VBScript

Programs written in VBScript—or in pretty much any other language, for that matter—are hierarchical structures. A fully-fledged VBScript program is built from a number of smaller units, each of which is written to accomplish a specific part of the overall task. These smaller units are built from even smaller ones, and so on until the very lowest level is reached: the units provided by VBScript itself. The large-scale, high-level units are designed to carry out highly specific tasks. To accomplish this, they make heavy use of a number of smaller units. In contrast, the smaller units are more generic. They do less but can be used in more situations.

For example, consider a VBScript program designed to produce a set of lottery numbers. At the highest level is the script itself: It performs the very specific and relatively complex task of producing a set of six numbers and printing them in the desired format. At the next level down might be a number of smaller units that actually carry out the components of the task. For example, one unit might produce a set of random numbers. This in turn might call on the services of even lower-level code, such as a unit responsible for generating a single random number within a specified range. Finally, this unit uses VBScript's built-in functions and operators (tiny units) to perform arithmetic calculations.

However complex or sophisticated a program, it is ultimately built from very simple building blocks. In this section of the chapter, we introduce each of the main building blocks of VBScript in turn and describe their use. We start with the most fundamental units and then move on to see how they can be combined to form more sophisticated structures.

Statements

A statement is exactly what it says it is: a semantically complete assertion, or the equivalent of a single-clause sentence in English. Because the function of a programming language is to carry out a set of commands, a statement can be thought of as being equivalent to a command.

Note: Imperative Languages

Not all programming languages are designed to carry out sets of commands (but most are). Languages that are in the category of being able to do so, such as VBScript, are known as imperative languages. ◆

A single statement is the smallest syntactically valid unit that you can write in a script. The following is an example of one of the shortest scripts you could possibly write:

```
WScript.Quit
```

It consists of a single statement, a command that means "Stop running the script."

Each statement in VBScript must either start on a new line or be separated from the previous line by a colon (:). VBScript assumes that the beginning of a new line always corresponds to the start of a new statement. If you want a single statement to be split over two lines (for example, if it is too long to fit on a single line), use the underscore character (_) at the end of the previous line to signify a continuation.

To clarify, consider the following example. It's a two-line script that displays the message "Good morning!" and then exits:

```
WScript.Echo "Good Morning!"
WScript.Quit
```

As you have probably guessed, `WScript.Echo` is a command that displays a dialog box and some text. This could also be written as

```
WScript.Echo "Good Morning!" : WScript.Quit
```

The following version is syntactically incorrect, because a single statement spans two lines. Attempting to write this in a script would cause an error.

```
WScript.Echo
"Good Morning!"
WScript.Quit
```

This one, however, works just fine:

```
Wscript.Echo _
    "Good Morning!"
WScript.Quit
```

You will notice that the second line is indented. This is not necessary, but this convention is often used to make it clear that the line "belongs" to the preceding one.

Any line that starts with an apostrophe (`'`) is a comment. VBScript ignores such lines, so they can contain any text at all; it doesn't have to be valid VBScript syntax. The purpose of comments is to allow annotation of code. In this four-line example, the first and third lines are comments:

```
'First I am going to say good morning
WScript.Echo "Good Morning!"
'Now I am going to quit VBScript
WScript.Quit
```

In this example, the comments are somewhat superfluous, because it is completely obvious what the script does. When used judiciously, however, comments can make a long, complex script much easier to read and understand.

Apart from comments, the only other lines that VBScript ignores are those that contain nothing but white space. Like comments, putting white space between sections of your code can make it a lot easier to read.

Both of the statements presented in the preceding examples are simple commands, but the first is slightly more complex than the second because the command `Wscript.Echo` takes an *argument* or *parameter*. In other words, it relies on an extra bit of data in order to carry out its task. In this case, the argument is the value to display. The true significance of *arguments* or *parameters* will become apparent later in this chapter.

Operators and Expressions

VBScript can do much more than merely display messages in dialogs. One of the things you might often need to do is display something that depends on the outcome of a calculation. To accommodate this, VBScript provides a set of *operators* that allow you to manipulate data.

Arithmetic Operators

Among the most commonly used operators are the *arithmetic operators,* which mimic the basic functions of a pocket calculator. For example, look at the following one-line script, which prints the number 7 in a window:

```
WScript.Echo 3 + 4
```

The following line prints 59:

```
WScript.Echo 30 * 2 - 1
```

Just as when you perform mathematical calculations with a pocket calculator—or on paper, for that matter—VBScript obeys certain *precedence rules* that specify the order in which arithmetic operations (or any other type of operation) are executed. In the preceding example, the multiplication (*) is carried out before the subtraction (-). Confusion is easy to avoid, however, because precedence rules can always be overridden with pairs of parentheses. Operations inside parentheses are carried out before operations *between* parentheses. This is demonstrated by this more-complex example, whose output is 6:

```
WScript.Echo ((3 + 17) / (1 + 3 - 2) - (2 ^ 3))  * 3
```

Just as is implied by the standard mathematical notation, this example adds 3 and 17 (giving 20), divides the result by 1 plus 3 minus 2 (giving 10), subtracts 2 to the power of 3 (giving 2, and multiplies the result by 3 (giving 6).

The commonly used arithmetic operators are described in Table 2.1.

Table 2.1 Arithmetic Operators

Operator	Description
+	Adds the values on either side of the operator.
-	Subtracts the value on the right from the value on the left. Alternatively, when there is nothing on the left (such as –5), negates the value.
*	Multiplies the values on either side.
/	Divides the value on the left by the value on the right.
\	Divides the value on the left by the value on the right, but rounds down to the nearest whole number.
mod	Divides the value on the left by the value on the right, and keeps only the *remainder*. For example, 5 mod 6 gives 1, because 5/6 gives 0 with a remainder of 1.

Operator	Description
^	Raises the value on the left to the power of the value on the right. This is the *exponent* operator.

There is an important difference between the arguments given to the `Wscript.Echo` command in these examples and the ones in the preceding section. In the earlier examples, VBScript merely displays the string *literal* `Good Morning!`. In the previous example, it displays the text exactly as it appears in the script. For example, the command `Wscript.Echo 4` displays the numeric *literal* `4`. In contrast, `Wscript.Echo 3 + 4` does not display `3+4`; instead, it evaluates the expression `3+4` to display `7`. Unlike a statement, an expression cannot stand as an entity in its own right. A line containing nothing but `3 + 4` is a syntax error. To use a linguistic analogy, an expression is a clause, not a sentence.

Note: Literal

Literal is a term used in programming to refer to a fixed value that represents only itself. For example, "goose" is a literal, as is 17, because if either of them appears in a program listing, they literally mean "goose" and 17 respectively, regardless of the context. ◆

If you are wondering what would happen if you typed `WScript.Echo "Good" / "Morning"`, the answer is simple: Attempting to use an arithmetic operator on a string of text is clearly nonsensical and would result in a runtime error. The only exception to this rule concerns the `+` operator: `WScript.Echo "Good" + "Morning"` would produce the result `GoodMorning`, because the `+` operator is *overloaded* to concatenate strings as well as perform arithmetic addition. This dual function can sometimes lead to confusion. For example, does `"3" + 2` produce 5 or 32? There is, in fact, a definitive answer to this question, because the behavior of VBScript in these ambiguous circumstances is always defined (see table 2.2). Our advice, however, is to avoid potential ambiguity by following one simple rule: *Never* use the `+` operator to concatenate two strings. Instead, use the concatenation operator (`&`). In the present context, the behavior of `+` and `&` is identical.

Table 2.2 Result of Concatenating Numeric and String Expressions

Expression1	Expression2	Result
String	String	Concatenation of two strings
String	Number	Addition of the two
Number	Number	Addition

Comparison Operators

It is not often that a system administration's script involves extensive computation, so you will probably rarely use most of the arithmetic operators. The *comparison operators,* on the other hand, are among the most useful tools in the armory! A comparison operator does exactly what the name implies: It sits between two values or expressions and compares them in some way that evaluates to true or false, depending on the outcome of the comparison.

VBScript offers a number of comparison operators. Here are the most commonly used ones:

>	Greater than
<	Less than
=	Equal to
<>	Not equal to
>=	Greater than or equal to
<=	Less than or equal to

To see how they work, consider the following expressions:

```
3 < 4
```

evaluates to true, whereas

```
3 > 4
```

evaluates to false.

```
"fish" = "chips"
```

evaluates to false, whereas

```
"fish" = "fish"
```

evaluates to true.

Because these are all expressions, they can be put in your script anywhere that an expression is allowed, so `WScript.Echo "hello" = "goodbye"` is perfectly syntactically correct.

The values `true` and `false` are not represented in VBScript by the words "true" and "false," but by the numeric values –1 and 0, respectively. Therefore, the line `Wscript.Echo "hello" = "goodbye"` displays 0. In contrast, `Wscript.Echo "hello" = "hello"` displays –1.

At this stage, all of these comparisons might seem rather pointless, because you could probably figure out without the aid of a script that 3 < 4, or even that (3*4)^2 >= 45—if, that is, you would even want to! However, when you consider variables and conditional execution, described next, the power of comparison operators will soon become obvious.

You might wonder what the evaluation of a comparison such `"fish" > "chips"` would be, or, for that matter, `15 =< "goose"`. The answer in the first case is that comparisons carried out on text strings are always evaluated according to alphabetical order, so `"fish" > "chips"` means “Fish comes after chips in alphabetical order”—which, of course, is true (–1). As for the second case, comparing 15 and “goose” is utterly ridiculous. Attempting to do so would create a runtime error. In contrast, `"15" =< "goose"` evaluates to true (–1), because here the `"15"` is treated as a text string rather than as a number. In other words, there is a fundamental difference between the way VBScript treats text and numbers. You can always tell which is which because text string literals are always enclosed in quotation marks, whereas numeric literals are not. In a text context, letters are always considered larger than numbers. `"a" > "999999"` is true, and `"p" < "1"` is false. Of course, `"a" > 999999` evaluates to nothing; it produces a syntax error. Letters are compared according to their ASCII character values, so `"A"` is smaller than `"a"`.

Logical Operators

The final group of operators we will consider are the *logical operators,* such as `AND`, `OR`, and `NOT`. Reassuringly, these perform exactly the functions you might expect. Here are some characteristics of these operators:

- `AND` is used to join two expressions. The combination evaluates to true only if both of the expressions are true.
- `OR` is used to join two expressions. The combination evaluates to true if either of the expressions is true.
- `NOT` is used to negate an expression. Any true expression prefixed by not becomes false, and any false expression prefixed by not becomes true.

A few examples should make this plain:

`3 = 3 AND 4 = 4` evaluates to true.

`3 = 3 AND 4 = 5` evaluates to false.

`3 = 3 OR 4 = 5` evaluates to true.

`3 = 4 OR 4 = 5` evaluates to false.

`3 = 4 OR NOT 4 = 5` evaluates to true.

Table 2.3 shows the complete *truth tables* for `AND`. Table 2.4 shows the complete truth tables for `OR`.

Table 2.3 Truth Table for AND

Value One	Value Two	Result
False	False	False
False	True	False
True	False	False
True	True	True

Table 2.4 Truth Table for OR

Value One	Value Two	Result
False	False	False
False	True	True
True	False	True
True	True	True

There are other logical operators too, such as `XOR`, `EQV`, and `IMP`, but you are unlikely to need these for writing system administration scripts, so they are not discussed here.

Variables

All the expressions we have considered so far have involved string or numeric literals. For example, we gave the words "Good Morning!" as an argument to the `WScript.Echo` command and evaluated whether 3 is larger than 4. In the real world, however, you want your scripts to behave rather more generically than this. You rarely need to compare the numbers 3 and 4 in code, because you can figure that out yourself. However, you will often want a script that compares two numbers that are passed to it. Imagine, for example, a script that needs to check whether the size of a series of files exceeds storage space on a device. The same can be said of comparisons of string literals. You will rarely need to compare string literals with comparison operators, but there are plenty of occasions when you want a script that can make use of some value that is passed to it, such as the name of a user, and compare that with something. In short, what you need is some way of writing code that includes placeholders so that the values—but not the computation—can be supplied later. This need is filled by variables.

Note: Placeholders

In the sections that follow, and throughout the rest of the book, we use angle brackets (<>) to indicate placeholders. When interpreting this, either in the text or in code, you should replace such placeholders with real, valid values. For example, `Dim <variable name>` *is not valid VBScript. If you see it in this book, you should replace* `<variable name>` *(including the angle brackets) with a name of your choice.* ◆

In VBScript, variables fulfill three important functions:

- They allow the writing of generic scripts that can perform the same operations using different data.
- In cases where the same string or numeric literal is required several times in a script, they allow that literal to be assigned to a variable once and then be referred to by the variable name. (For example, a script that needs to know that there are seven days in a week might assign the number 7 to a variable called `NumDays` and then refer to this variable rather than the numeric literal in computations.) This use of variables, similar to the use of environment variables in DOS batch files or at the command prompt, helps you avoid errors and inconsistencies within scripts.
- They can be used to control program flow, either by providing conditions for conditional execution or loop counters. (This use is discussed later in this chapter.)

The life cycle of a variable has four stages:

1. **The variable is initialized.** This process involves telling VBScript to create the variable and give it a name. This is accomplished with statements of the form `Dim <variable_name>`, where `<variable_name>` is replaced with the name by which you want to refer to the variable later. A variable name can be any word that is not already in use as a VBScript keyword. It can consist of any alphabetic or numeric characters, plus the underscore character (_). The only other restriction is that it cannot be any of the VBScript *reserved words*. This means that it cannot be a language keyword (such as and) or an operator (+).
2. **A value is assigned to the variable.** When it's first initialized, although the variable might "exist," it has no value. As soon as a variable has been assigned, it represents that value until explicitly changed. Assigning a variable is accomplished using expressions of the form `<variable_name> = <value>`, where `<value>` can be a string literal, a

numeric literal, or another variable name. If you assign another variable name, the value is copied from one to the other. After a value has been assigned to a variable, it can be changed either by assigning a new value explicitly or as the result of a computation.

3. **A value is unassigned.** After a value has been assigned, it persists until either a new value is assigned, the variable falls out of scope (discussed in a moment), or it is explicitly unassigned. Unassignment can be accomplished by setting the value to `empty` (with a statement of the form `<variable_name> = empty`). This action effectively returns the variable to its initialized but unassigned state.

Note: Unassigning Variables

Explicitly unassigning a value from a variable is not normally necessary. However, there are two situations in which you might want to do this. First, you might want to test whether a variable is empty and perform a conditional execution based on the test's outcome (see the later section "Conditional Execution"). Second, if a variable contains a large amount of data, such as the contents of a multimegabyte text-based log, you should unassign the data after you have finished using it to save memory. ◆

4. **The variable falls out of scope.** As soon as a variable falls out of scope, it has effectively ceased to exist. Most variables in VBScript have global scope, which means that they exist from the moment they are initialized until the moment the script stops executing. Some variables, however, do not behave in this way (see the "Subroutines" section later in this chapter).

After a variable has been initialized and a value assigned, it can be used in a script as though it were a literal. In other words, wherever a numeric literal appears, it can be replaced with a variable that represents the number. Whenever a string literal appears, it can be replaced with a variable that represents the string. To use a variable within a script, you simply refer to it by name.

The reason why string literals *always* must be enclosed in quotation marks should now be clear: VBScript could confuse an unenclosed string literal for a variable name or, for that matter, a built in keyword.

The following sample script should help clarify all this. It demonstrates the initialization, assignation, and use of variables:

```
Dim name
Dim age
Dim soonAge
name = "Matthew"
age = 25
```

```
soonAge = age + 5
WScript.Echo "Hello. Your name is " & name
WScript.Echo "You are " & age & "years old."
WScript.Echo "In 5 years time, you will be " & soonAge & _
      " years old."
```

The output of this code would be

```
Hello. Your name is Matthew
You are 25 years old.
In 5 years time, you will be 30 years old.
```

Note that variables and numeric literals can be used together in operations (`soonAge = age + 5`) and that literal strings and variables can be interchangeably concatenated to produce longer output strings (`"You are " & age & "years old."`).

If you are wondering why it is worth bothering with the calculation `soonAge = age + 5` when it would be just as easy in this case to write `soonAge = 30`, consider the changes you would have to make if you discovered that `age` should really be 26. In this code example, you would simply change the single assignment statement that sets up the `age` variable, and `soonAge` will automatically be correct; had `soonAge` been hard-wired, you would have to change that too. In addition, suppose you want to extend the script, maybe to pop up a box asking people to enter their age and setting the variable accordingly. Only by specifying everything else in the script in terms of the `age` variable can you make this work.

A little while ago we pointed out the probably obvious point that expressions of the form `"fish" * 3` are meaningless, because you cannot perform arithmetic operations on string literals. This mistake might seem very difficult to make, but exactly the same rule applies to variables, where it is much easier to fall into a trap. Consider this code fragment:

```
Dim age
Dim soonAge
age = "four"
... [many lines of code could go here] ...
SoonAge = age + 5
```

Oops! Unless you can actually see the assignment statement for `age` when you type the second statement, you might well assume that the variable contained a numeric value rather than a string literal. You would be wrong!

One way of avoiding this sort of mistake is to always label your variables with names that indicate whether they should be used for numeric or string values. Many programmers use prefixes to make the type of a variable clear: `age` becomes `numAge`; `name` becomes `strName`.

Very soon you will be ready to try out a fully-fledged code example and run it on the Windows Scripting Host. First, however, to make the example more interesting, you need to know one more thing—namely, how to pop up a dialog box, ask a user to provide some information, and assign that information to a variable. Luckily, this is incredibly simple due to a built-in function in VBScript called `InputBox`. The syntax for using this function follows the standard syntax for function calls described later in this chapter. For now, all that matters is that a function runs some code and then evaluates to an expression, normally based on the outcome of running the code. Therefore, a function can be placed anywhere in code that an expression would normally fit. The purpose of `InputBox` is to pop up a dialog box containing a message string, a user-editable text box, an OK button, and a Cancel button. When OK is clicked, it evaluates to the contents of the text box. If Cancel is clicked, it evaluates to an empty string (`""`). You invoke this function using the following syntax:

```
<variable_name> = InputBox(<text_string>)
```

Note: Placeholders

In the sections that follow, and throughout the rest of the book, we use angle brackets (<>) to indicate placeholders. When interpreting this, either in the text or in code, you should replace such placeholders with real, valid values. For example, `Dim <variable name>` *is not valid VBScript. If you see it in this book, you should replace* `<variable name>` *(including the angle brackets) with a name of your choice.* ◆

In the example, `<variable_name>` is the name of the variable that will hold the return value of the function, and `<text_string>` is the text of the message to display to the user. The value of `<text_string>` can, of course, be either a variable holding a string value or a string literal; the following two code fragments are equivalent:

```
'the first fragment
strAnswer = InputBox("Please enter your name and click OK")

'the second fragment
strQuestion = "Please enter your name and click OK"
strAnswer = InputBox(strQuestion)
```

Notice that arguments passed to a function are enclosed in parentheses.

The result of including either of these code fragments in a script would be a dialog box that looks very much like the one shown in Figure 2.1.

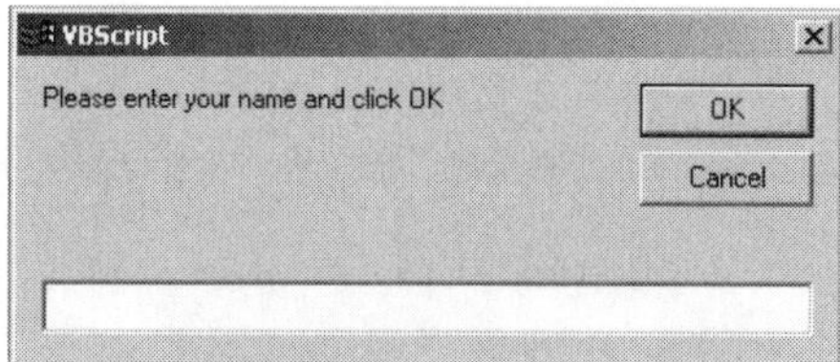

Figure 2.1 *An input box.*

Although input boxes are by no means the only mechanism for assigning values to variables at runtime, they are simple to use and visually appealing. We will introduce you to other more sophisticated methods later in this book.

A Fully-Fledged Example

At last you are ready to write a full-scale sample script and run it using the Windows Scripting Host. Your script will put together some of the code fragments you have already used by carrying out the following procedure:

1. It will pop up input boxes to ask the user to enter a name and age.
2. Using this information, it will calculate how old the user will be in 5 years' time and display the answer.
3. It will pop up a further pair of input boxes, each asking the user to enter a number.
4. It will calculate the sum, difference, and product of those numbers and display the answer in a series of dialog boxes.

Open a text editor, such as Notepad, and type the following script exactly as it appears here. If you want to, you can leave out the comments (the lines beginning with an apostrophe), because they are only there to explain what the script is doing.

```
'The line below forces VBScript to complain if we forget
'to explicitly initialize all variables (i.e. use a variable name
'without dimensioning them first).

option explicit

'Initialize all the variables we need
Dim strName
Dim numAge
Dim numFirstNum
Dim numSecondNum

'Ask the first pair of questions
strName = InputBox("Please enter your name and click OK")
numAge = InputBox("Please enter your age and click OK")
```

```
'now greet the user and tell them their age and their
'age in 5 years time
WScript.echo "Hello, " & strName
WScript.echo "You have told me that you are " & numAge & _
      " years old."
WScript.echo "In 5 years, you will be " & numAge + 5 & _
      " years old."

'now ask for a pair of numbers
numFirstNum = InputBox("Please enter any number and click OK")
numSecondNum = InputBox("Please enter a second number" _
      & " and click OK")

'finally calculate and display the sum, difference and product
WScript.echo "The sum of your numbers is " & _
      numFirstNum + numSecondNum
WScript.echo "The difference of your numbers is " & _
      numFirstNum - numSecondNum
WScript.echo "The product of your numbers is " & _
      numFirstNum * numSecondNum
```

After you have typed this script in full, save the file with the name script.vbs. To run it, open a command shell (by typing `cmd` into the Run dialog box), change to the directory where you saved the script, and type `wscript script.vbs`. Assuming that you typed everything correctly, you should see the first dialog box pop up. If you are running on a platform other than Windows 2000, you should first ensure that the Windows Scripting Host is properly installed. (See Appendix A, "WMI on Other Microsoft Platforms.")

You can try running any of the script fragments in this chapter using this technique (provided that they are syntactically complete): Type them into a text editor, save them with an appropriate filename and a .vbs extension, and run them with the Windows Scripting Host.

There are several things worth noting about the script:

- **All variables are given "sensible" names.** In other words, not only can you tell from the name what type of data the variable stores (string or number), but the name also reflects the data's function.
- **VBScript is not case-sensitive.** It does not care what combination of upPeR and LoWeRcase letters you use, but code is more readable if you stick to a consistent convention. In this script, variable names always begin with a lowercase prefix and then capitalize the first letter of every "word" or concept (such as `strSecondNum`). Statements other than those that start with a variable name begin with a capital letter. VBScript keywords are written using a convention similar to variable names, where capitalization follows "word" boundaries (such as `InputBox`).

- **A few statements are split to two lines because they are too long for the printed page.** Note that an underscore character appends every incomplete line. Continuation lines are indented for visual clarity. It is important to note that we never split a literal string to two lines using an underscore. Underscores are perfectly legitimate characters to contain within a string, so they cannot also be used to indicate a split statement. If you need to split a string literal, as we do on one occasion in this script, write it as two strings, separated with an ampersand (`&`) operator prior to the line break.
- **Different commands can be combined within a line.** Arithmetic operations and string-based concatenation can be combined in a single line. We did not need, for example, a variable called `numDifferenceOfNumbers`. We could work it out on-the-fly.

A final thing you have probably noticed about the script, if you have run it, is that it contains a bug! The dialog box that is meant to display the sum of the numbers actually displays a concatenation of the numbers. In other words, VBScript treats the numbers as strings, because the `InputBox` function returns a string value. We have a real example here of the problem first mentioned in the "Arithmetic Operators" section—namely, that unlike the – and `*` operators, the `+` operator is ambiguous: It can be used for both addition and string concatenation. There are several ways to tell VBScript to treat `numFirstNum` and `numSecondNum` as numbers and, therefore, to perform an addition operation rather than a concatenation operation. The simplest is to prefix the intended addition with a numeric literal that will not affect the result. Replace:

```
WScript.echo "The sum of your numbers is " & _
      numFirstNum + numSecondNum
```

with:

```
WScript.echo "The sum of your numbers is " & _
      0 + numFirstNum + numSecondNum
```

You will suddenly find that the script works as it should.

Note: Strong Typing in other Programming Languages

Many programming languages avoid this sort of problem by having strong typing for variables. This means that rather than simply initializing "a variable", you initialize "a string variable" or "a numeric variable" (actually, numeric is normally split further into "integer," "double," "float," and so on). An attempt to assign, say, a string value to an integer variable will simply produce an error. If you ever need to treat a string as a number, which is exactly what you need to do when

continues ▸

▶ *continued*

performing calculations based on the output of an `InputBox`, *you would normally explicitly cast from one type to another. The comparatively few languages that do use dynamically typed variables, such as Perl, tend to ensure that arithmetic addition and string concatenation use different operators. Why VBScript does not is quite beyond us!* ◆

Conditional Execution

The script might now be bug-free, but it certainly still has its problems. Consider, for example, what would happen if a user encountering the dialog box "Please enter your age and click OK" decided to submit a nonnumeric answer such as "hibiscus." VBScript would attempt to add 5 to "hibiscus," causing a runtime error. Arguably, a user who types `hibiscus` in response to a question about his age deserves for the script to fail! However, it is the job of a good programmer to anticipate problems that could occur as a result of user interaction with a script by ensuring, for example, that arithmetic calculations are carried out only on numbers. Conditional execution makes this possible by allowing you to choose whether to execute code, or even which code to execute, based on the evaluation of an expression.

The simplest form of conditional execution is the single-line `If` statement. It takes the following form:

```
If <condition> then <statement>
```

The `<condition>` can be substituted with any Boolean expression—that is, an expression that can evaluate to either true (–1) or false (0). This, of course, includes any expression involving a comparison operator. At execution time, if the expression evaluates to true, the statement is executed; otherwise, it is not.

Consider the following pair of script fragments. The first displays the phrase "I shall execute," and the second does not:

```
'this one will display the text
If 4 > 3 then WScript.echo "I shall execute"

'this one will not
If 3 > 4 then WScript.echo "I shall not execute"
```

Of course, in this particular case, you need hardly bother with the condition, because the outcome is utterly obvious. A more plausible scenario might be to compare a numeric literal with the contents of a variable whose value is assigned at runtime. The following little script, for example, asks a user to enter her age and displays the text "You cannot be telling the truth" if the answer given is more than 250. After all, very few people have lived to be more than 250 years old since Biblical days.

```
Dim numAge
numAge = InputBox("Please enter your age and click OK")
If numAge > 250 then WScript.echo "You cannot be telling" _
      & " the truth."
```

The expression `numAge > 250` is guaranteed to be Boolean, because it uses the conditional operator `>`. If you want to try out this little script, simply type it into your text editor, save it with a .vbs extension, and run it in the same way as the previous example.

Sometimes, you might want to carry out more than one command as a result of an evaluation. One way to achieve this is to have a series of single-line `If` statements, each of which tests the same condition. However, this would be very inefficient (because you would be testing the same thing several times) and could also lead to inconsistency if the evaluation changed for some reason while the script ran. The solution is to use a multiline `If` block of the following form:

```
If <condition> then
      <statement>
      ' ... as many statements as you like can go here
End if
```

Although it isn't necessary, it is conventional to indent statement lines to provide a clear indication that they constitute a block of code that is subordinate to the `If`. The `End if` statement tells VBScript that it has reached the end of the statements that should be executed conditionally. All lines following the `End If` will execute, regardless of the evaluation. As an example, you can extend the following little script so that if a user gives her age as more than 250 years old, not only is a message displayed, but `numAge` is given a *default* value of 32:

```
Dim numAge
numAge = InputBox("Please enter your age and click OK")
If numAge > 250 then
      WScript.echo "You cannot be telling the truth"
      numAge = 32
End if
```

Frequently, it is not good enough to execute code only if a condition is met; rather, you want to choose which code to execute depending on the outcome of a condition. For this, you use an `If-Else` block:

```
If <condition> then
      '... statements here are executed if condition is true
Else
      '... statements here are executed if condition is false
End if
```

There are times when the behavior of a script should depend not just on a single condition but on combinations of different ones. VBScript provides a number of mechanisms for dealing with such eventualities.

If you need conditional execution to depend on two or more conditions, they can simply be specified as a compound separated by the logical `AND` or `OR` operator. For example, a condition that tested whether a person was eligible for a discount at a store might read `numAge < 18 OR numAge > 65`. This expression would evaluate to true unless `numAge` was between 18 and 65. (People under 18 or over 65 are often eligible for discounts.)

If minors (people under 18) were eligible for a different discount than seniors (people over 65), you might want to use an `If-Elseif-Else` block, which takes the following form:

```
If <condition> then
      '...statements go here
Elseif <condition>
      '...statements go here
Elseif <condition>
      '...statements go here
'... As many more "Elseif" blocks as you need go here
Else
      '...statement here will be executed if ALL conditions
      ' evaluated to false
End If
```

VBScript executes this type of block by testing each condition in turn until one of them evaluates to true. As soon as a true evaluation is found, all the statements in the relevant code block are executed, after which execution continues from the next statement that appears after the `End If`. The important thing to remember here is that with an `If-Elseif-Else` block, one and only one block of statements will execute.

Note: Select Case

Where all the expressions are of the form `<expression> = <value>` *and* `<expression>` *is the same for every case (such as if you want to execute different statements depending on whether a variable stores the string* `"abacus"`, `"rhubarb"`, `"custard"`, *or* `"treacle"`*), you can use a special construction called* `Select Case` *instead of an* `If-Elseif-Else` *block. Although* `Select Case` *is a more elegant solution, we do not discuss it here, because it adds unnecessary complications at this stage for something that accomplishes nothing that cannot also be accomplished with the other syntax. We will meet* `Select Case` *in later chapters.* ◆

A final point to note is that conditional execution blocks can contain literally anything that can occur anywhere else in a script. This includes more conditional execution blocks! It is possible to build quite sophisticated patterns of conditional execution by nesting `If` statements. We leave the details to your imagination.

We will end this section by introducing a rather useful VBScript built-in function, `IsNumeric`. This function takes as an argument any valid expression and evaluates to true if and only if the expression can be evaluated as a number. For example, this entire expression evaluates to true, because 95 is a numeric literal:

```
IsNumeric(95)
```

In addition, this next one also evaluates to true, because the string literal `"95"` can be interpreted numerically:

```
IsNumeric("95")
```

This, however, evaluates to false:

```
IsNumeric("fish")
```

To see why this function is so very useful, think back to the full script presented in the preceding section. Although after you fixed the bug the script appeared to work very well, in reality it is rather fragile. As we suggested at the start of this section, it would be easy for a user to crash it simply by typing something silly into the "Please enter your age and click OK" dialog. The example we gave was someone typing `hibiscus` into the box, which would break the script at this line:

```
WScript.echo "In 5 years, you will be " & numAge + 5 & _
      " years old."
```

However hard it tries, VBScript can't add 5 to `hibiscus`! Using `IsNumeric` in conjunction with conditional execution, you can avoid this eventuality by making sure that numeric calculations are carried out only on numbers, as promised at the start of this section.

The following is a slightly modified version of the earlier script. The difference here is that you use a combination of `IsNumeric` and an `If-Else-End If` block to warn the user and exit gracefully if a nonnumeric value is typed into the dialog box when a number is required:

```
'Force VBScript to complain if we forget
'to explicitly initialize all variables
option explicit

'Initialize all the variables we need
Dim strName
```

```
Dim numAge
Dim numFirstNum
Dim numSecondNum

'Ask the first pair of questions
strName = InputBox("Please enter your name and click OK")
numAge = InputBox("Please enter your age and click OK")

'now check that numAge really is a number
'if it is, continue with the script
If IsNumeric(numAge) then
      'greet the user and tell them their age and their
      'age in 5 years time
      WScript.echo "Hello, " & strName
      WSCript.echo "You have told me that you are " & numAge & _
             " years old."
      WScript.echo "In 5 years, you will be " & numAge + 5 & _
             " years old."
Else
      'tell the user that they are mad, and exit
      WScript.echo "You have entered a non-numeric age! " & _
             "Are you insane?"
      WScript.Quit
End If

'now ask for a pair of numbers
numFirstNum = InputBox("Please enter any number and click OK")
numSecondNum = InputBox("Please enter a second number" _
       & " and click OK")

'Check they entered two numeric values and if so
'calculate and display the sum, difference and product
If IsNumeric(numFirstNum) AND IsNumeric(numSecondNum) then
      WScript.echo "The sum of your numbers is " & _
             numFirstNum + numSecondNum
      WScript.echo "The difference of your numbers is " & _
             numFirstNum - numSecondNum
      WScript.echo "The product of your numbers is " &  _
             numFirstNum * numSecondNum
Else
      WScript.echo "You did not enter two numbers."
End If
```

Notice that in the second half of the script, we use the logical AND operator to test both numbers at once. Also, it is worth noting that we didn't need to explicitly tell the scripting host to exit in the `Else` block of the second half, because there were no further instructions to execute anyway.

Loops

Although the combination of IsNumeric and conditional execution improves the script immeasurably, it is still far from ideal. Although you can guarantee that the code won't display nonsense, it is hardly very user-friendly to quit as soon as someone gets something wrong! Rather than displaying a rude message and exiting when a nonnumeric value is typed into the dialog box, it would surely be far better to simply pop up the dialog box again. In fact, what you really want is for the dialog to keep on popping up persistently until the user types a valid number. You can achieve exactly this effect with a conditional loop—more specifically, a Do...Until loop.

Do...Until

A Do...Until loop consists of a code block and a Boolean expression (a condition). When VBScript encounters such a loop, it executes all the instructions in the code block and then evaluates the condition. If the condition is true, execution continues from the next instruction following the loop. If the condition is false, the cycle begins again. In other words, the code "loops until" the condition becomes true.

The syntax for a Do...Until loop takes the following form:

```
Do
        'The code block
        <statement>
        ...
        <statement>
Until <condition>
```

<statement> can be replaced with any number of valid VBScript statements, and <condition> can be any expression that evaluates to a Boolean.

Such a loop is exactly what you need to improve the script. Instead of using an If-Else-End If block to conditionally execute calculations, you can write something like this:

```
Do
        numAge = InputBox("Please enter your age and click OK")
Until IsNumeric(numAge)
'...rest of script goes here
```

VBScript interprets this by popping up the input box and then evaluating IsNumeric(numAge). If numAge contains a number, the expression is true, and execution can continue. If it does not, the expression is false, and the dialog is displayed again, after which IsNumeric(numAge) is evaluated again, and so on, ad infinitum!

Do...While

Another commonly used loop, and one that appears frequently throughout this book, is `Do...While`. It is almost identical conceptually to the `Do...Until` loop, with one exception. Whereas the `Do...Until` loop repeatedly executes the code within the loop until the condition at the end evaluates to true, the `Do...While` loop executes until the condition at the end evaluates to false. In other words, `Do...While` executes code while the condition remains true—hence its name. The syntax for specifying a `Do...While` loop is exactly as you might have predicted:

```
Do
      <statement>
      ...
      <statement>
While <condition>
```

You might have noticed that these loops can be used interchangeably if you merely negate the condition. For example, in the case of our script, the `Do...Until` says "Pop up a dialog box until the user enters a valid number," whereas the `Do...While` says "Pop up a dialog box while the user persists in entering an invalid number." In code terms, to replace the `Do[el]Until` with a `Do...While`, you would replace this:

```
Do
      numAge = InputBox("Please enter your age and click OK")
Until IsNumeric(numAge)
'...rest of script goes here
```

with this:

```
Do
      numAge = InputBox("Please enter your age and click OK")
While Not IsNumeric(numAge)
'...rest of script goes here
```

Which one is better? Well, to be honest, it doesn't really matter! Use whichever you prefer. Normally, the rule is to write the code that is easiest to understand. In practice, this means to use the loop that fits the task most logically. If you find yourself writing things such as `While Not IsNumeric(numAge)`, you probably really mean `Until IsNumeric(numAge)`, so use that form instead.

Note: Why Do the Two "Do" Loops Exist?

The existence of the two forms is what programmer types might call "syntactic sugar." This doesn't add any new functionality, but it does make programs easier to read if you choose the logically most appropriate loop. ◆

While...Wend

Both the Do...Until and Do...While loops are guaranteed to execute the code within the loop at least once, because the condition is tested at the end. There are times, however, when this is not very helpful. A classic example is if you want to read the contents of a text file into memory. A standard approach is to write a loop that reads a single line and appends it to a variable. You repeatedly loop over this code until no more lines are left. (Alternatively, you repeatedly loop through the code while there are still more lines to read.) At first glance, this seems like a classic case for Do...Until or Do...While, but unfortunately there is a snag: If the file is totally empty (if it contains no lines at all), you will not find out until after the code within the loop has executed once, by which time the program will have probably crashed!

The solution, clearly, is to test the condition at the start of the loop. This can be accomplished with a While[el]Wend loop, whose syntax is as follows:

```
While <condition>
      <statement>
      ...
      <statement>
Wend
```

We leave an example to your imagination.

For...Next

A final type of loop is worth mentioning at this stage—namely, For...Next, which is conceptually somewhat different than the others. Whereas all the loops we have seen so far have been controlled by a condition, the For...Next loop iterates over the value of a variable. It is used whenever you want a block of code to execute a specific number of times. The For...Next loop takes the following form:

```
For <variable> = <num1> to <num2>
      <statement>
      ...
      <statement>
Next
```

<variable> can be any variable name, <num1> is the start of the iteration, and <num2> is the end of the iteration. Between the For and Next statements is the code block to be looped. Except in very special circumstances (as discussed

in a moment), `<num2>` must always be larger than `<num1>`. When VBScript encounters one of these loops, it performs the following procedure:

1. The value of `<variable>` is set to the value of `<num1>`.
2. If the value of `<variable>` is smaller than or equal to `<num2>`, all statements in the loop are executed. Otherwise, execution continues from the statement immediately following `Next`, and that is the end of the loop.
3. The value of `<variable>` is incremented by 1 (that is, VBScript performs the calculation `<variable> = <variable> + 1`), and the process begins again.

To clarify, here is a trivial example that uses a `For...Next` loop to display the word "hello" 10 times:

```
Dim numIterator
For numIterator = 1 to 10
      WScript.echo "Hello"
Next
```

If you need to carry out an operation several times, but you don't want to specify the number of iterations until runtime, you can still use a `For...Next` loop. To do so, merely replace `<num2>` with a numeric variable whose value is supplied when the script is run.

If the code inside the loop needs to know how many iterations have passed, it can read the value of `<variable>`, because this value increases by 1 every iteration. For example, a trivial modification can improve the preceding script fragment by making it tell the user how many times it has said "Hello":

```
Dim numCounter
For numCounter = 1 to 10
      WScript.echo "Hello. I have now said hello " & _
             numCounter & " times."
Next
```

This example has a minor cosmetic bug. The first time through, it displays "Hello. I have now said hello 1 times." This is grammatically incorrect, because it should not have an "s". To correct this, you need to modify the script so that the "s" in "times" appears only after the first iteration. A little string manipulation coupled with conditional execution can solve this problem. Here is a sample script that fixes this problem:

```
Dim numCounter
Dim strMessage
For numCounter = 1 to 10
      strMessage = "Hello. I have now said hello " & _
```

```
            numCounter & " time"
        If numCounter > 1 then strMessage = strMessage + "s"
        strMessage = strMessage + "."
        WScript.echo strMessage
Next
```

So far, all the `For...Next` loops you have seen have been just a mechanism for executing a block of code a given number of times. Our use of the counter variable within the code block has been exclusively cosmetic. It is possible, of course, to make more sophisticated use of the loop, such as by using the counter in arithmetic computations. In such situations, you might want the loop to exhibit slightly more complex behavior than simply counting from 1 to some other value. You can use two techniques to make its behavior somewhat more interesting:

- Change the value of `<num1>` to something other than 1.
- Use the `step` keyword.

Just as you can set the value of `<num2>`, you can also set `<num1>` to something other than 1. If, for example, you wanted to add all the numbers between 14 and 17, you could write this:

```
Dim numCounter
Dim numAnswer
numAnswer = 0
For numCounter = 14 to 17
      numAnswer = numAnswer + numCounter
Next
WScript.echo numAnswer
```

Of course, if you are writing this sort of thing, you need to be careful that `<num1>` is never larger than `<num2>`. Otherwise, the code in the loop will not execute at all!

By default, the value of `<variable>` is incremented by 1 every time the loop iterates. It is possible, however, to tell VBScript to change this increment by any value using the `step` keyword. This can be seen in the following code fragment, which adds all the even numbers between 2 and 20:

```
Dim numCounter
Dim numAnswer
numAnswer = 0
For numCounter = 2 to 20 step 2
      numAnswer = numAnswer + numCounter
Next
WScript.echo numAnswer
```

As a variation on this theme, if you need your loop to count backwards, just supply a negative `step` value (such as `For numCounter = 10 to 1 step -1`). Using a negative step value is the only time you ever want `<num2>` to be smaller than `<num1>`.

Note: Counting and Conditions

You will be relieved to hear that the discussion of loops is coming to an end. Before we leave them completely, however, let's consider one small point: We stated that a `For...Next` *loop is conceptually quite different from the conditional loops described earlier, because one is concerned with conditions and the other with counting. Certainly, the syntax for the two types of loops looks quite different. On a theoretical level, however, both types are extremely similar. Consider how a* `For...Next` *loop operates: It keeps incrementing a counter and decides whether to loop depending on the value of that counter. In other words, execution of the code in the loop depends on the value of the counter. To give a VBScript example, this code:*

```
Dim numCounter
For numCounter = 1 to 10
        'Do something in here
Next
```

does exactly the same as this:

```
Dim numCounter
numCounter = 1
While numCounter <= 10
        'Do something in here
        numCounter = numCounter + 1
Wend ◆
```

So why have a special `For...Next` loop with its own name and its own syntax when a `While...Wend` does the same job? For exactly the same reason that there is a `Do...Until` and a `Do...While`—to make scripts more readable. VBScript provides all these options so that the script's syntax can match the concept being expressed as closely as possible. The fact that they all effectively do the same thing is unimportant. So which loop should you use in any given situation? It all depends on your motivation for using it.

Subroutines

Imagine that everyone in your department is about to get an 11.2% pay raise. Just for fun, you want to write a quick script that figures out what each person's increase in monthly income will be. The easiest thing would be just to write the simple calculation once for every employee. A fragment of the script might look something like this:

```
'employee 1 - bob
numAmount = (15000 * 0.112) / 12
WScript.echo "Cool Bob! You will have another " & _
      numAmount & " to spend each month"
```

```
'employee 2 - frank
numAmount = (26000 * 0.112) / 12
WScript.echo "Cool Frank! You will have another " & _
      numAmount & " to spend each month"

'...and the same again for each employee
```

Even ignoring the fact that writing scripts that pop up dialog boxes announcing the amount of extra salary people will get is a bad thing to do, this script is horrific for a number of reasons:

- It is very difficult for someone to look at it and figure out what it does. Although you might guess that every "block" of code is performing the same calculation and then displaying the answer, the only way to be sure would be to look at every one. Imagine if there were 100 employees!
- You could easily make mistakes. On the 75th employee, your fingers might be getting tired, not to mention your brain, so you could accidentally type the calculation wrong (and, yes, that sort of thing can happen even if you're using cut and paste).
- It would be very tedious to maintain a script like this. Suppose you got the amount wrong—it was meant to be an 11.1% pay raise. You might have to change 100 lines of code.

In short, you don't want to write things like this! Whenever you find yourself repeatedly writing what is effectively the same code block—or using cut and paste in your program—you know it's time to write a subroutine.

Subroutines are self-contained blocks of code that can be called from anywhere in your script, like miniprograms in their own right. What makes them so powerful is that you can pass them arguments that control how they operate. Any number or text string passed as an argument appears to the subroutine itself as a variable.

A subroutine is defined using this syntax:

```
Sub <name> (<arg1>, <arg2>, etc...)
      <Statement>
      ...
      <Statement>
End Sub
```

<name> is the name used to refer to that subroutine from elsewhere in the program, and the various <arg>s are the names of variables that are used inside it to refer to the arguments. Between Sub and the End Sub can be any number of valid VBScript statements, except for the declaration of another subroutine. Although it is perfectly acceptable for a subroutine to *call* another as part of its work, it is not valid for a subroutine declaration (a Sub statement) to be nested within another.

To call a subroutine, you simply type its name, followed by any arguments separated by commas:

```
<name> <arg1>,<arg2> ...
```

The number of arguments you specify when calling a subroutine must exactly match the number defined by the subroutine itself; if it does not, a syntax error occurs. Syntactically, a call to a subroutine is a complete statement.

To write the income calculator with a subroutine, you would first define one that performs that calculation in terms of a variable, such as `numCurrentSalary`, and then displays the answer in terms of `strEmployeeName`; for each employee, you would then call it. The complete code would look similar to this:

```
'first define the subroutine
Sub CalculateIncome(numCurrentSalary,strEmployeeName)
      numAmount = (numCurrentSalary * 0.112) / 12
      WScript.echo "Cool " & strEmployeeName & _
             "! You will have another " & _
             numAmount & " to spend each month"
End Sub

The syntax to use it for each employee is:
CalculateIncome 15000, "Bob"
CalculateIncome 26000, "Frank"
'... etc for each employee
```

Every time you call `CalculateIncome` with the two arguments, the values are automatically assigned to `numCurrentSalary` and `strEmployeeName` so that they can be used in the calculation. Notice that the two variables are not (and must not be) explicitly declared with a `Dim` statement; defining them as arguments is enough to make them exist. The advantages of this method should be clear:

- The script is a fraction of the length, and anyone with VBScript knowledge could easily figure out what it does.
- Changing the calculation would be trivial: You simply change it in the subroutine, and it will work for everyone.
- You are far less susceptible to errors. For each new employee line you want to add to the list, you simply provide the two bits of information that are unique to that employee—salary and name. You don't have to worry about anything else.

Writing a subroutine can be thought of as extending the VBScript language itself: As soon as it is written, you simply have a custom facility that can be used in your script as easily as a built-in keyword. Although you have probably already guessed, it is worth noting that the effect of supplying a number where a text string argument is needed or vice versa has exactly the same effect as it would have anywhere else in VBScript: You get a syntax error.

If a subroutine is particularly long and complex, it might be desirable—or even necessary—to use variables inside it, just like in any other block of code. The difference is that you might not want those variables to be visible from outside the subroutine itself. You can do this by declaring the variables inside the subroutine as follows:

```
'this subroutine takes no arguments
Sub MySub()
      'First declare a variable
      Dim strPrivate
      strPrivate = "I cannot be accessed from outside the sub"
      WScript.echo strPrivate
End Sub
```

The variable `strPrivate` simply does not exist outside the subroutine. Instead, it is initialized each time it is called. As soon as the code inside has ended, it falls out of scope.

Functions

The final VBScript language element that needs to be introduced in this chapter is the function. In many ways, a function is identical to a subroutine. The only difference between a function and a subroutine is that a function returns a value. In practice, this means that whereas a subroutine is syntactically a statement, a function is syntactically an expression. You can define a function whenever you repeatedly carry out a series of operations whose result you want to retrieve.

In a vein similar to subroutines, functions are defined using the following syntax:

```
Function <name> (<arg1>, <arg2>, ...etc)
      <statement>
      ...
      <statement>
      <name> = <value>
End Function
```

Just as with a subroutine, a function must have a name and can optionally define a number of arguments. Between the declaration line and `End Function` can be any valid VBScript statements, except for another function definition. The major difference to note is that the final line of a function must be of the form `<name> = <value>`, where `<name>` is the name of the function itself. `<value>` is the value that the function *returns* when it exits. In other words, the function call expression *evaluates* to that value. Often, the value to which a function evaluates is called its *return value*.

Once defined, a function can be called with the following syntax:

```
<variable> = <function_name>(<arg1>,<arg2>,etc)
```

Here, `<variable>` is the name of a variable in which the return value is stored when the function exits. Notice that the syntax is not the same as that for a subroutine call, because here the comma-separated arguments are placed within parentheses. If you are calling a function that does not take any arguments, you should supply an empty set of parentheses.

The definition and use of functions is illustrated by the following short example, which uses a function to add two values and return a result:

```
'We define the function here
Function addNumbers(numFirst,numSecond)
    addNumbers = numFirst + numSecond
End Function

'and use it here
WScript.Echo addNumbers(3,4)
```

Running this script displays the number 7. Of course, this particular example is rather pointless, because a script that wants to add 3 and 4 could consist merely of the line `Wscript.Echo 3 + 4`. However, this more-concise version would not have demonstrated function use! More substantial functions will be presented frequently throughout this book. Their value will soon become obvious.

Just to make matters slightly more complicated, a second syntax can be used to invoke functions. It takes the following form:

```
<function name> <arg1> <arg2> <etc...>
```

In other words, you can call a function as though it were in fact a subroutine. If you do this, there is no way of discovering the return value, so the preceding example is utterly useless. There are, however, circumstances in which you might want to use a function to carry out some task but do not care about the value that is returned. You will see examples as this book progresses.

This section will end with a little nostalgia. Earlier in this chapter, we demonstrated a script that asks a user to enter his or her name. This script then uses that value to greet the person. The script fragment in question looked something like this:

```
Dim strName
strName = InputBox("Please enter your name and click OK")
WScript.echo "Hello " & strName
```

In retrospect, you can see that `InputBox` is nothing more than a *built-in function*. Such a function works identically to one that you can write yourself. The major difference is that it has already been written for you, and you cannot see the code inside it! These lines of code, then, are a paradigmatic example of function use: You want a value to be assigned to `strName`. You achieve this goal by using a function that pops up a dialog box, displays a message that you pass to it as an argument, reads a text string that the user enters, and returns it. As soon as the function has been written (which, in this case, it has—by the VBScript team) all of this activity can be encapsulated in a single, elegant line of code.

Accessing WMI from VBScript

If you have read and understood the entirety of the previous section, you know pretty much all you need to know about the basics of the VBScript language. You know how to write syntactically correct code, and you have an idea of what is good style and what is bad. You could not really claim to be a VBScript expert at this stage (unless, of course, you already were before you started reading this book), because there are several language features that we haven't yet mentioned, as well as some subtleties to learn about the ones we have! However, you certainly know almost enough to start making use of VBScript to write administration scripts. The one thing missing is knowledge of how VBScript can interact with Windows 2000 in a useful way. In short, you need to know how to access WMI components from scripts. Because the rest of this book is all about how to use VBScript and WMI to administer Windows-based networks, we do not want to go into too many details at this stage. However, we felt that this chapter seemed somewhat incomplete without at least a glimpse of what is to come. This final section, therefore, provides a very brief introduction to accessing WMI components from scripts.

VBScript and COM

You will remember from the previous chapter that WMI implements COM, a technology specifically designed to integrate with tools such as scripting languages. It should come as no surprise, then, that VBScript can access COM objects transparently. In fact, you have already come across a COM object—`WScript`. When you write `WScript.Echo "hello"`, you are not calling some weirdly named built-in subroutine; you are invoking the `Echo` method of the `WScript` object.

The word `WScript` when used within VBScript is in reality an *object reference*. An object reference is essentially just a variable, but instead of pointing to a string or a number, it points to an object. Just as you can refer to a string or numeric literal by the name of a variable that points to it, you can refer to an object by the reference that points to it. Just like variables, object references have to be *declared* and values *assigned* before they can be useful. The only reason why you didn't have to do this with `WScript` is that VBScript automatically makes this particular object reference available without your having to do anything.

As soon as you have a valid object reference (an object reference that has a value assigned), you can access its *properties* and *methods* (see Chapter 1, "Introduction to WMI,") by appending a dot to its name and then suffixing it with the property or method name in question. As you have seen, the `Echo` method of `WScript` is therefore referred to as `WScript.Echo <parameter>`.

Object properties behave syntactically in exactly the same way as a variable behaves. This means that they can be placed either on the left or the right side of an assignment statement, depending on whether you want to get or set the value. For example, `WScript` has a property called `Version`, which stores the version number of the Windows Scripting Host on your system. If you wanted to find out the version number, you might write this short script:

```
Dim numVersion
numVersion = WScript.Version
WScript.echo "Version is " & numVersion
```

If you wanted to be more concise, you could simply write this:

```
WScript.echo "Version is " & WScript.Version
```

Theoretically, if you wanted to change the value of this property, you would write something along these lines:

```
WScript.Version = 6.7
```

The only snag is that (unsurprisingly) `Version` is a read-only property; this attempt to change it raises a runtime error.

You have already seen that a method can be used almost identically to a subroutine, using this syntax:

```
<objectref>.<methodname> <arg1>, <arg2> etc.
```

In addition, however, some methods return values. In this case, they are used like functions:

```
<variable> = <objectref>.<methodname>(<arg1>, <arg2>, etc)
```

Object properties may be accessed and used just like any other variables, but object references themselves do not behave quite like other variables. They are declared using the conventional syntax:

```
Dim <objectref>
```

But assignment is not the same at all. Whereas variable assignment takes the form `<name> = <value>`, object reference assignment is accomplished with the special keyword `Set`:

```
Set <objectrefname> = <object>
```

If you want to dereference an object (unassign the reference), the syntax is also slightly different from other types of variables. Whereas to unassign a variable you would type `<name> = Empty`, an object is dereferenced with the `Nothing` keyword:

```
Set <objectrefname> = Nothing
```

It is good practice to always dereference an object after you have finished using it. Depending on who created it, VBScript might be able to reclaim memory used by an object that is no longer needed. The same could be said for variables (it is, in fact, good practice to declare variables as `Empty` when you no longer need them), but the average object takes up considerably more memory than the average variable.

This syntactic distinction reflects a fundamental difference between variables and object references—namely, that variables are assigned by value, whereas object references are assigned by reference. To understand what this difference actually means, consider this code fragment:

```
Dim numSomeNumber
Dim numAnotherNumber

numSomeNumber = 20
numAnotherNumber = numSomeNumber
numSomeNumber = 50

WScript.echo "Some number is " & numSomeNumber & _
      " and another number is " & numAnotherNumber
```

If you run this script, it will pop up a dialog box displaying the text "Some number is 50 and another number is 20". The reason for this is that when you assign the value of `numSomeNumber` to `numAnotherNumber`, you are assigning it by value; you are literally copying the value and storing that copy somewhere else.

On the other hand, imagine that you have an ActiveX object that has a single property called `Value`. You could try writing a script similar to the one just shown, but this time using references to the ActiveX object instead of variables to store the number. (Because we have not yet explained how to create objects or get references to them, assume for this code fragment that `refSomeNumber` has already been correctly initialized and assigned, just like the `WScript` reference.)

```
Dim refAnotherNumber
'first set the value of refSomeNumber to 20
refSomeNumber.value = 20

'now make refAnotherNumber point to refSomeNumber
Set refAnotherNumber = refSomeNumber

'now change the Value of refSomeNumber
refSomeNumber.value = 50

WScript.echo "Some number is " & refSomeNumber.value & _
      " and another number is " & refAnotherNumber.value
```

The output of this script is "Some number is 50 and another number is 50". The reason? When we assigned `refSomeNumber` to `refAnotherNumber`, we did not make a copy of the object itself; all we did was point another name at the same object. `refSomeNumber` and `refAnotherNumber` are two names for exactly the same thing.

If you are still confused by this, consider this short script:

```
Dim refGoose
Set refGoose = WScript
refGoose.echo "I am a goose!"
```

This is perfectly correct VBScript syntax that would work just fine. All it does is initialize a variable, `refGoose`, assign an object to it, and use a method of that object to display the text "I am a goose!". Clearly, what we have done here is made a second reference to the object normally referred to as `WScript`. However, we haven't copied that object; there is still just one Windows Scripting Host on your computer. Likewise, consider a WMI object that represents a hard disk in your computer. If objects were assigned by value, we could manufacture new hard disks very cheaply like this (this code assumes that `refHD` already points correctly to the hard disk object):

```
Dim refAnotherHD
Dim refAndAnotherHD
Dim refAndYetAnotherHD

Set refAnotherHD = refHD
Set refAndAnotherHD = refHD
Set refAndYetAnotherHD = refHD
```

Sadly, such a ploy would not work. You would simply have four references to the same hard disk object. Oh, well. Back to the shop.

Referencing a WMI Object

It should now be clear that as soon as you have a reference to an object, accessing its properties and using its methods is extremely simple. The last remaining question, then, is how do you get a reference in the first place?

As you have already seen, an extremely simple way to get a reference is to take a reference from another one. However, this leaves you with something of a bootstrapping problem! Unfortunately, there is no single answer to the question of how you initialize and reference an object, because it depends on what the object is and where it comes from. Even if we restrict ourselves to consideration of WMI objects, the way to get a reference depends on a host of factors, such as whether you know the exact name of the object you are looking for, whether you need to issue a WQL query, and whether your script and the object reside on the same computer. It can even depend on the use you want to make out of the object reference when you have it. Having said this, in the simplest scenario, getting a reference to a WMI object can be as trivial as specifying the name of the object you want in a moniker string and passing that moniker string as an argument to VBScript's built-in `GetObject()` function.

VBScript cannot access WMI objects itself, because it knows nothing about the WMI providers that create them. VBScript doesn't even know about the CIM Object Manager that normally brokers WMI objects. Therefore, if a VBScript script needs access to such a beast, it has to call on the services of a *moniker,* a special type of object that can act as an intermediary between VBScript and a system that can provide the desired reference. A *moniker string* is a text string that tells VBScript which moniker to call on and then tells the moniker what object is required. The `GetObject()` built-in VBScript function can use a moniker string to ask a moniker to get the reference.

So, the syntax for getting an object reference is

```
Set <objectrefname> = GetObject(<moniker>)
```

In this example, `<objectref>` is the name of a variable to which the object will be assigned, and `<moniker>` is the moniker string. The moniker string itself consists of two parts, separated by a colon. The first part tells `GetObject` which moniker to use; the second, moniker-specific part tells the moniker what to do.

The moniker associated with WMI has the text name `WINMGMTS`, which presumably stands for "Windows Management Services." These letters, therefore, constitute the first part of any moniker string destined to retrieve a reference to a WMI object. The second part of the string—the bit interpreted by the `WINMGMTS` moniker—can be somewhat more complicated. The simplest incantation, however, consists merely of the object path to a WMI object (see Chapter 1). An entire moniker string required to retrieve a reference to the WMI object representing the C: drive on a Windows 2000 box would be as follows:

```
WINMGMTS:Win32_LogicalDisk='c:'
```

This means "Ask the `WINMGMTS` moniker to get a reference to the object in the default namespace of type `Win32_LogicalDisk` whose key value is C:." To get a reference to the WMI object in question, all you need is a two-line script:

```
Dim refMyHardDisk
Set refMyHardDisk = GetObject("WINMGMTS:Win32_LogicalDisk='C:'")
```

It really is as easy as that!

Note: Quoting a Quotation Mark

You might notice that within the moniker string itself, we have used apostrophes (') in place of quotation marks (") to demark a string literal. Quotation marks are allowed according to the moniker string syntax, but in VBScript, their use presents a rather ugly problem: The moniker itself (which is a string literal) needs to contain quotation marks. VBScript would not know that the second quotation mark was a nested quotation and would interpret it as the end of the whole moniker string—with unfortunate results! If you ever need to quote a quotation mark literally, as it were, this is possible within VBScript: You escape it with yet another quotation mark! In other words, inside a string, `"` *becomes* `""`*. If you ever need to assign to a variable a string literal that contains only a pair of quotation marks, you will find yourself writing something like this:*

```
Dim strStupid
StrStupid = """"""
```

Why the developers of VBScript decided on such a ludicrously illegible strategy is a total mystery.

The problem of quoting quotes is obviously common to all languages, not just VBScript. Most, however, use an escape character that isn't itself a quotation mark. For example, C uses \ as its escape symbol. Of course, this means that a literal \ has to be escaped as \\, but this is clearer and a far less regular occurrence than the double quoting in VBScript.

We can thank the designers of WMI for the fact that we can avoid all this nonsense by simply using apostrophes to quote string literals within WMI object paths. ◆

We will end this chapter with a short, simple script that gets a reference to the WMI object corresponding to the C: drive on a computer and reads one of its values to display a dialog box containing the size of the disk in bytes. The script should work if you type it exactly as is and run it with the Windows Scripting Host, but this depends on the security settings on your workstation (WMI security issues are discussed in Chapter 5, "WMI Security"). If the script does not work for you, make sure that you are a member of the Administrators group, and try again.

```
'How big is your C: drive? Let's find out
Dim refDrive
Set refDrive = GetObject("WINMGMTS:Win32_LogicalDisk='C:'")
WScript.echo "Your drive is " & refDrive.Size & " bytes."
Set refDrive = Nothing
```

In reality, the final line of the script that releases the reference to `refDrive` is not actually needed, because as soon as the variable goes *out of scope,* which it does when the script stops executing, VBScript automatically performs this step for you. However, explicitly freeing an object reference that you have stopped using is considered good practice, even in cases where it is not strictly necessary.

If you have come this far and can understand within reason what is going on, you are well on your way to becoming a WMI/VBScript guru. The details can be much more complex when you write more powerful scripts and access WMI in more sophisticated ways, but the conceptual basis remains unaltered.

Summary

This chapter introduced the VBScript language. It explained the basics of VBScript syntax and the fundamental building blocks of a script, including statements, operators, variables, conditional execution, loops, subroutines, and functions. In addition, it demonstrated how, for a simple case, WMI objects can be accessed from VBScript with only a few lines of code. This basic knowledge was intended to impart the knowledge of VBScript required to understand the rest of this book. Discussion of some of VBScript's more interesting features and its extensive built-in functions will be developed in conjunction with consideration of WMI as this book progresses.

3

Examining the Filesystem with WMI

Having spent the first two chapters introducing the core WMI concepts and the basics of the VBScript programming language, we will now start putting it all to work. In this chapter, we will investigate the fundamentals of the Windows 2000 filesystem as seen from a WMI perspective. More importantly, we will use the filesystem to investigate how WMI works in a real computing environment. You will see how the various components of WMI fit together, how WMI objects are related to each other, and how VBScript can be used to control them.

Filesystem Basics

At its most basic, a filesystem is quite simply a collection of files, hierarchically organized into folders (or directories). It should come as no surprise, then, that two fundamental classes of WMI objects represent a filesystem. One represents a file, and the other represents a directory.

Properties of Files

A file is represented in WMI by a `CIM_DataFile` object. Every single file on a Windows 2000 system is represented by one of these objects. Each such object can be identified uniquely by its *primary key*. The primary key of a `CIM_DataFile` is its `Name` property. Unsurprisingly, the value of this property is the fully-qualified path to the file being represented. For example, the `CIM_DataFile` object representing boot.ini, a file that can be found in the C:\ directory of all standard Windows 2000 machines, has the name `"c:\boot.ini"`.

Using VBScript, you can get a reference to a `CIM_DataFile` object with the following code fragment:

```
Dim refFile
Set refFile = GetObject("winMgmts:CIM_DataFile.Name='c:\boot.ini'")
```

This code tells VBScript to ask the `winMgmts` service (that is, WMI) to find an object of type `CIM_DataFile` whose name is `'c:\boot.ini'`. In reality, the object is not so much "found" as "created," because `CIM_DataFile` objects are dynamic—they are created as and when they are needed.

Tip: Language Reminder

Notice that `'c:\boot.ini'` *is placed in single quotes rather than double quotes. The reason for this is that it is actually embedded within a string, a series of characters encapsulated in another set of quotes. If we had used double quotes around* `c:\boot.ini`*, VBScript would have had no way of knowing which were the complement pairs. If you ever need to embed a double-quote character in a string, it must be escaped with a second double-quote character. For example,* `""""` *represents the string literal* `"`.◆

As soon as you have a reference to a `CIM_DataFile`, it is easy to find out most of that file's vital statistics, because these are exposed as properties of the object. For example, you can find out the size, attributes, and creation, modification, and access dates of boot.ini using this simple code example:

```
'basicfileinfo.vbs - show basic information about boot.ini
'force VBScript to complain about use of undeclared variables
Option explicit
'declare a variable to be used as an object reference
Dim refFile
'use GetObject() to set the object reference
Set refFile = GetObject("winMgmts:CIM_DataFile.Name='c:\boot.ini'")
'output the file's name and size
Wscript.echo "File name is: " & refFile.Name
Wscript.echo "File size is: " & refFile.FileSize & " bytes"
'use conditional execution to report on any set attributes
If refFile.Archive then WScript.echo "The archive bit is set"
If refFile.Hidden then WScript.echo "This file is hidden"
If refFile.System then WScript.echo "This is a system file"
'output date information
Wscript.echo "The file was created on: " & refFile.CreationDate
Wscript.echo "The file was last modified on: " & refFile.LastModified
Wscript.echo "The file was last accessed on: " & refFile.LastAccessed
Set refFile = Nothing
```

This is a complete, executable script. Type it into a text editor, save it with a .vbs extension, and you can run it from the command line using the Windows Scripting Host.

Tip: Setting the Windows Scripting Host Default Host Mode

If you rely on Windows file associations to run this script (that is, you run it without explicitly typing `cscript scriptname.vbs`*, where* `scriptname` *is the script's filename), you might find that the Windows Scripting Host defaults to graphical mode, and each of the* `Wscript.echo` *lines causes an irritating dialog box to pop up on the screen with the data in it. You could, of course, fix this problem by compiling a very long string containing all the data and then invoking* `WScript.echo` *just once. However, a better solution for this script—and for many in this book—is to ensure that your Windows Scripting Host is configured to default to text mode (where output is displayed in the command window). You can do this by invoking the following from the command line:*

```
cscript //h:cscript
```
◆

Remember that the first line, `Option Explicit`, is not part of the script as such. It's an instruction to the VBScript interpreter, telling it to complain if you ever use a variable name without first declaring it with a `Dim` statement. Although this line does not affect the script's runtime behavior, it prevents you from accidentally referring to nonexistent variables later. Having declared the variable `refFile` and set it to reference the WMI object that represents c:\boot.ini, you can start extracting information by reading its *properties*. Most of the information you extract is textual (such as `Name`) or numerical (such as `FileSize`) and can be displayed directly using `WScript.echo`. The `Archive`, `Hidden`, and `System` properties, in contrast, are *Boolean:* They return either true or false. Although we could have written `WScript.echo "Archive bit:" & refFile.Archive` (and, in this case, caused the script to display `Archive bit: false`), it seemed much neater to take advantage of the Boolean nature of the `Archive` property and use a conditional in the code:

```
If refFile.Archive then WScript.echo "The archive bit is set"
```

This code will display `The archive bit is set` if and only if `refFile.Archive` returns a value of true. Note that as the last step, we set `refFile` to the special value of `Nothing`, telling VBScript that we no longer need a reference to the object and that resources allocated to it can be released.

Dates and Times

If you ran the script, you might be puzzling over one minor problem: The time and date information extracted from the `CreationDate`, `LastModified`, and `LastAccessed` properties is utterly incomprehensible. Rather than a sanely formatted date, you see a very large number! The reason for this is that the WMI date format is entirely different from the VBScript date format (and, for that matter, from the Windows 2000 internal date format). This large number is in fact nothing more than a long string of the form `"yyyymmddHHMMSS.mmmmmmsUUU"`, where `yyyy` is the four-digit year; `mm` and `dd` are the two-digit month and date, respectively; `HHMMSS` represents hours, minutes, and seconds; `mmmmmm` represents microseconds(!); and `sUUU` represents the offset from GMT (Greenwich Mean Time).

If you are wondering why on earth Microsoft would choose such an alien representation for its WMI dates, the answer is that this platform-independent format is actually part of the WBEM specification as defined by the Distributed Management Task Force (DMTF), so Microsoft had no choice here. If, on the other hand, you are wondering about the more practical matter of how you can turn this mess into a civilized, readable date, the answer is that this is actually rather simple—it just requires a little bit of string manipulation and a couple of VBScript conversion functions. Sadly, a detailed discussion of string manipulation in VBScript would take us a little too far from the matter at hand, so we will simply present here a short function that solves the problem, without dwelling too much on the details:

```
Function GetVBDate(wd)
    GetVBDate = DateSerial(left(wd,4),mid(wd,5,2),mid(wd,7,2)) _
              + TimeSerial(mid(wd,9,2),mid(wd,11,2),mid(wd,13,2))
End Function
```

If you append these lines to the end of your script, this function can be used to convert the WMI dates to VBScript format, thereby giving you a sane output. To use this function, simply replace these lines:

```
Wscript.echo "The file was created on: " & refFile.CreationDate
Wscript.echo "The file was last modified on: " & refFile.LastModified
Wscript.echo "The file was last accessed on: " & refFile.LastAccessed
```

with these:

```
Wscript.echo "The file was created on: " & GetVBDate(refFile.CreationDate)
Wscript.echo "The file was last modified on: " & _
                GetVBDate(refFile.LastModified)
Wscript.echo "The file was last accessed on: " & _
                GetVBDate(refFile.LastAccessed)
```

This syntax means "Evaluate `refFile.LastAccessed`, pass it as a parameter to the `GetVBDate()` function, which is defined further down in the script, and echo the value that this function returns." Forgetting to paste the function itself into the script and attempting to run this code results in a VBScript runtime error of the form `Type mismatch:'GetVBDate'`. Or, if you start your script with the `Option Explicit` directive, you see the equally helpful runtime error `Variable Undefined`.

VB Date *and String Functions Used in* GetVBDate

A date in VBScript is not just a string or a number. It is actually a special type of thing in its own right. This allows VBScript to store a date internally in a way that is convenient for performing calculations (such as working out differences between two dates) but display it in a format appropriate not only for humans in general, but also for the locale that a computer happens to be using. Our `GetVBDate()` *function turns a WMI date string into a bona fide VBScript date using two functions that are built into the VBScript language:*

- `DateSerial()` *takes three numeric parameters—a year, a month, and a day—and returns a VBScript date representing that year, month, and day. For example,* `DateSerial(2001,1,10)` *would return a date of 10th January 2001.*
- `TimeSerial()` *takes three numeric parameters—hours, minutes, and seconds—and returns a VBScript date representing that time. For example,* `TimeSerial(10,15,0)` *would return a "date" of* `10.15am` *exactly.*

Because VBScript dates can be added together, a combination of `DateSerial()` *and* `TimeSerial()` *can be used to create a date that represents any year, month, day, hour, minute, and second. Using* `DateSerial()` *and* `TimeSerial()` *to create a date from a WMI date string simply requires a means to extract the year, month, day, hour, minute, and second information from the string so that they can be given as parameters. This task is accomplished with two of VBScript's string manipulation functions:*

- `Left()` *takes two parameters—a string and a number (n)—and returns the left n characters of the string. For example,* `Left("goose",2)` *evaluates to* `go`.
- `Mid()` *takes three parameters—a string and two numbers (p and n)—and returns n characters from the string, starting from the character in position p. For example,* `Mid("goose",2,2)` *returns* `oo`.

VBScript also has a `Right()` *function; we leave you to guess its purpose!* ◆

Further File Properties

You can use a `CIM_DataFile` to find out a lot more about the file it represents than merely the size, attributes, and access times. It can also reveal whether the file has been compressed (and, if so, with what algorithm) and whether it has been encrypted (and, if so, using what method). It can also show what the filename would look like under DOS (that is, the 8.3 filename), and it can reveal the file type (as defined by file associations), the path, and even whether the user querying the `CIM_DataFile` can read and write to the file in question. The following script uses these facilities to give a more encyclopedic insight into the boot.ini file on a system:

```
'file_info.vbs - print out information about boot.ini
Option Explicit
Dim refFile
Set refFile = GetObject("winMgmts:CIM_DataFile.Name='c:\boot.ini'")
WScript.echo "Information about " & refFile.Name
With refFile
    WScript.echo "Name: " & .Name
    WScript.echo "Size: " & .FileSize
    WScript.echo "Created on " & GetVBDate(.CreationDate)
    WScript.echo "Last modified on " & GetVBDate(.LastModified)
    WScript.echo "Last accessed on " & GetVBDate(.LastAccessed)
    WScript.echo "Short filename: " & .EightDotThreeFileName
    WScript.echo "Filetype: " & .FileType
    WScript.echo "Extension: " & .Extension
    WScript.echo "Path: " & .Path
    WScript.echo "Drive: " & .Drive
    If .Archive then WScript.echo "Archive bit set"
    If .Hidden then WScript.echo "File is hidden"
    If .System then WScript.echo "System File"
    If .Compressed then WScript.echo "Compressed with " & .CompressionMethod
    If .Encrypted then WScript.echo "Encrypted with " & .EncryptionMethod
    If .Readable then
        WScript.echo "You may read this file"
    Else
        WScript.echo "You may not read this file."
    End If
    If .Writeable then
        WScript.echo "You may write to this file"
    Else
        WScript.echo "You may not write to this file"
    End If
End With
Set refFile = Nothing

'Don't forget to include this function...
Function GetVBDate(wd)
    GetVBDate = DateSerial(left(wd,4),mid(wd,5,2),mid(wd,7,2)) _
              + TimeSerial(mid(wd,9,2),mid(wd,11,2),mid(wd,13,2))
End Function
```

Running this script on a system gives you a very good idea of boot.ini's vital statistics!

Notice that the script introduces a new feature of the VBScript language—the `With...End With` construct. This construct offers a convenient way of performing a set of operations on a single object without having to invoke the object name repeatedly. Code placed within a `With...End With` block acts in exactly the same way as code placed anywhere else, with the exception that any word prefixed by a dot (.) is interpreted as a property or method of the object declared with `With`. In other words, the following two code fragments are functionally identical:

```
'Fragment one - refFile used explicitly
WScript.Echo refFile.FileSize
WScript.Echo refFile.FileType
WScript.Echo refFile.FileName

'Fragment two - refFile implied by With...End With block
With refFile
    WScript.Echo .FileSize
    WScript.Echo .FileType
    WScript.Echo .FileName
End With
```

All other aspects of the script should now be self-explanatory.

Tip: Layout of If _Statements_

Whenever an `If` *statement constitutes the start of a block (that is, it is accompanied by an* `End If`*), the* `Then` *must be followed immediately by a carriage return. Even if the block consists of only a single statement, that statement must be placed on the following line.* ◆

Manipulating Files

In addition to providing information about the underlying files that they represent, `CIM_DataFile` objects can be used to perform a number of simple housekeeping tasks.

`CIM_DataFile` objects have methods to support most of the actions that you would expect to be supported at the filesystem level—namely, copying, moving, renaming, and deleting. In addition, there are methods to control a file's compression status and to manipulate security on an NTFS filesystem. The following script fragments demonstrate the use of these methods (with the exception of the security-related methods, which are discussed in Chapter 5, "WMI Security"). Because some of these methods are really quite destructive, it is probably best not to use a file as important as boot.ini as the example if you intend to try anything out!

Simple Manipulation

The `Copy()` method is invoked exactly as might be expected: It takes a single parameter—namely, a string representing the destination path. So, assuming that `refFile` has been set to point to a valid `CIM_DataFile`, you could invoke `Copy` like this:

```
refFile.Copy "c:\temp\copy-of-file.txt"
```

Despite the evident simplicity, there are a few idiosyncrasies to note. First, the destination path must always be given in full; you may not omit the filename if you're copying to a different directory, and you may not omit the directory name if you're copying to a different filename in the same directory. After all, a `CIM_DataFile` has no concept of "working directory." Second, the `Copy()` method cannot be used to overwrite an existing file. This limitation seems somewhat strange given that there are many circumstances under which overwriting a file with a copy operation is exactly what you want to do. No doubt, Microsoft had their reasons. Another caveat is that the intended destination directory must exist, because it will not be created on-the-fly. This behavior, however, is unsurprising and should not catch too many people off guard!

The `Rename()` method can be used either to rename or move a file. Its invocation is identical to that of `Copy()`, and its use is subject to exactly the same limitations. The two uses are illustrated in the following script fragment, which invokes `Rename` on a `refFile` that has been previously initialized to represent `"c:\temp\goose.txt"`:

```
'This command will rename the file as "albatross.txt" while
'leaving it in its current location
refFile.Rename "c:\temp\albatross.txt"

'This command will move the file, preserving its name
refFile.Rename "c:\matthew\goose.txt"
```

Invocation of the `Delete()` method is even more straightforward, requiring no parameters:

```
refFile.Delete
```

There are, of course, a number of caveats to consider when invoking `Delete()` on a `CIM_DataFile` object, because the operations that can be performed by a file through WMI are subject to the same set of restrictions as those that govern file manipulation anywhere else. For example, you cannot delete a read-only file or one for which you do not have the relevant permissions. We will discuss mechanisms for detecting such problems in the next section.

In a real script, it is always sensible to *dereference* a `CIM_DataFile` object immediately after invoking its `Delete()` method (that is, set the relevant object reference to `Nothing`):

```
refFile.Delete
Set refFile = Nothing
```

Failure to do this can lead to rather strange results. You can see this by using Notepad to create a file in c:\temp called deleteme.txt, adding a few lines of text, saving it, and then running the following script:

```
'deleteme.vbs - demonstrate strange delete behavior
Option Explicit
Dim refFile
Set refFile = GetObject("winMgmts:CIM_DataFile.Name='c:\temp\deleteme.txt'")
WScript.echo "Hello. I am a file called " & refFile.Name
WScript.echo "I am about to be deleted"
refFile.Delete
WScript.echo "Hello again. I am still a file called " & refFile.Name
WScript.echo "And I even have a size: " & refFile.FileSize
WScript.echo "And now the program will crash..."
refFile.Delete
'the line below will not be called
set refFile = Nothing
```

This produces output very similar to the following:

```
Hello. I am a file called c:\temp\deleteme.txt
I am about to be deleted
Hello again. I am still a file called c:\temp\deleteme.txt
And I even have a size: 28
And now the program will crash...
C:\wmibook\oops.vbs(10,1) SWbemObject: Not found
```

Oops! Even after the file has been deleted, the `CIM_DataFile` object is more than happy to continue providing information about it, because this information is cached and can be read without reference to the underlying filesystem. You find out that something has gone dramatically wrong only when you attempt to carry out an action that forces the `CIM_DataFile` to interact with the underlying filesystem. At this point, the object realizes that it is nothing but a ghost, representing something that does not actually exist. WMI throws an error, and the script exits.

This scenario reveals something extremely important about WMI objects and their relationship with the underlying structures they represent: *WMI objects are populated with data that is accurate at the time the object is constructed. If the underlying structure changes after this time, these changes will not be reflected in the WMI object.*

An artifact of the same phenomenon is illustrated by the following code fragment:

```
WScript.Echo "My name is " & refFile.Name
refFile.Rename "c:\temp\goose.txt"
WScript.Echo "My new name is " & refFile.Name
```

If this code is called on a `CIM_DataFile` that represents a file called c:\temp\albatross.txt, its output would be

```
My name is c:\temp\albatross.txt
My new name is c:\temp\albatross.txt
```

Despite the fact that the file is now really called goose.txt, the `CIM_DataFile` knows nothing of this novelty. In the trivial examples shown here, the mistakes are easy enough to spot, but in longer, more complex scripts, confusing mistakes are much easier to make. Luckily, you can avoid these pitfalls altogether by following one simple rule: If you invoke a method on an object that causes an inconsistency to appear between the object and the structure it represents, always dereference the WMI object immediately after the invocation. An attempt to access properties of a dereferenced object will cause VBScript to raise an error but will never lead to inconsistent, bizarre results.

Note: WMI Event Model

WMI provides a very sophisticated mechanism for detecting and reacting to changes in modeled structures—the WMI Event Model. This is a complex topic that is discussed later in this book. In addition, VBScript has support (albeit limited) for handling errors and preventing them from causing a fatal crash. Again, this is discussed later. ◆

Detecting Errors

An attempt to perform an operation on a nonexistent entity, such as invoking `Delete()` twice on a `CIM_DataFile`, causes WMI to raise an error that terminates script execution (unless it is handled). This reaction occurs because WMI encounters a situation with which it cannot cope. Not all failed operations evoke such drastic reactions, however; under normal circumstances, a failed attempt to invoke `Copy()`, `Move()`, or `Delete()` appears to evoke no reaction at all. If, for example, an attempt is made to copy a file to a nonexistent directory, the copy will fail, but the WMI provider that is responsible for executing this method has been explicitly written to cope with such an eventuality and will not complain. To understand this point, try running the following script:

```
'silentfailure.vbs - demonstrate silent copy failure
Option Explicit
Dim refFile
Set refFile = GetObject("winMgmts:CIM_DataFile.Name='c:\boot.ini'")
WScript.Echo "About to do something stupid"
refFile.Copy "z:\pterodactyl\triceretop\z\x\q.txt"
WScript.echo "The script still seems to be running"
Set refFile = Nothing
```

Unless you happen to have a directory on your system whose path is z:\pterodactyl\triceretop\z\x, the copy will undoubtedly fail, but the script will continue to run.

Tip: Omitting the Primary Key

So far, each time we have used `GetObject()` *to retrieve a* `CIM_DataFile`, *we have written the moniker string in full, using the format* `winMgmts:ObjectType.PrimaryKey='value'`. *It is equally valid to omit* `.PrimaryKey`, *however, giving a slightly shorter string of the form* `winMgmts:ObjectType='value'`. *The primary key is implied.* ◆

Although it is good to know that a failed copy or move operation will not crash a script, it is often equally good to know whether an operation succeeds! In common with many WMI methods, `CIM_DataFile` methods reveal this information in the form of a return value. So far, we have been using these methods as though they were subroutines—self-contained blocks of code that perform an action but return no value. As far as VBScript syntax is concerned, we have been invoking them as statements. However, it is equally possible to use them as functions—self-contained blocks of code that return a value. Syntactically, they would become VBScript expressions. Unlike our own `GetVBDate()` function, whose main purpose is to return a value, the primary purpose of the `CIM_DataFile` methods when used as functions is still to carry out an action, but as an added bonus, they return a value—namely, an error code.

The following script, like its companion (just shown), is highly likely to fail:

```
'anotherfailure.vbs - another demonstration of copy failure
Option Explicit
Dim refFile
Dim numErrorCode
Set refFile = GetObject("winMgmts:CIM_DataFile.Name='c:\boot.ini'")
numErrorCode = refFile.Copy("z:\pterodactyl\triceretop\z\x\q.txt")
WScript.echo "Error code: " & numErrorCode
Set refFile = Nothing
```

Running it produces the following output:

```
Error code: 9
```

According to the `CIM_DatFile` specification, this code means that "the name specified was invalid." Table 3.1 is a complete listing of error codes returned by `CIM_DataFile` methods, along with their meanings. All of these methods share the same collection of error codes, although clearly not all of them are applicable to every operation!

Table 3.1 CIM_DataFile *Method Error Codes*

Code	Meaning
2	You do not have access to perform the operation.
8	The operation failed for an undefined reason.
9	The name specified as a target does not point to a real file or directory.
10	The file or directory specified as a target already exists and cannot be overwritten.
11	You have attempted to perform an NTFS operation on a non-NTFS filesystem.
12	You have attempted to perform an NT/2000-specific operation on a non-NT/2000 platform.
13	You have attempted to perform an operation across drives that can be carried out within only a single drive.
14	You have attempted to delete a directory that is not empty.
15	There has been a sharing violation; another process is using the file you are attempting to manipulate.
16	You are attempting to act on a nonexistent file.
17	You do not have the relevant NT security privileges to carry out the operation.
21	You have supplied an invalid parameter to the method.

So far, we have been treating the file manipulation methods as subroutines. However, if instead we treat them as functions, we can read these error codes from within our script. The file manipulation methods, in common with virtually *all* WMI methods, present an error code as a return value. A value of 0 indicates a successful operation. A minor modification to our script, then, can make it report on the success or failure of the attempted operation:

```
'copycheck.vbs - copy a file, demonstrating use of error return code
Option Explicit
Dim refFile
Dim numErrorCode
Set refFile = GetObject("winMgmts:CIM_DataFile='c:\boot.ini'")
numErrorCode = refFile.Copy("z:\pterodactyl\triceretop\z\x\q.txt")
If numErrorCode = 0 then
    WScript.Echo "File copied successfully"
Else WScript.Echo "Copy failed with error code " & numErrorCode
End If
Set refFile = Nothing
```

Of course, we could make this code more user-friendly by testing `numErrorCode` for each possible value and reporting in text format exactly which error occurred. For the moment, though, this hardly seems necessary.

Note that in this script and the immediately preceding one, the syntax of the `Copy()` invocation has changed to reflect the fact that we are using it as a function. Omitting the parentheses around its parameters would constitute a syntax error.

Tip: Checking Success Without Reporting an Error Code

If you do not want to report the actual error code, but you only care whether the operation was successful, you could make the script more concise by dispensing with the variable `numErrorCode`*:*

```
'copyandreport.vbs - copy a file and report operation success or
failure
Option Explicit
Dim refFile

Set refFile = GetObject("winMgmts:CIM_DataFile='c:\boot.ini'")
If refFile.Copy("z:\pterodactyl\triceretop\z\x\q.txt") = 0 then _
    WScript.echo "File copied successfully"
Else
    WScript.echo "Copy failed"
End If
Set refFile = Nothing ◆
```

File Compression

Before we move on to discuss the handling of multiple files simultaneously, we will look briefly at one more pair of file operations that can be executed with methods of `CIM_DataFile`—namely, those concerned with compression. Unsurprisingly, these operations are carried out by `Compress()` and `Uncompress()`, neither of which takes any parameters. Although these methods barely warrant a script example of their own, we will present one nonetheless as an excuse to consolidate some of the issues discussed so far in this section—namely, error handling and consistency. The following script retrieves a `CIM_DataFile` object representing the file c:\temp\albatross.txt, compresses it if it is not already compressed, decompresses it if it is compressed, and reports its success. Notice that immediately after a successful call to `Compress()` or `Uncompress()`, you dereference the object, precluding the possibility of any consistency errors, even though you know you will not make any mistakes in a script this simple.

```
'compress.vbs - toggle compression status of a file
Option Explicit
Dim refFile
Set refFile = GetObject("winMgmts:CIM_DataFile='c:\temp\albatross.txt'")
```

```
If Not refFile.Compressed then
    If refFile.Compress = 0 Then
        WScript.echo "File compressed successfully"
        Set refFile = Nothing
    Else
        WScript.echo "File could not be compressed"
    End If
Else
    If refFile.Uncompress = 0 Then
        WScript.echo "File uncompressed successfully"
        Set refFile = Nothing
    Else
        WScript.echo "File could not be uncompressed"
    End If
End If
'if we were to invoke a property of refFile here we may get a runtime error
'if refFile has been set to nothing, but we know that we will never get
'incorrect information
Set refFile = Nothing
```

Manipulating Multiple Files: WQL and Collections

Although it is often useful to be able to find out about various aspects of files and to carry out basic maintenance, this hardly requires the use of WMI. Windows Explorer provides a perfectly good, significantly simpler, and arguably more powerful interface for accomplishing these tasks! The true benefits of WMI become immediately apparent, however, where there is a need to perform operations on multiple files chosen according to arbitrary criteria. In this section, we demonstrate the ease with which `CIM_DataFiles`—and, by extension, any WMI objects—can be selected and manipulated in bulk. In so doing, we introduce one of the most useful features of WMI—the WMI Query Language (WQL).

So far, whenever we have needed a reference to a `CIM_DataFile` object, we have used VBScript's `GetObject()` function. This function does not know anything about `CIM_DataFile` itself. Behind the scenes, it asks the WMI service, via COM, to interpret the moniker string and return the relevant object.

There is, however, an alternative approach to retrieving such a reference. Rather than asking `GetObject()` to act as an intermediary, we could have asked WMI for the object directly, as in this code fragment:

```
Set refWMIService = GetObject("winMgmts:")
Set refFile = refWMIService.Get("CIM_DataFile.Name='c:\boot.ini'")
```

This fragment still uses the `GetObject()` function, but not in conjunction with a full object-specifying moniker string. By specifying only `"winMgmts:"` as the moniker string, our script tells `GetObject()` that we are interested in the services of WMI. However, it does *not* give any further information about what we want the WMI service to return. The result of such a call is for WMI to locate and return the default `SWbemServices` object. `SWbemServices` is not a WMI object as such; it does not live in the CIMOM Repository and is not defined by the CIM schema. Rather, it is an interface to the WMI services on a machine. More specifically, it is an interface to the default namespace of the WMI services on a machine. In other words, `SWbemServices` is an object representation of the WMI service (`winMgmts`) itself. As soon as we have a reference to this object, we can use its methods to interact further with WMI. In the fragment just shown, we use the `Get()` method to retrieve the `CIM_DataFile` (as illustrated in the second line of code).

At first glance, this approach hardly seems radically different from the one we have been using. All we have done is use two lines of VBScript where previously one sufficed. There is an important difference, however. As soon as you have a reference to an `SWbemServices` object, you can ask it directly for any further WMI objects that you need. Before, we were giving `GetObject()` our shopping list and asking it to go shopping for us; now we are going shopping ourselves. In real life, it might often be convenient to send a friend to buy a single item for you. On the other hand, if your shopping list is long or complex, there is never a substitute for going yourself. WMI is no different. `GetObject()` is perfectly able to retrieve a single WMI object for you, but if you have a more complex request, you better talk to `SWbemServices` directly!

The `Get()` method of `SWbemServices` is not particularly interesting. It merely takes an object path (a moniker string without the `winMgmts:` prefix) and returns the matching object. Another `SWbemService` method, however—namely, `ExecQuery()`—is quite a different matter. If using `Get()` is like going shopping yourself, using `ExecQuery()` is like speaking to a highly knowledgeable expert store assistant and explaining your exact requirements. Whereas `Get()` returns a single WMI object when given an object path, `ExecQuery()` returns a *collection* of objects when given a query written in WQL.

Note: ExecQuery() _Returns an_ SWbemObjectSet

If we are being pedantic, we should say that `ExecQuery()` *returns an* `SWbemObjectSet`*, a particular type of collection defined by WMI, but this distinction is not of particular relevance here.* ◆

WMI Query Language is a subset of ANSI SQL, the language used to query databases. It is an extremely simple language to learn, because it is basically a highly formalized subset of plain English. A generic WQL query looks something like this:

```
SELECT * FROM <CLASSNAME> WHERE <PROPERTY> <OPERATOR> <VALUE>
```

This means "Get me every object of type `<CLASSNAME>` whose `<PROPERTY>` property has a value that is related to `<VALUE>` by some `<OPERATOR>`." An example will probably make this clearer:

```
SELECT * FROM CIM_DataFile WHERE Name = 'c:\\boot.ini'
```

This means "Get me every object of type `CIM_DataFile` whose `Name` property is c:\boot.ini." Note that the `\` character must *always* be escaped in the `WHERE` clause of a query string, so c:\boot.ini becomes c:\\boot.ini. This query, when passed as a parameter to `ExecQuery()`, returns a collection that contains a single object, the `CIM_DataFile` representing c:\boot.ini.

The power of WQL becomes much more obvious in a slightly more complex query:

```
SELECT * FROM CIM_DataFile WHERE FileSize < '1024'
```

This query returns a collection that contains `CIM_DataFiles` representing all the files on a system that are smaller than 1024 bytes. The VBScript code to execute the query would look something like this:

```
set refWMIService = GetObject("winMgmts:")
set colSmallFiles = refWMIService.ExecQuery _
        ("SELECT * FROM CIM_DataFile WHERE FileSize < '1024'")
```

Note: The col *Prefix*

Notice that the variable name for the collection has been given a `col` *prefix. Just like our use of* `num`*,* `str`*, and* `ref` *throughout this book, this is a convention that we find helpful. VBScript doesn't care what you call them!* ◆

An obvious question to ask at this stage is "How do you access the objects inside a collection?". It's all very well having a reference to a collection, but it's useless unless you can look inside it. As with many things in the world of programming, the answer is that there are many ways, but probably the most common method—and the one we will use here—is to loop through the objects using VBScript's built-in collection-iterating syntax, `For Each...Next`:

```
For Each <item> In <collection>
    <statements>
        ...
    <statements>
Next
```

This construct operates in a manner very similar to that of the `For...Next` loop: All code within the statement block executes sequentially and loops a certain number of times. The difference is that in a `For...Next` loop, the number of iterations is determined by a numeric variable whose value increases each time through the loop until a maximum is reached. In contrast, the number of iterations in a `For Each...Next` loop is determined by the number of objects in the collection, and an object variable, `<item>`, is set to a different object on every iteration.

Use of the `SWbemServices` object, WMI Query Language, and the `For Each...Next` loop is illustrated in the following script, which prints the names of all files on a computer that are smaller than 14 bytes:

```
'smallfiles.vbs - print names of all files smaller than 14 bytes
Option Explicit
Dim refWMIService
Dim colSmallFiles
Dim refItem
'get a reference to the SWbemServices object
set refWMIService = GetObject("winMgmts:")

'Execute a WQL query - this may take some time...
'it should return a collection of all CIM_DataFile objects
'representing all files smaller than 14 bytes
set colSmallFiles = refWMIService.ExecQuery _
       ("SELECT * FROM CIM_DataFile WHERE FileSize < '14'")

'Now loop through the collection and invoke CIM_DataFile.Name
For Each refItem in colSmallFiles
    WScript.echo refItem.Name
Next
Set colSmallFiles = Nothing
Set refWMIService = Nothing
```

Tip: Finding All Objects of a Certain Type

Just like its SQL counterpart, a WQL query does not necessarily have to contain a `WHERE` *clause. The query* `SELECT * FROM CIM_DataFile` *is perfectly valid. It means "Give me a collection of all objects of type* `CIM_DataFile`*."*

If you want to retrieve all instances of a particular class of object, however, the `SWbemServices` *object provides a simpler mechanism—an* `InstancesOf()` *method. This method takes a class name as a parameter and returns all instances of the named class. For example, the following code fragment, when* `refWMIService` *has been set appropriately, returns a collection of all* `CIM_DataFile` *objects on a system. That is, it returns a collection containing one* `CIM_DataFile` *object for every file on a computer's hard disks, mapped drives, floppies, and so on:*

```
Set colAllFiles = refWMIService.InstancesOf("CIM_DataFile")
```

Running a line of code such as this could take quite a long time! ◆

As promised, we end this section with a script that could actually be useful in a real-world computing environment! It saves disk space by compressing all files that have not been accessed for more recently than one month before the script is run. Any failure to compress a file is reported. Thanks to WQL, this script is very straightforward. We can delegate the task of finding all currently uncompressed files that have not been accessed for a month to `SWbemServices`, giving it instructions with a single WQL string. There is only one slight complication to contend with: In order to figure out whether a file has been accessed within the last month, we need to compare two dates—one from VBScript and one from WMI. If this comparison is to work, both must be in the same format. Unfortunately, we cannot use our `GetVBDate()` function here, because the comparison is being carried out by WMI, not by VBScript. Instead, we need to write a function that does the exact opposite and converts a `VBDate` into a WMI date. This function, and a small helper function that it uses, is included in the code listing. As you can see, the function takes two parameters—a `VBDate` and an offset from GMT:

```
'compressrare.vbs - compress rarely used files
Option Explicit
Dim refWMIService
Dim colRarelyUsedFiles
Dim refItem
Dim strQuery

set refWMIService = GetObject("winMgmts:")

'build the query string and execute the query
strQuery = "SELECT * FROM CIM_DataFile WHERE LastAccessed < '" & _
           GetWMIDate(DateAdd("m",-1,Now),"+000") & _
           "' AND Compressed = 'False'"
set colRarelyUsedFiles = refWMIService.ExecQuery(strQuery)

'Now loop through the collection and attempt compression
'Report success or failure with WScript.echo
For Each refItem in colRarelyUsedFiles
    If refItem.Compress = 0 then
        WScript.echo refItem.Name & "compressed successfully"
    Else WScript.echo "Compression of " & refItem.Name " failed"
    End If
Next

'release objects
set colRarelyUsedFiles = Nothing
set refWMIService = Nothing


'This function turns a VBDate into a WMI date
Function GetWMIDate(vd,strOffset)
    GetWMIDate = Year(vd) & AddZero(Month(vd)) & AddZero(Day(vd)) & _
```

```
                AddZero(Hour(vd)) & AddZero(Minute(vd)) & _
                AddZero(Second(vd)) & ".000000" & strOffset
End Function

'This function turns a one-digit number into a two-character string
'It is used by GetWMIDate
Function AddZero(pNum)
    If pNum <= 9 then
        AddZero = "0" & pNum
    Else AddZero = pNum
    End If
End Function
```

And there you have it. Run this script on your servers once a week, and see how much space you save.

Warning: Compressing Files

Before you decide to compress files on a production system, you should be sure to think about the consequences. Will it cause any problems for users trying to read their files on older platforms? Will performance be fast enough?

Hopefully, you can now see the potential of WMI as a system administration tool. We have managed to perform operations on a set of files chosen according to relatively complex criteria, and we have not even had to meet WMI's representation of a directory yet!

We end this section with one small note of caution: A WQL query that has to trawl through a filesystem, checking the modification times of every file, could take a long time to execute and involves relatively heavy I/O usage. In a production environment, a script like this should be run late at night as a timed job (using at.exe or one of its colleagues) rather than in the middle of the business day. A related point to note is that WMI queries execute *out of process*. They do not run as part of your script, but as part of the WMI process. This means that you should not be surprised if terminating script execution in the middle of a long query does not stop query running. Your hard disk will carry on crunching regardless, until the query is complete.

Tip: Rogue Queries

If you really do need to stop a query that is running wild, the only solution is to stop the WMI service on the computer in question. This can be accomplished just as with any other service, such as through the Service Control Manager or with a `net` *command.* ◆

Note: VBScript Functions Used in GetWMIDate

`GetWMIDate` *uses a series of VBScript date manipulation functions to extract numeric representations of the individual components that make up a date (years, months, days, hours, minutes, and seconds). It concatenates the output of these functions to produce a string in the format required by WMI. These functions, whose purpose is self-explanatory, are* `Year()`, `Month()`, `Day()`, `Hour()`, `Minute()`, *and* `Second()`.

WMI requires that all fields except the year be encoded as a two-character string. Unfortunately, if we simply concatenate the output of the VBScript date functions, we cannot guarantee constructing a string of the requisite length, because any of the functions except `Year()` *could return a single digit. Hence our little* `AddZero()` *function. This function takes a number and returns that same number as a string prefixed with 0 if the original number consists of only a single digit.* ◆

Directories in WMI

Every directory on a filesystem is represented in WMI by a `Win32_Directory` object, whose primary key is a `Name` property. Unsurprisingly, the value of this property, just like that of a `CIM_DataFile`, corresponds to the fully-qualified directory name. For example, the `Win32_Directory` object representing C:\Winnt on a system has the name C:\winnt.

The similarity between a `Win32_Directory` and a `CIM_DataFile` does not stop with the fact that both have a `Name` property. In fact, a `Win32_Directory` possesses every single property and method that a `CIM_DataFile` does, and vice versa. In other words, our entire discussion of `CIM_DataFile` objects applies equally to `Win32_Directory` objects. This similarity is not a coincidence. The reason for it is that in terms of the CIM schema, both these types of objects *derive* from the same *superclass*—`CIM_LogicalFile`. It is this superclass that defines the methods and properties that both `CIM_DataFile` and `Win32_Directory` *inherit*. In turn, even the `CIM_LogicalFile` class itself inherits some of its properties from a superclass, `CIM_LogicalElement`, and ultimately from `CIM_ManagedSystemElement` (see Figure 3.1). The `Name` property, for example, is defined by this top-level class, and hence appears in a vast number of WMI objects.

Although this zoo of class relationships that explains the similarity between `CIM_LogicalFile` objects and `Win32_Directory` objects might seem somewhat confusing, it does reveal a lot about the way WMI models the world. Components of a computer system are modeled in a hierarchical tree structure. At the leaves are the real objects—directories, files, disks, network cards—that make up a living, working system. Further up the trunk, as branches begin to converge, are more and more abstract representations of those objects. Whenever someone wants to add a new class to the CIM schema, he has to decide where exactly in the tree his class should live, whether it can join an existing branch at some level, or whether it must form a new root. This multiroot hierarchy is an excellent reflection of reality. Rarely is a device or software component of a computer system truly new; usually, new things are merely extensions and adaptations of items that already exist.

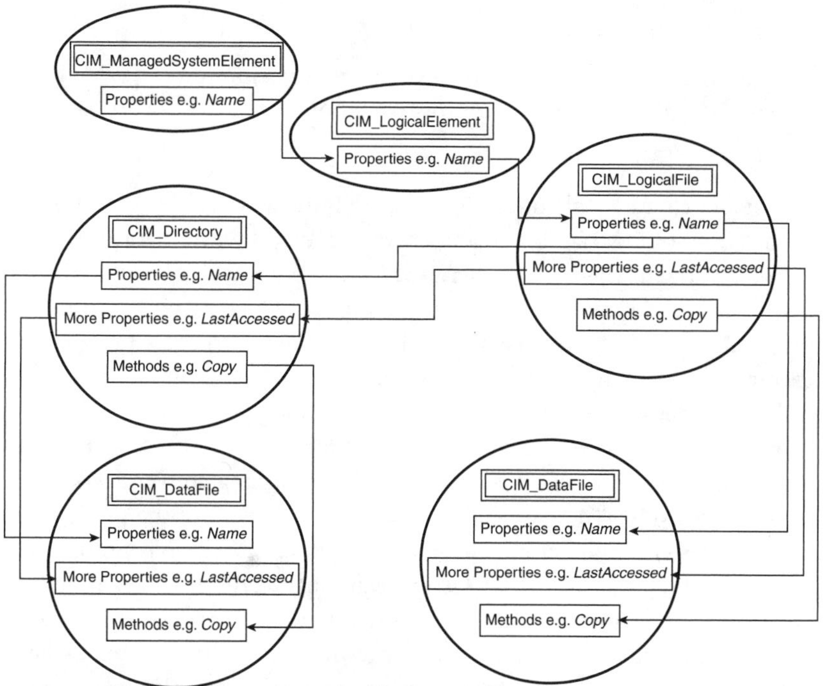

Figure 3.1 *The WMI class hierarchy: derivation of* `Win32_Directory`.

This class hierarchy is not merely of aesthetic value. It also offers significant practical benefits. Perhaps the most important of these is that any WMI object can be considered to be of the type defined by its own class *or that of any of its superclasses*. For example, a `Win32_Directory` object can be treated as a `Win32_Directory` object, a `CIM_Directory` object (its immediate superclass), a `CIM_LogicalFile`, a `CIM_LogicalElement`, or a `CIM_ManagedSystemElement`. This means that if you want to get a reference to every file *and* directory on a system, you can do so with a single WQL query:

```
SELECT * FROM CIM_LogicalFile
```

You could even get a collection of virtually every interesting WMI object on an entire computer system with this trivial query:

```
SELECT * FROM CIM_ManagedSystemElement
```

Of course, running this query would take quite a while. More importantly, at that level of abstraction, a script would have to waste a lot of time working out what subclass of `CIM_ManagedSystemElement` each object really was before any useful management information could be extracted from it! The principle, however, remains: WMI's hierarchical abstraction presents an extremely powerful way of conceptually grouping and finding instances of different types of system elements.

Before we return to the more mundane matter of `Win32_Directory` objects, we should make one small point about WMI naming conventions. You will have noticed that whereas objects representing files have the prefix `CIM`, those representing directories have the prefix `Win32`. There is nothing particularly significant about this. Classes beginning with `CIM` were defined by the Distributed Management Task Force (DMTF). They are part of the generic CIM schema and can be found on any WBEM-compliant system. Classes with a `Win32` prefix, in contrast, were defined by Microsoft and are specific to Win32 systems.

Luckily, little needs to be said about the behavior of `Win32_Directory` objects that has not already been said about `CIM_DataFile` objects—another advantage of the hierarchical structure of WMI! It is worth noting, however, that the behavior of a couple of the properties is slightly different. The `FileSize` property of a directory is `empty` (it contains no value), and the `FileType` is always `File Folder`. In addition, methods such as copy and compress operate recursively, on the named directory and on all files and subdirectories within it.

Conspicuously missing from the definition of a `Win32_Directory` is any reference to its contents. It is not at all obvious from looking at such an object that directories are containers! At first sight, this might seem like a somewhat strange omission, but, as you have probably guessed, WMI has its own special way of representing relationships between different WMI objects, such as that between a file and its parent directory. These are represented by associators.

WMI Associators

An *associator* is a WMI object containing two properties, each of which stores an object path to a specific type of object. A pair of WMI objects are related if there exists an associator containing their object paths in its properties. There are several different classes of associators to represent different types of relationships. The names of the two properties in which the object paths are stored describe how the referenced objects are related. As always with WMI, an example should make all of this clearer.

The relationship between a file and its parent directory is defined by a `CIM_DirectoryContainsFile` associator. This associator has two interesting properties:

- The `GroupComponent` property stores an object path to a `CIM_Directory` (from which `Win32_Directory` inherits).
- The `PartComponent` property stores an object path to a `CIM_DataFile`.

Every file in a directory has a unique `CIM_DirectoryContainsFile` associator whose `GroupComponent` contains a reference to the directory and whose `PartComponent` contains a reference to the file. This is illustrated in Figure 3.2.

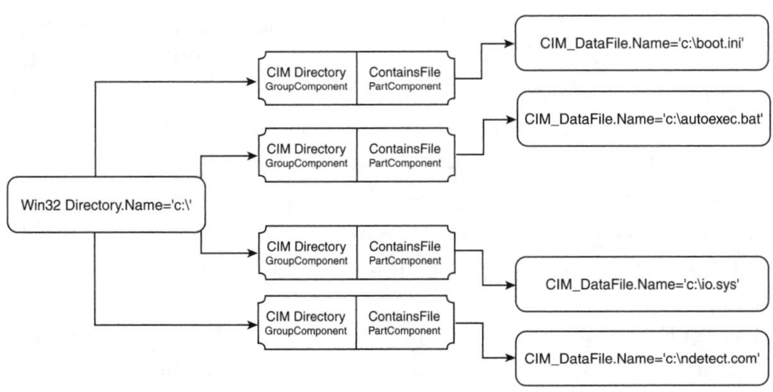

Figure 3.2 *Associator* `CIM_DirectoryContainsFile`.

If you wanted a reference to the WMI objects representing all the files contained in the directory c:\temp on a given computer, you could do this in two stages:

1. Find all the `CIM_DirectoryContainsFile` associators whose `GroupComponent` points to `Win32_Directory.Name='c:\temp'`.
2. Extract the object path from the `PartComponent` property of each one and use `GetObject()` to retrieve a reference to the file.

Although in principle this method would retrieve the references, you would not use it in reality. The designers of the WBEM concept realized that nobody would ever be interested in associators as objects in their own right, but only as a means of retrieving instances of associated classes. Therefore, they provided a mechanism for retrieving collections of associated objects in a single step, without the bother of having to retrieve references to the associators first and manually read their properties.

Associator Queries

This one-step operation can be accomplished with an `ASSOCIATORS OF` WQL query, whose simplest incarnation takes the following form:

```
ASSOCIATORS OF {<object>}
```

For example, all objects associated with the directory `Win32_Directory.Name='c:\temp'` can be retrieved with the following code fragment:

```
set ColObjects = refWMIService.ExecQuery _
    ("ASSOCIATORS OF {Win32_Directory.Name='c:\temp'}")
```

There is, however, a slight snag! This query will certainly give us all the objects associated with `Win32_Directory.Name='c:\temp'`, but this collection will not be restricted to files. It will contain objects representing files, subdirectories, the parent directory, security settings, and shares, to name but a few. We asked for a set of associators, but we did not specify what sort of associations we were interested in finding, so we got the lot! This small nightmare reveals the power of associators as a mechanism for representing relationships between objects: Any WMI object can be associated with any number of different objects in any number of ways. All it takes is an associator object linking pairs.

The WQL `ASSOCIATORS OF` syntax provides several phrases that can be placed in a `WHERE` clause to refine a search and restrict the type of object returned. The most useful of these are `AssocClass`, `ResultClass`, `ResultRole`, and `Role`.

- The `AssocClass` qualifier specifies the type of associator that should be found. For example, a query containing the qualifier. `AssocClass=CIM_DirectoryContainsFile` would return only objects that are associated through a `CIM_DirectoryContainsFile` associator.
- The `ResultClass` qualifier specifies the type of object that should be returned. For example, `ResultClass=CIM_DataFile` would return only `CIM_DataFile` objects.
- The `ResultRole` qualifier specifies the role that a returned object should play in the association (such as `PartComponent` or `GroupComponent`).
- The `Role` qualifier specifies the role that the source should play in the association.

Between them, these four qualifiers are almost always sufficient for achieving the desired result. Using a combination of them, you can write a query that really will return all the WMI objects representing files within c:\temp and *nothing else:*

```
ASSOCIATORS OF {Win32_Directory='c:\temp'} WHERE
    AssocClass=CIM_DirectoryContainsFile
    ResultRole=PartComponent
```

Literally, this query means "Find all WMI objects that are referenced in the `PartComponent` property of `CIM_DirectoryContainsFile` associations involving the `Win32_Directory` representing c:\temp." You know that these objects will all be `CIM_DataFiles` because this is a feature of the `CIM_DirectoryContainsFile` associator. An alternative query producing the same result could substitute `ResultClass` for `ResultRole`:

```
ASSOCIATORS OF {Win32_Directory='c:\temp'} WHERE
    AssocClass=CIM_DirectoryContainsFile
    ResultClass=CIM_DataFile
```

In English, this means "Find all `CIM_DataFile` objects that are referenced in `CIM_DirectoryContainsFile` associations involving the `Win32_Directory` representing c:\temp."

In this case, the two results return an identical collection, because the `PartComponent` of a `CIM_DirectoryContainsFile` associator *always* points to a `CIM_DataFile`. There are times when this equivalence does not hold, however: `ResultClass` can be useful if you need to restrict a result set to objects of a type that is a `subclass` of the `PartComponent`.

You have probably noticed that despite having multiple conditions after the WHERE clause, neither of these two queries contains the keyword AND. This is not an oversight! Multiple qualifiers in an ASSOCIATORS OF query follow each other directly, *without* an AND. The following query is syntactically incorrect and would fail:

```
ASSOCIATORS OF {Win32_Directory='c:\temp'} WHERE
    AssocClass=CIM_DirectoryContainsFile
    AND ResultClass=CIM_DataFile
```

Why the syntax here has to be so different from that of a SELECT query is beyond us—it seems completely counterintuitive. Nonetheless, we can't change WMI, so this is just something to remember!

Tip: Judicious Use of Qualifiers

It is rarely necessary to use all the qualifiers simultaneously. Sometimes, being too specific can cause problems, and some combinations produce nonsensical queries. For example, consider this query:

```
ASSOCIATORS OF {Win32_Directory='c:\temp'} WHERE
    AssocClass=CIM_DirectoryContainsFile
    ResultClass=CIM_DataFile
    ResultRole=GroupComponent
```

This is clearly nonsense: If the associator is a CIM_DirectoryContainsFile *and the* ResultClass *is a* CIM_DataFile, *the* ResultRole *cannot ever be a* GroupComponent*!* ◆

The PartComponent of a CIM_DirectoryContainsFile must be a CIM_DataFile (or one of its subclasses) rather than a CIM_LogicalFile, so this type of associator cannot be used to retrieve a list of WMI objects representing subdirectories of a Win32_Directory. Instead, the relationship between a directory and its parent—or a directory and its subdirectories—is handled by a Win32_SubDirectory associator. The two properties of a Win32_SubDirectory associator, just like those of a CIM_DirectoryContainsFile, are GroupComponent and PartComponent. GroupComponent contains a reference to the parent directory, and PartComponent contains a reference to the child. A collection of Win32_Directory objects representing all the subdirectories of c:\winnt on a system, then, can be retrieved using a trivial query:

```
ASSOCIATORS OF {Win32_Directory='c:\winnt'} WHERE
    AssocClass=Win32_SubDirectory
    ResultRole=PartComponent
```

This, of course, means "Find all WMI objects that are referenced in the PartComponent property of a Win32_SubDirectory associator connected with the Win32_Directory object representing c:\winnt." Note that specifying a

`ResultClass` of `Win32_Directory` would not help limit the scope of the query, because the components of a `Win32_SubDirectory` associator are *always* `Win32_Directory` objects.

Note: The AssociatorsOf() *Method*

As ever with WMI, there is more than one way to retrieve a collection of objects linked by an associator. If you do not like the look of `ASSOCIATORS OF` *queries, you can achieve the same results with the* `AssociatorsOf()` *method of an* `SWbemServices` *object. This method has one required parameter—a source object path—and several optional parameters that refine the search. In its simplest form, a call to the method might look something like this:*

```
set colDirectories =
refWMIService.AssociatorsOf("Win32_Directory='c:'")
```

This has exactly the same effect as the equivalent `ASSOCIATORS OF` *query with no* `WHERE CLAUSE`. *The most interesting optional parameters also mirror their equivalents in WQL, defining an association class, result class, result role, and role. This WQL query:*

```
ASSOCIATORS OF {Win32_Directory='c:\temp'} WHERE
     AssocClass=CIM_DirectoryContainsFile
     ResultClass=CIM_DataFile
     ResultRole=PartComponent
     Role=GroupComponent
```

can be replaced with the following invocation of `AssociatorsOf`*:*

```
set colDirectories = refWMIService.AssociatorsOf( _
                        "Win32_Directory='c:\temp'", _
                        "CIM_DirectoryContainsFile", _
                        "CIM_DataFile", _
                        "PartComponent", _
                        "GroupComponent") ◆
```

A Fully-Fledged Example

To end this chapter, we present a script that calculates the size (in bytes) of a directory, including all its files and subdirectories. As it goes along, it provides a running total of the size of each subdirectory's contents. This script demonstrates the relationship between WMI objects, associators, and queries in a reasonably complex context. This is accomplished using the following procedure:

1. Get a reference to the WMI object representing the directory we would like to know about.

2. Use an `ASSOCIATORS OF` query to find `CIM_DataFile` objects representing all the files contained in that directory.
3. Loop through the collection of `CIM_DataFile` objects, read the `FileSize` property of each one, and add it to a running total.
4. Use an `ASSOCIATORS OF` query to find `Win32_Directory` objects representing all the subdirectories of the directory we are looking at.
5. Loop through the collection of `Win32_Directory` objects, and perform this entire procedure for each one. Add the results to the running total.
6. Display the running total.

This series of steps introduces one small programming subtlety, hidden in the phrase "perform this entire procedure for each one." The problem here is how to script a procedure "for each one" when we have no idea in advance how many there will be! No amount of conditional logic or complex program flow will get around this one. The solution is to use a programming concept known as *recursion*. With recursion, you write a function that adds up the sizes of all files in a directory whose name is passed as a parameter. This function then calls *itself* once for each subdirectory, adding the return value of each function call to the running total. From the perspective of the function, which we will call `getDirectorySize()`, the process of calculating directory size can be described as follows:

> Add up the sizes of all files *and* directories contained in the directory whose name I have been passed. I can add up the file sizes by querying each file object in turn; I can add up the directory sizes by calling `getDirectorySize()` on each directory in turn. After I have added everything up, return the total.

Having written a function that calls itself recursively in this way, writing a script that can traverse a directory tree and figure out the total file size is easy. It is simply a question of printing the output of a single call to `getDirectorySize()` on the directory you want to know about!

Here, then, is the full script listing. This script reports the size of c:\program files (you can change this by modifying the value of `strDirName`). It would, of course, be much more convenient if the directory name could be provided as a command-line parameter, something that is perfectly possible with VBScript. This chapter, however, is quite long enough already, so the use of a command line must remain a mystery until Chapter 4, "Remote Administration."

```
'dirsize.vbs - prints the size of all directories on a system
Option Explicit
Dim refWMIService
Dim strDirName
Dim refDirectory
```

```
'put the name of the directory you wish to find the size of here
strDirName="c:\program files"

'get reference to WMI. Also get a direct reference to the directory
'we want to know about
set refWMIService = GetObject("winMgmts:")
set refDirectory = GetObject("winMgmts:Win32_Directory='" & strDirName & "'")

'fire our recursive function and display results
WScript.echo "Size of " & strDirName & " is " & _
             getDirectorySize(refDirectory) & " bytes."

'clean up
set refDirectory = Nothing
set refWMIService = Nothing

'------- End of script --------

'This function returns the aggregated size
'of all files in a directory and its subdirectories
Function getDirectorySize(pCurrentDir)
    Dim numFSize
    Dim numDSize
    Dim strQuery
    Dim refItem
    Dim colFiles
    Dim colSubdirs
    numFSize = 0
    numDSize = 0

    'first get a reference to all files in the directory
    strQuery = "ASSOCIATORS OF {Win32_Directory='" & _
               pCurrentDir.Name & "'} WHERE " & _
               "AssocClass=CIM_DirectoryContainsFile " & _
               "Role=GroupComponent ResultRole=PartComponent"
     set colFiles = refWMIService.ExecQuery(strQuery)

    'loop through each file and add the size of each to numFSize
    For Each refItem In colFiles
        numFSize = numFSize + refItem.FileSize
    Next
    set colFiles = Nothing

    'now get a reference to all the subdirectories
    strQuery = "ASSOCIATORS OF {Win32_Directory='" & _
               pCurrentDir.Name & "'} WHERE " & _
               "AssocClass=Win32_SubDirectory " & _
               "ResultRole=PartComponent"
    set colSubDirs = refWMIService.ExecQuery(strQuery)

    'loop through each subdirectory, and add its
    'size to numDSize by recursively calling this function
    For Each refItem in colSubDirs
```

```
        numDSize = numDSize + getDirectorySize(refItem)
    Next
    set colSubdirs = Nothing

    'finally, print stats and return the total size
    WScript.echo pCurrentDir.Name & ": " & numFSize & _
                 " bytes in files - " & numDSize & _
                 " bytes in subdirs"
    getDirectorySize = numFSize + numDSize
End Function
```

Type this script into a text editor and run it in the Windows Scripting Host. You will find out how much space is taken up with all those programs you installed! In order to keep a permanent log, pipe the output of the script to a file by typing something like this at the command prompt:

```
dirsize.vbs > log.txt
```

Note: Compressed Versus Uncompressed Filesize

This program gives you the uncompressed size of the files. If you use compression, the actual disk space used could be significantly less. ◆

This might seem like a rather complicated script for a terribly simple task. After all, if you are not interested in the per-subdirectory running totals, and you only want to find out the total amount of space taken up by the contents of a directory, you can accomplish this much more conveniently and quickly with Windows Explorer! As you will discover as this book progresses, plenty of useful things can be accomplished with WMI that simply cannot be done any other way. If you understand how this script works, you will be able to do them all.

Summary

This chapter investigated the basics of filesystem representation in WMI. It described the WMI objects that represent files and directories, as well as the relationships between them. More usefully, this chapter illustrated the use of several core WMI mechanisms and structures, an understanding of which is crucial to making use of WMI in a real-world computing environment. These concepts include properties, methods, primary keys, collections, WQL SELECT queries, associators, WQL associator queries, and inheritance.

In the next chapter, you will see how these can control computers across a network.

4

Remote Administration

As you have encountered it so far, WMI represents a new, unified way of modeling the components of a computer system. Despite this ability, from the perspective of the system administrator, WMI does not help accomplish anything that could not be handled equally well with conventional tools. The most exciting feature of WMI, however, is one that you have yet to encounter—namely, the ability to perform any function remotely just as easily as on a local machine! It is perhaps this one feature that makes WMI truly powerful as a system administration tool. This chapter introduces WMI's facilities for remote administration and presents examples of tasks that make use of them.

Connecting to a Remote Machine

Accessing WMI objects on a remote machine, executing queries, and retrieving collections can be accomplished in exactly the same way as they are done locally. First you get a reference to a `SWbemServices` object on the remote machine, and then you use that `SWbemServices` object to service all further WMI requests. Performing the first step merely involves a call to `GetObject()` with a slightly extended moniker string; performing all further steps is absolutely identical to performing them locally.

So far in this book, we have been finding `SWbemServices` objects by passing the word `"winMgmts:"` as a moniker string to `GetObject()`. As we have already noted, this string is actually a shorthand notation for "the `SWbemServices` object that services the default namespace on the local machine." Retrieving a reference to a `SWbemServices` object that can service the default namespace on a remote machine merely involves providing the machine name as part of the moniker, using the syntax `"winMgmts:\\<MACHINE-NAME>"` or `"winMgmts://<MACHINE-NAME>"`. The direction of the slashes is unimportant, because both are supported. The following

VBScript fragment retrieves a reference to the `CIM_DataFile` representing boot.ini on a Windows 2000 workstation called STYX:

```
Set refWMI = GetObject("winMgmts:\\STYX")
Set refBootIni = refWMI.Get("CIM_DataFile.Name='c:\boot.ini'")
```

In the spirit of the Windows 2000 concessions to IP, a moniker string can substitute for the traditional NetBIOS machine name a DNS host name (`"winMgmts:\\styx.stones.com"`) or even an IP address (`"winMgmts:\\192.168.1.64"`). And that really is the only difference between local and remote use of WMI! Thanks to COM (the technical architecture underlying WMI), a script could theoretically retrieve WMI objects from a computer on the other side of the world without noticing that anything extraordinary is happening.

You will recall from Chapter 1,"Introduction to WMI," that WMI objects are implemented as Component Object Model (COM) components. COM—or, more specifically, Distributed COM (DCOM)—uses remote procedure calls to communicate with COM objects across a network. The result is that an invocation of `GetObject()` with a moniker string that includes a host name or IP address can call upon the services of DCOM to handle all the magic required to return what looks like an ordinary object reference but is in fact a proxy for an object sitting on a remote machine. All attempts to interact with properties or methods of the referenced object are transparently brokered by DCOM and passed on to the remote machine. The remote machine, in turn, passes on the request to the object in question and returns data as required.

Tip: Remote Direct Object Access

It is possible to retrieve a WMI object directly from a remote machine using a single call to `GetObject()` *without retrieving a* `SWbemServices` *object first. However, a moniker string for such a call must specify not only the machine name but also the namespace in which the object is found. For example, a* `CIM_DataFile` *retrieving boot.ini could be retrieved in a single line of VBScript as follows:*

```
Set refBootIni = GetObject _
    ("winMgmts:\\STYX\root\cimv2:CIM_DataFile='c:\boot.ini'")
```

But the following line would result in an error:

```
Set refBootIni =
GetObject("winMgmts:\\STYX:CIM_DataFile='c:\boot.ini'")
```

In fact, the preceding line of code would not work even if you ran it on STYX itself, because the object path syntax requires that the only thing that can immediately follow a computer name is a namespace specification. ◆

As a quick demonstration of how easy remote administration can be, we present a short script that reboots a remote computer. It accomplishes this task in two phases. First, it connects to the WMI service of the machine in question and retrieves a `Win32_OperatingSystem` object. Second, it calls its `reboot()` method.

As the name implies, `Win32_OperatingSystem`, which derives from `CIM_OperatingSystem` (which in turn derives from `CIM_LogicalElement` and `CIM_ManagedSystemElement`), represents the operating system on a Windows computer. In common with all `CIM_ManagedSystemElement` subclasses, a `Win32_OperatingSystem` can be identified uniquely by its `Name` property, the primary key. Hence, getting a reference to such an object can, in theory, be as simple as calling `GetObject()` with an appropriate object path. Unfortunately, in contrast to all of the objects we have met so far, the `Name` property of a `CIM_OperatingSystem` is so unwieldy that it is virtually unusable! It is constructed from an amalgam of the OS name (such as `"Windows 2000 Professional"`), the Windows directory (such as `"C:\WINNT"`), and the disk partition on which the OS lives (such as `"\Device\HardDisk0\Partition1"`), all separated by | characters.

In order to save ourselves the trouble of having to correctly type an absurdly long string into a script while specifying the object path, we use a different approach to retrieve a reference to the `Win32_OperatingSystem` object. Instead of specifying an object path involving a primary key, we use a WQL query to return a *collection* of `Win32_OperatingSystem` objects. We can then use a `For Each...Next` loop to call `reboot()` on each one in turn. This is not as absurd as it seems, because we know that there will be only one such object on any given machine!

The `reboot()` method itself and its companion method, `shutdown()`, perform exactly the functions you might expect—they reboot and shut down a machine, respectively. Neither requires any parameters. Both return a value of 0 if execution is successful or another number if an error occurs.

The entire script for rebooting a remote machine appears in the following code. Note the use of a WQL query to retrieve what is actually a single instance of a `Win32_OperatingSystem`, and the checking of the return value from `reboot()`. If you want to try this out, ensure that you are logged into your workstation with an account that has Administrator privileges on the remote machine (such as a Domain Admin account). Bear in mind, however, that the script will work *only* on a remote machine; an attempt to use it to reboot your own workstation will fail! The reasons for this will become evident later in this chapter.

```
'reboot.vbs - reboot STYX
Option Explicit
Dim refWMIService
Dim colComputers
Dim refComputer

Set refWMIService = GetObject("winMgmts:\\STYX")
'Do this because primary key is absurdly unweildy!
Set colComputers = refWMIService.ExecQuery("SELECT * FROM Win32_OperatingSystem")
For Each refComputer In colComputers
    If refComputer.reboot() = 0 Then
       Wscript.echo "Computer rebooted"
    Else
       Wscript.echo "Reboot failed"
    End If
Next

Set refComputer = Nothing
Set colComputers = Nothing
Set refWMIService = Nothing
```

Later in this chapter, we describe a variety of techniques for invoking a script such as this not only on a single machine, but on an entire network.

The Win32Shutdown() *Method*

For more fine-grained control over a shutdown or reboot, `Win32_OperatingSystem` *provides the more sophisticated* `Win32Shutdown()` *method. In addition to being used to reboot and shut down a machine, it can also be used to invoke a soft poweroff or to log off a logged-in user. Like its two colleagues,* `reboot()` *and* `shutdown()`*, this method returns 0 if execution succeeds or some other number—usually 1—if it fails. Unlike its colleagues, it takes a numeric parameter, whose value determines the action taken. Possible values are listed in Table 4.1.*

Table 4.1 Win32Shutdown() *Method Parameters*

Parameter	Meaning
0	Logs off the current user.
1	Shuts down the machine.
2	Reboots the machine.
4	Forces a logoff, shutdown, or reboot, even if the user has unsaved work.
8	Powers down the machine.
10	Forces a logoff, shutdown, or reboot, even if software currently running has hung and does not respond to an End Task request.

These values are called flags*—numbers that can be combined to encode several parameters in a single value. To use the method, you specify its behavior by* *choosing a value representing logoff (0), shutdown (1), reboot (2), or powerdown (8). In addition, you can* add *a value representing one of the two levels of "force." These force values (4 and 10) are qualifiers: They make no sense when used alone, but when added to one of the other values, they qualify its behavior. For example, invoking* `Win32Shutdown(8)` *powers down the machine, but if a user happens to be working at the time, shutdown occurs only if all the applications are happy to quit (that is, if there is no unsaved work). You can force shutdown by adding 4 to the parameter:* `Win32Shutdown(8+4)` *shuts down the machine regardless of whether there is unsaved work. Likewise,* `Win32Shutdown(2+10)` *forces a reboot even if running software has stopped responding entirely.*

Passing any value other than the ones just listed, or a sensible combination of them, will cause the method to fail. Flags like this are often used in function calls to the Windows API (which is essentially what `Win32Shutdown()` *really is), because they are a convenient and efficient way of encoding behavior.*

A word of warning: If you do not use one of the force options, and unsaved work does prevent a logoff, reboot, or shut down from occurring, `Win32Shutdown()` *will return a success code of 0 rather than an error.* ◆

You have seen that connecting to the WMI service on remote machines is utterly trivial—provided, of course, that you have the relevant permissions (see Chapter 5, "WMI Security"). There is, however, one minor snag: There are many more chances for things to go wrong! When running a script as an administrator on your own machine, provided that the script is written sensibly, everything is likely to work as expected. In contrast, when you run a script remotely, a whole host of factors can contribute to unexpected behavior. For example, a machine might be disconnected from the network or even switched off, your script might not have the security clearance it needs to carry out the tasks it is asked to do, an unexpected surge in network traffic might cause the network connection to time out, or a DNS or WINS anomaly might prevent the connection from being made in the first place. Any or all of these problems could cause a script to fail anywhere in the code at any time. Such behavior hardly makes for a reliable system administration scenario.

Thankfully, you can use several techniques to prevent, detect, and respond to errors in a safe, civilized way before they manage to halt script execution. The next section discusses their use, both to handle problems specifically associated with remote administration and to tackle errors that can haunt you when running WMI locally or remotely.

Handling Errors

As you saw both in Chapter 3, "Examining the Filesystem with WMI," and in the previous script, many WMI methods return a value that indicates whether they succeeded. Whenever a script takes an action that depends on that value, it is performing a kind of error handling. The previous script, for example, reboots a remote machine and uses the return value of the `Reboot()` method to spark conditional execution. If the reboot succeeds, it runs a line of code that outputs `Computer rebooted`. If the reboot fails, it handles the error by outputting `Reboot failed`. (This description does not hold if you attempt to run the script without relevant permissions, though.)

When working with WMI and VBScript, you will encounter only two types of errors. One type is exemplified by the previous script: A WMI method fails to carry out its task and returns an error value. Sometimes the error value is not particularly informative, merely telling you that a failure has occurred. At other times, such as with the `CIM_LogicalFile` methods, the values are highly informative and can be interpreted to tell you exactly what has gone wrong. In either case, however, the crucial thing to note is that as far as VBScript is concerned, there is no error; there is merely a function with a return value.

In contrast, the other type of error is that which really upsets VBScript and, unless handled, causes a script to abort execution. Errors of this type occur when VBScript encounters a situation with which it absolutely cannot cope or if WMI encounters such a situation and passes the crisis back to VBScript. Such situations arise with monotonous regularity. In fact, if you tried running all the scripts in the preceding chapter, you might well already have encountered some of these problems. The good news is that these errors are normally the result of fixable human programmer mistakes and under such circumstances are easy to correct! Three regular contenders are listed here, along with script fragments and sample error output:

- A moniker string or a WQL query is not formatted correctly. This could happen as the result of a programming error when the string is compiled from fragments within the code, particularly if part of the string is supplied at runtime (that is, as a command-line parameter). For example, a WQL string of the form `SELECT * FROM CIM_DataFile WHERE` would cause the `ExecQuery()` method of a `SWbemServices` object to throw a fatal error: `C:\wmibook\oops.vbs(2, 1) 0x80041017`. This rather uninformative output—an error returned to VBScript by WMI—means "The query was not syntactically valid." You can figure this out by looking in the WMI Error Codes reference documentation, which can be found at `http://msdn.microsoft.com/library/psdk/wmisdk/errorwmi_4bxv.htm`.

Similarly, an attempt to find references to a nonexistent class (such as `SELECT * FROM Win32_IdoNotExist`) would raise an error of type 0x80041017, meaning "The specified class is invalid." Either way, the crucial problem is that such an error will halt script execution.

- An attempt is made to read a nonexistent property or invoke a nonexistent method of an object. For example, an attempt to call `refItem.Reboot()` where `refItem` is actually a `CIM_DataFile` would raise the following error:

```
C:\oops.vbs(5, 1) Microsoft VBScript runtime error: Object doesn't
support this property or method: 'reboot'.
```

  Although you would be forgiven for thinking that this is a rather ludicrous mistake to make—and, in many ways, it is—you might occasionally fall into a trap when dealing with a large collection of objects of different types. This can happen when you make a WQL query that requests all objects of a class that has a large number of subclasses, and you erroneously attribute a method of a subclass to the base class.

- An attempt to connect to a remote machine fails. This can either be because the name provided in the moniker string does not correspond to a real machine on the network, or because the computer in question is switched off, disconnected from the network, or otherwise unresponsive. This situation could arise during an attempt to execute code such as

```
set refWMI = GetObject("winMgmts:\\NON-EXISTENT-MACHINE")
```

  This would result in the following fatal error:

```
C:\wmibook\oops.vbs(2, 1) Microsoft VBScript runtime error: The remote
server machine does not exist or is unavailable: 'GetObject.'
```

Note: Empty Collections

Contrary to what you might expect, an attempt to loop through a collection after executing a query that returns no objects does not raise an error. If `ExecQuery()` *cannot find any instances that satisfy the criteria for a WQL search, it simply returns an empty collection. The VBScript* `For Each...Next` *construct will happily loop zero times through an empty collection. In other words, no code within the loop is executed.* ◆

The most appropriate way to handle the first two examples is to preempt and avoid the errors in the first place! When reading properties and invoking methods, try to think about all the circumstances in which the code might run, and ensure that it is always likely to work. When constructing strings to pass to `GetObject()` or `ExecQuery()`, ensure that any fragments of strings generated at runtime produce syntactically correct moniker strings or WQL queries. The third example, however, cannot be handled in this way. It is simply not possible to predict or check in advance that a call to `GetObject()`, particularly sent to a remote machine, will actually work. The only option is to attempt the call, let VBScript raise an error, and handle it before the script aborts. There are two steps involved in handling unavoidable runtime problems: instructing VBScript not to complain when they occur, and taking appropriate action when something appears to have gone wrong.

The first, and simplest, of these steps is accomplished by issuing the `On Error Resume Next` directive. This directive means exactly what it implies: If any error occurs at any time after this directive has been issued, VBScript ignores the error and resumes script execution at the next statement. This behavior is illustrated in the following script example, where an attempt to connect to WMI on a remote machine fails because of a badly formatted IP address in the moniker string. However, the script still merrily outputs the message `Successfully connected!`.

```
'continueonfail.vbs - demonstrate use of On Error Resume Next
Option Explicit
On Error Resume Next
Dim refWMI

Set refWMI = GetObject("winMgmts:\\192.168.G.999")
'line below will execute despite error
Wscript.echo "Successfully connected!"
```

In a more extended script, the line following the failed `GetObject()` call would probably be unable to execute, because it would probably depend on `refWMI`'s being set correctly. This is not a problem, however, because VBScript keeps skipping to the next line of execution until it finds one that *can* execute—unless, of course, the script finishes first! As soon as the `On Error Resume Next` directive has been issued, VBScript ignores every error that occurs and attempts to execute every line of code until either the end of the script has been reached or a further directive, `On Error Goto 0`, has been issued. Issuing this latter directive tells VBScript to stop ignoring errors and to respond to mishaps in its usual way—namely, by aborting script execution.

`On Error Resume Next` is, of course, only part of the story. It is one thing to tell VBScript to ignore errors, but quite another to behave sensibly when a mishap occurs. After all, it might not be particularly desirable for a script to abort if it cannot connect to a remote computer, but it is surely equally undesirable for it to fail silently before merrily reporting `Operation completed successfully` or some other similar lie! Even if VBScript ignores errors, we need a way to respond to them ourselves or, at the very least, figure out when they have occurred. A means to achieve this is provided by the `Err` object.

Just like the `WScript` object that you have met at several points throughout this book, an `Err` object does not have to be created. Every script has one, and, as you might have guessed, its purpose is to provide information about the last error that occurred. `Err` objects have five properties—`Number`, `Description`, `Source`, `HelpContext`, and `Helpfile`—and two methods—`Clear()` and `Raise()`. The first three properties provide information about the error. `Number` is a unique internal description of the error type, `Description` gives a textual description of this error type, and `Source` states which object caused the error to be raised. The final two properties are interesting for developers of larger programs, because they allow an error to be linked to an entry in an online help system; these are not discussed further here. The `Clear()` method resets `Number` to 0 and the other two properties to null-length strings (`""`). In other words, it resets `Err`'s properties to the state in which they should be if no error has occurred. The `Raise()` method is used to provoke an error from within a script. Effective use of this method involves relatively advanced programming considerations, so it is not discussed further here. Its use is mentioned briefly in Chapter 10, "Script Development and Deployment."

Consider the following error, which was responsible for halting script execution earlier:

```
C:\wmibook\oops.vbs(2, 1) Microsoft VBScript runtime error: The remote server
machine does not exist or is unavailable: 'GetObject.'
```

This would have been represented by an `Err` object with a `Description` of `The remote server machine does not exist or is unavailable` and a `Source` of `GetObject`. Because this is a VBScript internal error, as opposed to one raised by an external object from WMI, the error `Number` is not printed on the output. However, a quick glance at the VBScript Run-time Error Reference reveals that this is Error 462.

After an invocation of `On Error Resume Next`, script execution does not halt if a problem is encountered, but the properties of the `Err` object *are* set to reflect the most recent error that has occurred. Next, we present once more the script that reboots a remote computer named STYX. Here, however, the script is modified so that if STYX cannot be contacted, it produces a helpful explanatory message rather than failing miserably:

```
'advancedreboot.vbs - reboot STYX and report success or failure
Option Explicit
On Error Resume Next
Dim refWMIService
Dim colComputers
Dim refComputer

Set refWMIService = GetObject("winMgmts:\\STYX")

'The line above may well fail, so we must check Err
If Err.Number = 0 Then
    'good - we managed to connect without error
    Set colComputers = refWMIService.ExecQuery( _
                  "SELECT * FROM Win32_OperatingSystem")
    For Each refComputer In colComputers
       If refComputer.Reboot() <> 0 Then
          WScript.Echo "Reboot failed"
       Else
          WScript.Echo "Computer rebooted"
       End If
    Next
Else

    'we have an error, so report it and clear it
    WScript.Echo "Could not connect to remote computer"
    WScript.Echo "Error details: " & Err.Description & _
                 "(" & Err.Number & ")"
    Err.Clear()
End If

Set refComputer = Nothing
Set refWMIService = Nothing
```

As you can see, the addition of error handling required only minor modifications to the script: it merely involved adding an `On Error Resume Next` directive, followed by checking for a nonzero `Err.Number` at the point where we expected an error to occur. Note that having found an error, we call `Err.Clear()` to ensure that a further check on `Err.Number` would return 0. Here, of course, this was not exactly necessary, because we did not intend to read `Err.Number` again. However, calling this method is a good habit to get into, because in a longer script with lots of error handling, you do not want to accidentally respond to the same error twice! Had we not bothered checking `Err.Number` in the script, and just relied on `On Error Resume Next` to prevent a fatal halt, failure to connect to STYX would have resulted in the somewhat ridiculous message `Computer rebooted`.

Another change that you might have noticed is that these lines in the original script:

```
If refComputer.Reboot() = 0 Then
    WScript.Echo "Computer rebooted"
Else
    WScript.Echo "Reboot failed"
End If
```

have been inverted:

```
If refComputer.Reboot() <> 0 Then
    WScript.Echo "Reboot failed"
Else
    WScript.Echo "Computer rebooted"
End If
```

If you have religiously followed the instructions for running scripts presented in this chapter and you ran the code with administrative privileges, you would not notice any difference between the behavior of the two examples. If, however, you attempted to run the script *without* administrative privileges, there would be one extremely important difference. In both cases, the call to `refComputer.Reboot()` would fail because of lack of sufficient privileges, and, thanks to `On Error Resume Next`, the line of code following this call would be executed. In the second example, that line would cause `Reboot failed` to be printed on the screen. As it happens, this is perfectly appropriate behavior. In contrast, the first example would print `Computer rebooted`, which is not true at all!

This difference in behavior is highly revealing: *If an error occurs during the evaluation of a conditional execution statement, the effect of* `On Error Resume Next` *is the same as the effect of the statement that evaluated to true.* Hence, an error during an `If` statement causes the `If` block rather than the `Else` block to be executed. An error during the evaluation of a `While` condition will end up looping forever. Of course, in this example, we could have avoided the issue entirely by checking the value of `Err.Number` just after the call that has the potential to fail. However, inverting the sense of the conditional execution statements was a more concise way of achieving the same end.

In this script example, the addition of error handling didn't achieve very much. We simply replaced a rather aesthetically displeasing abort message from VBScript with a more helpful and relevant one of our own and, of course, prevented an erroneous announcement about rebooting. In a longer script, however, such error handling can be invaluable. For example, a script that performs an action on a whole set of machines could use error handling to ensure that a small number of unresponsive machines do not prevent the rest from being manipulated. Such a technique is illustrated later in this chapter.

Err.Number

`Err.Number` is the default *property of the `Err` object. This means that an attempt to read `Err` as though it were a straightforward numeric variable automatically uses the `Err.Number` property. The following two code fragments, therefore, are functionally identical:*

```
'fragment one
If Err.Number <> 0 Then WScript.Echo "we have an error"

'fragment two
If Err <> 0 Then WScript.Echo "we have an error"
```

The second incantation is more concise and therefore tends to be used rather regularly in VBScript code. We advise, however, that you use default properties only in cases where their meaning is obvious and unambiguous, because overuse can lead to rather confusing code. ◆

In terms of its potential use in a script, `Err.Number` performs exactly the same function as an error return value from a method. In the preceding example, `Err.Number` was used as a basic check to see whether an error had occurred. If the likelihood of certain types of errors occurring can be anticipated in advance, however, it is perfectly possible to check for specific values of `Err.Number` and have conditional execution blocks behave differentially depending on the error that occurred. The following script fragment, for example, combines a `For...Next` loop with more sophisticated checking of `Err.Number` when attempting to connect to the WMI service on a remote machine called STYX. If a call to `GetObject()` fails because the machine is unavailable, the script keeps trying up to a maximum of five times. If it fails for any other reason, however, an error message is displayed, and the script exits:

```
On Error Resume Next
For i = 1 To 5
    Err.Clear()
    Set refWMI = GetObject("winMgmts:\\STYX")
    If Err.Number = 0 Then
        'no error - break out of loop
         Exit For
    Else
        'an error number of 462 means the machine is unavailable
        'so we don't want it to cause a fatal error
        If Err.Number <> 462 Then
             'an unexpected error occurred - we will quit
             WScript.Echo "We have an odd problem (" & Err.Number & ")"
             WScript.Quit
        End If
    End If
```

```
        WScript.Sleep(5000)
    Next

    If Err.Number <> 0 then
        WScript.Echo "Despite 5 attempts, we have failed to connect"
        WScript.Quit
    End If
    'rest of script, which can safely use refWMI, continues below
```

There are several things to note about this script fragment. First, each time through the loop, `Err.Clear()` is called, ensuring that any error that is detected really does come from the most recent call to `GetObject()`. Second, as soon as we manage to connect, we use `Exit For`, a VBScript construct that has not been mentioned so far in this book. This construct, which is syntactically valid only within a `For` loop, tells VBScript to break out of the loop and resume execution from the statement following `Next`. Notice also that the statement following `Next` is yet another test of the error condition. If we omitted this, a fifth failure to connect would not be detected. When an error is found here, `WScript.Quit` is invoked to halt script execution. Having failed to connect, we do not want the rest of the script, which needs a valid `refWMI`, to attempt to run! A final thing to note is that we have used the `Sleep()` method of `WScript` at the end of each cycle through the loop. This method pauses script execution for a given number of milliseconds. In this case, we wait 5 seconds before trying to connect again to an unresponsive machine.

Error handling, then, is actually rather simple to accomplish. There is nothing more to it than invoking a few VBScript incantations and deciding what to do when a problem crops up. *Effective* error handling, in contrast, is somewhat harder to achieve. It requires figuring out when it is most appropriate to check for an error. If you check too frequently, the script will be a large, unwieldy mess of conditional execution blocks. If you check too infrequently, an important problem might be overlooked. Unfortunately, there are no absolute rules for determining when it is sensible to check for errors. It's just a question of anticipating where a problem is likely to occur or deciding where you would really like to know about one if it does crop up. Here are a few basic rules to bear in mind when deciding where to check `Err.Number`:

- A call to `GetObject()` could fail for a number of reasons. Therefore, always check for errors after such a call.
- Even after a successful call to `GetObject()`, a reference to the WMI service on a remote machine might fail. For example, someone might reboot a machine after you have retrieved a reference to its WMI service but before you have finished using it! There is probably no point

in checking for errors after every single call to every method or property of any WMI object, but it probably *is* worth checking once for each object that you retrieve a reference for (for example, once for every `For Each...Next` loop), particularly if undetected failure would have serious repercussions.

- Nothing in the world of programming is ever guaranteed. Failure happens where you least expect it!

The only real way to decide how to implement error handling is to practice, make mistakes, and build up heuristics. With error handling, as with many other things in life, there is no better guide than experience! All scripts from now on in this book will include error-handling code, to a greater or lesser extent, so there will be plenty of examples on which to draw as you read on. One final piece of advice we want to offer before leaving this topic is to *never* switch on error handling when first developing and debugging a script. When trying to write and test a script, you *want* VBScript to complain when things go wrong. What you *don't* want is for all problems to be silently ignored!

Representation of Processes in WMI

Having discussed the principles and techniques involved in implementing scripts that invoke WMI on remote machines, it seems appropriate to illustrate situations in which this can be useful, and develop some scripting techniques that can help with successful remote administration of multiple machines. As an example of a facet of a computer system that could usefully be managed remotely, we take a process—a program running on a remote computer.

Processes are represented in WMI by instances of the `Win32_Process` class. This is derived from `CIM_Process`, which in turn is derived from `CIM_LogicalElement`, which we have met several times already. The primary key of a `Win32_Process` object is its `Handle` property; this value represents a numeric identifier that the operating system assigns to a process when it is created. Every process running on a computer at any given time has a different handle; the operating system uses this number to uniquely identify each process. Hence, you can easily retrieve a WMI object representing a process whose ID you know using code such as this:

```
Set refExistingProcess = GetObject( _
                         "winmgmts:Win32_Process.Handle='1000'")
```

Superb! From a practical point of view, however, there is one slight problem: A system administrator is likely to want to get a reference to a Win32_Process object representing an instance of a specified application, but how do we find out its ProcessID in order to retrieve it? We have a bootstrapping problem! In common with all the subclasses of CIM_LogicalElement and, in fact, its superclass CIM_ManagedSystemElement, the Win32_Process class has a Name property. Unlike the filesystem objects discussed in the preceding chapter, the Name property of a Win32_Process is not unique and cannot be used in a moniker string. After all, there could be several instances of a single program running on a computer! The solution, of course, is to use a query to retrieve all instances of Win32_Process with a specified name. This is illustrated in the following fragment, which retrieves a collection of processes representing all running copies of Internet Explorer:

```
Set colProcesses = refWMI.ExecQuery( _
        "Select * from Win32_Process Where Name='IEXPLORE.exe'")
```

If you want to hone the collection further, you can draw on one of the many other properties of Win32_Process. For example, CreationDate, as the name implies, specifies the date a process first came into being. You can retrieve a collection of Win32_Process objects representing running copies of Internet Explorer that have been launched within the last 30 minutes with a code fragment such as this:

```
Set colProcesses = refWMI.ExecQuery( _
  "SELECT * FROM Win32_Process WHERE Name='iexplore.exe' AND " & _
  "CreationDate < '" & GetWMIDate(DateAdd("n",-30,Now),"+000") & "'"
```

Note that this fragment uses the GetWMIDate() function introduced in the preceding chapter.

Having retrieved a collection of Win32_Process objects, you can manipulate them within a For Each...Next loop in the usual way.

Manipulating Processes Remotely

The past few months have seen widespread press coverage (at least in the UK) of the playing of Quake on corporate networks. According to our newspapers, millions of dollars are wasted as employees spend time, money, and resources on Quake. Many companies apparently struggle to control its use. Thus, it seems appropriate to begin our discussion of process manipulation with a script that can terminate Quake sessions on a network!

The key to this is the Win32_Process Terminate() method, which, as the name implies, terminates the process on which it is called. This method, just like many of the others we have already encountered, returns an error code of 0 if successful or another number if the call fails. This method takes a single, optional parameter—an `Exit` code with which the process should terminate. This parameter is not used for most system administration purposes. The following short script example illustrates the use of the `Terminate()` method by killing all instances of Quake running on a local machine:

```
'killquake.vbs - terminate quake process on local machine
Option Explicit
On Error Resume Next
Dim refWMI
Dim strQuery
Dim colProcesses
Dim refItem

Set refWMI = GetObject("winMgmts:")
If Err <> 0 Then
    WScript.Echo "Could not connect to WMI"
    WScript.Quit
End If
StrQuery = "SELECT * FROM Win32_Process WHERE Name='quake.exe'"
Set colProcesses = refWMI.ExecQuery(strQuery)
For Each refItem In colProcesses
    If Err = 0 Then
        RefItem.Terminate()
    End If
Next
Set colProcesses = Nothing
Set refWMI = Nothing
```

To make this script truly useful, we need one more feature: the ability to run the script on whole groups of machines remotely without having to rewrite a line of the script for every machine! Next, we explore several ways in which this can be achieved.

Machine Names as Command-Line Arguments

Perhaps the easiest way to provide runtime information to a script is to give it command-line arguments. For example, if you could adapt the preceding script to read, say, a process name and a list of machines from the command line, you could create a much more useful tool. Because WSH has a built-in facility for handling command-line arguments, this is easy to accomplish.

Command-line arguments passed to WSH at runtime are available in the `Arguments` property of `WScript`. This property is in fact a `wshArguments` collection, each of whose elements is a whitespace-separated argument. For example, an invocation such as the following would start a script whose `WScript.Arguments` contains four items: `goose.exe`, `Erasmus`, `albatross`, and `romeo`:

```
c:>argtest.vbs goose.exe erasmus albatross romeo
```

Within this script, we can loop through the arguments with a `For Each...Next` loop, as in this code fragment:

```
For Each strItem in Wscript.Arguments
   Wscript.echo "Argument: " & strItem
Next
```

In common with all collections, elements of a `wshArguments` collection can be accessed individually via the `Item` property. This property is somewhat different from the ones you have met so far in that it behaves more like a method because it takes a parameter—an imply index that uniquely identifies the item you want to retrieve. This index is usually either a number or a text string. We have not used the `Item` property to retrieve individual members of collections so far because when WMI returns a collection, you do not necessarily know the index of the item you want to retrieve. In any event, iterating through a `For Each...Next` loop ensures that you never miss an object that you were not expecting! In the case of `wshArguments`, however, the items are all indexed numerically: The first command-line argument is stored in `WScript.Arguments.Item(0)`, the second in `WScript.Arguments.Item(1)`, and so on. Thus, if you know how many arguments there are, it is easy to address each directly without wasting time writing loops.

A second property of all collections, including `wshArguments`, is `Count`, which reports the number of items in the collection. Given that the first command-line argument passed to a script has an index of 0, the final argument has an index of `WScript.Arguments.Count - 1`. The following code fragment loops through each command-line argument again, this time using a `For...Next` loop in conjunction with the `Count` property:

```
For i = 0 to WScript.Arguments.Count - 1
    WScript.Echo "Argument " & i & ":" & _
                 WScript.Arguments.Item(i)
Next
```

This fragment outputs lines such as `Argument 0: goose.exe`.

`Item` is the default property of a collection. This means that a line such as this:

```
WScript.Arguments.Item(i)
```

can be made slightly more concise:

```
WScript.Arguments(i)
```

We will use this second syntax from now on.

When you loop through all the command-line arguments, a combination of `Count` and `Item(index)` is no more convenient and a lot less concise than a `For Each...Next` loop. The direct index method becomes extremely useful, however, when you want to treat arguments individually. For example, a sensible use of command-line arguments for the Quake-killing script would be to make the first argument the name of a process to kill and any number of remaining arguments a set of computers on which to kill it. This can be accomplished with the following code fragment:

```
strProcessName = WScript.Arguments(0)
For i = 1 to WScript.Arguments.Count - 1
    strMachine = WScript.Arguments(i)
    'Main body of script goes here
Next
```

This code generates an error if an attempt is made to execute it without supplying an argument. This, of course, can be handled using the `Err` object, as described earlier in this chapter. Alternatively, a more graceful approach would be to check the value of `WScript.Arguments.Count`; if it is 0, no arguments have been provided!

The following code shows a script that puts all of this together. It takes as its parameters a process name followed by any number of machine names. Its job is to terminate any instance of the named process found on any of the machines. To terminate all Quake sessions on a group of networked machines, you might consider using the script with a command line such as this:

```
c:\>terminate.vbs quake.exe finance1 finance2 finance3
```

This script works by attempting to connect to each named machine (provided as command-line arguments after the process name) and then to get a reference to any `Win32_Process` objects representing processes whose names match the first command-line argument (`quake.exe`). For each reference it finds, it calls the `terminate()` method to kill the represented process. Note that in addition to providing the upper bounds for the loop, `WScript.Arguments.Count` is used to perform some basic error-avoidance checks, as well as using the `Err` object where it is required.

```
'killit.vbs - terminate a named process on a set of computers
Option Explicit
On Error Resume Next
Dim refWMI
Dim colProcesses
Dim refProcess
Dim strMoniker
Dim strQuery
Dim i

'check to see that we have supplied at least two arguments
'if not, then print a usage message and quit
If WScript.Arguments.Count < 2 Then
```

```
    WScript.Echo "Usage: killit.vbs <process name> [<machine name>]"
    WScript.Quit
End If

'build the query string using the first command line argument
'this query will be used on all machines
strQuery = "select * from Win32_Process where Name='" _
           & WScript.Arguments(0) & "'"

'loop through each of the remaining command-line arguments
'these are assumed to be machine names (or, of course, IP addresses)
For i = 1 to WScript.Arguments.Count - 1
    'reset the Err object to ensure that any non-zero Err.Number comes
    'from this part of the code
    Err.Clear()
    'build a moniker string for the machine and try to get
    'an object reference
    strMoniker = "winmgmts:\\" & WScript.Arguments(i)
    set refWMI = GetObject(strMoniker)
    'did we successfully connect to the machine?
    If Err.Number <> 0 Then
        WScript.Echo "Failed to connect to " & WScript.Arguments(i)
    Else
        'good - we did. Get a collection of all relevant process objects
        Set colProcesses = refWMI.ExecQuery(strQuery)
        If colProcesses.Count=0 Then
            'none was found - we perform this check even though it is
            'not strictly necessary (For Each ... Next would not error out
            'on Count=0) because it allows us to print this friendly message
            WScript.Echo WScript.Arguments(0) & " - Not found on " _
            & WScript.Arguments(i)
        Else
            'we have some process objects, so loop through and terminate them
            For Each refProcess in colProcesses
                If refProcess.Terminate()=0 Then
                    WScript.Echo "(PID " & refProcess.Handle & ") " _
                                & refProcess.Name & " Terminated on - " _
                                & WScript.Arguments(i)
                Else
                    WScript.Echo "Unable to terminate - " _
                                 & refProcess.Name & " on " _
                                 & WScript.Arguments(i)
                End If
            Next
        End If
    End If
    Set colProcesses = Nothing
    Set refWMI = Nothing
Next
```

So, now you can terminate any process running on one or more machines on your network. Fantastic!

Although this technique is ideal for running a script that performs actions on a small, named group of machines, it is highly impractical for carrying out bulk activities on a large network. Using our script to stop Quake on several hundred machines would take an excessively long command line and would be extraordinarily unwieldy.

Multiple Machines as an IP Address Range

As you will recall from the start of this chapter, a moniker string will happily take an IP number in place of the machine name. Therefore, one possible approach to running a script on a large number of computers would be to loop through an entire IP address range, attempting to connect to each address in turn. You could do this by simply creating moniker strings that include an IP number instead of a machine name. The following script demonstrates how this can be done. The core is identical to the one we just saw, but this time, the command-line parameters consist of the name of the process we want terminated, followed by two IP addresses, representing each end of an IP address range. The script will be invoked with a command line such as this:

```
c:>terminate_all.vbs quake.exe 192.168.18.1 192.168.20.254
```

This constructs a moniker string to connect to WMI on every IP address within the given range. Error handling here is, of course, essential, because it is highly likely that several of the IP numbers will not correspond to Windows 2000 boxes—or, in fact, anything at all!

The core of the script works in exactly the same way as the previous one did: It takes a given range and iterates its way through a loop until it has checked every machine in the desired range. There is one slight complication, however: An IP address is not a number as such, but a string representation of 4 bytes. An attempt to write code such as this:

```
For i = 192.168.18.1 to 192.168.20.254
    'do stuff
Next
```

is obviously nonsense and will result in an error—a type mismatch, to be precise! The solution to this problem is to convert the two IP addresses into true numeric values and loop through these values instead. Within the loop, each value can be converted back to an IP address string before being passed to WMI as part of a moniker. We accomplish this translation with two functions, `IPToNum()` and `NumToIP()`.

`IPToNum()` takes a string representation of an IP address and converts it into the 32-bit integer represented by that string. For example, `IPToNum(192.168.16.10)` and `IPToNum(192.168.16.20)` evaluate to 3232239626 and 3232239636, respectively. As you can see, these numbers are 10 apart, as are the addresses from which they were generated. In this form, however, we can easily loop through the entire range with reckless disregard for subnet boundaries. If passed an illegal IP address, the function returns a nonzero error code that we can trap in the main script. The second function, `NumToIP()`, reverses this transformation and converts the IP number back to its dotted notation. Thus, as we cycle our way through the `For...Next` loop, we can use this function, along with the loops counter variable, to help generate a sane moniker string.

Here, then, is the full code listing. The main body of the script appears first, followed by the definitions of `IPToNum()` and `NumToIP()`:

```
'killitIP.vbs - terminate a named process on computers in a given
'IP address range
Option Explicit
On Error Resume Next

Dim colProcesses
Dim refProcess
Dim refWMI
Dim strMoniker
Dim strQuery
Dim numLow
Dim numHigh
Dim i

'check that we have the right number of command-line args
'if not, then quit with a usage message
If WScript.Arguments.Count <> 3 Then
    WScript.Echo "Usage: killitIP.vbs <process> <lower IP> <upper IP>"
    WScript.Quit
End If

'Convert the second and third command-line argument into numbers
'using IPToNum() and store their results
numLow = IPToNUm(WScript.Arguments(1))
numHigh = IPToNUm(WScript.Arguments(2))
'check that numLow and numHigh are valid (IPToNum() returns -1 if not)
If numLow < 0 Or numHigh < 0 Then
    WScript.Echo "Incorrect IP address range"
    WScript.Quit
End If
'check that numLow is smaller than numHigh!
If numLow > numHigh Then
    WScript.Echo "The second IP address must be higher than the first."
    WScript.Quit
End If

'Build query string based on process name provided as first cmd-line arg
strQuery = "SELECT * FROM Win32_Process WHERE " & _
           "Name='" & WScript.Arguments(0) & "'"
```

```
'loop through address range
For i = numLow To numHigh
    Err.Clear()
    'try to connect to machine with given address
    'NumToIP() converts the counter value back to a textual address
    strMoniker = "winmgmts:\\" & NumToIP(i)
    Set refWMI = GetObject(strMoniker)
    If Err.Number <> 0 Then
        WScript.Echo "Failed to connect to " & NumToIP(i)
    Else
        'get a collection of Win32_Process objects
        Set colProcesses = refWMI.ExecQuery(strQuery)
        If colProcesses.Count=0 Then
            WScript.Echo WScript.Arguments(0) & _
                        " - Not found on "  & NumToIP(i)
        Else
            'there are some matching process, so loop through and kill
            For Each refProcess in colProcesses
                If refProcess.Terminate()=0 Then
                   WScript.Echo "(PID " & refProcess.Handle & ") " & _
                                refProcess.Name & _
                                " Terminated on - " & NumToIP(i)
                Else
                   WScript.Echo "Unable to terminate - " & _
                                refProcess.Name & " on " & NumToIP(i)
                End If
            Next
        End If
    End If
    Set colProcesses = Nothing
    Set refWMI = Nothing
Next


'IPToNum() function - turns a textual IP address into a 32-bit number
Function IPToNum(strIP)
    Dim numOctetsArray
    Dim i
    numOctetsArray = Split(strIP,".")

    'sanity checks
    If UBound(numOctetsArray) <> 3 Then
        'oops = wrong number of octets
        IPToNum = -1
        Exit Function
    End If
    For i = 0 to 3
        If Not IsNumeric(numOctetsArray(i)) Then
            'oops - not an IP address
            IPToNum = -2
            Exit Function
        End If
        If numOctetsArray(i) > 254 Then
```

```
            'oops - octet out of range
            IPToNum = -3
            Exit Function
        End If
    Next

    'now compile a number
    IPToNum = numOctetsArray(0) * (2^24)
    IPToNum = IPToNum + numOctetsArray(1) * (2^16)
    IPToNum = IPToNum + numOctetsArray(2) * (2^8)
    IPToNum = IPToNum + numOctetsArray(3)
End Function

'NumToIP() function - turns a 32-bit number into an IP address
Function NumToIP(numNum)
    Dim numOctetsArray(4)
    Dim param 'simulate passbyval
    Dim i
    param = numNum
   'don't bother with sanity checks here because
   'we are always passing something created by IPToNum
    numOctetsArray(0) = Int(param / (2^24))
    param = param - (numOctetsArray(0) * (2^24))
    numOctetsArray(1) = Int(param / (2^16))
    param = param - (numOctetsArray(1) * (2^16))
    numOctetsArray(2) = Int(param / (2^8))
    numOctetsArray(3) = param - (numOctetsArray(2) * (2^8))
    NumToIP = numOctetsArray(0) & "." & numOctetsArray(1) & _
              "." & numOctetsArray(2) & "." & numOctetsArray(3)
End Function
```

We hope you will agree that this technique for connecting to WMI on whole ranges of machines is really rather powerful!

Note: IPToNUM *and* NumToIP

`IPToNum()` *starts by performing some basic sanity checks: it uses VBScript's built-in* `Split()` *function to turn the IP string into an array of segments, delimited by .. It then uses the built-in* `UBound()` *function to check the size of the array and* `IsNumeric()` *to check that each array item really is a number. Having carried out these checks, it converts the four numbers representing each octet of the address into a single 32-bit integer. This is done, effectively, by considering the array as a four-digit number in base 256: the "column" on the right represents units, the second from the right "256es", the third from the right "256-times-256es," and the left column "256-times-256-times-256es". Each array element is multiplied by the requisite number of 256es before the total is added together to produce a single number.*

continues ▶

▶ *continued*

NumToIP() *performs the reverse process. It does not carry out any error checking, because in the context of the script, it knows for sure that any number passed to it is a valid IP address generated by* IPToNum()*. It first splits the single number into an array of four "digits" in base 256, using a combination of division and subtraction. It then concatenates the array into a dot-separated string.* ◆

Specifying Machines in a File

There are, of course, many ways to get a job done, and finding ways to pass machine names to scripts is no exception. Before leaving this topic, however, we will demonstrate one final approach—reading a list of machine names (or IP addresses) from a text file.

VBScript includes support for reading and writing files not through a built-in function but via the FileSystemObject. A FileSystemObject object can be created within a script using the built-in CreateObject() function. This function is similar to the GetObject() that you have seen several times before, but with one important difference: Whereas GetObject() is used to retrieve a reference to an existing object (or one that is transparently created on-demand by a DCOM server), CreateObject() asks an application to explicitly *create* an object on the client's behalf. The syntax for CreateObject() is as follows:

```
Set refObject = CreateObject("<application>.<classname>.<version>")
```

If you either do not know or do not care about the specific version, a shorter syntax uses the default version on a system:

```
Set refObject = CreateObject("<application>.<classname>")
```

<application> is the registered name of the *COM server* providing the object (the registered name of the executable file or library containing the code that defines and implements the class in question). <classname> is the name of the class of object to create. The registered name of the COM server providing the FileSystemObject class is Scripting, so an object of this type is created with a code fragment such as this:

```
Set refFSO = CreateObject("Scripting.FileSystemObject")
```

Only one instance of this object can be created at any one time from within any given script. This makes sense, of course, because the FileSystemObject represents the filesystem within a script, and there is always only one filesystem!

In order to read the contents of a text file, we first use the `OpenTextFile()` method of a `FileSystemObject` to retrieve a reference to a `TextStream`. The `ReadLine()` method of the `TextStream` can be used to read the file one line at a time.

`OpenTextFile()` requires a single parameter—the name of the file to open. This can be either a fully-qualified path and filename or the name of a file in the working directory. In addition, there are three optional parameters. The first specifies whether the file should be opened for reading, writing, or appending (values 1, 2, and 8, respectively); the second is a flag indicating whether a nonexistent file should be created; the third specifies whether the file should be opened in Unicode or ASCII mode. Given that we are interested only in reading here, we can ignore all but the first optional parameter. Thus, the code fragment required to open a text file for reading given a `FileSystemObject` reference is

```
Set refInputFile = refFSO.OpenTextFile("input.txt", 1)
```

Having retrieved a reference to a `TextStream`, lines can be read in turn with a call to `ReadLine()`. This method, which takes no parameters, returns a string corresponding to the first unread line in a file; each time it is called, it returns the next line. Thus, reading each line of a file in turn into a string variable simply requires multiple calls to the method.

An attempt to call `ReadLine()` when there are no more lines to read results, unsurprisingly, in an error! There is never a need to handle the error, though, because a `TextStream` has an `AtEndOfStream` property that can be read prior to a call to `ReadLine()` to check whether there are any lines left to read:

```
If Not refStream.AtEndOfStream Then strLine = refStream.ReadLine()
```

In order to loop through a file, reading each line in turn, we can place the call to `ReadLine()` within a `While...Wend` loop whose condition is `Not refStream.AtEndOfStream`. This is all illustrated in the following script, which opens a command-line-specified file, reads computer names from it line by line, and creates a WMI moniker string from each:

```
'killitfile.vbs - terminate a named process on all machines whose names
'are listed in a given file
Option Explicit
On Error Resume Next
Dim refFSO
Dim refInputFile
Dim strMoniker

'Check that an argument has been provided
If WScript.Arguments.Count < 1 Then
    WScript.Echo "You must provide a filename!"
    WScript.Quit
End If
```

```
'create a FileSystemObject object
Set refFSO = CreateObject("Scripting.FileSystemObject")
Set refInputFile = refFSO.OpenTextFile(WScript.Arguments(0),1)
If Err<>0 then
    WScript.Echo "Could not find the file " & WScript.Arguments(0)
Else
    While Not refInputFile.AtEndOfStream
        StrMoniker = "winMgmts:\\" & refInputFile.ReadLine()
        Wscript.echo strMoniker
        'do something useful in here
    Wend
    refInputFile.Close
    Set refInputFile = Nothing
End If
Set refFSO = Nothing
```

We leave it to your imagination to work out how a script structure like this can be used in conjunction with some of the examples you have already seen to perform remote administration on a set of computers!

Note that before setting `refInputFile` to `Nothing`, we sneaked in a new method called `Close()`, which tells the underlying operating system that we no longer need a handle to the file, so it can sever our links with it and allocate any used resources to someone else.

Creating Processes

Having demonstrated at length techniques that can be used to terminate processes running on remote machines, it seemed appropriate to discuss briefly the converse activity—namely, creating new processes on remote machines. As you might expect by now, the procedure for doing this is not at all complex, but it is conceptually different from anything you have encountered so far in this book.

All the methods we have applied thus far in the book work on *instances* of a given class. For example, the `Terminate()` method of `Win32_Process` destroys the instance upon which it is called. To create a new process, however, you have to use a *static* method—one that is called on the class itself. The reason is obvious: Before a process is created, there *is* no `Win32_Process` object that represents it! The method in question is `Create()`, and in order to call it, we need a reference to an object representing the `Win32_Process` class itself.

Retrieving such a reference is simple: It merely involves a call to `GetObject()` or the `Get()` method of a `SWbemServices` object, specifying a class object path rather than an instance object path (see Chapter 1, "Introduction to WMI"). A class object path looks exactly the same as an instance object path, except that it does not include the `Key=value` part that uniquely identifies an instance of a class. An object representing the `Win32_Process` class, then, can be retrieved with the following code fragment:

```
Set refProcessClass = GetObject("winMgmts:Win32_Process")
```

Once retrieved, `Create()`can be called just like any other method. It takes four parameters: the executable name of the program to launch, the startup directory, a reference to a `STARTUPINFO` structure, and a numeric variable whose value is unimportant.

The meaning of the first two parameters is self-explanatory. The first is simply the name of the program (including the fully-qualified path), and the second is the fully-qualified path of a directory that should be used as the program's working directory. This second parameter can safely be set to `null`, which means "no specified value." In this case, the new process will have the same working directory as the caller (our script).

Currently, the third parameter of the `Create()` method is not described by the Microsoft MSDN documentation. In fact, its existence is not mentioned at all! In the absence of any indication to the contrary, we assume that, in common with the Win32 API `CreateProcess()` function, it is used to specify the size and shape of the main window of the new process. It can safely be set to `null`, which is what we advise until the documentation is fixed.

The final parameter deserves further explanation. It is rather different from anything we have met so far, because it is an "out" parameter. Rather than being used to provide information to the *method,* it is used *by* the method to provide information to the *caller*. Specifically, if the method executes successfully and starts a new process, this variable contains the process ID (handle) of the newly created process. This information is invaluable, because it allows us to retrieve a reference to a `Win32_Process` object representing the newly created process. Why doesn't `Create()` simply *return* the process ID? Because, in common with many other WMI methods that we have already encountered, it uses the return value to specify an error code. It returns 0 for success and any other number for failure.

The following script illustrates the creation of a new process and the subsequent retrieval of the `Win32_Process` object that represents it. For the purposes of conciseness, it does not loop through a list of machines, creating series of processes based on complex criteria; instead, it merely launches a copy of Internet Explorer on the local machine. We hope it is now clear how this script could be combined with the techniques presented earlier to create processes on remote machines.

```
'createproc.vbs - launch IExplore.exe
Option Explicit
On Error Resume Next
Dim refProcClass
Dim numProcID
Dim refIEProcess

Set refProcClass = GetObject("winMgmts:Win32_Process")
If Err <> 0 Then
    WScript.echo "Could not connect to WMI"
    WScript.quit
```

```
End If
If refProcClass.Create( _
 "C:\Program Files\Internet Explorer\iexplore.exe", _
 null,null,numProcID) = 0 Then
    set refIEProcess = GetObject("winMgmts:Win32_Process.Handle='" _
                        & numProcID & "'")
Else
    WScript.Echo "Could not launch IE"
End If
Set refProcClass = Nothing

'now we can test that refIEProcess is a valid reference and use it
set refIEProcess = Nothing
```

For the record, we should point out that creating instances of Internet Explorer on a local machine is not a suitable task for WMI; this sort of task is better done through Windows Explorer. Creating instances of Internet Explorer on a remote machine is probably even more stupid in most situations, and certainly rather confusing for a user sitting at the remote machine: they will suddenly find an Internet Explorer window appearing on the desktop for no apparent reason! In fact, such a situation has far more serious ramifications than mere confusion at a user's desktop; it can also pose a rather nasty security risk. Thanks to DCOM impersonation (see Chapter 5 - "WMI Security") a remote application will run with the identity and permissions of the person who launched it (for example, you); this means that the Internet Explorer window that randomly pops up on the remote user's screen allows him to open files and run code with your credentials. If you do not think that this sounds particularly serious, consider the implications if instead of Internet Explorer you launch a command-shell on a remote machine!

Note: GUI-Based Remote Processes Persist Across Logins

If you launch a GUI-based application remotely, it will remain on the remote user's desktop until explicitly killed. Unlike programs that are launched locally, it will persist even after the user has logged out; in other words, it will still be there next time the user logs in and, more alarmingly, will appear on the desktop of any other user who logs on to the remote machine. Microsoft are aware of this problem; it is due to be fixed in Service Pack 3. ◆

Despite the dangers of running GUI-based applications on remotely, there are plenty of situations in which the ability to launch processes remotely is invaluable. For example, you might want to launch a network analyzer program on a remote machine, or start up a server application such as Apache; if the application runs in the background and is not GUI-based, it does not pose the security risk outlined above. There are even times when launching a GUI-based application remotely can be useful; you may actually *want* to allow a user to run a specific application with your credentials. We cannot say for sure under what circumstances you will need to launch remote processes on your particular network, but we can say with utter certainty that the ability to do so is an extremely valuable tool in a system administrator's armory.

Win32_Process Associators

`Win32_Process` objects are involved in associations with two other classes of object—`CIM_DataFile` and `Win32_ComputerSystem`. The associators that define these relationships are `CIM_ProcessExecutable` and `Win32_SystemProcesses`, respectively.

`Win32_SystemProcesses` is a subclass of `CIM_SystemComponent` and ultimately of `CIM_Component`. As the name implies, it associates a process (`PartComponent`) with the machine upon which it is running (`GroupComponent`). If you already have a reference to a `Win32_Process` object, the `Win32_SystemProcesses` associator is unlikely to be very useful, because it tells you nothing about a process that you do not already know or could easily find out through other means! It could, however, be used as a mechanism for finding a list of all processes running on a given computer. Whether a query such as

```
ASSOCIATORS OF {Win32_ComputerSystem} WHERE
        AssocClass=Win32_SystemProcesses
```

is actually better or more convenient than

```
SELECT * FROM Win32_Process
```

is a moot point, but as we have said many times, with WMI there is always more than one way!

`CIM_ProcessExecutable` connects a process with `CIM_DataFile` objects representing the program itself and any libraries with which it links. `CIM_ProcessExecutable` is a subclass of `CIM_Dependency`. It attaches a `Win32_Process` (referenced in a `Dependent` property) to a `CIM_DataFile` (referenced in an `Antecedent` property). We will end this chapter with a small script that illustrates its use. This script takes two command-line options—a machine name and the name of a process. It prints a list of all executable files upon which the process depends.

```
'whatuses.vbs - list the program files and libraries
'referenced by a given process on a given machine
Option Explicit
On Error Resume Next
Dim refWMI
Dim colProcesses
Dim refProcess
Dim colFiles
Dim refFile
```

```
If WScript.Arguments.Count <> 2 Then
    WScript.Echo "Usage: whatuses.vbs <machine> <process name>"
    WScript.Quit
End If

set refWMI = GetObject("winMgmts:\\" & WScript.Arguments(0))
If Err <> 0 Then
    WScript.Echo "Could not connect to WMI on " & WScript.Arguments(0)
    WScript.Quit
End If

set colProcesses = refWMI.ExecQuery( _
                "SELECT * FROM Win32_Process WHERE Name='" & _
                                  wscript.arguments(1) & "'")

For Each refProcess in colProcesses
    WScript.Echo refProcess.Name & "(" & refProcess.Handle & ") depends on:"
    set colFiles = refWMI.ExecQuery(_
                  "ASSOCIATORS OF {Win32_Process='" & _
                  refProcess.handle & "'} WHERE " & _
                  "AssocClass=CIM_ProcessExecutable ")
    For Each refFile in colFiles
        WScript.Echo refFile.Name
    Next
Next

set colFiles = Nothing
set colProcesses = Nothing
set refWMI = Nothing
```

Open a copy of Internet Explorer on your machine, and run the script with your machine name and `iexplore.exe` as command-line arguments. You might be surprised at just how many shared libraries it takes to get IE off the ground!

Summary

This chapter has focused on issues associated with using WMI on remote machines. We started by demonstrating how to connect to the WMI service of a remote machine and retrieve and manipulate references to remote WMI objects. This was followed by a discussion of error handling with WMI and VBScript. We showed a variety of techniques and tricks that can be used to ensure that scripts run smoothly even when connecting to WMI over a network. In the final section, we considered how to write scripts that can perform actions on a fleet of machines specified by name or IP address. These issues were all illustrated with an examination of `Win32_Process`, a WMI object that represents the programs running on a Windows 2000 box.

5

WMI Security

During the course of Chapter 3, "Examining the Filesystem with WMI", you copied, moved, and deleted files from an NTFS filesystem; in Chapter 4, "Remote Administration", you rebooted computers remotely and played havoc with remotely running processes. It is perhaps disturbing to contemplate that you have done all of this without having to cross a single security hurdle! In practice, of course, this situation is not as frightening as it sounds. We have not had any security problems because we have been running all scripts with Administrator privileges. You will be relieved to hear that WMI does, in fact, have a security model that is theoretically very secure and flexible.

WMI implements security on three levels. At the highest level, the WMI service itself (winmgmts.exe) can authorize or decline an attempted WMI operation based on the credentials of the serviced user. DCOM, the architecture underlying WMI, can accept or reject connections to WMI. It supplies security credentials to the WMI service on behalf of a user it accepts. At the very lowest level, WMI providers are all beholden to Windows 2000 native security and NTFS permissions. Any process is restricted in its operation by the security limitations placed on it by the operating system; winmgmts.exe is no exception.

Security at the WMI Level

At the WMI level, security is based on standard NT security descriptors, which are essentially Access Control Lists (ACLs) combined with information about the scope of their application. An ACL contains a series of Access Control Entries (ACEs), each of which associates a user or group with a set of rights. In an NTFS filesystem, ACEs give users or groups rights to read, write, execute, or otherwise tamper with a file. ACEs that form part of the WMI security descriptors give users or groups various rights to manipulate WMI objects within a namespace.

Note: Namespace Reminder

A namespace in WMI is a logical grouping of objects and classes. A `SWbemServices` *object is always associated with a specific namespace, meaning that it can see all classes and objects within that namespace but nothing beyond it. All the standard WMI classes defined as part of the CIM schema live in a namespace called \root\CIMv2; this is usually the default namespace on a system. Other common namespaces include \root\directory (the LDAP namespace), \root\WMI (the namespace where internal WMI objects live), and \root\SECURITY (where objects controlling WMI security live). This book deals almost exclusively with objects that live in \root\CIMv2.* ◆

WMI-level security for a machine is configured using a tool that you have not yet met—the WMI Control MMC component. This can be found in the computer management control panel under the Services and Applications tree. Go into the Control Panel folder, open the Administrative Tools subfolder, and open the Computer Management panel. Then look in the Services and Applications part of the tree and select WMI Control. Alternatively, you can directly invoke the component by running wmimgmt.msc from either a command prompt or Explorer's Run menu. All the configurable elements are found in the property sheet, which you can access by right-clicking the WMI Control icon and choosing Properties from the context menu. The sheet has five property pages, which present options to configure WMI's logging capability and the default namespace, to back up and restore the Repository, and to configure security. We are only interested in the Security tab, shown in Figure 5.1.

Most of the working area of this tab is filled with a listing of the WMI namespaces on a machine. Notice that these are organized hierarchically under a single Root namespace. To configure security for one of the namespaces, select its icon and click the Security button. To configure security for the standard WMI namespace that is the subject of the majority of this book, select CIMV2.

The security dialog that pops up should look remarkably familiar, because it is exactly the same interface as that used to configure NTFS file security, and it works in exactly the same way. In the top half is a list of the users or groups with permissions on the namespace; in the bottom half is a list of the permissions that they have been assigned (or explicitly denied). Just like its NTFS counterpart, it has an Advanced button, providing access to a dialog with finer-grained control (see Figure 5.2). Specifically, this dialog allows the administrator to specify whether permissions assigned to a namespace are hierarchically disseminated. In other words, it specifies whether permissions apply to only one level of a namespace or are inherited by all of its subnamespaces. By default, permissions always apply both to a namespace and are inherited by all of its subnamespaces.

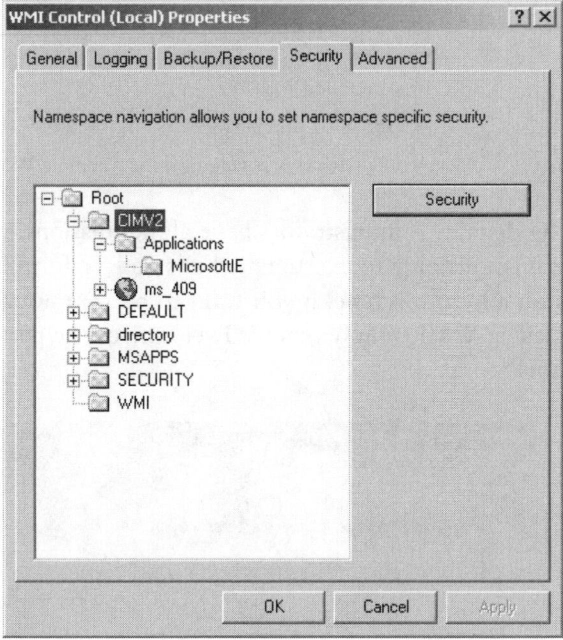

Figure 5.1 *The Security tab of the WMI Control (Local) Properties dialog.*

The main difference between an NTFS permissions dialog and this one controlling access to WMI namespaces is that this one offers a completely different choice of permissions to apply. These permissions, whose meaning is not entirely self-evident from their names, are listed and described in Table 5.1.

Table 5.1 *WMI Namespace Permissions*

Permission	Meaning
Execute Methods	A user with this permission can execute methods of WMI objects.
Full Write	A user with this permission can read, write, or delete objects or even class definitions from the CIM Repository. (You have not yet read about write or delete operations, but you will do so in later chapters.)
Partial Write	This permission allows a user to write to static objects in the Repository (see Chapter 8, "Proactive Troubleshooting with WMI Events" and Chapter 11, "WIM Internals".
Provider Write	This permission allows a user to write to dynamic objects managed by providers (see Chapter 11).

continues ▶

Table 5.1 continued

Enable Account	This, the most basic permission, allows a user to retrieve objects from WMI and read their properties.
Remote Enable	This is not a permission as such, but more like a flag. If it is set, a user is allowed to access WMI from a remote machine. When connected remotely, he or she will have permissions as if connecting locally.
Read Security	A user with this permission may read WMI security settings.
Edit Security	A user with this permission may change WMI security settings.

Note that by default, Administrators have all permissions, whereas everyone else has permissions only to execute methods and perform limited write operations on a local machine. If you want to prevent nonadministrative users from using WMI, simply remove Everyone or the permissions associated with this group.

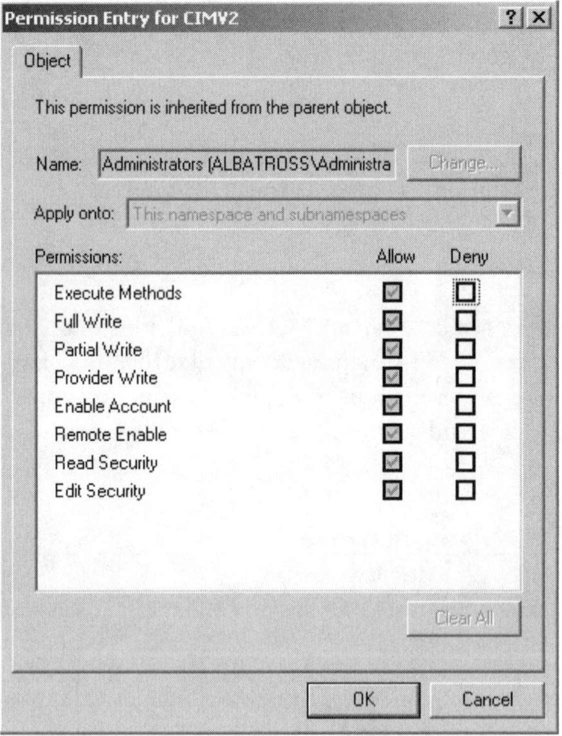

Figure 5.2 *Namespace permissions.*

Warning: Changing WMI Namespace Security

The WMI control panel makes it very easy to tamper with namespace security settings. It should be noted, however, that WMI security is reasonably complex, so it is extremely easy to get things wrong! The default security configuration on Windows 2000 machines (workstations and servers) is surprisingly sane, so unless and until you have very good reason to change it, we advise leaving these defaults as they are—particularly for namespaces outside of \root\CIMv2. ◆

Note that this security configuration—and, in fact, all of the options within the WMI Control console—refers to the WMI *service* on a machine. In other words, if you are using WMI to connect to a namespace on a remote machine, you will need the relevant permissions on that machine regardless of how your local workstation is configured.

DCOM Security

As we have already intimated, security at the WMI level is only part of the story. It is all very well for WMI to decide which operations should be allowed for different groups of users, but this works in practice only if WMI has a way of knowing who is trying to use it! This problem is handled by the DCOM security model, which not only has mechanisms for authenticating attempted connections (locally or remotely) but also can provide a DCOM application (in this case, winmgmt.exe) with the caller's credentials. It can even allow this application to impersonate the caller, giving the application permissions it would not otherwise have. If this sounds rather confusing, the next few paragraphs should make it more clear.

Consider once more a very familiar line of VBScript:

```
Set refWMI = GetObject("winMgmts:\\STYX")
```

This code is, of course, a request to connect to the WMI service on a machine called STYX. To be more pedantic, it is a request to connect to the default namespace (usually \root\cimv2) of the WMI service on a machine called STYX. Now we will be *really* pedantic: This line of code is, in reality, a request to DCOM to attempt to connect to the winMgmts DCOM application on a machine called STYX, using a default impersonation level, a default authentication level, and no special privileges. It is the job of winMgmts to read the remainder of the moniker string and return the requested object. Because the remainder of the moniker string is in this case blank, winMgmts interprets the call as a request for a `SWbemServices` object connected to the default namespace. Wow!

DCOM Impersonation Level

The most interesting concept in all of this is the impersonation level, which determines the effective permissions with which the WMI service itself runs when servicing a call. The best way to understand its operation is to consider the relationship between users, processes, and permissions. Under Windows 2000, just as with Windows NT 4.0, every running process has an owner. Processes do not just run; they run under an account. That account might have certain rights on a system and might appear in various Access Control Lists; these rights are automatically inherited by processes that the account runs. For example, I saved the Word document containing the text of this chapter on a network drive at work, and I set the NTFS permissions so that only I can read or write to the document. If someone else logs on to the network and tries to read it, he will be stopped by an `Access Denied` error. This is not so much because the person attempting to read the file does not have the relevant permissions, but rather because the application that is asking the filesystem to open the file does not have the relevant permissions. The reason why the application does not have permissions is, of course, because it is running as a person who does not have permissions (but this is beside the point).

When considering WMI—or any other DCOM application, for that matter—the situation is more complex. When I use VBScript to connect to WMI either locally or on a remote machine, my script is just like any other application: It runs as me, with my permissions. In order to do anything useful, however, my script requires the services of winMgmt.exe, the WMI service. This service is *not* running as me at all; it is running as System. When I invoke a method on a WMI object, that method is really invoked by winmgmt.exe, which means that it can do what the System account can do, *not* what I can do. This situation can cause two related problems. First, it can be annoyingly inhibitive, preventing me from using WMI to perform tasks that I normally have permissions to perform. Second, it can theoretically be a security risk, allowing users who are normally highly restricted in their activities to use WMI to perform any task that System has permission to execute. If you are wondering how this can be true, considering that we merrily manipulated the filesystem throughout Chapter 3, please be patient; all will soon be revealed.

The solution to this quagmire is impersonation. When an application or script makes a call through DCOM, it specifies which of four impersonation levels should be used for the call. Possibilities are anonymous, identify, impersonate, and delegate. The impersonation level determines what the *callee* (the COM object being called) is allowed to know about the *caller* (the program that is calling the object) and how the callee is seen by the operating system when it services the calls.

The following list describes the four impersonation levels and their effects on DCOM communication:

- If a caller chooses to remain *anonymous,* DCOM tells the callee nothing about the caller's identity. The callee is free to honor or reject the call, but it has no way of determining whether it should do so! WMI refuses to honor anonymous requests for service, because it needs to know the caller's identity in order to perform the security checks outlined earlier in this chapter.
- A caller who is prepared to allow the callee to know his or her identity uses the *identify* impersonation level. As you can probably guess, a DCOM application such as winMgmt.exe can ask DCOM to reveal the identity of a caller who uses this level. WMI can use this information to decide, using its own security mechanism, whether the call should be honored. Nonetheless, if a call to WMI is made using this impersonation level, winMgmt.exe continues to run with the permission of System (or as whatever user the administrator has configured for the service).
- Someone who wants to make effective use of WMI is likely to use the *impersonate* impersonation level. This level goes one stage above identify and instructs DCOM to allow the callee to run *with the caller's credentials*. In other words, whenever WMI performs an action on behalf of a caller who has requested an impersonation level of impersonate, that action is carried out *as the caller*. For the duration of the action, winMgmt.exe has the permissions associated with the caller in every respect. As far as the operating system is concerned, it *is* the caller (or at least a process running as the caller) performing the action. On Windows 2000, impersonate is the default impersonation level for WMI. It is for this reason that our earlier manipulation of the filesystem did not fail.
- The fourth impersonation level, *delegate,* is more powerful still. It allows the callee not only to perform actions with the caller's credentials, but also to connect to other DCOM services on remote machines and allow *them* to perform actions with the caller's credentials. This level can have serious security implications for the caller, because a rogue DCOM application could run amok, causing damage across a network and attributing it all to the caller! The worst-case scenario for a rogue application called with impersonate (which can also pose a security risk) is that it performs evil actions on a single machine.

The DCOM impersonation level can be set as part of the moniker string in a call to `GetObject()` using the following syntax:

```
WinMgmts:{impersonationLevel=<level>}!<namespace>:<objectpath>
```

`<level>` is `anonymous`, `identify`, `impersonate`, or `delegate`. For example, here is a fully-specified moniker string for retrieving the `CIM_DataFile` object associated with c:\boot.ini on a machine called STYX from the \root\CIMv2 namespace using `impersonate` as an impersonation level:

```
WinMgmts:{impersonationLevel=Impersonate}!\\STYX\root\cimv2:
CIM_DataFile.Name='c:\boot.ini'
```

The fully-specified moniker string to retrieve a `SWbemServices` object connected to the root\CIMv2 namespace on STYX is illustrated in the following VBScript fragment:

```
Set refWMI = GetObject( _
        "winMgmts:{impersonationLevel=Impersonate}!\\STYX\root\cimv2")
```

Thanks to the default namespace being \root\CIMv2 and the default impersonation level being impersonate, we have been able to get away so far with the rather shorter `winMgmts:\\STYX`!

DCOM Authentication Level

In addition to the impersonation level, DCOM also allows specification of an authentication level, which determines the number of times authentication checks are carried out when servicing requests. This term is slightly misleading, because the authentication level does not determine the "level" of authentication as such, but rather the frequency with which authentication checks are made. The seven levels are described in Table 5.2.

Table 5.2 *DCOM Authentication Levels*

Level	Meaning
Default	DCOM uses the default authentication level set for Windows 2000.
None	No authentication. The caller's credentials are not checked for authenticity.
Connect	When the caller first makes a DCOM request, authentication checks are carried out. As soon as a caller is connected, however (has a reference to a `SWbemServices` object), no further checks are carried out.
Call	Every time a call is made, the caller's authenticity is checked.
Pkt	Authentication checks are made against every packet sent.

Level	Meaning
PktIntegrity	Not only are authentication checks made against every packet sent, but also checksums are used to ensure that packets have not been modified en route between client and server.
PktPrivacy	All packets are authenticated, checksummed, and encrypted in transit.

This plethora of options and the degree of security offered by PktIntegrity and PktPrivacy are invaluable for a system that uses DCOM to ship highly sensitive data around a network, but they are somewhat extreme for most uses of WMI. Given the extra load that authentication, check summing, and encryption place on the system, we do not recommend using them for WMI unless you have a very good reason to do so. The default authentication level, which is usually Connect, is entirely adequate for almost all purposes. If you are considering using authentication levels other than the default, bear in mind that unlike impersonation level, the authentication level used for a connection is negotiated by both the client and the server. This is because a security breach would affect both. If client and server specify different authentication levels for a connection, the stricter of the two possibilities is used.

Note: DCOM and Network Protocols

The Connect and Call authentication levels make sense only if DCOM is using a connection-based (point-to-point) network protocol to communicate with remote hosts. By default, Windows 2000 attempts to connect using TCP/IP, which is indeed a connection-based protocol. It is possible, however, to change this default. If a connectionless protocol such as UDP/IP is selected, the default authentication level becomes Pkt.

The default protocol for DCOM connections can be changed in the Component Services control panel. Open the Control Panel folder, choose Administrative Tools, and then choose Component Services. Find the My Computer icon (under Component Services, Computers in tree view) and right-click Properties. The DCOM property sheet is displayed. Choose the Default Protocols property page. This contains a list of all the network protocols that DCOM will attempt to use for connections, in decreasing order of priority. Note that by default, all *of these protocols are connection-based. An Add button allows you to add from a list of available protocols, including connectionless ones such as UDP. In addition, the usual Move Up, Move Down, and Delete buttons let you move individual protocols within the priority hierarchy and even remove them entirely.*

We strongly recommend that you do not tamper with the default list of protocols. In particular, do not allow the use of connectionless protocols unless you really understand what you are doing and have a very good reason for doing so. ◆

Authentication level is specified in the moniker string, just after impersonation level; the two are comma-delimited. A moniker string specifying both takes the following form:

```
WinMgmts:{impersonationLevel=<level>,AuthenticationLevel=<level>}!
<namespace>:<objectpath>
```

Here is a fully-specified moniker string for retrieving the `CIM_DataFile` object associated with c:\boot.ini on a machine called STYX, from the \root\CIMv2 namespace using `impersonate` as an impersonation level and `connect` as an authentication level:

```
WinMgmts:{impersonationLevel=impersonate,authenticationLevel=connect}!
                    \\STYX\root\cimv2:CIM_DataFile.Name='c:\boot.ini'
```

Note: Shorter Notation for Specifying DCOM Security in Moniker Strings

You can make fully-specified moniker strings slightly more concise by employing a useful shorthand: The `impersonationLevel=` *and* `authenticationLevel=` *strings can actually be omitted. For example, the following is a perfectly valid, fully specified moniker string:*

```
WinMgmts:{impersonate,connect}!\\STYX\root\cimv2
```
◆

DCOM Privileges

The final element of WMI security provided by DCOM is the privilege set. Windows 2000 has certain operations that require a caller to have specific privileges, and those privileges must be explicitly enabled prior to the call. For example, clearing the Security Event Log can only be done by a user with a special Security privilege. Windows 2000, just like Windows NT 4.0, requires not only that a user attempting to clear this log hold the requisite privilege, but also that the application enable the privilege by making an API call that tells Windows "I would now like to use my Security privilege." Just like impersonation level and authentication level, privileges can be specified as part of a moniker string, using the following syntax:

```
WinMgmts:{impersonationLevel=<level>,AuthenticationLevel=<level>,
                  (<priv1>,<priv2>,...)}!<namespace>:<objectpath>
```

In this example, the braces contain a comma-delimited set of privileges. For example, the following moniker string gives you security privileges when you're connected to the root\CIMv2 namespace on STYX:

```
WinMgmts:{impersonate,connect,(Security)}!\\STYX\root\cimv2
```

In the rare case when you want to explicitly revoke a privilege, you can do so by preceding the privilege name with an `!`. (For example, `!Security` would revoke a previously-held security privilege.) Privileges are not a concept specific to WMI or to DCOM, but are a part of the operation of Windows 2000. Therefore, we provide no complete list of them here. As this book progresses, however, we will set and revoke permissions whenever necessary.

Note: Shutdown Privileges Are Not Always Needed

One task that requires a special privilege to be invoked is shutting down or rebooting a workstation. This privilege is, unsurprisingly, called `Shutdown`. *Yet the script earlier in this chapter successfully managed to reboot a remote machine without explicitly invoking this privilege. The reason? The Win32 provider code on the server (which calls the real Win32 API* `shutdown` *command) enables the privilege before it attempts the operation. If, however, we had attempted to use the script to reboot our* own *local workstation, the script would have failed, complaining of insufficient privileges. On a local workstation, both of the applications that are implicated in initiating shutdown (the script and the provider) must explicitly enable the privilege.* ◆

Impersonation level, authentication level, and privileges can all be specified in any moniker string. As soon as your script has a reference to a `SWbemServices` object with a specific impersonation level, authentication level, and privilege set, all collections, objects, and classes retrieved via that `SWbemServices` will possess exactly the same set. In other words, as soon as security has been defined for a session, the settings apply for all further operations. In virtually every situation, this behavior is exactly what you want. If for some reason you do want to change the impersonation level, authentication level, or privilege set that applies to a `SWbemServices` object after it has been retrieved, or you want to adjust the security for just a single object or a single operation, you can do so by manipulating the properties of an associated `SWbemSecurity` object. This procedure is discussed in Chapter 11.

Underlying Operating System Security

WMI's namespace-based security model, coupled with facilities provided by the DCOM layer upon which it is built, comprises a reasonably flexible and comprehensive way to control access to a Windows 2000 computer as seen by WMI. Only one more aspect of security needs to be considered—namely, the way in which these various security layers interact with authentication and restriction mechanisms present in the underlying operating system. One obvious interaction is that concepts such as "users," "groups," and "credentials" are not unique to WMI and DCOM! Using the WMI control snap-in involves adding Windows 2000 users to the Access Control Lists for various WMI namespaces. At this level, WMI is clearly using authentication mechanisms provided by the operating system to implement its security.

Beyond this, however, there is no special relationship between WMI and the operating system. Just like any other program, winMgmts.exe, the application that services WMI requests, is subject to any restrictions that the operating system happens to impose. Whenever a user connects using the `identify` impersonation level (the lowest level allowed by WMI itself) it cannot do anything that the System account cannot do. For example, when WMI is servicing a client using this level, it cannot perform any manipulation of the filesystem except that allowed by any process running as System (or whatever the administrator has configured winmgmts.exe to run as). In the more usual case, when a user connects to WMI using the `impersonate` impersonation level, winmgmts.exe cannot carry out any activity on behalf of the user that the user himself could not carry out through other means. Crucially, then, the management power of WMI and its potential availability to any user does not in itself present a security risk because *WMI cannot be used to carry out an action that the operating system would not permit through other means.*

Security Representation Within WMI

A discussion of WMI security would hardly be complete without at least a mention of how security is represented within WMI itself. One of the most striking things about security representation within WMI is that it is quite unlike everything else that we have encountered so far! To be sure, there are WMI objects to represent various facets of Windows 2000 security, such as SIDs (Security IDs), Access Control Lists, and trustees, but these objects are often impossible to retrieve directly from the Repository. They can be beyond the reach of any amount of creative WQL wizardry. The only way to retrieve a security object from WMI is often through methods of the objects whose security they represent. The remainder of this chapter is devoted to an investigation of security within WMI. Specifically, we will look once more at processes, files, and directories—this time from the perspective of security.

Process Security and SIDs

As we noted in the preceding section, the restrictions imposed on a process by the operating system are determined by the credentials of the user running the process (the process's owner). An owner's identity can be retrieved using two methods of `Win32_Process` that you have not yet met—`GetOwner()` and `GetOwnerSID()`. `GetOwner()` does not return an owner object, or even a string representation of a user. Instead, it returns an error value (0 for success or nonzero for failure). Details of a process's owner and domain are stored in two string variables that must be provided as "out" parameters to the function. This is illustrated by the following VBScript fragment, which prints either the name of a process's owner or an error message:

```
If refProcess.GetOwner(strOwner,strDomain) = 0 Then
    WScript.Echo "This process is owned by " & strOwner
Else
    WScript.Echo "Oh dear; I could not find the owner of this process"
End If
```

Similarly, `GetOwnerSID()` returns a success value and stores a string representation of a SID in an "out" parameter:

```
refProcess.GetOwnerSID(strSID)
WScript.Echo "Owner SID is " & strSID
```

The use of both of these functions is illustrated in the following script. This script produces a list of all processes running on the local computer in conjunction with the name of the process's owner. Having successfully connected to the WMI service on the machine in question, the script retrieves a collection of `Win32_Process` objects. For each object, it attempts to find the owner, domain, and owner SID. If calls to both `GetOwner()` and `GetOwnerSID()` are successful, the script outputs a line (using `WScript.Echo`) of the following format:

```
<processname> is owned by \\<domain>\<user> (SID)
```

If either of the two calls fails, an error is printed.

```
'listprocowner.vbs - list the names and owners of all processes running
'on the local machine
Option Explicit
On Error Resume Next
Dim refWMI
Dim colProcesses
Dim refItem
Dim strUser
Dim strDomain
Dim strSID

'try to connect to STYX
set refWMI = GetObject("winMgmts:")
If Err <> 0 Then
    WScript.Echo "I could not connect to WMI"
    WScript.Quit
End If
```

```
'Get a list of all processes and iterate through each
'printing name and SID. Use return values from GetOwner()
'and GetOwnerSID() as error handling device
' -main code section-
Set colProcesses = refWMI.ExecQuery("SELECT * FROM Win32_Process")
For Each refItem In colProcesses
    If refItem.GetOwner(strUser,strDomain) = 0 Then
        If refItem.GetOwnerSid(strSID) = 0 Then
            WScript.Echo refItem.Name & " is owned by \\" & strDomain & _
                         "\" & strUser & " (" & strSID & ")"
        End If
    Else
        WScript.Echo "Could not retrieve user info for " & refItem.Name
    End If
Next
'-end of main code section-

Set colProcesses = Nothing
Set refWMI = Nothing
```

Notice that a WMI object is not returned by either of these functions; all you get is a string representation of user, domain, and SID. One slightly curious aspect of this is that there is such a thing as a `Win32_SID` class, but `GetOwnerSID()` chooses not to return an instance of it!

SIDs are utterly fundamental to Windows 2000 security, because they are effectively passports—or ID cards—for their bearers. It is probably wise, therefore, for you to know what they look like from WMI's perspective! `Win32_SID` objects are extremely simple, possessing only five properties: `AccountName`, `BinaryRepresentation`, `ReferencedDomainName`, `SID`, and `SidLength`. The primary key is `SID`, a string representation of the SID itself. `BinaryRepresentation` stores an array representing the SID in binary format. `ReferencedDomainName` is the name of the domain in which the account lives. The meaning of the other properties should be self-explanatory.

To illustrate a simple use of `Win32_SID` objects, we can write a replacement for the main loop of the process-owner-finding code just shown. In that example, we used the `GetOwner()` method of `Win32_Process` to retrieve the account name associated with a running process. In contrast, here we can use `GetOwnerSID()` to retrieve a string representation of the SID and then use that to retrieve a `Win32_SID` object corresponding to the account. The account name can then be read from the `Win32_SID` object. The code fragment needed to achieve all this appears next. It slips into the full code listing just shown by replacing everything between the comments `-main code section-` and `-end of main code section-`.

```
'first, declare refSID, as this was not used in the previous example
Dim refSID
'get a list of all processes. For each one, find the SID, use it to
```

```
'retrieve a Win32_SID object, and output the details of that object
Set colProcesses = refWMI.ExecQuery("SELECT * FROM Win32_Process")
For Each refItem In colProcesses
    If refItem.GetOwnerSID(strSID) = 0 Then
        set refSID = refWMI.Get("Win32_SID.SID='" & strSID & "'")
        If Err = 0 Then
            WScript.Echo refItem.Name & " is owned by " & _
                         "\\" & refSid.ReferencedDomainName & _
                          "\" & refSid.AccountName & " (" & _
                           refSid.SID & ")"
        Else
            WScript.Echo "could not find a Win32_SID"
        End If
    Else
        WScript.Echo "Could not retrieve user info for " & _
                                  refItem.Name
    End If
Next
Set refSID = Nothing
```

This fragment is slightly more verbose than its equivalent in our original script and would probably take slightly longer to execute, but at least it gets authoritative account information from bona fide `Win32_SID` objects!

You should expect `Win32_SID` objects to be ubiquitous, appearing all over the Repository. To satiate your curiosity, it might be interesting to write a short script that retrieves every instance of a `Win32_SID` and then examines its associations. Such a script might start something like this:

```
Option Explicit
Dim refWMI
Dim colSIDs

Set refWMI = GetObject("winMgmts:\\STYX")
Set colSIDs = refWMI.ExecQuery("SELECT * FROM Win32_SID")
```

Unfortunately, this script would not work! The `Win32_SID` class cannot be enumerated, because it is not possible to retrieve a collection of SID objects via WMI. An attempt to do so will lead to error 0x80041024, `provider not capable`, meaning that the security provider does not support enumeration of the `Win32_SID` class.

Filesystem Security

At first glance, filesystem security as seen from a WMI perspective can seem extremely daunting. Various aspects of security and ownership information about files and directories are represented by a vast menagerie of classes and objects, all connected by a web of associators. WMI itself should not be blamed for this amazing jungle, though. In fact, the inventors of the WMI security classes have done an incredible job of designing a transparent and comprehensible view of Windows 2000 security. The problem is that Windows 2000 security, just like that of Windows NT 4.0, is extremely complicated. It is no accident that several books have been dedicated solely to the subject of programming NT security! Rather than attempting a comprehensive flyby of every facet of the security provider's offerings (something that would take a great many pages and would not be that interesting to most people reading this book), we will concentrate here on a core subset of objects needed in order to manipulate filesystem security. Everything discussed in these sections is applicable to only NTFS filesystems.

The security of a file or directory (or any `CIM_LogicalFile`, in fact) is represented by a `Win32_LogicalFileSecuritySetting` whose primary key, the `Path` property, contains the fully qualified path of the file or directory to which the `Win32_LogicalFileSecuritySetting` belongs. If you think this class name is absurdly long, you have seen nothing yet: `Win32_LogicalFileSecuritySetting` objects are related to `CIM_LogicalFile` objects through `Win32_SecuritySettingOfLogicalFile` associators. This associator class derives from `Win32_SecuritySettingOfObject`, which, in turn, derives from the more concisely named `CIM_ElementSetting`. Its two properties, which are inherited from `CIM_ElementSetting`, are `Element` (which points to a `CIM_LogicalFile`) and `Setting` (which points to a `Win32_LogicalFileSecuritySetting`). To clarify all of this, we present two code fragments. The first finds the `Win32_LogicalFileSecuritySetting` associated with c:\boot.ini directly, using the `Path` property. The second accomplishes the same task by retrieving a collection of such objects via an associator query.

```
'fragment one
set refSecurity = refWMI.Get("Win32_LogicalFileSecuritySetting='c:\boot.ini'")

'fragment two
set colSecurities = refWMI.ExecQuery( _
                    "ASSOCIATORS OF {CIM_DataFile='c:\boot.ini'} WHERE " & _
                    "AssocClass=Win32_SecuritySettingOfLogicalFile " & _
                    "ResultRole=Setting")
For Each refSecurity In colSecurities
    '<use the security object>
Next
```

Perversely, having retrieved a `Win32_LogicalFileSecuritySetting` object, you cannot find out very much from it directly. In fact, apart from its primary key, it possesses only two properties that tell you anything about security at all! The first is `ControlFlags`, which yields information about the propagation of the security setting (such as whether it is inherited or shared by other objects). This setting performs the same function as the `AccessMask` property of the `Win32_ACE` class, which you will meet shortly. The other is a Boolean property, `OwnerPermissions`, that returns true if the user currently referencing the `Win32_LogicalFileSecuritySetting` in question is the owner of the file whose security it represents.

Perhaps surprisingly, a `Win32_LogicalFileSecuritySetting` class does not possess properties or methods that can tell you directly who owns the `CIM_LogicalFile` to which it relates. Instead, this information can be found indirectly through `Win32_LogicalFileOwner`, an associator that links a `Win32_LogicalFileSecuritySetting` to a `Win32_SID`. As you might have guessed, the two properties of a `Win32_LogicalFileOwner` are `Owner` and `SecuritySetting`. Both of these are inherited from the superclass `Win32_SecuritySettingOwner`. These relationships are illustrated in Figure 5.3.

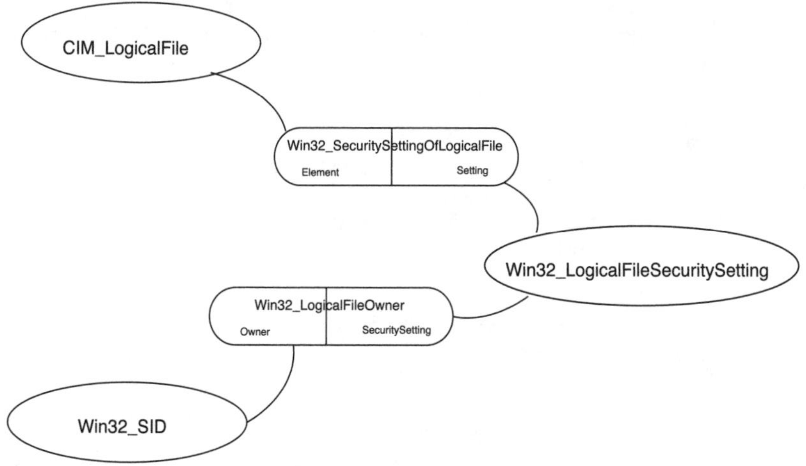

Figure 5.3 *The relationship between* `CIM_LogicalFile`, `Win32_SecuritySettingOfLogicalFile`, `Win32_LogicalFileSecuritySetting`, `Win32_LogicalFileOwner`, *and* `Win32_SID`.

Despite this labyrinthine indirection, you can identify the owner of a file or directory relatively easily using the following procedure:

1. Perform an `ASSOCIATORS OF` query on the relevant `Win32_LogicalFileSecuritySetting` class to retrieve a `Win32_SID` object representing the owner.
2. Read the owner's identity from the `AccountName` property of `Win32_SID`.

The following script demonstrates this procedure. It takes a single command-line argument—the name of a file or directory—and returns the identity of the owner (or an error message):

```
'checkowner.vbs - outputs the owner name of a file passed as a command-line
'parameter, or gives an error if it cannot
Option Explicit
```

```
On Error Resume Next
Dim refWMI
Dim strQuery
Dim colOwner
Dim refItem

'check command-line argument seems sane
If WScript.Arguments.Count <> 1 Then
    WScript.Echo"Usage: checkowner.vbs <path>"
    WScript.Quit
End If

'connect to WMI or quit with error
set refWMI = GetObject("winMgmts:")
If Err <> 0 Then
    WScript.Echo "Oh dear. Could not connect to WMI. Error: " & Err.Description
    WScript.Quit
End If

'get reference
strQuery = "ASSOCIATORS OF {Win32_LogicalFileSecuritySetting=" & _
           "'" & WScript.arguments.item(0) & "'} WHERE " & _
           "AssocClass=Win32_LogicalFileOwner " & _
           "ResultRole=Owner"
set colOwner = refWMI.ExecQuery(strQuery)

'finally, read the owner info from Win32_SID
For Each refItem In colOwner
    If Err = 0 Then
        WScript.Echo WScript.arguments.item(0) & _
          " is owned by " & refItem.AccountName
    Else
        WScript.Echo "Cannot find owner for " & WScript.arguments.item(0)
    End If
Next

Set colOwner = Nothing
set refWMI = Nothing
```

Because `CIM_DataFile` objects and `Win32_Directory` are both subclasses of `CIM_LogicalFile`, we do not have to differentiate between the two here.

Unfortunately, it is not possible to reverse this script to find a list of files owned by a specific user, because the `SecuritySetting` property of `Win32_LogicalFileOwner` cannot be enumerated. If you need convincing of this point, try retrieving a `Win32_SID` object and then using an `ASSOCIATORS OF` query to get a collection of `Win32_LogicalFileSecuritySetting` objects. Assuming that you have a `Win32_SID` referenced in a variable called `refSID`, the query string would look like this:

```
"ASSOCIATORS OF {Win32_SID.SID='" & refSID.SID & "'} " & _
"WHERE AssocClass=Win32_LogicalFileOwner " & _
"ResultRole=SecuritySetting"
```

You will find that this query runs happily and returns an empty collection. Whether this limitation is a security feature or whether its rationale in fact lies in the difficulty of extracting information from the underlying operating system we do not know.

Relationships between files and users in Windows 2000 are not limited simply to ownership. Access Control Lists allow any number of users or groups to be given various levels of access to either. As far as WMI is concerned, nonowner users or groups are related to files and directories via `Win32_LogicalFileAccess` associator objects. More specifically, a `Win32_LogicalFileAccess` associator links a `Win32_LogicalFileSecuritySetting` object (via its `SecuritySetting` key property) with a `Win32_SID` object (via its `Trustee` key property). You could retrieve a collection of `Win32_SID` objects corresponding to all users and groups with rights to c:\boot.ini by using the following query:

```
ASSOCIATORS OF {Win32_LogicalFileSecuritySetting='c:\boot.ini'} WHERE
    AssocClass=Win32_LogicalFileAccess
    ResultRole=Trustee
```

Note: Win32_LogicalFileAccess *Implementation*

`Win32_LogicalFileAccess` *objects are unlike any of the other associators you have met so far, because in addition to their two keys, they have a number of other properties. In other words, as well as forming an association between two other objects, these associators are of interest in their own right. Nominally, these properties can be used to discover details of permissions that apply to a trustee's access to an object. Unfortunately, however, it seems that the security provider—that is, the code responsible for* `Win32_LogicalFileAccess` *objects—does not implement these properties. Attempts to read them return null.* ◆

`Win32_LogicalFileSecuritySetting` objects and their associators provide us with a simple way of finding a list of users and groups who have ownership of or access to a filesystem object (a file or directory). Finding out more detailed security information, such as what specific rights a particular user has on an object (or actually altering security settings) requires reading and manipulating a Windows 2000 security descriptor, represented in WMI by a `Win32_SecurityDescriptor` object.

A `Win32_SecurityDescriptor` is a rather special class of object. It has no key properties and cannot be retrieved directly from the Repository either via a call to `GetObject()` or via any kind of query. A subclass of `Win32_MethodParameterClass`, the only way to access one of these objects is via a call to the `GetSecurityDescriptor()` method of the object representing the entity whose security it describes. In the case of a file or directory,

`GetSecurityDescriptor()` is called not directly on a `CIM_LogicalFile` subclass but on a `Win32_LogicalFileSecuritySetting` object. `GetSecurityDescriptor()` takes a single "out" parameter: a variable to which the `Win32_SecurityDesciptor` object should be assigned. Like many other WMI methods, it returns a success value.

`Win32_SecurityDescriptors` are different from most of the other WMI objects that you have met so far in another respect too: All but one of their properties are containers for one or more embedded objects. Rather than storing numbers, text strings, or associator-style object paths, the properties actually hold other WMI objects, each of which describes some facet of the security descriptor. A `Win32_SecurityDescriptor` possesses five properties in all: `Owner`, `Group`, `DACL`, `SACL`, and `ControlFlags`. Between them, these encapsulate every aspect of Windows 2000 filesystem security. Each is discussed in turn in the following sections.

Owner

As you can guess from the name, the `Owner` property identifies the owner of an object protected by a `Win32_SecurityDescriptor`. The owner is represented by an embedded `Win32_Trustee` object, which, like its container, is a subclass of `Win32_MethodParameterClass`. `Win32_Trustee` has five properties: `Domain`, `Name`, `SID`, `SIDLength`, and `SIDString`. `Domain` and `Name` specify the domain in which the account lives and the name of the account itself. `SID` contains an array of numbers representing the SID itself. `SIDString` specifies the length of this array, and `SIDString` holds the SID in the standard textual format, with sections separated by hyphens.

Retrieving a reference to the `Win32_Trustee` object representing the owner of a file or directory is simply a matter of retrieving the relevant `Win32_SecurityDescriptor` from the `CIM_LogicalFile` object and setting an object variable. As an illustration, the following short script outputs the name of the owner of c:\boot.ini on a system, without reference to any `Win32_LogicalFileOwner` associators. Instead, it finds the information from the `Owner` property of a `Win32_SecurityDescriptor`. (For the sake of brevity, most error-handling code is omitted from this and a few subsequent examples.)

```
'ownerNoLFO.vbs - retrieve the name of c:\boot.ini's owner
'without using Win32_LogicalFileOwner
Option Explicit
Dim refSetting
Dim refSD
Dim refOwner

Set refSetting = GetObject( _
        "winMgmts:Win32_LogicalFileSecuritySetting='c:\boot.ini'")
```

```
If refSetting.GetSecurityDescriptor(refSD) = 0 Then
    'operation was successful
    Set refOwner = refSD.Owner
    WScript.Echo refSetting.Path & " is owned by " & refOwner.Name
    Set refOwner = Nothing
    Set refSD = Nothing
End If
Set refSetting = Nothing
```

This code is significantly more compact than the script we presented earlier, which found out ownership by traversing associators. We could, however, make it more compact still by removing all references to `refOwner`. Properties of embedded objects, such as the `Win32_Trustee` embedded within a `Win32_SecurityDescriptor`, can be invoked directly from the container object using the following syntax:

```
OuterObject.PropertyContainingEmbeddedObject.PropertyOfEmbeddedObject
```

Using this syntax, our script could look like this:

```
'ownerReallyShort.vbs - output owner of c:\boot.ini in a
'REALLY concise way!
Option Explicit
Dim refSetting
Dim refSD

Set refSetting =
GetObject("winMgmts:Win32_LogicalFileSecuritySetting='C:\boot.ini'")
If refSetting.GetSecurityDescriptor(refSD) = 0 Then
    WScript.Echo refSetting.Path & " is owned by " & refSD.Owner.Name
    Set refSD = Nothing
End If
Set refSetting = Nothing
```

From here on, we will tend to use this second, more-convenient syntax in our script examples.

Group

Windows 2000 security descriptors (and therefore `Win32_SecurityDescriptor` objects) are not just restricted to controlling NTFS file permissions. Permissions associated with processes and even with WMI itself are described by security descriptors that can be read and manipulated through WMI. Some of these objects are associated not only with an owner, but also with a group. Group information can be read from the `Group` property of a `Win32_SecurityDescriptor`. Like its `Owner` counterpart, this property contains a `Win32_Trustee`.

Because NTFS filesystem security descriptors do not include group information, the `Group` property of a `Win32_SecurityDescriptor` retrieved from a `Win32_LogicalFileSecuritySetting` is always null (it contains no object).

Hence, a line such as

```
Wscript.Echo refSD.Group.Name
```

will produce an error.

DACL

This property contains a representation of the Discretionary Access Control List (DACL) associated with a security descriptor. DACLs consist of a series of Access Control Entries (ACEs), each of which allows or denies a user or group with a specific set of rights with regard to the protected object. In terms of WMI, the DACL property is an array of `Win32_ACE` objects. A `Win32_ACE` object is yet another subclass of `Win32_MethodParameterClass`, so you will not find any of them directly in the Repository! Each has a number of properties, four of which are of interest to us here: `Trustee`, `AceType`, `AccessMask`, and `AceFlags`.

Win32_ACE.Trustee

As you might have guessed, the `Trustee` property contains an embedded `Win32_Trustee` object that represents the user or group for which the ACE applies. Therefore, iterating through each `Win32_ACE` in the DACL and reading the `Name` property of the `Win32_Trustee` object embedded within its `Trustee` property provide a mechanism for enumerating all users and groups with specified rights to a file or directory without using a `Win32_LogicalFileAccess` associator. The following short script demonstrates this. Note that in VBScript, a WMI array can be treated just like a collection. Retrieving a reference to each member of the array can be accomplished with a `For Each...Next` loop.

```
'trustees.vbs - output the names of all trustees with rights to boot.ini
Option Explicit
Dim refSetting
Dim refSD
Dim refItem

Set refSetting = GetObject( _
"winMgmts:Win32_LogicalFileSecuritySetting='c:\boot.ini'")
If refSetting.GetSecurityDescriptor(refSD) = 0 Then
    For Each refItem In refSD.DACL
        WScript.Echo refItem.Trustee.Name
    Next
    Set refSD = Nothing
End If
Set refSetting = Nothing
```

Again, this information could have been retrieved through associators of `Win32_LogicalFileSecuritySetting` objects, but this code is considerably more concise.

The true power of this method, however, lies not so much in its conciseness, but in the fact that it gives access to the three other properties of each `Win32_ACE` in a `DACL`: `AceType`, `AccessMask`, and `AceFlags`.

Win32_ACE.AceType

The `AceType` property is the simplest of the three. It provides a particularly important piece of information—namely, whether the `Win32_ACE` object allows access to the named trustee (a value of 0) or denies access (a value of 1).

Win32_ACE.AccessMask

By far the most interesting property is the `AccessMask`, a value that describes the exact nature of rights conferred (or denied) by a given `Win32_ACE` to a given trustee. The `AccessMask` looks like a 32-bit integer (a number), but it is actually a *bitmask*, or a set of flags.

The concept of bitmask can be best understood by considering what exactly is meant by the term "32-bit integer." On one level, a 32-bit integer is a number—or, more precisely, a block of memory that a programming language such as VBScript has demarked as containing a numeric value between 0 and 4294967295 (if the integer in question is *unsigned*) or between –2147483648 and 2147483647 (if it is *signed*). However, in literal terms, a 32-bit integer can also be seen as nothing more than a row of 32 bits. A bitmask is a way of viewing the 32-bit integer that ignores the fact that it represents a numeric value and instead interprets its bits as a series of 32 independent switches. In the case of the `AccessMask` property, each of the bits represents a specific permission that can be either on (the bit is set to 1) or off (the bit is set to 0).

VBScript, in common with most programming languages, does not provide a syntax for directly manipulating the individual bits that make up the representation of a number, so you cannot *set* (1) or *clear* (0) to an individual bit as though it were, say, an element of an array. It is, however, simple to set or clear an individual bit or find out its status using the operators `AND`, `OR`, and `NOT`.

You have seen all of these operators several times throughout this book, but so far we have always used them as *logical* operators that specify a conjunction of expressions whose values are either true or false. For example, the following code fragment outputs `Hello` and then `Goodbye`:

```
If 3 = 3 And 4 = 4 Then WScript.Echo "Hello"
If 3 = 4 Or 4 = 4 Then WScript.Echo "Goodbye"
```

The reason it outputs `Hello`, of course, is that `3 = 3` and `4 = 4` are both true, so the conjunction is equally true. As for `Goodbye`, `3 = 4` is false, but `4 = 4` is true, so the logical `OR` condition is satisfied.

These operators can also have quite a different purpose: They can be used as *bitwise operators*. Consider, for example, this tiny script fragment, which is perfectly valid VBScript syntax:

```
WScript.Echo 1 Or 2
```

Clearly this code is nonsense if you consider the `OR` as a logical operator, but as a bitwise expression, it makes perfect sense. The bitwise expression `1 Or 2` simply means "Take the binary representations of the numbers 1 and 2, and for each bit in turn, perform a logical `OR` operation. Store the result in the corresponding bit position of the result." In other words, for each bit that is *set* in the binary representation of the number 1 *or* in the binary representation of the number 2, set the equivalent bit in the result. In binary, 1 is represented as a number with only a single bit set—the *least-significant bit;* 2 is also represented as a number with only a single bit set—the *second-least-significant bit.* The result of performing a bitwise `OR` operation on these numbers is a number whose binary representation has the least-significant and second-least-significant bits set; this number is 3. This is all made clearer in Table 5.3, which shows the numbers 1, 2, and 3 in conjunction with their 32-bit binary representations.

Table 5.3 Binary Representations

Numeric Representation	Binary Representation
1	00000000000000000000000000000001
2	00000000000000000000000000000010
3	00000000000000000000000000000011

This table illustrates two important concepts. First, it gives a graphical illustration of the way in which bitwise `OR` combines numbers. Second, it shows a symmetry between representations: Just as a number is represented by a string of bits, any combination of 32 1s and 0s can be represented as a plain, ordinary number! Within this second observation lies the attraction of bitmasks: They allow a huge, unwieldy set of switches to be represented concisely as a single number.

The `AccessMask` property of a `Win32_Ace` does not use all 32 bits to represent permissions; it uses only 14. Any combination of any permissions, then, can be specified simply by `OR`ing together the numeric representations of each bit associated with each permission that the mask should grant or deny. For example, permission to read a file or list the contents of a directory is encoded by the value 1, and permission to write to a file or add a file to a directory is encoded by the value 2. An `AccessMask` that encoded read and write permissions but *nothing else* would have the aggregate value of `1`

`OR 2` (which, as it happens, is 3). The crucial thing to remember with a bit-mask is that *every possible combination of permissions produces a unique number when* `OR`*ed together*. Table 5.4 lists the 14 permissions and their unique numeric representations.

Table 5.4 AccessMask *Values*

Value	Permission Description
1	Reads the contents of a file or directory listing
2	Writes to a file or adds a file to a directory
4	Appends data to a file or adds a subdirectory to a directory
8	Reads a file's extended attributes
16	Writes a file's extended attributes
32	Executes a file or traverses a directory
64	Deletes a directory and its contents
128	Reads standard file attributes
256	Writes standard file attributes
65536	Deletes a file 131072 Reads security information
262144	Writes to the Access Control List
524288	Writes owner information
1048576	Synchronizes—a facility of interest only to programmers who want to manipulate a filesystem dynamically

To reiterate, combining *any* combination of *any* number in the preceding permission table with a bitwise `OR` produces a number that uniquely identifies that set of permissions. Or, to put it in a slightly different way, the `AccessMask` property of a `Win32_ACE` has a value comprised of the bitwise `OR` of a particular set of the numbers in the table. The next question to ask, then, is how you can extract the individual values from this combined value.

The answer is the *bitwise* `AND` operator. As you have probably guessed, bitwise `AND` sets each bit of the result if and only if that bit is set in the binary representations of *both* the numbers being conjoined. For example, `1` (binary 01) `AND 2` (binary 10) `= 0` (binary 00) because 1 and 2 do not share a common set bit. If you want to know whether any particular bit is set in the binary representation of a number, all that is required is to perform a bitwise `AND` operation on the number in question and another bitmask whose binary representation consists exclusively of 0s except for a single 1 in the bit position you want to know about. The result of this operation will be nonzero if and only if the bit in question was set in the number you are interested in. For example, if you want to know whether the third bit was set in any given number, you perform a bitwise `AND` operation on this number and binary 100 (represented numerically as 4). Only if the corresponding bit is set in the number you want to know about will the result be nonzero. So `3 AND 4 = 0` (false), but `5 AND 4 <> 0` (true). This can be seen in Table 5.5, which shows the numeric and binary representations of these numbers (this time, without the 32-bit padding).

Table 5.5 Binary Representations

Numeric Representation	Binary Representation
3	011
4	100
5	101

The following VBScript example clarifies all of this by demonstrating how to create and then read an `AccessMask`. It starts by creating an `AccessMask` that gives `Read`, `Write`, `Append`, and `Delete` privileges. The second part of the script decodes the mask and displays the list of privileges that were encoded. Of course, the script is of little practical value, because it decodes a mask whose component values we know in advance, but it illustrates the procedure nonetheless!

```
'encodethendecode.vbs - create an AccessMask with
'Read, Write, Append and Delete permissions by using logical OR.
'Then decode the mask with logical AND.
Option Explicit
Dim m

'create a mask with Read, Write, Append and Delete permissions
m = 1 OR 2 OR 4 OR 65535

'now decipher the mask
WScript.Echo "The following permissions are set:"
If m AND 1048576 Then WScript.Echo "Synchronize"
If m AND 524288 Then WScript.Echo "Write owner"
If m AND 262144  Then WScript.Echo "Write ACL"
If m AND 131072  Then WScript.Echo "Read Security"
If m AND 65536  Then WScript.Echo "Delete"
If m AND 256  Then WScript.Echo "Write Attr"
If m AND 128  Then WScript.Echo "Read Attr"
If m AND 64  Then WScript.Echo "Delete Dir"
If m AND 32  Then WScript.Echo "Execute"
If m AND 16  Then WScript.Echo "Write ExtAttr"
If m AND 8  Then WScript.Echo "Read ExtAttr"
If m AND 4  Then WScript.Echo "Append"
If m AND 2  Then WScript.Echo "Write"
If m AND 1  Then WScript.Echo "Read"
```

If after running this script you need further convincing, try changing the original value of `m` and giving it another go! Later in this chapter, we will use the same code in a real-world script example.

Win32_ACE.AceFlags

The final `Win32_ACE` property of interest is `AceFlags`. This is another bitmask. It specifies how the access permissions specified by the `AccessMask` are inherited by child objects and reports on whether they were themselves inherited. Although it is represented as a 32-bit integer, only five values are actually used. The official documentation defining these flags is probably the most confusingly opaque description of anything we have ever seen! We offer our translation in Table 5.6.

Table 5.6 *Explanation of the* AceFlags *Bitmask*

Value	Description
1	Child objects that are not themselves containers (files but not directories) inherit these permissions. Child objects that are containers inherit the ability to pass these permissions on to their children but are not themselves subject to them.
2	Child objects that are containers inherit these permissions and pass them on to their children.
4	Child objects that inherit these permissions do not pass them on to their children. This setting overrides the propagation behavior implied by values 1 and 2.
8	The object is not affected by these permissions, but it *does* pass them on to its children. This value is set for objects that have inherited permissions from a parent whose inheritance includes value 1.
16	Any object whose permissions have been inherited has this value set.

If you find this confusing, that is because it is! As we said earlier in this chapter, Windows 2000 filesystem security is nothing if not complex.

SACL

The DACL is not the only Access Control List contained in a `Win32_SecurityDescriptor`. There is also a Security Audit Control List (SACL). This list, like its DACL counterpart, contains an array of `Win32_ACE` objects. This time, however, rather than describing rights that a trustee is allowed or denied with respect to an object, these `Win32_ACE`s specify which actions should be audited in the security log. Information contained in a SACL is accessed in exactly the same way as that within a DACL. There is only one difference between `Win32_ACE` objects contained in a DACL and those contained in a SACL: the `AceType` property. Rather than having a value of 0 (allow) or 1 (deny), this has a value of 2, meaning "audit."

ControlFlags

There is only one more property of Win32_SecurityDescriptor objects that you have not yet encountered—ControlFlags. Unlike all the other properties, this one does not contain any embedded objects, but a straightforward value. In fact, as the name implies, it contains yet another bitmask! This mask specifies how a security descriptor should behave when it is written to an object. This is explained later.

Putting the Security Descriptor Back Together

In order to consolidate this menagerie of objects, we present a script that uses a Win32_SecurityDescriptor to display all the security information associated with a file or directory. It lists the owner and then the contents of the DACL and SACL. For each ACE, it outputs the Win32_Trustee to whom the security applies, the type (allow, deny, or audit), the set of permissions defined by the access mask, and an interpretation of the inheritance flags. The AccessMask is decoded using exactly the same procedure as in the earlier example, except that here the code to accomplish this is placed in its own function for tidiness. Rather than outputting with WScript.Echo directly, the function returns a comma-separated string of permissions. A second function performs the same analysis for AceFlags. The script takes a single command-line parameter—the file or directory for which ACL information should be displayed. If you ever want to be *really* sure of who has what level of access to an object, run this script. It is possibly the first example of WMI filesystem manipulation in this book in which the script is probably more convenient to use than Explorer!

```
'showperms.vbs - display all security information about a named
'file or directory
Option Explicit
On Error Resume Next
Dim refSetting
Dim refSD
Dim refItem

'check that arguments are valid
If WScript.arguments.count <> 1 Then
    WScript.Echo "Usage: showperms.vbs <object>"
    WScript.quit
End If

'attempt to retrieve a Win32_LogicalFileSecuritySetting for
'the file or directory specified on the command line
Set refSetting = GetObject("winMgmts:{(Security,Restore)}" & _
                          "Win32_LogicalFileSecuritySetting='" & _
                          WScript.arguments.item(0) & "'")
If Err <> 0 Then
```

```
        WScript.Echo "Cannot get security for " & WScript.arguments.item(0)
        WScript.quit
    End If

    'output owner name
    If refSetting.GetSecurityDescriptor(refSD) = 0 Then
        WScript.Echo refSetting.Path & " owned by " & refSD.Owner.Name
        'loop through the DACL - for each Trustee, output the name and a decoded
        'textual representation of the AccessMask and AceFlags
        For Each refItem In refSD.DACL
            WScript.Echo " Access Control Entry for " & refItem.Trustee.Name
            If refItem.AceType = 0 Then
                WScript.Echo "  The following rights are conferred:-"
            Else
                WScript.Echo "  The following rights are denied:-"
            End If
            WScript.Echo "    " & decodeAccessMask(refItem.AccessMask)
            WScript.Echo " ACE inheritance controlled as follows:-"
            WScript.Echo "    " & decodeAceFlags(refItem.AceFlags)
        Next
        'now do the same for the SACL
        For Each refItem In refSD.SACL
            If Err <> 0 Then
                'there is no SACL
                WScript.Echo "SACL is NULL: Nothing will be audited"
            Else
                Wscript.Echo " The following actions will be audited for " & _
                             refItem.Trustee.Name
                WScript.Echo "  " & decodeAccessMask(refItem.AccessMask)
                WScript.Echo " ACE inheritance controlled as follows:-"
                WScript.Echo "  " & decodeAceFlags(refItem.AceFlags)
            End If
        Next
        Set refSD = Nothing
    End If
    Set refSetting = Nothing

    'decodeAccessMask() turns an AccessMask bitmask into a textual
    'representation
    Function decodeAccessMask(m)
        Dim s
        If m AND 1048576  Then s = s + "Synchronize,"
        If m AND 524288  Then s = s + "Write owner,"
        If m AND 262144  Then s = s + "Write ACL,"
        If m AND 131072  Then s = s + "Read Security,"
        If m AND 65536  Then s = s + "Delete,"
        If m AND 256 Then s = s + "Write Attr,"
        If m AND 128 Then s = s + "Read Attr,"
        If m AND 64 Then s = s + "Delete Dir,"
        If m AND 32 Then s = s + "Execute,"
        If m AND 16 Then s = s + "Write ExtAttr,"
        If m AND 8 Then s = s + "Read ExtAttr,"    If m AND 4 Then s = s + "Append,"
    If m AND 2 Then s = s + "Write,"    If m AND 1 Then s = s + "Read."
```

```
    decodeAccessMask = s
End Function

'decodeAceFlags() turns an AceFlags bitmask into a textual
'representation
Function decodeAceFlags(m)
    Dim s
    If m AND 16  Then s = s + "Has been inherited,"
    If m AND 8  Then s = s + "Not effective will be inherited,"
    If m AND 4  Then s = s + "Children will not pass on,"
    If m AND 2  Then s = s + "Containers will inherit and pass on,"
    If m AND 1  Then _
              s = s + "Non-containers will inherit and pass on."
    decodeAceFlags = s
End Function
```

By default, a security descriptor often does not contain a SACL, in which case the `SACL` property of a `Win32_SecurityDescriptor` object is null. An attempt to loop through a null array produces an error, which we catch in the script and then output `SACL is NULL: Nothing will be audited.` DACLs can also be null; a null DACL means that *anyone* can access the "secured" object in any way. For obvious reasons, an object never has a null DACL by default, so we do not bother to test for it in the script. Another point to note about this script is that we have explicitly enabled the Security and Restore privileges, both of which are required to retrieve ACEs from security descriptors. Contrary to the official WMI documentation, it would appear that a user with Administrator privileges does *not* need to explicitly enable these, but it does no harm to do so anyway!

To end this section, we present Figure 5.4, which shows the various classes that make up a `Win32_SecurityDescriptor` and the relationships between them.

Note: Null and Empty DACLs

A null DACL is not the same as an empty *one. If an object is secured by an* empty *DACL, nobody has any access; if a DACL is* null, *everybody has access. The Explorer security pop-up dialog does not offer the facility for creating a null DACL. You can achieve this effect programmatically, however, by altering the Security Descriptor's* `ControlFlags` *property (discussed near the end of this chapter).* ◆

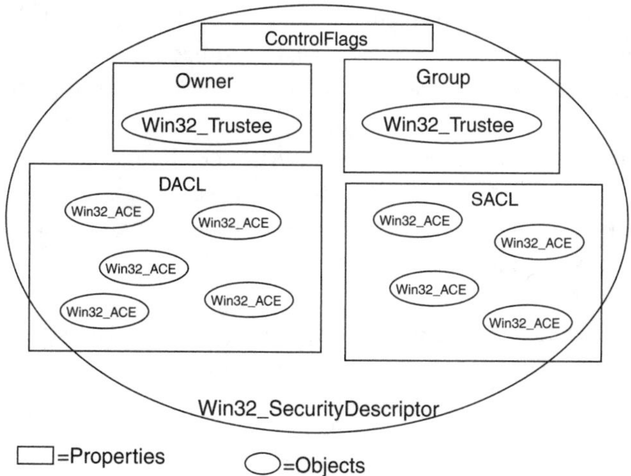

Figure 5.4 *Objects inside a* `Win32_SecurityDescriptor`.

Manipulating Security Descriptors

It seems appropriate to end our discussion of security descriptors by considering how their properties can be altered within WMI. In this, the final section of this chapter, we explain how to make alterations to an ACE, add or remove an ACE from a security descriptor, and create a new ACE from scratch.

Altering an existing ACE is very straightforward. The most likely change you will want to make is to alter the value of the access mask. If you understand how access masks work, you can do this easily! All you need to do is change the `AccessMask` property of the `Win32_ACE` object in question and then save the changed `Win32_SecurityDescriptor` with a call to the `SetSecurityDescriptor()` method of the object from which it originated. Changing a property is simply a matter of assigning a new value using the following syntax:

```
Object.Property = value
```

For example, if you have a reference to a `Win32_ACE` in a variable called `refACE`, you can change its value to read-only using the following code fragment:

```
RefACE.AccessMask = 1
```

As soon as the `Win32_SecurityDescriptor` is written back to the secured object with a call to `SetSecurityDescriptor()`, the altered ACE takes effect.

The following script demonstrates this procedure in full. It attempts to get a `Win32_LogicalFileSecuritySetting` object for a file or directory given as the first command-line parameter. It then loops through the DACL, looking for a `Win32_ACE` object whose `Win32_Trustee` embedded object has a name that corresponds to the second command-line parameter. If it finds one, it changes the `AccessMask` to a value of 2032127 (the value you get when all the flags are set) and then attempts to write the changes back to the `Win32_LogicalFileSecuritySetting`. Note that we invoke the Security and Restore privileges in the script. Because we are writing the security descriptor, they really *are* required!

```
'fullcontrol.vbs - gives full control over a given file or directory
'to a given account, but only if that account already exists within the DACL
Option Explicit
On Error Resume Next
Dim refSetting
Dim refSD
Dim refItem
Dim boolFoundIt

'check that command-line arguments are same
If WScript.arguments.count <> 2 Then
    WScript.Echo "Usage: fullcontrol.vbs <object> <account>"
    WScript.quit
End If

'try to retrieve a Win32_LogicalFileSecuritySetting for the file
'or directory in question
Set refSetting = GetObject("winMgmts:{(Security,Restore)}"& _
    "Win32_LogicalFileSecuritySetting='" &_
     WScript.arguments.item(0) & "'")
If Err <> 0 Then
    WScript.Echo "Cannot get security for " & WScript.arguments.item(0)
    WScript.quit
End If

If refSetting.GetSecurityDescriptor(refSD) = 0 Then
    'loop through the DACL. If we find an entry for the given
    'account, change its AccessMask to full control and set
    'boolFoundIt to true
    boolFoundIt = False
    For Each refItem In refSD.DACL
        If refItem.Trustee.Name = WScript.arguments.item(1) Then
            refItem.AccessMask = 2032127
            boolFoundIt = True
        End If
    Next
    'if there was no appropriate DACL entry, report failure
    If Not boolFoundIt Then
        WScript.Echo "Could not find an ACE for " & _ WScript.arguments.item(1)
    Else
        'try to write back security descriptor and report success
        'or failure
        If refSetting.SetSecurityDescriptor(refSD) = 0 Then
```

```
            WScript.Echo "Security Descriptor changed successfully"
        Else
            WScript.Echo "Failed to write back changed security descriptor"
        End If
    End If

Else
    'oh dear - could not get SD
    WScript.Echo "Cannot retrieve Security Descriptor"
End If
Set refSetting = Nothing
```

Note that we use a Boolean value in the `For Each...Next` loop as a quick way of checking whether the relevant `Win32_ACE` object has been found and reporting this back to the script's user. To run the script, type something like `full_control.vbs c:\temp\somefile.txt Bart`. This gives a user named Bart full control over the file c:\temp\somefile.txt. If Bart is not already mentioned in the DACL for c:\temp\somefile.txt, the script reports this fact as an error.

In an ideal world, we would want a script to not only alter the `AccessMask` for a Bart who is already mentioned in a DACL, but also create a *new* `Win32_ACE` object for Bart if one does not already exist. This, too, can be accomplished reasonably easily, using the following procedure:

1. Find out the SID and domain of the user for whom an ACE will be created.
2. Create a new, blank Win32_Trustee object, and set its properties to the appropriate values.
3. Create a new, blank Win32_ACE object, and set its properties to the desired values. Its Trustee property should point to the newly created Win32_Trustee.
4. Add the Win32_ACE to the DACL.
5. Write back the `Win32_SecurityDescriptor` as before.

The first step, then, is to find the user's vital statistics. The easiest way to do this is via a `Win32_Account` object, which, as the name implies, represents information about a user account. Such objects have two key properties—`Domain` and `Name`. They have one other property of interest to us—`SID`, a string representation of the account SID. Assuming that we already have a reference to a `SWbemServices` object, we can retrieve a `Win32_Account` object representing the user Bart at domain SIMPSONS with a code fragment such as this:

```
Set colUsers = refWMI.ExecQuery( _
    "SELECT * FROM Win32_ACCOUNT WHERE Domain='SIMPSONS' AND Name='BART'")
```

```
For Each refUser in colUsers
    Set refBart = refUser
Next
```

When it comes to creating a new Win32_Trustee, we need the SID in both string and binary representations (see the description of the Win32_Trustee class in the "Owner" section). Unfortunately, the Win32_Account object we have retrieved gives us only a string representation. Although it is perfectly possible to convert a string representation into a binary one with creative use of VBScript's string manipulation and conversion functions, the easiest way of getting the data into the form we need is to locate the Win32_SID object associated with the Win32_Account. Win32_SID contains *all* the information needed to fill in the properties of a Win32_Trustee. There are two obvious ways to retrieve the required Win32_SID. The first is to use a Win32_AccountSID associator, which associates a Win32_Account (through its Element property) with a Win32_SID (through its Setting property). The second, possibly even easier way is to use the SID property of the Win32_Account object as a key for retrieving the Win32_SID directly. This is demonstrated in the following code fragment:

```
Set refSID = refWMI.Get("Win32_SID.SID='" & refBart.SID & "'")
```

Stage two of our security descriptor manipulation procedure involves creating a new WMI object, something that we have not seen in this book so far. This two-stage process is incredibly straightforward. First, retrieve a reference to the Win32_Trustee class itself. Next, invoke one of the "internal" methods that all SWbemObjects possess—namely, SpawnInstance_(). As we noted when discussing Win32_Process objects in Chapter 4, retrieving a reference to a class merely involves specifying an object path with no key identifier:

```
Set refTrusteeClass = refWMI.Get("Win32_Trustee")
```

Having retrieved a reference, we can create the new Win32_Trustee object with the following code fragment:

```
Set refTrustee = refTrusteeClass.SpawnInstance_()
```

Then we merely set its properties with values from the Win32_SID, as shown in this code snippet:

```
With refTrustee
    .Domain = refSID.ReferenceAccountDomainName
    .Name = refSID.AccountName
    .SID = refSID.BinaryRepresentation
    .SidLength = refSID.SidLength
    .SIDString = refSID.SID.
End With
```

Easy! The third stage in our process, creating and populating a Win32_ACE, follows exactly the same pattern. First, we retrieve a reference to the Win32_ACE class and spawn a new instance with SpawnInstance_(). Then we set the Trustee property to the newly created Win32_Trustee and fill in the other properties as desired. We need only worry about AccessMask, Trustee, and AceType, because the others set themselves to appropriate default values. The full procedure required to spawn a new Win32_Ace and set its properties is demonstrated in this code fragment:

```
Set refACEClass = refWMI.Get("Win32_ACE")
Set refACE = refACEClass.SpawnInstance_()
Set refACEClass = Nothing
With refACE
    .AccessMask = 2032127
    .Trustee = refTrustee
    .AceType = 0
End With
```

Tip: Spawning New Instances

If you want to retrieve a reference to a class simply for the purposes of spawning a new instance and are not actually interested in keeping a reference to the Win32_ACE *class itself, you just need it long enough to spawn a new instance. Given that this is the case, we could have used the following shorthand syntax, which saves us from having to declare and then free* refACEClass*:*

```
Set refACE = refWMI.Get("Win32_ACE").SpawnInstance_()
```
◆

Finally, we are ready to add the new Win32_ACE object to the DACL and save the Win32_SecurityDescriptor. If the new Win32_ACE object will *replace* an existing one, all we have to do is assign it to the array element currently containing the one we want to replace. For example, we can replace the first entry in the DACL with a new ACE using a line of code such as this:

```
Set refSD.DACL(0) = refACE
```

Unfortunately, *adding* a Win32_ACE object to a DACL while keeping all of the existing ones is not so trivial, because it involves resizing an array. This is a problem, because most arrays cannot be resized after they are created. Those returned by WMI are no exception! The solution is to create a new array of the right size, copy the contents of the DACL and the new Win32_ACE into it, and then replace the DACL with the new one. In terms of coding, there are several ways in which to carry out this task, but possibly the simplest is via a Dictionary object.

Dictionaries are a facility provided by VBScript for storing an arbitrary set of objects, each of which is indexed by a key. In other words, they are a type of collection. You create a `Dictionary` object from within code by calling `CreateObject()` with the string `"Scripting.Dictionary"` (see Chapter 4). In addition to the standard properties that all collections possess (such as `Item` and `Count`), dictionaries include several methods for adding, removing, and retrieving items. It will come us no shock to discover that items can be added to a dictionary using its `Add()` method. This method takes two parameters: an index (either numeric or a string) and an item. After an item has been `Add()`ed, it can be retrieved using the standard `refItem = refDictionary.Item(index)` that is common to all collections. A complementary method, `Remove()`, performs the converse action: It takes an item out of the dictionary. An item is specified for removal by its index (such as `refDictionary.Remove(0)`). There are several other methods, but they are of no particular interest here, so we will not discuss them!

When collating a set of objects, such as the `Win32_ACE` objects that reside in a DACL, `Dictionary` objects offer one significant advantage over arrays—the ease with which elements can be added and removed. There is no need to specify the size of a dictionary when it is created; it simply grows or shrinks as items are added and removed. It is important to note, however, that dictionaries and arrays are *not* interchangeable. You can definitely not set the DACL property of a `Win32_SecurityDescriptor` to be one! However, dictionaries do have an extremely convenient method, `Items()`, that returns the elements as an array. Hence, by using a dictionary to construct your replacement DACL, you can combine the convenience of a mutable collection with the ability to return a structure of the required type! You can add a `Win32_ACE` to a DACL, then, using the following VBScript code (assuming that `refSD` and `refACE` point to a `Win32_SecurityDescriptor` and a `Win32_ACE`, respectively):

```
set refDictionary = CreateObject("Scripting.Dictionary")
For i = LBound(refSD.DACL) To UBound(refSD.DACL)
    refDictionary.Add i, refSD.DACL(i)
Next
refDictionary.Add refDictionary.Count, refACE
refSD.DACL = refDictionary.Items
```

In this code fragment, we create a `Dictionary` object and then loop through the existing DACL array, adding the elements to the dictionary one at a time. We use the existing array indexes as indexes for the dictionary. Then we add the new `Win32_ACE` to the dictionary, using the current number of elements as an index. This produces the same index as would `UBound(refSD.DACL) + 1`. Finally, we copy the elements of `refDictionary` into an array that is assigned to `refSD.DACL`.

To end this chapter, we present an extended script that puts all of this together. Its purpose is to manipulate the ownership information and the

DACL of a security descriptor associated with a file or directory. The script takes four command-line parameters: `<machine>`, `<object>`, `<account>`, and `<action>`. `<machine>` specifies the name of a computer on which the actions are to be performed. `<object>` is the name of a file or directory whose security descriptor is to be manipulated. `<account>` specifies the name of a user whose relationship with the security descriptor is to be changed. `<action>` can be one of `OWN`, `FULL`, `READ`, or `REMOVE`. When `OWN` is specified, the script attempts to make `<person>` the owner of `<object>` on `<machine>`. `FULL` attempts to give `<person>` full permissions on `<object>` on `<machine>`. `READ` attempts to give `<person>` the standard set of permissions that correspond to Read & Execute in the Windows 2000 NTFS permissions dialog. If either `FULL` or `READ` is specified, the script either changes the `AccessMask` of an existing ACE or (if no existing ACE is found) creates a new one and adds it to the DACL. The `REMOVE` action attempts to remove any ACEs from the DACL that refer to `<person>`. A command-line invocation of this script would look something like this:

```
c:>changeownerandperms.vbs STYX c:\temp bart FULL
```

This code attempts to give a user named Bart full control of c:\temp on a machine called STYX. We have not provided a facility for specifying `AceFlags` on the command line. Instead, any newly created ACEs are hard-coded to propagate to all files and subfolders (given a value of 3).

Because this script is somewhat longer than the ones we have presented so far, it is structured somewhat differently. Instead of being a single flow from top to bottom with perhaps a short function or two to fulfill specific tasks, it is clearly split into segments. The main body handles the large-scale control flow only. It parses the command-line arguments, retrieves references to the main WMI objects, and reports errors. Most of the real work, meanwhile, is handled by three functions—`changeDACL()`, `makeOwner()`, and `createTrustee()`. The purposes of `changeDACL()` and `makeOwner()` should be obvious from their names. `createTrustee()` is a helper function, used by the other two to create a `Win32_Trustee` object corresponding to a user for cases in which one is unavailable from an existing `Win32_ACE`. Following the example of many WMI methods, all three of these functions return success values (0 for success or some other number for failure). Again, following the example set by WMI methods, `createTrustee()` delivers a created `Win32_Trustee` object to the caller via an "out" parameter to the function.

Much of the code in the script should look very familiar, because it follows the procedures outlined in the past few pages. There are, however, a few interesting things to note. First, `changeDACL()` makes extensive use of a dictionary. Its very first action is to put the contents of a DACL into a dictionary. The only time it refers to the actual DACL array again is when it assigns the dictionary's items to it. Unlike the previous example, the `Win32_ACE` objects are not indexed numerically, but by the `Name` property of their trustee. This allows you to make use of a method of `Dictionary` objects that you have not yet met—`Exists()`. This method takes a single parameter, an index. It returns true if an object in the dictionary corresponds to the index or false if not. Using `Exists()`, we can easily find out whether a DACL contains a `Win32_ACE` corresponding to a particular user with a single line of code:

```
If refDictionary.Exists("Fred") Then WScript.Echo "Fred has an ACE!"
```

There is one extremely important caveat to note when using a dictionary in this way, however: Keys are case-sensitive. In other words, an item added with the key `"fred"` will *not* be returned by `refDictionary.Exists("Fred")`. In terms of our script, unless the account name provided on the command line is exactly the same as that stored in a nominally matching `Win32_ACE` object, the dictionary would be unable to spot the match. To avoid this problem, we employ VBScript's built-in `UCase()` function, which converts all the characters of a string into their uppercase equivalents. For example, `WScript.Echo UCase("fish")` displays the string `"FISH"`. We use this function to ensure that all interactions with `Dictionary` objects involve only uppercase keys, avoiding any potential pitfalls.

Another notable feature of the script is that it introduces a new VBScript construct: the `Select Case` block. This construct provides a convenient replacement for a series of `If...Else` statements in the special case where different evaluations of the same expression should lead to conditional execution. In the case of our script, the `Select Case` block is used to read the final command-line argument (`<action>`) and spark different behavior depending on the argument's value. The syntax of a `Select Case` block is as follows:

```
Select Case <expression>
Case <value1>
    'block 1
Case <value2>
    'block 2
Case Else
    'block 3
End Select
```

If `<expression>` evaluates to `<value1>`, the code in `block 1` is executed. If it evaluates to `<value2>`, `block 2` is executed. If it evaluates to anything else, the code in `block 3` is executed. Hence, `Case Else` is a catchall for unanticipated or default values. Of course, the same behavior could have been achieved with `If`, `Then`, and `Else`:

```
If <expression> = <value1> Then
```

```
    'block1
Else
    If <expression> = <value2> Then
        'block2
    Else
        'block3
    End If
End If
```

However, `Select Case` clearly offers the neater solution!

The script is presented in full next. Note that after a few initial sanity checks and a bit of WMI object retrieval, `Select Case` is responsible for the large-scale logic of the program flow:

```
'changeownerandperm.vbs -- change the owner of
'a specified file or directory on a specified machine
'or change the permissions that a specified user has over
'that file or directory
Option Explicit
On Error Resume Next
Dim refWMI
Dim refSetting
Dim refSD
Dim strMachine
Dim strObject
Dim strPerson
Dim strAction
Dim numSuccess

If WScript.arguments.count <> 4 Then
    WScript.Echo _
        "Usage: changeownerandperms.vbs <machine> <object> <person> <action>"
    WScript.Echo "   where <action> is OWN, FULL, READ, or REMOVE"
    WScript.quit
End If

'assign arguments to named variables for clarity later on
strMachine = WScript.arguments(0)
strObject = WScript.arguments(1)
strPerson = WScript.arguments(2)
strAction = WScript.arguments(3)

'connect to WMI
set refWMI = GetObject("winMgmts:{(Security,Restore)}!\\" & strMachine)
If Err <> 0 Then
    WScript.Echo "Could not connect to machine " & strMachine
End If

'find a LogicalFileSecuritySetting
Set refSetting = refWMI.Get("Win32_LogicalFileSecuritySetting='" & _
                                                      strObject & "'")
If Err <> 0 Then
    WScript.Echo "Cannot find a LogicalFileSecuritySetting for " & strObject
```

```
        set refWMI = Nothing
        WScript.quit
    End If

    'get security descriptor
    If refSetting.GetSecurityDescriptor(refSD) <> 0 Then
        WScript.Echo "Cannot retrieve the security descriptor for " & strObject
    End If

    'work out what to do
    Select Case strAction
        Case "OWN":
            WScript.Echo "Attempting to make " & strPerson & _
                         " owner of " & strObject
            numSuccess = makeOwner(strPerson, refSD, refWMI)
        Case "FULL":
            WScript.Echo "Attempting to give Full Control of " & _
                         strObject & " to " & strPerson
            numSuccess = changeDACL(strPerson, refSD, refWMI,2032127)
        Case "READ":
            WScript.Echo "Attempting to give Read Access of " & _
                         strObject & " to " & strPerson
            numSuccess = changeDACL(strPerson, refSD, refWMI,131245)
        Case "REMOVE":
            WScript.Echo "Attempting to remove " & strPerson & _
                         " from the DACL of " & strObject
            numSuccess = changeDACL(strPerson, refSD, refWMI,0)
        Case Else:
            WScript.Echo "Action must be one of: OWN, FULL, READ, REMOVE"
            set refSD = Nothing
            set refSetting = Nothing
            set refWMI = Nothing
            WScript.quit
    End Select

    If numSuccess <> 0 Then
        WScript.Echo "Failed to manipulate security descriptor."
    Else
        If refSetting.SetSecurityDescriptor(refSD) <> 0 Then
            WScript.Echo "Failed to re-write Security Descriptor."
        Else
            WScript.Echo "Operation successful!"
        End If
    End If

    set refSD = Nothing
    Set refSetting = Nothing
    Set refWMI = Nothing

    '--- END OF MAIN SCRIPT ---

    Function changeDACL(strPerson, refSD, refWMI,numPerms)
        On Error Resume Next
        Dim refDictionary
```

```
Dim refItem
Dim refTrustee
Dim refACE

'create a dictionary and populate it with DACL
'index by Trustee.Name
set refDictionary = CreateObject("Scripting.Dictionary")
For Each refItem In refSD.DACL
    refDictionary.add UCase(refItem.Trustee.Name), refItem
Next

'First deal with case when ACE should be removed
If numPerms = 0 Then
    'if there is an ACE corresponding to the person
    'delete it from dictionary
    If refDictionary.Exists(UCase(strPerson)) Then
        refDictionary.Remove(UCase(strPerson))
        refSD.DACL = refDictionary.Items
    End If
    'that's all we need to do
    ChangeDACL = Err
    set refDictionary = Nothing
    Exit Function
End If

'If we got here, we need an ACE. So if there isn't one
'already, we must create it
If Not refDictionary.Exists(UCase(strPerson)) Then
    'don't check return value here because it'll be caught
    createTrustee strPerson,refWMI,refTrustee

    'create ACE
    set refACE = refWMI.Get("Win32_ACE").SpawnInstance_()
    With refACE
        .AceType = 0
        .AceFlags = 3
        .Trustee = refTrustee
    End With

    'did it work?!
    If Err <> 0 Then
        ChangeDACL = Err
        set refTrustee = Nothing
        set refACE = Nothing
        set refDictionary = Nothing
        Exit Function
    End If

    'cool - it worked. Add it to the dictionary
    refDictionary.add UCase(strPerson),refACE
Else
    'we have an ACE, so get a ref to it
    set refACE = refDictionary.item(UCase(strPerson))
End If
```

```
    'now alter the access mask and copy back to DACL
    refACE.AccessMask = numPerms
    refSD.DACL = refDictionary.Items
    changeDACL = Err
    set refACE = Nothing
    set refTrustee = Nothing
End Function


Function makeOwner(strPerson,refSD,refWMI)
    On Error Resume Next
    Dim refTrustee
    Dim numError

    'create a Trustee or die
    numError =  createTrustee(strPerson,refWMI,refTrustee)
    If numError <> 0 Then
        makeOwner = numError
        Exit Function
    End If

    'set owner
    set refSD.Owner = refTrustee
End Function


Function createTrustee(strPerson,refWMI,refTrustee)
    On Error Resume Next
    Dim colWinAcc
    Dim refSID
    Dim refItem

    'find a SID
    set colWinAcc = refWMI.ExecQuery("SELECT * FROM Win32_ACCOUNT " & _
                                    "WHERE Name='" & strPerson & "'")
    For Each refItem in colWinAcc
        set refSID = refWMI.Get("Win32_SID='" & refItem.SID & "'")
    Next

    'create trustee
    Set refTrustee = refWMI.Get("Win32_Trustee").spawnInstance_()
    With refTrustee
        .Domain = refSID.ReferencedDomainName
        .Name = refSID.AccountName
        .SID = refSID.BinaryRepresentation
        .SidLength = refSID.SidLength
        .SIDString = refSID.SID
    End With
    createTrustee = Err
End Function
```

It should be noted that this script can take several seconds to execute and, of course, it will not do anything useful on non-NTFS filesystems. You could make plenty of additions to the script to make it more useful. For example, you could add a facility for adding `DENY ACEs` to a DACL (the present script handles only `ALLOW ACEs`). You could also add options for manipulating the Security Audit Control Lists. Apart from adding extra features, you could improve the script by adding more comprehensive error reporting. Although errors are *handled* and the script should never actually crash or abort its mission, it does not return very helpful information. You could improve this dramatically by making use of the functions' return values. Had we incorporated these features here, however, the script would have been considerably longer and probably of little more pedagogical value. With the information in this chapter, you can always add any extra functionality you need!

Before leaving this chapter, we turn, as promised, to a property of `Win32_SecurityDescriptor` objects that we have not yet considered—the `ControlFlags` bitmask. The value of this mask controls the behavior of a security descriptor when it is written back to the secured object with a call to `SetSecurityDescriptor()`. Various flags control which parts of the `Win32_SecurityDescriptor` object are actually written back to the underlying security descriptor and how inheritance information is propagated to children. Understanding the subtleties of the various `ControlFlags` and their influence on a security descriptor's behavior is a particularly complex subject and is of real interest only to programmers writing sophisticated tools. For a system administrator who merely wants to alter the properties of `Win32_SecurityDescriptor` objects rather than build them from scratch, it is almost always sensible to leave the `ControlFlags` in their default state. If you are hungry for fine-grained control over the behavior of security descriptors beyond that which we have discussed in this chapter, `ControlFlags` are a feast waiting to be gorged upon. If you do so, however, you do so alone in conjunction with the Microsoft documentation. A description of their meaning does not grace the pages of this book!

We end with a small note of warning: By presenting an interface to security descriptors, WMI offers an extremely powerful mechanism for manipulating NTFS file permissions. This power does not come without a price. A carelessly written script designed to perform a bulk security operation on a range of files could quite easily wreak havoc with your filesystem by decimating the security model that you have spent months setting up! Before running a new script on a production system, *always* check and then double-check that any manipulation of access masks, inheritance flags, and ACLs will really do what you think it will.

Summary

This chapter was concerned with WMI security. It started with a discussion of the various layers of security that control WMI's behavior and the tasks it can accomplish. Topics included WMI's own security model, DCOM security, and its relationship with Windows 2000. The second part of the chapter considered more programmatic aspects of security, focusing on a selection of WMI objects that represent concepts, users, and SIDs. The final section of this chapter was devoted to a discussion of security descriptors, the core of Windows 2000 security, and the behavior of the various WMI objects that represent them. It presented scripts that report on and write to the security descriptors, protecting files and directories in an NTFS filesystem.

6

Logs and Reports

If you have read this far, you have met almost all the concepts needed to harness the power of WMI for system administration tasks. The only major component not yet encountered is the capability to respond to system events when they occur, which is discussed in Chapter 8, "Proactive Troubleshooting with WMI Events" Hopefully you now have a good understanding of how the world looks from a WMI perspective, and an idea of the many ways in which VBScript can be used to view and interact with that world. It should by now be apparent that for a system administrator, one of the most powerful features of WMI is its capability to provide a consistent interface to information about computer systems; in this and the next chapter, we take a short break from heavy conceptualizing and pause to consider how this information can be compiled into presentable, useful reports. This chapter starts with an examination of the Windows Event Logs, and shows how WMI can be used both to manage them and report on their contents; it then moves on to a brief discussion of the Windows Installer and produces a report of all software installed under its auspices on machines across a network. Finally, it presents the WMI Object Browser, a graphical tool for investigating a computer's WMI Repository. You can use this tool to discover which objects exist on any given Windows 2000 machine, and determining what properties, methods, and associators each has. In short, the WMI Object Browser is the perfect tool for exploring the WMI world; it is a gold mine of management information.

Examining the Event Logs with WMI

The Event Logs on Windows 2000 and Windows NT are central repositories for log information generated by components of the operating system or, in fact, by any application that registers as an *event source*. On Windows 2000, and Windows NT computers, there are three Event Logs, each of which is intended to store information from different types of sources:

- The *system* log typically receives log entries from drivers and components of the operating system itself. For example, the Netlogon service (whose registered source name is `netlogon`) would report an inability to find a domain controller; the Print Spooler service (whose registered source name is `spooler`) would report the addition or removal of a printer. The Event Log service (registered as `eventlog`) also reports on its own operation here.
- The *application* log typically receives log entries from high-level components of the operating system, such as the Windows Installer or Explorer; in addition, it receives entries from any application software written to use it.
- The *security* log receives log entries about security-related events, such as logons and audit failures. The type and variation of events recorded here largely depends on the security auditing policies of any given computer or domain.

In addition to these three standard logs, Windows 2000 Server has additional ones for the DNS service, the File Replication service, and for directory services. There are also rumors of an IExplore log to handle reporting of IE problems. Presumably, the rationale for separating these was that each of the services generates a significant number of log entries, whose presence would quickly clutter up the system log if they were posted there.

Our use of the word *typically* in the preceding descriptions perhaps deserves further explanation: although the system log is *intended* for system-level log entries and the application log for application-related entries, this distinction is not enforced. Any application or driver written to make use of Event Logs can, in fact, write to either of them; all that is required is for the application or driver in question to register itself appropriately with the Event Log service.

Regardless of its source, every entry posted to one of the Event Logs has a consistent format, allowing all log data to be viewed and processed with the same tools; the consistency also helps a system administrator make an educated guess as to the meaning and importance of a message that he may never have met before! A log entry specifies the following information:

- The *date* and *time* that the entry was posted to the log.
- The registered name of the *source* that generated the entry.
- The *type*, which specifies the severity level of the event that caused the entry to be written. An entry that is merely providing noncritical

information is given a type of "information"; more important information that could require action from a system administrator is given a type of "warning"; when things go wrong, an "error" is written to the log. Two further types exist for entries relating to security audits: A successfully completed *audited* operation is given the type "success"; a failed one is logged as a "failure".

- The *computer* and, if applicable, the *user* account from which the event was posted.
- An *EventID*, which is a numeric value that uniquely differentiates the specific event type from all others that can be generated by the same *source*. In addition to this identifier, an event may belong to an application-defined *category*.
- A textual *description* of the event and the reason for its being posted. This may be accompanied by a chunk of binary data, at the discretion of the event *source*.

As most system administrators will know, the Event Logs can be browsed, filtered, and cleared with the graphical *Event Viewer* tool, which remains almost identical in its Windows 2000 incarnation to its original form in Windows NT. This tool, which can display the contents of Event Logs on local or remote machines, is an indispensable part of any system administrator's armory. Despite its powerful filtering capabilities and remote operation, however, it has two limitations that can be extremely irritating in environments with a large base of Windows machines. First, it does not provide a practical mechanism for backing up and clearing the logs on a large number of machines on a regular basis, something that many administrators consider to be an essential everyday maintenance task. Second, it provides no facility for exporting a set of log entries in a clear, readable format so that they can be viewed without the Event Viewer itself.

Fortunately, both of these limitations can be overcome trivially with WMI and VBScript thanks to the Event Log Provider, which provides a WMI interface both to the logs themselves and to the individual log records that they contain. The remainder of this section is devoted to demonstrating how WMI can be used to perform bulk management of logs on multiple machines, and to provide neat, customized reports of logged events.

Representation of an Event Log in WMI

Event Logs are represented by instances of the `Win32_NTEventLogFile` class, which is derived from `CIM_Datafile`. This inheritance chain is not as strange as it may seem at first: In literal terms, an Event Log is just a file on disk with an .evt extension, living in the c:\winnt\system32\config directory of a

Windows 2000 machine. For example, the application log is stored in c:\winnt\system32\config\appevent.evt. As a subclass of `CIM_DataFile`, an instance of `Win32_NTEventLogFile` can be investigated and manipulated using all the techniques discussed in Chapter 3, "Examining the Filesystem with WMI." Like its superclass, the primary key is the `Name` property.

`Win32_NTEventLogFile` objects have six properties in addition to those inherited from `CIM_DataFile`. These are described in Table 6.1.

Table 6.1 Win32_NTEventLog *Properties*

Property Name	Description
`LogFileName`	The name of the Event Log represented by this `Win32_NTEventLogFile` object (for instance, System, Application, Security). The Name property holds the name of the Event Log file containing the log (for instance, AppEvent.evt).
`MaxFileSize`	The size, in bytes, to which the file is allowed to grow before either old entries are overwritten or no new entries are added. The behavior when a log reaches this size depends on the logging policy in operation.
`NumberOfRecords`	The number of records currently in the log.
`OverwriteOutDated`	The number of days a record should be retained before it can be overwritten (as discussed later in this chapter).
`OverwritePolicy`	The policy governing rewriting behavior (as discussed later in this chapter).
`Sources`	A list of sources registered to post entries to the log represented by the `Win32_NTEventLogFile` objects.

The last three properties in the table probably deserve further explanation! `OverwriteOutDated` and `OverwritePolicy` represent the policies used by the Event Log service for deciding how to behave when `MaxFileSize` is reached. The most important of these is `OverwriteOutDated`, which either reports a number of days between 1 and 365, after which an entry can be overwritten, or else one of two special values, `0` and `4294967295`. If the property reports `0`, the Event Log service can overwrite an entry whenever it wants (that is, whenever `MaxFileSize` has been reached); if it reports `429467295`, the Event Log service can never overwrite an entry, regardless of its age. For the curious, `429467295` is not quite such a strange value as it may seem at first; it is the largest value that an unsigned 32-bit integer can represent (that is, 32 bits all set; see the discussion of bit masks in Chapter 5, "WMI Security").

`OverwritePolicy` is a peculiar addition to the property list because it does not provide any useful information whatsoever that cannot be deduced from `OverwriteOutDated`! It is a string value that gives a textual interpretation of the `OverwriteOutDated` property. If `OverwritePolicy` is `0`, it contains

WhenNeeded; if OverwritePolicy is between 1 and 365, it contains OutDated; or if OverwritePolicy is 4294967295, it displays Never. Quite why this information is provided as a separate property we simply do not know!

The Sources property is an array property containing a list of all the registered sources that are permitted to write to the Event Log. An application, driver, or even part of the operating system writes to a log by calling a Win32 API function; this function, in turn, calls on the Event Log service to actually perform the operation. The Event Log service will only honor a request to post an event if the request comes from a registered source; hence the Sources property is effectively an inventory of all the various sources of a log entry. As with all array properties, the VBScript For...Next loop can be used to read each of the items in turn. Assuming that the variable refEventLog holds a valid reference to a Win32_EventLogFile object, the following code fragment would display a list of sources registered to write to the log in question:

```
For Each strEntry In refEventLog.Sources
    WScript.Echo strEntry
Next
```

All of this is illustrated in the script presented here, which reports on the overwriting policy and displays a list of registered sources for all the Event Logs on a machine whose name or IP address is supplied as a command-line option. If no machine name is specified, the script provides information about the Event Logs on the local machine at which the script is run. First, the script attempts to connect to the WMI service of the named machine, and then uses the InstancesOf() method of the SWbemServices object to retrieve a collection of all Win32_NTEventLogFile objects (see Chapter 3 for details about InstancesOf()). In addition to the overwriting policy and the list of registered sources, it also reports basic information for each Event Log, such as the log's current size, maximum allowed size, and number of entries.

Before we present the script itself, there is one small complication to note. To display information about the overwriting policy, the script must read OverwritePolicy and determine whether it contains either of the special values (0 or 4294967295). The snag is that VBScript does not know about 32-bit unsigned integer values and interprets them incorrectly if they fall outside the standard integer range of –2147483648 to 2147483647; as you have probably deduced, 4294967295 *is* outside that range. When VBScript reads this value, then, represented in binary as 32 set bits, it interprets it not as 4294967295 but, somewhat confusingly, as -1! The general implications of this observation and the places in which you need to worry about it will be considered in Chapter 10, "Script Development and Deployment." For now, the point to note is that when you want to use VBScript to test whether `OverwritePolicy` holds the value 4294967295, you must test instead for the value –1.

```
'loginfo.vbs - display information about the overwrite policy and
'registered sources for each Event Log on a computer
Option Explicit
On Error Resume Next

Dim strMoniker
Dim refWMI
Dim colEventLogs
Dim refEventLog
Dim strSource

'moniker string stub - security privilege needed to get
'numrecords for Security log
strMoniker = "winMgmts:{(Security)}!"

'append to moniker string if a machine name has been given
If WScript.Arguments.Count = 1 Then _
    strMoniker = strMoniker & "\\" & WScript.Arguments(0) & ":"

'attempt to connect to WMI
Set refWMI = GetObject(strMoniker)
If Err <> 0 Then
    WScript.Echo "Could not connect to the WMI service."
    WScript.Quit
End If

'get a collection of Win32_NTEventLogFile objects
Set colEventLogs = refWMI.InstancesOf("Win32_NTEventLogFile")
If Err <> 0 Then
    WScript.Echo "Could not retrieve Event Log objects"
    WScript.Quit
End If

'iterate through each log and output information
For Each refEventLog In colEventLogs
    WScript.Echo "Information for the " & _
                 refEventLog.LogfileName & _
                 " log:"
    WScript.Echo " Current file size: " & refEventLog.FileSize
    WScript.Echo " Maximum file size: " & refEventLog.MaxFileSize
    WScript.Echo " The Log currently contains " & _
                 refEventLog.NumberOfRecords & " records"

    'output policy info in a friendly format using OverwriteOutDated,
    'as OverWritePolicy is utterly pointless.
    'note "-1" is the signed interpretation of 4294967295
    Select Case refEventLog.OverwriteOutDated
        Case 0 WScript.Echo _
               " Log entries may be overwritten as required"
        Case -1 WScript.Echo _
```

```
                " Log entries may NEVER be overwritten"
            Case Else WScript.Echo _
                    " Log entries may be overwritten after " & _
                    refEventLog.OverwriteOutDated & " days"
        End Select

        'now print out list of registered sources - note extra spaces
        'are for cosmetic reasons
        WScript.Echo " The following are registered Sources for this log:"
        For Each strSource In refEventLog.Sources
            WScript.Echo "    " & strSource
        Next
    Next


    Set refEventLog = Nothing
    Set colEventLogs = Nothing
    Set refWMI = Nothing
```

This script may not achieve anything that could not be accomplished through other means, but with a trivial modification to the script using the techniques discussed in Chapter 4, "Remote Administration," it suddenly provides a powerful way to gather basic information about your Event Log configuration and usage across an entire network! Note that we set the security privilege when connecting to WMI in this script; this privilege is required to read the `NumberOfRecords` property of the security Event Log.

Backing Up the Event Logs

As noted near the start of this chapter, a system administrator who is concerned about auditing and retention of log files would benefit enormously from an efficient mechanism for backing up Event Log files on a server or workstation farm to a central location and clearing their contents. The `Win32_NTEventLogFile` class, in addition to all the methods inherited from `CIM_DataFile`, provides two methods that enable you to do just this. These methods are the appropriately named `BackupEventLog()` and `ClearEventLog()`.

The `BackupEventlog()` method, as you will not be surprised to learn, backs up the Event Log represented by the `Win32_NTEventLogFile` on which it is called. It takes a single parameter, the name (and fully qualified path) of a file to which the archive should be written. Equally unsurprisingly, the `ClearEventLog()` method clears all entries from the log; this method can be called with no parameters. Typically, an administrator would want to perform a backup and then clear a log as a single operation. In WMI terms, this can obviously be accomplished by invoking `BackupEventLog()` followed by `ClearEventLog()`; there is an even simpler way, however: `ClearEventLog()` can optionally take a single parameter, the name (and fully qualified path) of an archive to which to archive the log. In other words, the following two fragments of VBScript, both of which assume that refEventLog is a valid reference to a Win32_NTEventLogFile, are almost functionally identical:

```
'fragment 1
refEventLog.BackupEventLog "c:\temp\oldlog.evt"
refEventLog.ClearEventLog
```

and

```
'fragment 2
refEventLog.ClearEventLog "c:\temp\oldlog.evt"
```

There is one minor difference, however: If the backup fails in the first fragment, it could still go ahead and clear the Event Log; in the second fragment, a failed backup will cause the clear to fail. In common with many WMI methods, both BackupEventLog() and ClearEventLog() return a success value. If method execution is successful, 0 is returned; failure is indicated by a non-0 value. An attempt to write a log archive to a nonexistent directory, or to overwrite an existing file, will fail. Hence, the preceding fragments could be rewritten as follows:

```
'fragment 1
If refEventLog.BackupEventLog("c:\temp\oldlog.evt") = 0 Then
    x=refEventLog.ClearEventLog()
End If
```

and

```
'fragment 2
x=refEventLog.ClearEventLog("c:\temp\oldlog.evt")
```

Now the two fragments are truly functionally identical, because the return value of BackupEventLog() in the first fragment ensures that ClearEventLog() is called only if the backup succeeds.

Note: Clearing the Security Log

The act of clearing all entries from the security log, whether through WMI, through the Event Viewer, or directly through the Win32 API, provokes the Security Provider into writing a new entry into the newly cleared log. This entry, whose source is "security" *and whose event ID is 517, logs when and by whom the log was cleared. The rationale for this entry, of course, is that clearing the security log is in itself a security event worthy of note!* ◆

The script illustrates the use of ClearEventLog() to make a backup and then to clear the contents of all Event Logs on a named machine. It requires two parameters: the name or IP address of the machine whose logs are to be cleared, and the name of a directory to which the archives should be saved. Archives are saved to this directory with automatically generated filenames that consist of machine name, log name, and the current date. For conciseness, responsibility for generating filenames is delegated to a separate function, `makeFileName()`.

To make life more interesting, the script's operation is optionally conditional on the log size. A third, numeric parameter can be provided on the command line; this is treated as a percentage value. If it is provided, the script compares the current size of each log (its `FileSize` property) with its maximum size (the `MaxFileSize` property); a backup and clear is performed only if the ratio of file size to maximum file size specified as a percentage exceeds the specified value. The calculation is handled by a short function, `shouldAct()`, which returns a non-0 value if the criteria for action have been met. Notice that this script is considerably longer than the fragments presented earlier. Most of this code, however, is concerned with checking command-line arguments, connecting to WMI, compiling log filenames and determining whether each log needs to be archived; the core functionality is implemented just as before, with a simple call to `ClearEventLog()`.

```
'archivelogs.vbs - make a backup and clear all Event Logs
'on a command-line specified computer. Back up to a command-line
'specified archive directory. Optionally only back up if a cmd-line
'specified threshold has been reached
Option Explicit
On Error Resume Next

Dim numThreshold
Dim strMachine
Dim strArchivePath
Dim strMoniker
Dim refWMI
Dim colEventLogs
Dim refEventLog

'how many cmd-line args?
If WScript.Arguments.Count < 2 Then
    WScript.Echo _
        "Usage: archivelogs.vbs <machine> <archive_path> [threshold]"
    WScript.Quit
End If

If WScript.Arguments.Count = 2 Then
    numThreshold = 0
Else
    'ensure that third arg is numeric and set threshold
    numThreshold = WScript.Arguments(2)
    If Not IsNumeric(numThreshold) Then
        WScript.Echo "The third parameter must be a number!"
        WScript.Quit
    End If
```

```
    If numThreshold < 0 OR numThreshold > 100 Then
        WScript.Echo "The third parameter must be in the range 0-100"
        WScript.Quit
    End If
End If

'save machine name and archive path
strMachine =  WScript.Arguments(0)
strArchivePath = WScript.Arguments(1)


'attempt to connect to WMI
strMoniker = "winMgmts:{(Backup,Security)}!\\" & strMachine
Set refWMI = GetObject(strMoniker)
If Err <> 0 Then
    WScript.Echo "Could not connect to the WMI service."
    WScript.Quit
End If

'get a collection of Win32_NTEventLogFile objects
Set colEventLogs = refWMI.InstancesOf("Win32_NTEventLogFile")
If Err <> 0 Then
    WScript.Echo "Could not retrieve Event Log objects"
    WScript.Quit
End If

'iterate through each log
For Each refEventLog In colEventLogs
    'if shouldAct() returns non-zero attempt to back up
    If shouldAct(refEventLog.FileSize,refEventLog.MaxFileSize) <> 0 Then
        If refEventLog.ClearEventLog( _
                    makeFileName(refEventLog.LogfileName)) = 0 Then
            WScript.Echo refEventLog.LogfileName & _
                        " archived successfully"
        Else
            WScript.Echo refEventLog.LogfileName & _
                        " could not be archived"
        End If
    Else
        WScript.Echo refEventLog.LogfileName & _
                        " has not exceeded the backup level"
    End If
Next

Set refEventLog = Nothing
Set colEventLogs = Nothing
Set refWMI = Nothing

'--- end of script

'shouldAct() calculates whether the backup and clear
'should be performed  based on cursize, maxsize and
'threshold. Returns 0 for "do not act", non-zero otherwise
Function shouldAct(numCurSize, numMaxSize)
```

```
    If (numCurSize/numMaxSize)*100 > numThreshold Then
        shouldAct = 1
    Else
        shouldAct = 0
    End If
End Function

'makeFileName() generates a string that can be used as an
'archive file name from the machine name, log name and date
Function makeFileName(strLogname)
    makeFileName = strArchivePath & "\" & _
        strMachine & "-" & strLogname & "-" & _
        Year(Now) & Month(Now) & Day(Now) & ".evt"
End Function
```

If you try running this script to back up an Event Log on a *remote* machine, you will notice one small problem: Although the script reports that it has operated successfully (assuming that it has), you will not find the archive files in the location you expect to find them! If you attempt to back up all logs on the machine STYX that are more than 10% full, for example, you might specify the following command line:

```
c:\>archivelogs.vbs STYX c:\temp 10
```

Assuming nothing goes wrong, the script will output the following:

```
Application archived successfully
System archived successfully
Security archived successfully
```

Unfortunately, however, there will be no archives in c:\temp on your workstation. The reason for this is that the archive path passed as a parameter to the `ClearEventLog()` method specifies a path *relative to the remote machine* rather than relative to the workstation that runs the script. The logs probably were archived successfully, but to c:\temp on STYX rather than to c:\temp on your own workstation. In most scenarios, that is really not terribly useful!

Theoretically, the solution to this problem is utterly trivial because `ClearEventLog()`, in common with its colleague `BackupEventLog()`, can take a UNC path as a parameter. Therefore, all that should be required to fix the script is to change the `strArchivePath` variable so that instead of specifying `c:\temp` as the backup location, it specifies something like `\\archiveserver\share` (where `archiveserver` is the name of a server on which you would like to store the archived logs and `share` is the name of a share to which you have read-write access on that server). In practice, however, life is not quite so simple.

As you might recall from Chapter 5, "WMI Security," WMI scripts run with a DCOM impersonation level of `impersonate` by default; this means that a WMI script executed by you will run as though it really were you, even if it happens to be running under the control of the WMI service on a remote machine. In other words, if *you* have permissions to back up Event Logs on a remote machine, so does the WMI service on the remote machine when it is running a script at *your* behest. After all, if this were not the case, most of the scripts presented in this book would fail to work. One thing that `impersonate` explicitly denies, however, is permission for a remote machine to give permission to yet another machine to use your credentials; the WMI service on a remote machine may be able to act in its own territory as if it were you, but it does not have the power to pass that luxury on to the rest of the world.

What is the relevance of all this to our script problem? By specifying a UNC name, we are asking a remote machine to use a network resource; in other words, we are asking one remote machine (machine A) to ask another machine (machine B) to provide access to a share. The limitations of `impersonate` mean that machine A cannot ask machine B to provide access with *your* credentials; instead, it must ask machine B to connect to the resource using its own true identity, namely the machine A SYSTEM account. This account is highly unlikely to have the security credentials necessary to use the network drive, so the script will fail. The solution, as you might have already guessed, is to use DCOM delegation.

Using DCOM Delegation

DCOM delegation was discussed briefly in Chapter 5; it is an impersonation level that allows a remote object not only to act with the credentials of its caller in its own territory, but also to extend this permission to any other machines on the network. With delegation, machine A can ask machine B to provide access to a share using permissions it borrowed from you. In short, setting up DCOM delegation allows a remote WMI machine to archive an Event Log to a network share, provided that *you* have permissions to write to that share. Exactly what we need!

We can specify the impersonation level to use when connecting to a WMI service in the moniker string passed to `GetObject()`. The following code fragment is an attempt to connect to the WMI service of a machine called STYX using delegation:

```
Set refWMI = GetObject("winMgmts:{impersonationLevel=delegate}!\\STYX")
```

Try including the string `{impersonationLevel=delegate}` in the moniker in the Event Log archive script, create a network share to which you have write permissions, change the value of `strArchivePath` to point to this share, and try running the script to archive a remote Event Log. You will find that it fails spectacularly, with a cryptic error message informing you of an internal error in the Security Provider. Oh dear! The reason for the failure is that delegation is a security-sensitive operation—it allows remote machines to allow any resources they like to masquerade as you—and a number of hurdles must be jumped before it will actually work. These hurdles are outlined here:

- All machines that need to delegate must be marked on your network as "trusted for delegation." In the case of our script, all machines whose event logs need archiving must be trusted. To trust a machine for delegation, find the icon representing its computer account in the Active Directory Users and Computers MMC panel, right-click and open its property sheet, and then tick the check box labeled Trust This Computer for Delegation.
- All users who are allowed to use delegation (in this case, system administrators allowed to run our script) also need to be trusted for delegation. Check the Account Is Trusted for Delegation option in the Accounts property page of their account details in the Active Directory.
- An `EnableDelegation` privilege needs to be specifically enabled in the moniker string used to connect to WMI in our script. The logic here is that delegation is a security-sensitive operation; just as backing up an Event Log requires a `Backup` privilege to be enabled specifically, delegation does too.
- All authentication must be carried out using Kerberos rather than the older NT LanManager system.

This final point deserves further explanation. Windows 2000 provides two different mechanisms for authentication: Kerberos and NTLM. Whereas the future of Windows 2000 authentication undoubtedly lies with Kerberos, there are still several services and subsystems that use the older NTLM system by default; DCOM, and therefore WMI, is one of these. For most purposes, the underlying authentication system need not be of concern to the application user; not so, alas, for DCOM delegation, which relies on a specific feature of Kerberos (delegating tickets) for its operation. Sadly, a full discussion of Kerberos authentication, its ticket granting mechanism, and interaction with DCOM is well beyond the scope of this book. What we will show, however, is how to specify Kerberos authentication to successfully use DCOM delegation.

Chapter 5 discussed various appendages to moniker strings that can be used to specify impersonation level, authentication level, and privileges. Here we introduce an additional appendage that is almost exclusively used in the context of delegation, namely the `authority` string. This string specifies which authentication system to use (Kerberos or NTLM) and provides additional information required by the security subsystem in question. Kerberos authentication requires a string of the following form:

```
Authority=kerberos:<domain>\<machinename>
```

Where `<domain>` is the name of your Windows 2000 domain in the full DNS form (for instance, `SEABREAM.COM`) and `<machinename>` is the host name part of the *Kerberos principal* of the machine to which you are trying to connect. In practice, this means the host name of the machine, in capital letters, suffixed by a dollar sign (for instance, `STYX$`). For the curious, Kerberos uses this information to ask the KDC for a "service ticket" giving access to the machine in question. The full moniker string needed to connect to a machine called STYX in a domain called SEABREAM.COM and allow that machine to impersonate using DCOM delegation and archive all the Event Logs looks like this:

```
WinMgmts:{impersonationLevel=delegate,
authority=kerberos:SEABREAM.COM\STYX$,
(Backup,Security,EnableDelegation)}!\\STYX
```

Wow! Armed with this information, we can finally fix the Event Log archiving script. All we need to do is replace the code that builds the moniker string so that it includes the relevant Kerberos incantations and use a UNC path in the parameter to `ClearEventLog()`. To run the script, ensure that the machines whose logs you want to archive are trusted for delegation, and that your own user account is trusted for delegation. Finally, in this script, notice that we have hard-coded the domain in a string constant; you will need to change this string to specify your own domain. The modified script is presented in full here:

```
'archivewithdelegation.vbs - make a backup and clear all Event Logs
'on a command-line specified computer. Back up to a command-line
'specified archive share. Optionally only back up if a cmd-line
'specified threshold has been reached
'This version actually works!!!
'Be sure to change MYDOMAIN to the Kerberos Realm of the machine
'you're trying to connect to!
Option Explicit
On Error Resume Next


Dim numThreshold
Dim strMachine
Dim strArchivePath
Dim strMoniker
Dim refWMI
Dim colEventLogs
Dim refEventLog
```

```
'change this to your own domain
Const MYDOMAIN="SEABREAM.COM"

'how many cmd-line args?
If WScript.Arguments.Count < 2 Then
    WScript.Echo _
        "Usage: archivelogs.vbs <machine> <archive_path> [threshold]"
    WScript.Quit
End If

If WScript.Arguments.Count = 2 Then
    numThreshold = 0
Else
    'ensure that third arg is numeric and set threshold
    numThreshold = CInt(WScript.Arguments(2))
    If Err <> 0 Then
        WScript.Echo "The third parameter must be in the range 0-100"
        WScript.Quit
    End If
End If

'save machine name and archive path
strMachine =  WScript.Arguments(0)
strArchivePath = WScript.Arguments(1)


'attempt to connect to WMI
'note the use of UCASE() to ensure that the machine name
'used for the Kerberos authority will be in capital letters
strMoniker = "winMgmts:{impersonationLevel=delegate," & _
             UCASE(strMachineName) & _
             "$,(Backup,Security,EnableDelegation)}!\\" & _
strMachine
Set refWMI = GetObject(strMoniker)
If Err <> 0 Then
    WScript.Echo "Could not connect to the WMI service."
    WScript.Quit
End If

'get a collection of Win32_NTEventLogFile objects
Set colEventLogs = refWMI.InstancesOf("Win32_NTEventLogFile")
If Err <> 0 Then
    WScript.Echo "Could not retrieve Event Log objects"
    WScript.Quit
End If

'iterate through each log
For Each refEventLog In colEventLogs
    'if shouldAct() returns non-zero attempt to back up
    If shouldAct(refEventLog.FileSize,refEventLog.MaxFileSize) <> 0 Then
        If refEventLog.clearEventLog( _
           makeFilename(refEventLogfileName)) = 0 Then
            WScript.Echo refEventLog.LogfileName & " archived successfully"
        Else
```

```
                WScript.Echo refEventLog.LogfileName & " could not be archived"
            End If
        Else
            WScript.Echo refEventLog.LogfileName & _
                           " has not exceeded the backup level"
        End If
    Next

    Set refEventLog = Nothing
    Set colEventLogs = Nothing
    Set refWMI = Nothing

    '--- end of script

    'shouldAct() calculates whether the backup and clear
    'should be performed  based on cursize, maxsize and
    'threshold. Returns 0 for "do not act", non-zero otherwise
    Function shouldAct(numCurSize, numMaxSize)
        If (numCurSize/numMaxSize)*100 > numThreshold Then
            shouldAct = 1
        Else
            shouldAct = 0
        End If
    End Function

    'makeFileName() generates a string that can be used as an
    'archive file name from the machine name, log name and date
    Function makeFileName(strLogname)
        makeFileName = strArchivePath & "\" & _
            strMachine & "-" & strLogname & "-" & _
            Year(Now) & Month(Now) & Day(Now) & ".evt"
    End Function
```

Of course, to make this script really useful, it needs to back up and clear Event Logs on a whole set of computers; we leave it as an exercise to the reader to adapt it to this task using one of the techniques discussed in Chapter 4.

Although the ability to perform housekeeping operations on remote Event Logs can often be useful, the ability to read the contents of the logs is arguably more so! You will probably not be surprised to discover, therefore, that WMI provides a representation not only of the Event Logs themselves but also of the individual records inside them. It is to this subject that we now turn.

Event Log Records in WMI

Each Event Log record is represented in WMI as an instance of the `Win32_NTLogEvent` class, which is not derived from any superclass. The primary key is defined by a combination of two properties: `Logfile`, whose value corresponds to the name of the log to which the event was written (for instance, Application, System, or Security); and RecordNumber, which uniquely identifies the record within this file. When a primary key consists of two or more properties, they can be specified in a moniker string as comma-separated values; a call to GetObject() whose purpose is to return the first record in the system log on the local machine would look like this:

```
Set refSingleEvent = GetObject( _
    "winmgmts:Win32_NTLogEvent.Logfile='application',RecordNumber='1'")
```

Win32_NTLogEvent does not define any methods, but has several properties, corresponding to the various components of an Event Log record, as described at the start of this chapter. We will not list all these properties here for two reasons: First, many of them are not particularly interesting except for very specific purposes; second, by the end of this chapter you will know a very quick way to work out what they are for yourself! Instead, we demonstrate a way in which Win32_NTLogEvent objects can be used to build a smart, Event Viewer–independent report of the contents of the Event Logs.

Generating a report containing a list of Event Log records with WMI is trivial. It merely requires writing a query capable of retrieving a collection of Win32_NTLogEvent objects representing a set of records that we want to know about, and displaying the contents of each in a human-readable format. In other words, there is nothing special about Win32_NTLogEvent objects; they can be retrieved and have their properties accessed just like anything else. This is illustrated in the following simple script, which retrieves a collection of all Win32_NTLogEvents representing error entries in the system Event Log, and uses WScript.Echo to display the record source and entry details.

The script uses two Win32_NTLogEvent properties in its query string: Logfile, which we have already discussed; and Type, which specifies the severity level (type) of the entry. Type is always one of error, warning, or information; in the security log, it can be audit success or audit failure. These two properties are enough to construct a query that will retrieve all events in the system log of type error. Having retrieved a collection of Win32_NTLogEvent objects, the script outputs the values of the SourceName and Message properties. As the name implies, SourceName represents the registered name of the application or operating system component that posted the event, whereas Message is the textual description of the event details. For the purposes of brevity, this script does not include any error-handling code:

```
'simplelogreport.vbs - lists the source and message of each
'error entry in the system log
Option Explicit
Dim refWMI
Dim strQuery
```

```
Dim colEvents
Dim refEvent

Set refWMI = GetObject(winMgmts:)
strQuery = SELECT * FROM Win32_NTLogEvent  &_
        "WHERE Logfile='System' and Type='error'
Set colEvents = refWMI.ExecQuery(strQuery)
For Each refEvent In colEvents
    WScript.Echo Event source:  & refEvent.SourceName
    WScript.Echo Event message:  & refEvent.Message
Next
Set colEvents = Nothing
Set refWMI = Nothing
```

This script, like most of the reporting type code that we have presented throughout the book, provides a quick and simple mechanism for producing a basic report. If the script is invoked with command-line redirection, the report can even be kept for posterity. For example, the following command-line invocation would run the script (assuming that it is saved as `simplelogreport.vbs`) and log its output to c:\temp\logfile.txt:

```
c:>simplelogreport.vbs > c:\temp\logfile.txt
```

Making a Smarter Report

The report that is generated may be functional, but is not very aesthetically pleasing; it is certainly not the kind of thing you would display proudly to your boss by way of explanation for the fact that you appear to have spent an entire day doing nothing but coding! There is an obvious way, however, to modify such a script so that it produces significantly smarter output: Make it write HTML and display the results in a browser. Creatively interspersing normal script output with calls to `WScript.Echo` that contain HTML tags can convert a lifeless, turgid list into a streamlined, impressive report. Unfortunately, there is one small downside: Littering your VBScript code with HTML tags can very quickly make it utterly unreadable, hard to debug, and extremely verbose. As a solution to this problem, we have written a small *Windows script component* called `SimpleReport` that hides all the HTML behind a clean programmatic interface.

A Windows script component is a self-contained class or series of classes that a script can call on to help it with a task. Just like the `FileSystemObject` that we have already discussed, using a Windows script components involves creating an object with the `CreateObject()` function and then calling properties and methods of the newly created object. The first step in using such a component is to install it on your computer. Copy the file WMIBook.wsc from the Component subdirectory of the accompanying CD-ROM into your %SystemRoot%\System32 directory. Then, using explorer, right-click the icon representing the newly installed component and click Register. After you have done this, the component is ready for use.

Our component contains only one class, whose registered name is WMIBook.SimpleReport. Objects of this class encapsulate an entire HTML report. A SimpleReport object can be created with a call to CreateObject(), such as this:

```
Set refSimpleReport = CreateObject("WMIBook.SimpleReport")
```

A SimpleReport has two properties: Title and Comment, both of which can be set as well as read. Title holds the text to be displayed in the <title> field of the HTML document; this value also displays as a level 1 header (<H1>) at the top of the report's <body>. Comment holds text to be displayed just below the title, such as a brief description of the report's contents.

Most of the functionality of SimpleReport lies in its four methods, namely AddEntry(), AddSection(), SaveAs(), and Browse().

AddEntry (*<index>*,*<short_description>*,*<long_description>*) adds an item into the report. *index* specifies a text string to be used as an index entry; SimpleReport uses this value to create a hyperlink-based index of all entries within the report. In a long report, it provides a quick way to find particular entries. *<Short_description>* specifies a text value to be used as the heading for each entry. *<Long_description>* is the full text of the entry.

- AddSection(*<Title>*) adds a new section to the report; in HTML terms, this means adding a horizontal rule and a new level 2 title. *<Title>* specifies the text for this title.
- SaveAs (*<filename>*) saves the full report as an HTML page. The parameter is, of course, the filename and path to which to save the report. It must be a fully qualified filename, as the component does *not* support relative paths. The SimpleReport uses the FileSystemObject internally to save the file; if a save attempt is not successful, the FileSystemObject raises an error that will propagate to the calling script. Such errors are not handled by SimpleReport itself.
- Browse (*<filename>*) is a convenience method. It saves the full report as an HTML page and then displays it in an Internet Explorer window. This method raises an error if Internet Explorer is not installed on your computer! Just as with the SaveAs() method, the filename must be a fully qualified path.

To make this clearer, we present a very short script that demonstrates how to use the SimpleReport component.

```
'simplereport.vbs - demonstrate use of WMIBook.SimpleReport
Option Explicit
Dim refReport
```

```
Set refReport = CreateObject("WMIBook.SimpleReport")

refReport.Title = "A sample report"
refReport.Comment = "This is an example of a report created " & _
                    "by the WMIBook.SimpleReport component"
refReport.AddSection "The first section"
refReport.AddEntry "Index item to first entry", _
                   "Title of first entry", _
                   "text of first entry. Blah, blah, blah"
refReport.AddEntry "Index item to second entry", _
                   "Title of second entry", _
                   "text of second entry. Blah, blah, blah"
refReport.browse "c:\myreport.html"
```

Figure 6.1 shows the result of running this script.

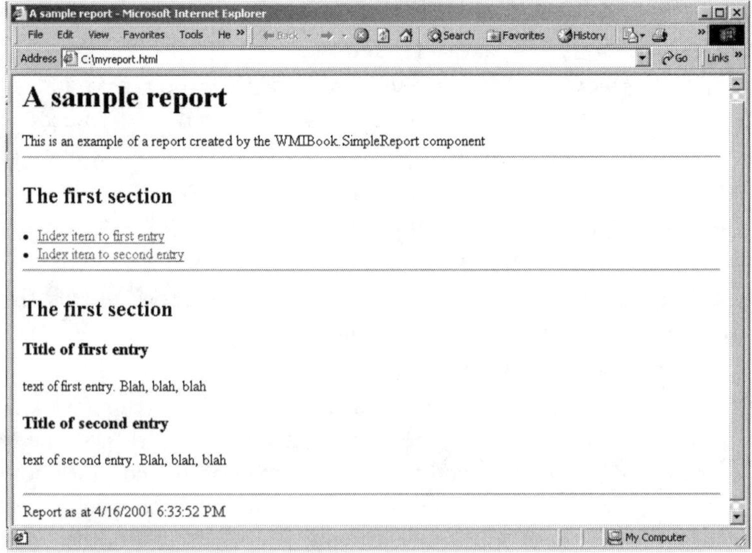

Figure 6.1 *Output from the* `SimpleReport` *component.*

Reporting *Win32_NTLogEvents* with *SimpleReport*

It should be clear by now that using the `SimpleReport` component is utterly trivial. Crucially for present concerns, it also allows us to harness the power of WMI to compile a report that lets us browse the contents of Event Logs offline, without the Event Viewer. This is demonstrated in the final script of this section, which uses the component to provide a listing of error events on a set of machines. The script requires two parameters: a filename to which the report will be saved, and the name of a machine whose logs are to be scrutinized. Any further parameters are interpreted as the names of other machines whose logs should be included in the report.

After checking for the required command-line parameters, the script creates a `SimpleReport` object and sets an appropriate title and comment. VBScript's built-in function `Now()` is used to record the date and time that the script is run. For each machine, a new section is added to the report (with the `addSection()` method), and a WQL query is used to retrieve a set of `Win32_NTLogEvent` objects whose type is `error`. Then, for each object, a report entry is created (using the `addEntry()` method) according to the following procedure:

1. The *`index`* is set to be the first 75 characters of the event record's `Message` property.
2. The *`short_description`* is set to be a concatenation of the event's `Logfile` and `SourceName` properties, both of which we have already discussed, and the time that the event was written to the log, which is stored in a `TimeWritten` property. We use the `GetVBScript()` function introduced in Chapter 3 to convert the WMI date stored in `TimeWritten` to a `VBDate`.
3. The *`long_description`* is set to the full text of the `Win32_NTLogEvent` object's `Message` property.

After all events have been reported on all the specified machines, the file is saved and displayed (using `SimpleReport`'s `Browse()` method). Here, then, is the script itself:

```
'coollogreport.vbs - create an HTML report of all Error events
'logged in the event logs on a set of computers
Option Explicit
On Error Resume Next

Dim strReportFile
Dim refReport
Dim colEvents
Dim refEntry
Dim refWMI
Dim strQuery
Dim i

'check cmd-line args
If WScript.Arguments.Count < 2 Then
    WScript.Echo "Usage: coollogreport.vbs <reportfile> " _
             & "<machine1> [machine2 machine3 etc.]"
    WScript.Quit
End If
strReportFile = WScript.Arguments(0)
```

```
'create and initialise a SimpleReport object
Set refReport = CreateObject("WMIBook.SimpleReport")
refReport.Title = "Report of 'Error' entries in the NT Event Logs"
refReport.Comment = "This report contains a list of 'Error' " & _
    "entries that appear in the NT Event Logs on a set of " & _
    "important machines on the network, as at " & Now()

strQuery = "SELECT * FROM Win32_NTLogEvent WHERE Type='Error'"

'loop through each machine in turn
For i = 1 to WScript.Arguments.Count -1
    'add a report section for the machine
    refReport.addSection "Machine: " & WScript.Arguments(i)
    'try to connect to WMI
    Set refWMI = GetObject("winMgmts:{(security)}!\\" & _
             WScript.arguments(i) & ":")
    If Err <> 0 Then
        refReport.addEntry "Connection Failure", _
                     "Unable to connect to WMI",""
    Else
        Set colEvents = refWMI.ExecQuery(strQuery)
        For Each refEntry In colEvents
            'add an index consisting of the first 75 chars of message
            'a title of Logfile - Source and then the full entry
            refReport.addEntry Left(refEntry.Message,75), _
                refEntry.Logfile & " - " & refEntry.SourceName & _
                "[" & GetVBDate(refEntry.TimeWritten) & "]", _
                refEntry.Message
        Next
    End If
Next

'save and display results
refReport.browse strReportFile
Set colEvents = Nothing
Set refWMI = Nothing
Set refReport = Nothing

'--- end of script

'turn a WMI date into a VBDate
Function GetVBDate(wd)
        GetVBDate = DateSerial(Left(wd,4),Mid(wd,5,2),Mid(wd,7,2)) _
        + TimeSerial(Mid(wd,9,2),Mid(wd,11,2),Mid(wd,13,2))
End Function
```

A section of a report produced by this script is presented in Figure 6.2; the displayed section shows the tail end of the index and a few Event Log entries for the machine on our network, whose IP address is 192.168.16.27.

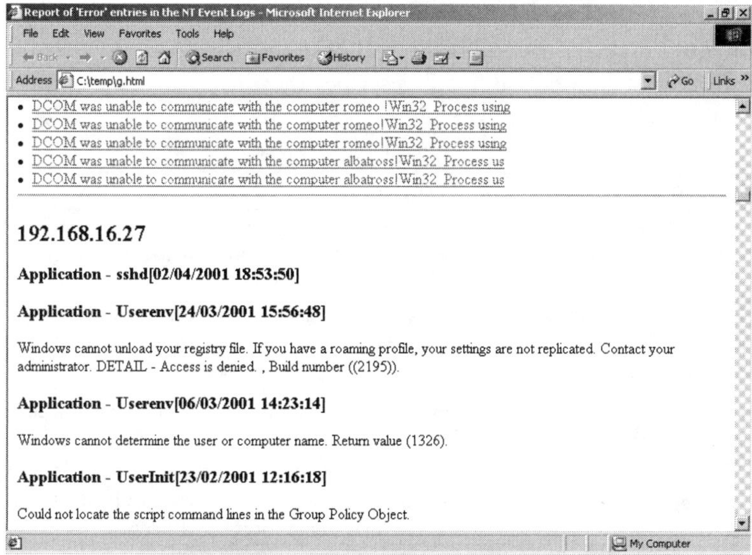

Figure 6.2 *Sample output from coollogreport.vbs.*

Of course the preceding script will not be appropriate for all Event Log reporting purposes, and there is a virtually unlimited number of ways in which it could usefully be modified; all that it takes is a need and some imagination! We leave this task as an exercise for the reader. To whet your appetite, however, we list three possibilities, in increasing order of interest:

- For a large number of machines, the command-line-specified list of names is impractical; change the code so that it reads a list of machine names from a file or so that it sweeps an IP address range.
- For any given purpose, you might not be interested in *all* the logs, but only one of them; you might really only be interested in log entries originating from a particular source. Add command-line options to control which logs, event types, and sources should appear in the report.
- The Event Logs, particularly those of servers, can store a vast amount of information in a large production environment. Much of this information could be useful in all sorts of ways with a good enough reporting tool. The power of any reporting tool lies in the flexibility of its searches, so write some alternative WQL queries for the code. For this you will probably want to know about all of `Win32_NTLogEvent`'s properties; the final section of this chapter explains how to find out.

Before we leave Event Logs entirely, there is one final point worthy of note that could make your modified script even more exciting: `Win32_NTLogEvents` has three associators. Table 6.2 describes these.

Table 6.2 Associators of Win32_NTLogEvent

Associator	Description
`Win32_NTLogEventLog`	Associates a `Win32_NTLogEvent` (referenced in a Record property) with a `Win32_NTEventLogFile` (in a Log property).
`Win32_NTLogEventComputer`	Associates a `Win32_NTLogEvent` (referenced in a Record property) with a `Win32_Computer` (referenced in a Computer property).
`Win32_NTLogEventUser`	Associates a `Win32_NTLogEvent` (referenced in a `Record` property) with a `Win32_User` (referenced in a User property). This associator is normally of relevance only to events in the application log that are evoked by the actions of a user.

We wish you happy reporting!

Reporting with the Windows Installer

The previous discussion has hopefully convinced you that in conjunction with a bit of HTML and some imagination, the wealth of information made available through WMI objects constitutes a powerful, flexible reporting tool. Our discussion focused on Event Logs because examination of their contents are of clear interest to any conscientious administrator. One of the very best features of WMI, however, is that it offers a consistent interface to a massively diverse range of subsystems and components; therefore it goes without saying that the suggestions we have made for producing well-formatted, human-readable output from Event Logs are equally applicable to anything else modeled within WMI. As an example, we now turn briefly to the Windows Installer service, and illustrate how the `SimpleReport` class introduced earlier can be used to report on the software products installed on a Windows 2000 computer.

The Windows Installer service is the first serious attempt by Microsoft to provide a consistent package management system for their platforms. It offers, among other things, a centralized database of packages that keeps tabs on their installation state, dependencies, and usage, a mechanism for rolling back failed installations, and for installing parts of packages on-demand if a user tries to do something that requires a component that has not been installed. A WMI interface to the array of facilities that the Installer offers is provided, unsurprisingly, by the Windows Installer

Provider; this provider defines a zoo of classes to represent products, features, installations, and much more besides. These classes allow two types of interaction with the Installer:

- They provide a mechanism for finding out about any software whose details are stored in the Installation service's database.
- They provide a mechanism for manipulating packages: There are methods for performing installations, configuring existing ones, and even removing an application from a machine.

The Windows Installer is sophisticated enough to warrant an entire book of its own, but fortunately, the WMI interface has been designed to make basic interaction extremely simple. In the next chapter, we show how WMI can be used to manage installation and maintenance of software. In this chapter, we merely dip our toes into the water and create a simple report of the software currently installed on a machine.

Product Representation Within WMI

As far as the Windows Installer is concerned, software is organized in a three-tier hierarchy: Products contain one or more software features; these features, in their turn, consist of one or more elements (see Figure 6.3)

Products sit at the top of the hierarchy. They represent complete, packaged applications or systems, such as Microsoft Office 2000 Professional. Within WMI, products are represented by instances of `Win32_Product`, a subclass of the `CIM_Product` class. Its primary key is a combination of three properties: a `Name`, a `Version`, and an `IdentifyingNumber`. All these properties are inherited from `CIM_Product`.

At the next level down in the hierarchy sit software features, represented in WMI by instances of `Win32_SoftwareFeature`, a class derived from `CIM_LogicalElement` and thence `CIM_ManagedSystemElement`. A feature is related to its parent product through a `Win32_ProductSoftwareFeatures` associator, a subclass of `CIM_Dependency`. Its primary key consists of four properties: a `Name`, a `Version`, an `IdentifyingNumber`, and a `ProductName`. This final property, as the name suggests, contains the name of the `Win32_Product` of which the feature is a part. Software features are meant to encapsulate components of a product that may be installed independently. In the case of Microsoft Office 2000 Professional, components such as Excel, Word, and Access are all features; so too are the Spell Checker, Thesaurus, and Export Filters. It might seem perverse that an entire application, such as Word, is placed in the same category as, say, a Spell Checker, but in the world of Windows Installer, both are independently installable components and so both are software features. The apparent problem of treating a fully blown word processor and a spell checker equally is solved by another feature of the Windows Installer, namely the capability to have hierarchies of features. In addition to being associated with a product, every feature also can be associated with parent features; in WMI, this association is represented by a `Win32_SoftwareFeatureParent` associator, a subclass of `CIM_Dependency`.

At the bottom of the hierarchy sit software elements, the individual sets of files that make up a feature. An element contains a set of files, folders, Registry entries, and the like that are always installed or removed atomically; in other words, they are the smallest unit that the Windows Installer is prepared to install on or remove from a system. Typically, the end user or system administrator never sees the elements of her software features individually; they are more important for the software developers, when working out dependencies. A single software element might be shared among many features or even many products. This is important, for example, in the case of shared libraries. Within WMI, elements are represented by instances of the `Win32_SoftwareElement` class. This class is not discussed further here.

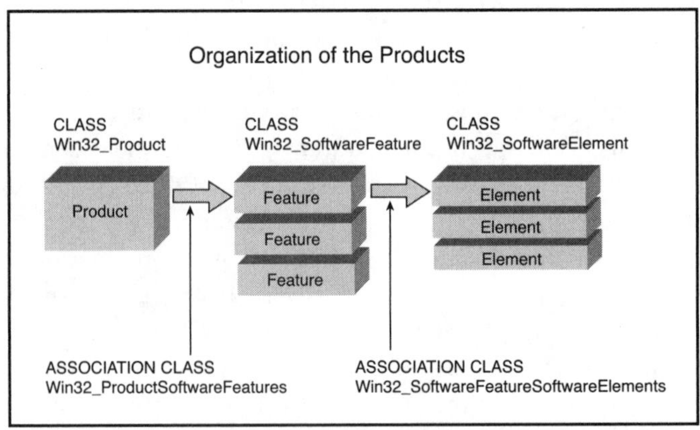

Figure 6.3 *Organization of products.*

Armed with this knowledge, we can now produce a basic script that will provide a report of installed applications on the local machine. The script uses an `InstancesOf()` call to request a collection of all `Win32_Product` objects; it then builds a report that displays the key properties and a description, a property that, as the name implies, provides a textual description of the product. The report is saved to c:\temp\mysoftware.html; and if c:\temp doesn't exist, an error is raised. This behavior could, of course, be changed trivially. The full code listing is presented here:

```
'productreport.vbs - create a simple report listing all products
'installed on a machine under the control of the Windows Installer
Option Explicit
On Error Resume Next
```

```
Dim refReport
Dim refWMI
Dim colInstProducts
Dim refProduct

'Initialize report
Set refReport = CreateObject("WMIBook.SimpleReport")
refReport.title = "Software on my computer"
refReport.comment = "This report lists all the software " & _
    "products installed on my computer under the control " & _
    "of the Windows Installer"

'connect to WMI and retrieve collection of Win32_Products
Set refWMI = GetObject("winmgmts:")
If Err <> 0 Then
    WScript.Echo "Could not connect to WMI"
    WScript.Quit
End If
Set colInstProducts = refWMI.InstancesOf("Win32_Product")

'Loop through Products adding report entries
For Each refProduct in colInstProducts
    refReport.addEntry refProduct.Name, _
            refProduct.Name, _
            "Version: " & refProduct.Version & "<br>" & _
            "IndentifyingNumber: " & refProduct.IdentifyingNumber & _
            "<br>" & "Description: " & refProduct.Description
Next

refReport.browse("c:\temp\mysoftware.html")

Set ColInstProducts = Nothing
Set refWMI = Nothing
Set refReport = Nothing
```

Note that for the *`long_description`* parameter of `SimpleReport`'s `addEntry()` method, we concatenate each of the properties we would like to include in a single string. To improve readability of the final report, we include an HTML `<BR>` tag between each; in HTML parlance, this inserts a line break.

It would, of course, be possible to improve this script by making it run on multiple machines and produce a listing of the installed product base across a network. The `SimpleReport` `addSection()` method could be used to provide a new section of the report for each machine; we leave you to write this modification.

Note: Limitations of Windows Installer Information

Only applications installed using the Windows Installer will be registered in the Installer database. While Microsoft is plugging the technology very hard, a large number of applications are still shipping with alternative installation systems. Such applications will not be accessible for reporting through the Installer Provider. ◆

Ideally, a report of an installed software base should list not only the products but also the features of those products. We can accomplish with a relatively simple alteration to our script: Instead of merely reporting the keys and Description property of each product, we also can report on each of its features by querying WMI for instances of the Win32_SoftwareProductFeatures associator. One way to achieve this would be to construct an ASSOCIATORS OF query for each product, using the Win32_Product primary keys to construct each query string. Such a query specified literally for Microsoft Office would look something like this:

```
ASSOCIATORS OF {Win32_Product.Name='MicrosoftOffice 2000
Premium,Version='9.00.2720',IdentifyingNumber="{00000409-78E1-11D2-B60F-
006097C998E7}"} WHERE AssocClass=Win32_SoftwareProductFeatures
```

Thanks to one of the elements of the primary key being IdentifyingNumber, the query looks particularly cumbersome. To make matters even worse, a peculiarity in the WQL parsing implementation means that a string containing braces ({}) within an ASSOCIATORS OF query has to be enclosed within double quotation marks rather than apostrophes. As you may remember from Chapter 2, "Using VBScript," a string within a string in VBScript is *escaped* with yet more quotation marks; the combination would reduce readability to approximately zero! Luckily, there is no need actually to specify all this in our script; we just build the string using the relevant properties of the Win32_Product object to which we already have a reference.

In fact, there is an even easier and neater alternative. Given that in our script we already have a reference to each Win32_Product that we care about, there is no need to specify it in a query; instead, we can use SWbemObject's Associators_() method that was discussed in Chapter 3. As a brief reminder, look at the following VBScript fragment. Assuming that refProduct is a valid reference to a Win32_Product object, this code will retrieve a collection of all Win32_SoftwareFeatures associated with that product:

```
Set colFeatures = refProduct.Associators_( _
                            "Win32_ProductSoftwareFeatures")
```

We are sure you will agree that this is far more concise and comprehensive than the equivalent ASSOCIATORS OF query! Having retrieved a set of Win32_SoftwareFeatures for each of the Win32_Products on our system, we can include the name and description of each in the report.

Before we can present a modified script that includes this data, note one final caveat: The Windows Installer database knows about *all* the features of a product, whether or not they are actually installed. The reason for this, of course, is so that once a product is installed, users can perform a *maintenance installation*, selecting additional features that they have chosen not to install originally. For our report, we want to know only about the features actually installed on each machine. The solution lies in the `InstallState` property of `Win32_SoftwareFeature` objects, which holds a numeric value representing the installation state of a feature. Table 6.3 lists possible values.

Table 6.3 Interpretation of InstallState *Value*

Value	Meaning
1	The feature is advertised as being available for on-demand installation but is not installed.
2	The feature is not installed.
3	The feature is installed locally.
4	The feature is installed, but is run remotely over the network from a CD-ROM source.
-1	The feature is unknown.
-2	An invalid argument has been passed to the installation function.
-6	The configuration is corrupt.

The three negative values seem rather odd; that is because they reflect states that a feature can be in during an installation process; the four positive values should be self-explanatory.

For our script, we list features whose `InstallState` has a value of `3`, meaning that they are installed locally. You may, of course, want to modify this to suit your own reporting needs.

Finally, we are ready to write our fully fledged reporting script designed to compile a report on the software installed on computers across a network. The script takes two command-line parameters: the name of a file to which the HTML report should be written, and the name of an input file containing the names or IP addresses of each machine whose software database is to be interrogated. This second file should contain one machine name or IP address per line, as described in Chapter 4. For each machine, the script retrieves a list of `Win32_Product` objects, uses the `Associators_()` method to retrieve a list of `Win32_SoftwareFeatures` for each product, and compiles a report entry for each features whose `InstallState` is `3`. If an error occurs while the script tries to connect to WMI on any machine, the error is reported with `WScript.Echo` and nothing is written to the report for that machine.

Before presented the code listing, we leave you with one word of warning: Running this script can take a *very* long time; the list of features for Microsoft Office 2000 Professional runs into hundreds of items!

```
'featurereport.vbs - create a report listing all products and
'features installed on a set of workstations whose names or
'IPs are specified in a file
Option Explicit
On Error Resume Next

Dim strReportFile
Dim strMachineFile
Dim strMachineName
Dim refFSO
Dim refMachineFile
Dim refReport
Dim refWMI
Dim colInstProducts
Dim refProduct
Dim colFeatures
Dim refFeature
Dim strFullDescription

'check cmd-line args for sanity and attempt to
'open input file
If WScript.Arguments.Count <> 2 Then
    WScript.Echo "Usage: featurereport.vbs <reportfilename> " & _
                 " <machinefilename>"
    WScript.Quit
End If
strReportFile = WScript.Arguments(0)
strMachineFile = WScript.Arguments(1)

'attempt to open machine file
Set refFSO = CreateObject("Scripting.FilesystemObject")
Set refMachineFile = refFSO.OpenTextFile(strMachineFile)
If Err <> 0 Then
     WScript.Echo "Sorry. Could not open machine file"
     WScript.Quit
End If

'Initialize report
Set refReport = CreateObject("WMIBook.SimpleReport")
refReport.title = "Software on my computer"
refReport.comment = "This report lists all the software " & _
    "products installed on my computer under the control " & _
    "of the Windows Installer"

'loop through each machine
While Not refMachineFile.AtEndOfStream
    'connect to WMI and retrieve collection of Win32_Products
    strMachineName = refMachineFile.readLine()
    Set refWMI = GetObject("winmgmts:\\" & strMachineName & ":")
    If Err <> 0 Then
        WScript.Echo "Could not connect to WMI on " & _
                     strMachineName
    Else
```

```
            'add new report section and report progress with WScript.Echo
            refReport.addSection(strMachineName)
            WScript.Echo "Getting data from " & strMachineName
            'Loop through Products
            Set colInstProducts = refWMI.InstancesOf("Win32_Product")
            For Each refProduct in colInstProducts
                'build product part of full_description for report
                strFullDescription = _
                  "Product version: " & refProduct.Version &  _
                  "<br> IndentifyingNumber: " & _
                  refProduct.IdentifyingNumber & _
                  "<br>Description: " & refProduct.Description & _
                  "<br>" & "Installed features: <br>"

                'now loop through features, appending Description
                'and version of all which are installed locally
                Set colFeatures = refProduct.Associators_( _
                                 "Win32_ProductSoftwareFeatures")
                For Each refFeature In colFeatures
                    If refFeature.InstallState = 3 Then
                        strFullDescription = strFullDescription & _
                            refFeature.Description & " (" & _
                                   refFeature.Version & _
                            "), "
                    End If
                Next
                'now add the report entry for this product on this machine
                refReport.addEntry refProduct.Name, _
                        refProduct.Name, strFullDescription
            Next
        End If
    Wend

    'finally, write and display report
    refReport.Browse(strReportFile)

    Set colFeatures = Nothing
    Set ColInstProducts = Nothing
    Set refWMI = Nothing
    Set refReport = Nothing
    Set refMachineFile = Nothing
    Set refFSO = Nothing
```

Notice that we have reported the `Description` and `Version` properties of `Win32_SoftwareFeature` objects but not the `Name`. The reason for this is that the `Name` property, although important to the Windows Installer internally, is not particularly human-friendly; a `Description` and `Version` are enough uniquely to identify each feature, so we report those instead. You are, of course, at liberty to change this to suit your own reporting needs.

The WMI Object Browser

As noted at the very start of this chapter, the reporting techniques discussed earlier do not apply only to Event Logs and the Windows Installer but to *any* system represented within WMI. Creative use of WQL queries, nested sets of collections, and a bit of string concatenation can produce any number of reports. All that is needed is knowledge of the WMI objects available on a system, their properties, their methods, and the associators that join them together. In this, the final section of the chapter, we introduce a tool that you can use to discover exactly what WMI objects are available on a system, and how they are related to each other. This tool is the WMI Object Browser.

The Object Browser is an ActiveX control, a COM component with a graphical interface, provided as part of the WMI Software Development Kit. It can be displayed in any graphical environment that can act as a COM *container*, such as Internet Explorer, and its purpose, as the name implies, is to provide a graphical representation of WMI objects and their connections. Objects are represented as nodes in a tree-like structure; nodes are connected together through associations. Therefore, the WMI Object Browser can be used to navigate through the components available to the WMI service on the machine to which it is connected by following the web of associations through which the objects are joined. There is nothing magical about the program's behavior; behind the scenes, all it is doing is using the WMI service to execute queries, retrieve collections, read object properties, and execute their methods.

Installing the Object Browser

The Object Browser is currently available only as part of the WMI SDK. You can download this freely from Microsoft's MSDN site at `http://msdn.microsoft.com/downloads/sdks/wmi`. This SDK contains a number of tools, and the WMI documentation, which is in itself an essential tool for anyone keen on taking WMI seriously. Installation follows the same pattern as all modern Microsoft software: It uses the Windows Installer, so we will not to go into the details here. The only advice we will give is that you must ensure that the WMI Tools feature is selected for installation, otherwise the Object Browser will not be installed. When installation is complete, an icon for the tool appears in the Start menu under Microsoft Platform SDK/WMI/Object Browser.

Using the Object Browser

As soon as you launch the Object Browser, you will encounter a dialog box prompting you to enter the path of a namespace to which the browser should connect. By default, \root\CIMV2 is suggested. If you are using the browser to investigate WMI on your own workstation, this default is almost certainly the namespace that you want. If you want to connect to WMI on a remote machine, merely specify this as part of the namespace path—that is, `\\to-the-wall\root\CIMV2`. After you have clicked away this dialog box, a second appears, this one dealing with security (see Figure 6.4). By default, it suggests attempting to log on to WMI with the current user's credentials; this is the only acceptable option if you have chosen to connect to the local WMI service. If you have chosen to connect to a remote namespace, however, you have the option of changing the logon credentials. In addition, this dialog box allows you to select DCOM impersonation and authentication levels for a session. A tick box enables all privileges, a convenient shorthand for setting all the NT security privileges. Remember that behind the scenes, the Object Browser relies on the WMI service for all of its functionality. Therefore, all the security issues that apply when connecting to WMI through VBScript apply equally when using the Object Browser. Refer to Chapter 5 for a discussion of what the various options actually mean.

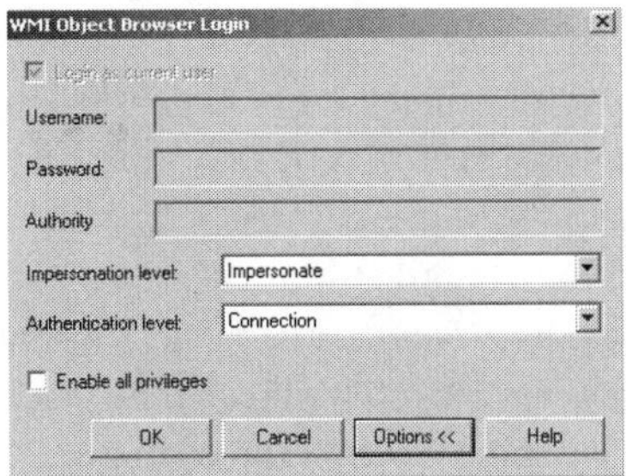

Figure 6.4 *WMI Object Browser Logon dialog box.*

Finally, having decided on the security settings and clicking OK, assuming logon succeeds, the main Browser window appears (see Figure 6.5). The main window has two distinct parts: on the left is the navigation pane, while on the right is the Object Viewer, a pane showing details of the currently selected object.

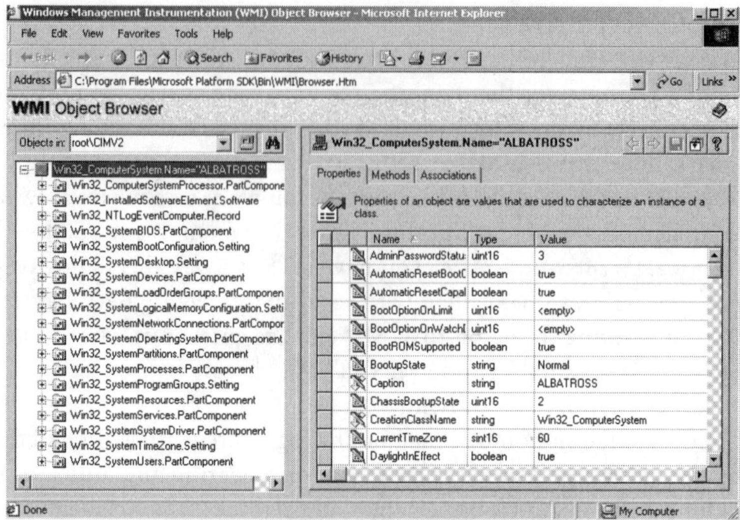

Figure 6.5 *WMI Object Browser main window.*

Understanding the Navigation Pane

On startup, the navigation pane reveals only one item, labeled `Win32_ComputerSystem`. This represents a `Win32_ComputerSystem` object, whose properties contain basic information about the computer system that it represents. Every computer has a single instance of `Win32_ComputerSystem`. The entire list of `Win32_ComputerSystem` properties are displayed in the Object Viewer on the right as, if you are currently looking at either the browser or Figure 6.5, you could hardly fail to notice! For now we are not interested in any of these properties, however. Instead, we will make one single observation about the `Win32_ComputerSystem` object that has extremely important ramifications for the working of the Object Browser: *Almost any WMI object representing any component of a computer system is associated with a* `Win32_ComputerSystem` *either directly or indirectly*. In other words, by tracing the associators of `Win32_ComputerSystem`, you can reach almost every WMI object available on a system. This process of tracking associators is exactly what the navigation pane of the WMI Object Browser does when you traverse down a tree.

The navigation pane's interface is immediately recognizable as an Explorer clone and operates as you might expect, so we will not dwell on navigation details. As you would expect, the plus sign (+) is used to expand a node, and double-clicking an item triggers its representation to appear in the Object Viewer. By contrast, the meaning of the various icons that appear as nodes in the tree view is not so obvious. Table 6.4 explains these icons.

Table 6.4 Icon Explanations

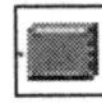	This type of node represents an actual instance of a WMI object. The label accompanying the icon shows the name of the class and the key property, in standard object path format. If such an object is selected, the Object Viewer pane displays a list of the object's properties and their values (see Figure 6.5)
	These nodes appear below an object node in the tree. They represent the set of all association classes that involve objects of the class represented by the parent node. Expanding the node represented by `Win32_ComputerSystem`, for example, reveals 19 association nodes, representing each of the associator classes that reference `Win32_ComputerSystem` objects in one of their properties. Double-clicking an association node sparks a WQL `ASSOCIATORS OF` query that retrieves all objects associated with the parent node through an associator of this type. For example, double-clicking the associator node under a `Win32_Computer` system that represents the `Win32_InstalledSoftwareElement` associator class sparks a query to retrieve all `Win32_SoftwareElement` objects associated through `Win32_InstalledSoftwareElement` associators with the `Win32_ComputerSystem` in question. A list of these objects and a summary of their property values displays in a table in the Object Viewer. We do not advise performing this particular query, however, because its execution could take several hours to complete; the average computer system will contain thousands of software elements. The text string accompanying icons of this type specify the name of the associator class and the role being played by the child nodes. We can use these names to work out, for example, that children of the `Win32_InstalledSoftwareElement.Softwarenode` will be software elements and not computer systems! Expanding associator nodes performs exactly the same query, and reveals a list of object and group nodes, which are described further in the next paragraph.

continues ▸

Table 6.4 continued

	Nodes of this type are group nodes. They do not represent WMI objects as such, but assist in the visual grouping of components within the navigation pane. Appearing below association nodes, these encapsulate all objects that are instances of the same class. This is best explained by example: Expanding the `Win32_SystemDevices` associator will reveal, among other things, an object node representing a `Win32_Keyboard` object. (There is, presumably, only one keyboard on your system.) It also will reveal a group node labeled `Win32_SerialPort`; expanding this node will produce a list of serial ports on the system. Because most computers have more than one serial port, objects representing each one are grouped under the umbrella of a single group node.

Note: Caching Results

The first time an association or group entry in the navigation pane is used to trigger a WQL query, the results appear to be cached. Although this might increase the speed of future expansions, it has an unfortunate side-effect: If a new object is created or one is deleted in the underlying CIM Repository, future attempts to expand a branch can produce erroneous results. A classic example of this unfortunate behavior can be seen by expanding the `Win32_SystemProcesses` *association node under* `Win32_ComputerSystem`*: Expand this node, close it, open a copy of Notepad, and expand the node again. The new process will not display. Oops!* ◆

Casual Browsing

The Object Browser is an excellent tool for, well, browsing! Using the tool is a bit like window shopping. We can use it to wander whimsically through WMI, expanding nodes, sparking associators, meeting objects, and seeing how they relate. The usefulness of this facility should not be underestimated: Investigating WMI in this way is possibly the very best way of getting a feel for WMI and fostering ideas for scripts. As an example, how about taking the following journey: Look down the list of `Win32_ComputerSystem` associators and one of the first ones you will stumble across is the association `Win32_NTLogEventComputer.Record`. Expand the entry to reveal a group node named `Win32_NTLogEvent`, expand this in turn, and you'll see a list of objects, all of which are of the class `Win32_NTLogEvent`. In other words, we have just found the WMI representation of the Event Logs. Choose one of them at random, say, the one whose name is `Application`.

Expand it to reveal yet more associations and then, suddenly, a group of `Win32_NTLogEntry` objects (see Figure 6.6). We have discovered the WMI representation of Event Logs almost by accident, using nothing more than the navigation pane of the WMI Object Browser. We haven't even used the Object Viewer yet!

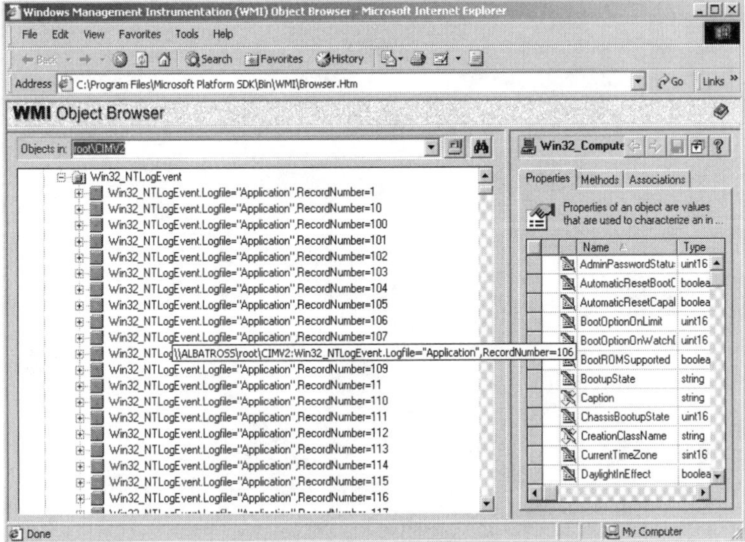

Figure 6.6 *A group of* `Win32_NTLogEntry` *objects.*

Resetting the Browse Root

If you are interested only in a small part of WMI object space, it is possible to reroot the tree so that it starts from a specified point. One way to do this is to right-click a node object and select Make Root from the context-sensitive menu. Alternatively, navigation can be avoided altogether by using the Browse for Instances feature.

This feature is launched from a button located at the upper-right corner of the navigation pane. It has an icon depicting a pair of binoculars. Launching the feature displays the Browse for Instances dialog box (see Figure 6.7), whose main feature is a pair of lists. By default, the left side presents a list of all available classes that can have instances. A combination of radio button gives the option of modifying the contents to display all classes regardless of whether they have instances; a check box specifies whether association classes should be included. On the right is another list that is initially empty. However, you can add items to it by selecting them on the left and clicking the Add button. Unsurprisingly, the Remove button removes a selected entry from the list on the right.

Clicking OK queries WMI for all instances of the classes listed in the rightmost column, and displays them as a list in another dialog box. Double-clicking an entry in this list sets that object as the new root of the Object Browser's navigation tree.

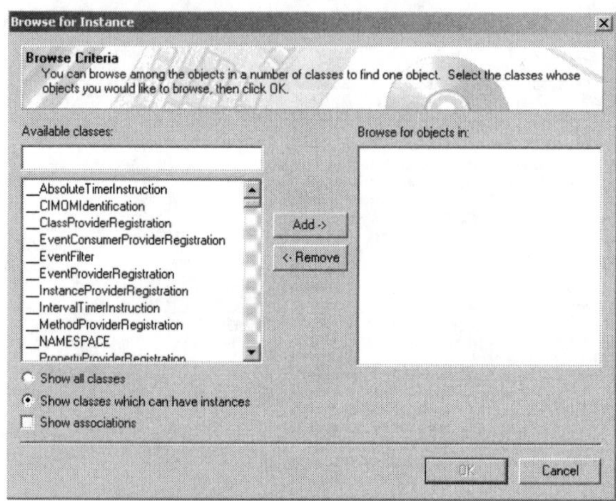

Figure 6.7 *Browse for instances.*

To reset the root back to `Win32_ComputerSystem`, just use Browse for Instances and select the `Win32_ComputerSystem` class. Alternatively, Internet Explorer's refresh action (F5 key) automatically restarts the WMI Object Browser.

Note: Permanently Changing the Tree Root

If you constantly find yourself rerooting the tree to a specific object, it is possible to change the default so that instead of pointing to `Win32_ComputerSystem`*, the Object Browser starts off rooted at your chosen point. This can be accomplished by right-clicking the object node that you want to set as the default tree root and selecting Make Initial Tree Root from the context-sensitive menu.* ◆

The Object Viewer Property Pages

The right pane of the Object Browser is where detailed information about the selected object, group, or association is displayed. This is referred to as the Object Viewer pane. As noted previously, the Object Viewer display for group and association nodes is merely a list of instances with a tabular listing of their properties. The real utility of the Object Viewer is to allow graphical interaction with the properties, methods, and associators of the WMI objects. This facility is activated when an object node is selected in the navigation pane.

Objects are depicted in the Object Viewer pane by three property pages. One pane presents the object's properties and their values, one presents its methods and allows their execution, and one shows a graphical representation of its associations.

In many ways, the most interesting of the three property pages is the one that displays a detailed analysis of a WMI object's properties. This is displayed by default when an object is first selected. For each property, it lists a name, type, and value. It also provides a number of symbols that specify whether the property is inherited, writeable, a system property, or part of the object's primary key. Table 6.5 lists the meanings of these.

Table 6.5 Object Properties

	This property is part of the object's primary key.
	This property is local to the object's class; in other words, it has not been inherited from a superclass.
	This property is declared to be writeable. A writeable property can have its value changed as well as read. It should be noted, however, that a value declared to be writeable in the CIM Schema is not necessarily actually writeable; the actual behavior on attempted write is dependent on the provider responsible for the object (see Chapter 7, "System Configuration").
	The definition of this property has been inherited from a superclass.
	This is a system property.

Figure 6.8 shows a typical view in this Property pane. Note that array properties do not have their values displayed directly. Instead, you can click the button to be presented with a dialog box containing a list of the elements of the array.

The Method pane displays a list of methods associated with the selected object. Figure 6.9 shows an example. It lists all of an object's methods and, just like the Property pane, denotes an inherited method with a yellow arrow symbol. An interesting feature of this pane is that it actually lets you execute methods! We have yet to find a serious use for this facility, but if you want to avail yourself of its services, you can. Right-click the method name and select the Execute option from the context-sensitive menu. A dialog box will then display, in a tabular form, a list of parameters expected by the method. Fill in the value (or values if there is more than one) and click the Execute Method button found at the lower right of the dialog box. The method will then execute and display the return value, if one is specified, in the text box found at the bottom of the dialog box.

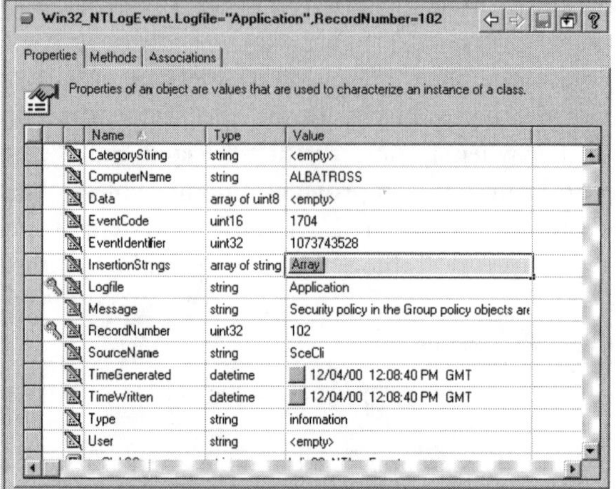

Figure 6.8 *Object Viewer Property pane.*

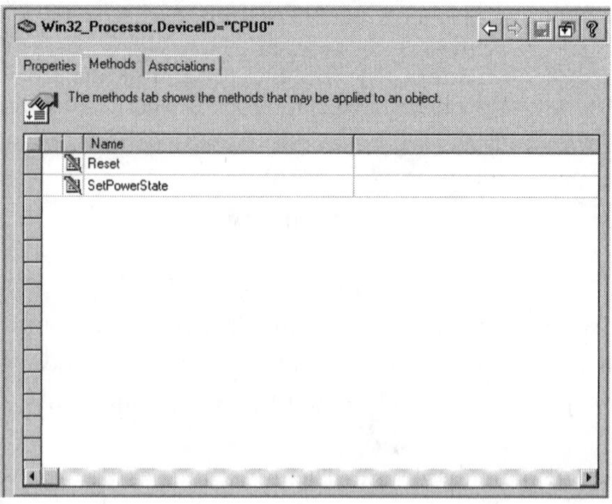

Figure 6.9 *Object Viewer Method pane.*

Note: WMI Qualifiers

If you have tried to execute a method, you have probably noticed that the context-sensitive menu presents a couple of other interesting options, offering to present Method Qualifiers and Object Qualifiers. Qualifiers are discussed in Chapter 11, "WMI Internals." For the moment, however, it is worth noting that the Method Qualifier dialog box contains one extremely useful bit of information: It lists the privileges required to execute the method. You might want to check this privilege list before you write your scripts! ◆

This final pane is a graphical display of the associations between the selected object and any associated objects (see Figure 6.10). This pane does not provide any information that cannot be gleaned just as easily from the navigation pane; the main difference is that the display it produces gives a slightly clearer view of the associations between objects. The pane can be used as a navigation tool in its own right; right-clicking any of the objects represented produces a context-sensitive menu offering the facility either to look at that object's properties, or make it the root object for navigation.

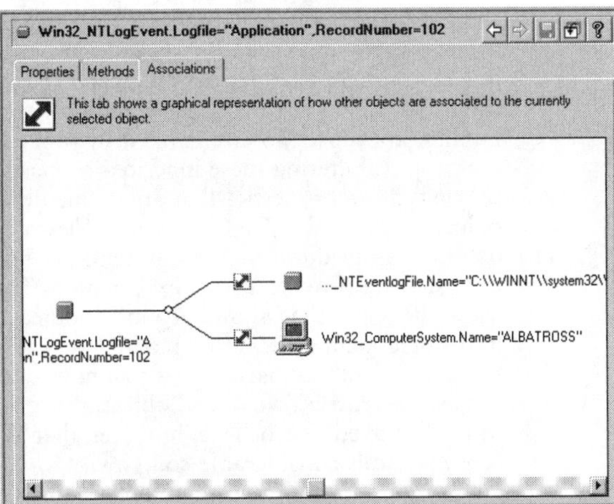

Figure 6.10 *Object Viewer Property pane.*

Above the Property, Method, and Association panes in the Object Viewer sits a set of five buttons that mediate the behavior of the Object Viewer. Table 6.6 describes these.

Table 6.6 Object Viewer Buttons

	This is the Help option. Contrary to what might be expected, it does not provide information about how to use the Object Browser itself. (This facility is provided by the book icon that sits on the title bar.) Instead, it provides help on the currently presented object. That is, it displays a list of all the properties and methods for the chosen object, giving a short explanation of each. Unfortunately, the explanations are often rather terse. In some cases, they verge on useless! However, they provide a useful quick reference to information such as the parameters required by a method, its return value, or the meaning of an otherwise obscure bit mask. In the highly likely event that the information provided here is not sufficient for writing VBScript code, you should refer to the WMI class documentation that also ships as part of the WMI SDK.
	This is the Views option. It allows the activation of two filters and a feature known as Customized Views. The two filters specify whether system properties and inherited properties are viewable in the property list. System properties are special properties common to all WMI objects that will be discussed in Chapter 11. Such properties are instantly recognizable because they are prefixed with two underscore characters. Displaying them does little harm; but if you do not like to see them clogging up the property list, switch on this filter and they will vanish! Inherited properties, as the name implies, are those that are defined by superclasses of the current object. Filtering these inherited properties allows you to see only those properties that are defined by the current object's class itself. The Customized Views option is almost definitely grayed out on your system; but for the sake of curiosity, we provide a brief explanation. There is a WMI Views Provider that allows groups of objects to be combined into single meta objects in a manner very similar to views in relational database parlance. If you have created views that involve the currently selected object, this option allows them to be displayed. We believe, however, that WMI Views is feature that adds considerable complexity to WMI for dubious advantage; they will not, therefore, be discussed in this book.
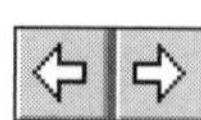	These are navigation buttons. They act just in the same way as the equivalent buttons in standard web browsers, allowing the user to navigate backward and forward through the display history.
	This is the Save option. If you change a writeable property, this button is used to write the changes back to the repository (see Chapter 7).

In short, that is about all there is to the WMI Object Browser. It presents a few extra nooks and crannies that we have not mentioned here, but we invite you to explore those at your leisure. As should now be abundantly clear, the WMI Object Browser is a tool that is certainly worth getting to know. Incidentally, if you are wondering why we have waited until Chapter 6 to introduce such a useful tool, the answer is merely that for someone with a good understanding of WMI, the tool is invaluable; on the other hand, for someone without this understanding, the tool can be a confusing nightmare. Believe us, we were there once!

Summary

This chapter began with a discussion of Windows Event Logs, demonstrating how WMI can be used to find out about the logs on a given workstation or server and to perform basic housekeeping operations on them. It then introduced `WMIBook.SimpleReport`, a Windows script component designed to help convert WMI output into neat HTML reports. More important than the component itself was the concept it represented: the idea that WMI and VBScript can be used as an extremely powerful, self-contained reporting tool. Another, very different kind of report was presented in the second section of the chapter, which showed how the Windows Installer Provider could be used to compile a report of all the software lurking on machines across a network. Finally, we discussed the WMI Object Browser, a graphical tool that can be used to find out what WMI objects are available on a computer system and how they are related to each other.

If there are two major system administration uses of WMI, they are reporting and configuring. In the next chapter, we investigate how WMI can be used to configure and manage remote machines.

7
System Configuration

Computer systems do not run by themselves. However careful we are with hardware and software purchases, and however carefully a system rollout is planned, a large network of computers runs smoothly only if it is given constant care and attention from its administrators. In many ways, system maintenance is to the corporate computer what fly-by-wire technology is to an aircraft. A modern plane may be able to fly itself with no user intervention to a large extent, but without a pilot regularly checking the controls, and the engineer performing safety checks on the ground, there is always a chance that the plane will fall out of the sky. Likewise, without constant monitoring and adjustment, computer systems soon start their uncontrolled decent to the ground.

So far in this book, we have used WMI mainly to examine and manipulate high-level components of a smoothly running operating system. In this chapter, we turn briefly to two aspects of lower level system configuration and maintenance, to suggest ways in which WMI can be used to keep a computer flying. Specifically, we demonstrate how to use WMI to control services and to tweak the Registry on local or remote machines. System configuration and maintenance can involve many different tasks, and requirements can vary dramatically between organizations; therefore, we have not tried to give you a comprehensive overview of the vast number of WMI objects that represent configurable parts of a computer system; these are best explored with a tool such as the Object Browser (see Chapter 6, "Logs and Reports"), and we strongly recommend you take time to do this. Instead, this chapter presents examples from two very different areas of the operating system, which will hopefully inspire you to develop configuration and maintenance solutions for your own environments.

Managing Services with WMI

Windows 2000 services are processes that generally do not interact with a user but instead provide core functionality on which components of the operating system, applications, and users can rely. For example, the Spooler service handles the queuing and scheduling of print jobs and the DNS service on Windows 2000 Server provides DNS services to a domain. Services such as the DNS server and spooler, which perform user-level tasks, are so-called Win32 services; they are written in accordance with specifications laid down by the Service Control Manager, which is the operating system component that controls their behavior. The term *service* also covers a rather different sort of beast, however, namely device drivers. As most readers will no doubt be well aware, device drivers are usually intended to provide an interface between the operating system and hardware devices.

At first glance, it seems rather strange that device drivers and Win32 services are so often bracketed under the same term; certainly, Windows is probably the only family of operating systems that draws this connection. However, the bracketing does make a certain degree of sense, because there is a lot of commonality between the operation of the two types of service:

- Both have various startup modes that determine whether they should start automatically, at some specified point in the boot sequence, or manually.
- Both have chains of dependencies without which they cannot operate.
- Both essentially perform the same function, namely to provide some service to other users, applications, or the operating system itself. Seen in this light, the difference between something that writes data to a disk and something that spools data for a printer is somewhat academic.

The following discussion focuses on Win32 services, because remote manipulation of device drivers may be considered somewhat unwise! In principle, however, much of the discussion applies equally to device drivers. As will shortly be revealed, the close relationship between the two types of service is well reflected in WMI. We assume here that the reader is familiar with the facilities offered by the graphical Service Control Manager tool or the service control facilities of NET.EXE.

Representation of Services in WMI

Win32 services are represented in WMI, unsurprisingly, by instances of the `Win32_Service` class; device drivers are represented by instances of `Win32_DeviceDriver`. Both of these classes are derived from `Win32_BaseService`, which is in turn derived from `CIM_Service`, then `CIM_LogicalElement`, and then `CIM_ManagedSystemElement`.

Most of properties of `Win32_Service` and `Win32_DeviceDriver` are inherited from `Win32_BaseService`; there are more than 20 such properties, encapsulating information about a service's configuration, its type, and its current operational state. In common with all descendents of `CIM_ManagedSystemElement`, a `Name` property acts as a primary key. All the properties are read-only; configuration tasks are accomplished through a set of methods. A discussion of every property and method presented by `Win32_BaseService` or its subclasses would bloat this chapter beyond all proportion; therefore, we concentrate here on the properties and method that are generally of most interest to a system administrator.

Arguably, a service's most vital statistics are its name, purpose, operational state, startup state, and user account under which it runs. Additionally, we might include in this list the extent to which a service can be manually controlled and a list of other services that depend on it. Table 7.1 lists some properties that yield some of this information.

Table 7.1 *Some Useful* Win32_BaseService *Properties*

Property	Description
`AcceptPause`	A Boolean indicating whether the service can accept the pause command.
`AcceptStop`	A Boolean indicating whether the service can accept a `stop` command.
`Description`	A textual description of the service; this is the value normally displayed as the service name in the Service Control Panel.
`Name`	The service's operational name; this is the value used to control a service using NET.EXE.
`PathName`	The full path and executable name of the binary providing the service's implementation.
`StartMode`	Indicates the startup mode for the service. There are three startup modes associated with services: **Auto:** The Service Control Manager starts the service automatically on system boot. **Manual:** The Service Control Manager starts the service only when a process requires it to be running. **Disabled:** The service is not started under any circumstances.
`StartName`	This is the account under which the service will run. The account can take the form of a domain account or a local account. If this property contains no value, the LocalSystem account is used.
`State`	Holds the current operational state of the service. The state can be one of the following: Stopped, Start Pending, Stop Pending, Running, Continue Pending, Pause Pending, Paused, Unknown.

Notably lacking from this list of properties is information about a service's dependencies; the reason for this omission will become apparent later in this section.

As for manipulating services, the most common actions that most administrators tend to perform are to start, stop, pause, or resume a service, and change its start mode. These actions are carried out with five methods, as detailed in Table 7.2.

Table 7.2 Some Useful Win32_Service *Methods*

Method	Purpose
`StartService()`	Starts a service.
`StopService()`	Stops a service.
`PauseService()`	Pauses a running service.
`ResumeService()`	Resumes a paused service.
`ChangeStartMode()`	Changes the start mode to Automatic, Manual, or Disabled.

None of `StartService()`, `StopService()`, `PauseService()`, or `ResumeService()` take any parameters; `ChangeStartMode()` takes a string that specifies the mode to set. This is illustrated in the following script fragment, which sets the start mode of the print Spooler service to `disabled`:

```
Set refSpooler = GetObject("winMgmts:Win32_Service.Name='spooler'")
refSpooler.ChangeStartMode("disabled")
```

Each of these methods returns either 0, if the operation was successful, or one of 24 error codes. A script that seeks to detect whether an operation has been carried out successfully could use a fragment such as this:

```
If refService.StartService() = 0 Then
    WScript.Echo "Service successfully started"
Else
    WScript.Echo "Service could not be started"
End If
```

If you are interested in discriminating between different kinds of errors, check out the WMI Software Development Kit documentation. It describes all 24 error codes.

Tip: Auto Versus Automatic

The `StartMode` *property refers to automatic start mode as* `"auto"`*, but the string required to specify automatic start mode with the* `ChangeStartMode()` *method is* `"automatic"`*. Somewhat counter intuitively, an attempt to call* `ChangeStartMode("auto")` *will fail.* ◆

The following script illustrates the use of `Win32_Service` in a real-world system administration context. It is designed as a simple tool that can be used to start, stop, pause, resume, or change the start mode of any service on any machine on a network. The script requires two parameters: the name of the machine whose services should be manipulated, and the name of a service; the service name should be given in the short form used by NET.EXE, rather than the longer form used by the Services MMC snap-in. When given these parameters alone, the script will report on the current status and start mode of the specified service on the specified machine. An optional third `"action"` parameter turns the script from a reporting tool into a configuration one: if this parameter is specified as `"start"`, `"stop"`, `"pause"`, or `"resume"`, it will attempt to perform the stated action. Alternatively, if an action of `"automatic"`, `"manual"`, or `"disabled"` is specified, the script will attempt to change the startup behavior of the service in question.

The script first connects to WMI on the specified machine and attempts to retrieve a reference to the specified service. If successful, it either displays the service's current state or, if an action has been specified, it calls the relevant `Win32_Service` method. A helper function, `SrvErrorCheck()`, interprets the return code from these methods and reports any error in a human-readable format.

```
'servicecontrol.vbs - find out about or control services
Option Explicit
On Error Resume Next

Dim refWMI
Dim refService
Dim strService
Dim strRequestedState
Dim strMachineName
Dim numResult
Dim strInfo

'check cmd-line arguments for sanity
If WScript.Arguments.Count < 2 Then
    WScript.Echo "Usage: ServiceControl.vbs <machine> <service> " & _
                 "[<requested state>]"
    WScript.Quit
End If

'turn WScript.Arguments into something more readable
strMachineName = WScript.Arguments(0)
strService = WScript.Arguments(1)
If WScript.Arguments.Count > 2 Then
    strRequestedState = LCase(WScript.Arguments(2))
End If

'connect to the WMI service
```

```
Set refWMI = GetObject("winMgmts:\\" & strMachineName)
If Err <> 0 Then
    WScript.Echo "Could not connect to the WMI service"
    WScript.Quit
End If

'attempt to retrieve a reference to the service
Set refService = refWMI.Get("Win32_Service.Name='" & strService & "'")
If Err <> 0 Then
    WScript.Echo "Could not find the " & strService & " service."
    WScript.Quit
End If


If IsEmpty(strRequestedState) Then
    'no change parameters were specified, so output current status
    WScript.Echo refService.Description
    WScript.Echo " The service is currently: " &  refService.State
        WScript.Echo " Start Mode: " & refService.StartMode
Else
    'an action has been requested - work out what an act accordingly
    Select Case strRequestedState
        Case "start" : WScript.Echo SrvErrorCheck( _
                       refService.StartService,strRequestedState)
        Case "stop"  : WScript.Echo SrvErrorCheck( _
                        refService.StopService,strRequestedState)
        Case "pause" : WScript.Echo SrvErrorCheck( _
                        refService.PauseService,strRequestedState)
        Case "resume": WScript.Echo SrvErrorCheck( _
                        refService.ResumeService,strRequestedState)
        Case Else:
            'assume its an attempt at setting startup state
            WScript.Echo SrvErrorCheck( _
              refService.ChangeStartMode( _
              strRequestedState), strRequestedState)
    End Select
End If

Set refService = Nothing
Set refWMI = Nothing

'srvErrorCheck function interprets common error codes returned
'by Win32_Service methods
Function SrvErrorCheck(numResult,strInfo)
    Select Case numResult
        Case 0 : srvErrorCheck = "Service State Changed to " & strInfo
        Case 1 : srvErrorCheck = "Request not supported"
        Case 3 : srvErrorCheck = "Not stopped - dependencies found"
        Case 10 : srvErrorCheck = "Service already running"
        Case 14 : srvErrorCheck = "Service is disabled"
        Case Else : srvErrorCheck = "Unkown Error - " & _
                    "Service state not changed to "& strInfo
    End Select
End Function
```

This script is extremely simple in WMI terms; strip away the error checking and cosmetics, and all that is left is an object retrieval, property read, and a few simple method calls. Yet, it is functionally far more useful than the traditional "net start" and "net stop" incantations! Once again, you see the power of WMI for system configuration.

Dependencies

As noted earlier in this section, services often cannot function as independent entities because of their dependence on other services. For example, the Netlogon service on a Windows 2000 workstation, which handles Windows network logons, is dependent on the lanmanworkstation service. An attempt to use the Win32_Service StopService() method on a service on which others depend will fail, as can be illustrated by attempting to use our script to stop the lanmanworkstation service.

Dependencies between services are represented in WMI by instances of the Win32_DependentService associator class. Win32_DependentService is a subclass of CIM_ServiceDependency, which in turn is a subclass of CIM_Dependency. It associates two Win32_BaseServices in antecedent and dependent properties. In a Win32_ServiceDependency association, the dependent service is the one that requires the antecedent for it to function.

A list of Win32_Service objects relying on the lanmanworkstation can be retrieved with the following ASSOCIATORS OF query:

```
ASSOCIATORS OF {Win32_Service.Name='lanmanserver'}
          WHERE AssocClass=Win32_DependentService
          ResultRole=Dependent
```

If you spend a lot of time controlling services on computers within your organization, you may want to incorporate such a query, or an Associators_() method call, to the servicecontrol.vbs script presented earlier. With a minor modification, it could not only report on the state and startup mode of a service, but also could list dependencies and antecedents.

WMI and the Registry

Traditionally, if we can call doing something for a few years a tradition, the Registry has been the savior of system administrators who, frustrated with a limited GUI interface, wanted to tweak the machines under their control. Ever since the launch of Windows 95, the Registry has been the primary location for vast swathes of configuration options that can be used to control operating system components with a precision that far exceeds that which can be accomplished through the GUI. A constant frustration, however, has always been that comparatively few of the useful Registry keys and values have ever been documented officially; administrators wanting to tweak them either had to resort to unofficial documentation, the web, or else work things out for themselves. We remember only too vividly the sense of joy experienced only three years ago, when we discovered that a machine's MAC address under NT 4.0 could be retrieved from the Registry key `HKLM\SOFTWARE\Microsoft\Rpc\UuidTemporaryData`. Obvious really, is it not?!

With WMI, of course, all this changes; if you need to find the MAC address of an Ethernet card, you merely read the `MACAddress` property of the `Win32_NetworkAdapter` object representing the card in question. In fact, one of the main attractions of WMI for the system administrator is that it obviates the need for obscure Registry hacks and similar tweaks. Despite this dramatic change, however, the Registry is still the primary repository under Windows for operating system and application configuration information; although many tasks that were once accomplished with Registry hacks can now be carried out with WMI, sometimes a script-savvy administrator will still want to manipulate the Registry directly for one reason or another. It should come as no surprise that the Registry is itself represented within WMI; this section considers how.

Representation of the Registry in WMI

The Registry is represented in WMI by an instance of the `Win32_Registry` class. This is derived from `CIM_LogicalElement`, which itself derived from `CIM_ManagedSystemElement`.

In addition to properties inherited from its superclass (such as `Name`, the primary key), `Win32_Registry`, defines three properties of its own:

- **`CurrentSize`** This read-only property indicates the size, in megabytes, of the Registry.
- **`MaximumSize`** This read-only property indicates the maximum allowable size to which the Registry can grow. Again, this is measured in megabytes. If the Registry grows beyond this size, the machine will crash.
- **`ProposedSize`** This is a read/write property used to propose a maximum size for the Registry. If this value is changed, Windows 2000 attempts to set the maximum size to the proposed value; if this cannot be done, the original maximum size is retained.

So far in this book, whenever we have needed to manipulate WMI objects, we have done so via method calls; properties have been used solely for retrieving information. One reason for this is that although many of the classes we have encountered define properties as read/write, the providers serving these classes have not implemented the write operation. This

ProposedSize property of Win32_Registry, however, is genuinely writeable; the Win32 Provider that services it does implement the write operation. Hence, for the first time, we can change a value just by assigning it, as in the following code fragment, which assumes that refRegistry holds a reference to a Win32_Registry object:

```
refRegistry.ProposedSize = 50
```

Assigning a value in this way, however, does not actually write any changes back to the Repository. Just as when you create a new object and assign values to its properties, the changes are written only after a call to the SWbemObject Put_() method. This is demonstrated in the following short script, which changes the proposed size of the Registry on the local machine to 50 MB. Error handling has been omitted for the sake of brevity.

```
'setregsize.vbs - set the registry proposed size to 50Mb
Option Explicit
Dim refWMI
Dim colRegistry
Dim refRegistry

Set refWMI = GetObject("winMgmts:")
Set colRegistry = refWMI.InstancesOf("Win32_Registry")

For Each refRegistry In colRegistry
    refRegistry.ProposedSize = 50
    refRegistry.Put_()
Next

Set colRegistry = Nothing
Set refWMI = Nothing
```

Note that the script actually retrieves a collection of Win32_Registry objects even though every Windows 2000 computer has only one such object. The reason for this is that retrieving this object directly using GetObject() would involve an absurdly long moniker string, because Win32_Registry's Name property (the primary key) consists of a concatenation of machine name, operating system type, and disk partition name. Alas, Win32_Registry is not a *singleton* class, which means it cannot be retrieved with the object path shorthand Win32_Registry=@.

The Win32_Registry object itself, as you have seen, is not particularly exciting! This is because the Registry's interest lies not in the object itself, but in it contents; that is, its hives, keys, and values. Surprisingly, these are not represented in WMI at all: there is no Win32_RegistryKey class or anything remotely resembling it. Perhaps the reason for this is that Microsoft wants to discourage Registry hacking as a system administrator's pastime; perhaps it is merely a question of the difficulty of representing something as labyrinthine as the Registry in WMI terms; perhaps it is a question of the performance problems that may result from having hypothetical key objects constantly polling the Registry for updated information. Whatever the reason, the WMI development team clearly realized that even in a WMI world, people would occasionally want to indulge in Registry hacking; to facilitate this, they have provided a *static class*, which provides all the methods necessary to create, delete, and enumerate keys and values. The class is *static* in that it has no instances; it has no properties. All it contains is a set of methods that allow programmatic access to the Registry. The class in question is called `StdRegProv`, and the following section explains its use. The discussion assumes knowledge of the basic Registry terminology and value types.

Using *StdRegProv* Class

The `StdRegProv` class is serviced by the Win32 Registry Provider, which is installed by default on Windows 2000 systems. Because it does not fit into the WMI hierarchy in the root\cimv2 namespace, it lives in another namespace altogether, namely root\default. As it is a static class, there are no instances to retrieve; instead, the first stage in performing any Registry operation is to retrieve a reference to the class itself. This can be accomplished with a simple line of VBScript code:

```
Set refRegistry = GetObject("winMgmts:root\default:StdRegProv")
```

Just as with any other WMI class, if a remote machine name is provided as part of the moniker string, the `StdRegProv` class retrieved allows manipulation of the remote machine's Registry.

The `StdRegProv` class presents 16 methods that allow the creation, deletion, and enumeration of keys and values. These will be described, according to the activities that they support, in the sections that follow.

Reading a Value

`StdRegProv` provides five methods for reading values from the Registry: `GetBinaryValue()`, `GetDWordValue()`, `GetExpandedStringValue()`, `GetMultipleStringValue()`, and `GetStringValue()`. These retrieve values of type `REG_BINARY`, `REG_DWORD`, `REG_EXPANDED_SZ`, `REG_MULTI_SZ`, and `REG_SZ`, respectively. Each method takes four parameters:

- A numeric constant representing the root key under which the value resides
- A string value corresponding to the Registry key under which the value resides
- The name of the value itself
- An `"out"` parameter into which the value is returned

The root key numeric constants are defined as hexadecimal numbers, as listed in Table 7.3.

Table 7.3 Root Key Values

Root Key	Hexadecimal Value
`HKEY_CLASSES_ROOT`	0x80000000
`HKEY_CURRENT_USER`	0x80000001
`HKEY_LOCAL_MACHINE`	0x80000002
`HKEY_USERS`	0x80000003
`HKEY_CURRENT_CONFIG`	0x80000005
`HKEY_DYN_DATA`	0x80000006

`HKEY_DYN_DATA` is not actually applicable to Windows 2000 Registries, because the key exists only on Windows 9x; it has been provided in the preceding table only for completeness.

Tip: Symbolic Constants

The easiest way of using root key values within a script is to define them as symbolic constants at the start and then refer to them by their mnemonic names. This is illustrated in the following code fragment, which first defines the value `HKEY_LOCAL_MACHINE` *and then uses it (in a somewhat pointless way):*

```
Const HKEY_LOCAL_MACHINE = &H80000002
WScript.Echo HKEY_LOCAL_MACHINE
```

Once defined, a symbolic constant can be used in place of the value. In this respect, it is similar to a variable, except that once defined, a constant cannot take on a new value. ◆

These methods all return a success value of 0, or some other number in case of failure. The problems that can occur correspond to the equivalent values returned by the Win32 API Registry functions.

The following script demonstrates the use of `GetBinaryValue()`, arguably the most difficult of the five methods to use because it returns an array of bytes, which means that further VBScript processing is required to make sense of the data returned. The purpose of the script is to display the digital product ID, a long hexadecimal string that uniquely identifies a licensed copy of Windows 2000. Although we cannot think of many situations in which this is actually useful, it provides a good example of reading binary values, because the digital ID is a suitably long binary array. The script works by retrieving a reference to the `StdRegProv` class, calling `GetBinaryValue()` to retrieve the `DigitalProductID` value in the

HKEY_LOCAL_MACHINE\SOFTWARE\Microsoft\Windows NT\CurrentVersion key, and then looping through the byte array converting it into "human-readable" format. Arguably, a long string of hexadecimal values is not particularly human-readable, but that is beside the point! To convert each byte into a string, you use the VBScript Hex() function, which formats a number as a hexadecimal string. To ensure that the string is exactly two characters long, you concatenate "00" with the value and use the VBScript Right()function to return the last two characters. To generate the full string representation of the digital product ID, you merely concatenate each converted byte, separating them with dashes. This procedure may seem slightly cumbersome and is not strictly relevant to the process of extracting information from the Registry, but we present the example anyway; if you can understand how it works, extracting and displaying any other type of data from the Registry will seem utterly trivial!

```
'digitalID.vbs
Option Explicit

Dim refRegistry
Dim arrValueData
Dim strValueData
Dim strSKPath
Dim strValueName
Dim i

'define symbolic constant for HKLM
Const HKEY_LOCAL_MACHINE = &H80000002

'retrieve StdRegProv class
Set refRegistry = GetObject("winmgmts:root\default:StdRegProv")

'prepare parameters for GetBinaryValue()
strSKPath = "SOFTWARE\Microsoft\Windows NT\CurrentVersion"
strValueName = "DigitalProductID"


If  refRegistry.GetBinaryValue( _
        HKEY_LOCAL_MACHINE, strSKPath , strValueName , arrValueData) = 0 Then
    'call was successful so loop through array
    'and create human-readable string with the VBScript Hex()
    'function, VBScript Right() function and string concatenation
    For i = LBound(arrValueData) to UBound (arrValueData)
        strValueData = strValueData & _
            Right("00" & Hex(arrValueData(i)),2) & "-"
    Next
    'remove trailing dash
    strValueData = Left(strValueData, Len(strValueData) - 1)

    'display value
    WScript.Echo "Digital Product ID: " & strValueData
```

```
Else
    'call to GetBinaryValue() failed
    WScript.Echo "Unable to find the appropriate value"
End If

Set refRegistry = Nothing
```

Provided you know the location of a Registry value, it is easy to retrieve. Retrieving string values is even easier, because there is no array to worry about.

Setting a Value

`StdRegProv` provides five `SetValue` methods for setting data of a given value type. Both in name and semantics, they mirror the various `GetValue*` methods. Their names are `SetBinaryValue()`, `SetDWORDValue()`, `SetExpandedStringValue()`, `SetMultipleStringValue()`, and `SetStringValue()`. As you might have guessed, they take four parameters, just like their retrieval counterparts. The only difference is that the fourth value, instead of *receiving* a value, is used to *specify* the value to write. If the third parameter specifies a value that does not actually exist, all the `SetValue*` methods create the necessary value and then write the data.

The following script demonstrates the use of `SetStringValue()` method. Its purpose is to change the wallpaper settings of the default user on a machine; the default user's wallpaper is displayed on the Windows 2000 logon screen, so it could be used to update corporate colors (or, of course, to annoy your colleagues). The script takes two parameters: a machine name, and the fully qualified name of a bitmap to be used as wallpaper.

```
'setdefaultwallpaper.vbs - set the default wallpaper of a remote machine
Option Explicit
On Error Resume Next

Dim refRegistry
Dim strSKPath
Dim strMoniker
Dim strMachineName
Dim StrWallPaper
Dim i

'set symbolic constant
Const HKEY_USERS = &H80000003

'check cmd-line args for sanity
If WScript.Arguments.Count <> 2 Then
    WScript.Echo "Usage: SetWallpaper.vbs <Machine> <wallpaper path>"
    WScript.Quit
End If
```

```
'prepare variables for writing value
strSKPath  = ".default\Control Panel\Desktop"
strMachineName = WScript.Arguments(0)
strWallPaper = WScript.Arguments(1)

'attempt to retrieve remote StdRegProv
strMoniker = "winMgmts:\\" & strMachineName & "\root\default:StdRegProv"
Set refRegistry = GetObject(strMoniker)
If Err<>0 Then
    WScript.Echo "Unable to locate registry - on " & strMachineName
    WScript.Quit
End If

'Set the WallPaper
If  refRegistry.SetStringValue( _
           HKEY_USERS, strSKPath , "WallPaper" ,strWallPaper) = 0 Then
    WScript.Echo "Wall paper Set on " & strMachineName
Else
    WScript.Echo "Unable to set wallpaper on " & strMachineName
End If

'set wallpaper so that it is tiled
If  refRegistry.SetStringValue( _
                HKEY_USERS , strSKPath , "TileWallpaper" ,1) = 0 Then
    WScript.Echo "Set wall paper to tiled on " & strMachineName
Else
    WScript.Echo "Unable to tile wallpaper on " & strMachineName
End If

Set refRegistry = Nothing
```

If you are tempted to use a script such as this in a corporate environment, you may want to refer back to Chapter 3, "Examining the Filesystem with WMI," and incorporate some code that checks to see that the specified bitmap file exists on the remote machine. If you are feeling more ambitious, you can even automatically copy the wallpaper on to the remote machine from a network share, using DCOM delegation (see Chapter 6, "Logs and Reports").

Enumerating Keys and Values

The `GetValue*` and `SetValue*` methods provide a simple and efficient interface for reading and writing to specific Registry values. They are useless, however, if you do not know the path of the value you need to read or write. `StdRegProv` provides two enumeration methods that can help you solve such problems by listing a key's subkeys and values.

Key enumeration is handled by an `EnumKey()` method. This method takes as parameters a root key, the path of a key to enumerate, and an empty variable; if enumeration is successful, it places an array of subkey names in the empty variable passed as a third parameter. This is illustrated in the following script fragment, which enumerates HKEY_LOCAL_MACHINE\SOFTWARE:

```
Const HKEY_LOCAL_MACHINE = &H80000002
If refRegObject.EnumKey(HKEY_LOCAL_MACHINE,"SOFTWARE",arrKeys) = 0 Then
    For Each strKey In arrKeys
        WScript.Echo strKey
    Next
End If
```

If you try to run this fragment, you will notice that the strings returned give the subkey names *relative to SOFTWARE*; in other words, there is a "Microsoft" entry, not a "SOFTWARE\Microsoft" entry.

In practical terms, EnumKey() does have one major limitation, namely it enumerates only one level of the key structure. In other words, it may be able to list the subkeys of HKLM\SOFTWARE\Microsoft, but cannot tell you whether these subkeys contain further subkeys. The following script demonstrates how this limitation can be overcome; the script enumerates the entire hierarchy of keys under HKLM\SOFTWARE. It achieves this by using a recursive subroutine call (see Chapter 3). The subroutine, called Enumerate(), takes three parameters: the name of a key within HKLM to enumerate (strKey), a reference to StdRegProv (refRegistry), and a number that denotes how many times Enumerate() has been called down a single set of nodes (numLevel). Each time it is called, it carries out the following activities:

- It constructs a string of numLevel spaces, and then displays this string followed by the key name.
- It uses StdRegProv's EnumKey() method to retrieve an array of strKey's subkeys.
- For each subkey, it generates a fully qualified key name string by concatenating strKey, a "\", and the subkey name, and recursively calls Enumerate() for the newly generated string, passing numLevel + 1 as the final parameter. The effect of passing numLevel + 1 is that subkeys at each level of the hierarchy will display with more indentation than those at the preceding level.

The main part of the script is extremely simple: It defines the HKEY_LOCAL_MACHINE constant, retrieves a reference to StdRegProv, and calls Enumerate(), passing "SOFTWARE\Microsoft" as the first parameter, its newly retrieved StdRegProv reference as the second, and 0 as the third. For the sake of brevity, the key hierarchy for enumeration is hard-coded into the script; to turn this into a really useful tool, you will want to replace this with command-line parameters. In addition, this script contains no error handling.

```
'enumkeys.vbs - recursively list the names of all
'keys under HKLM\SOFTWARE
Option Explicit
Dim refRegistry

Const HKEY_LOCAL_MACHINE = &H80000002
Set refRegistry = getobject("winmgmts:root\default:stdregprov")
Enumerate "SOFTWARE\Microsoft",refRegistry,0
Set refRegistry = Nothing


'recursive subroutine call
Sub Enumerate(strKey,refRegistry,numLevel)
    Dim arrSubKeys
    Dim strSubKey
    Dim strIndent
    Dim i

    'prefix output with correct indentation level
    strIndent = ""
    For i = 0 To numLevel
        strIndent = strIndent + " "
    Next

    'display output
    WScript.Echo strIndent & strKey

    'enumerate any subkeys
    If refRegistry.EnumKey( _
            HKEY_LOCAL_MACHINE, strKey, arrSubKeys) = 0 Then
        For Each strSubKey In arrSubKeys
            'recursively call ourselves
            Enumerate strKey & "\" & strSubKey, refRegistry, numLevel + 1
        Next
    Else
        WScript.Echo "Unable to enumerate. Sorry."
        WScript.Quit
    End If
End Sub
```

Try running this on your computer, and you will find a neatly structured list naming all the Registry keys under `HKLM\SOFTWARE\Microsoft`.

The second enumeration method provided by `StdRegProv` is `EnumValues()`. This method, as the name implies, enumerates the names of a key's values; at the same time, it also returns the data type of each value. It achieves this dual objective by having four parameters. As usual, the first specifies the root key and the second the path of the key whose values should be enumerated. The third, an output parameter, receives an array of names; the fourth receives an array of types. These two output arrays are synchronized so that the first member of the name's array corresponds to the first member of the type's array, and so on. Types are encoded numerically. Table 7.4 lists their interpretation.

Table 7.4 Numeric Encoding of Value Types

Type	Numeric Encoding
REG_SZ	1
REG_EXPAND_SZ	2
REG_BINARY	3
REG_DWORD	4
REG_MULTI_SZ	7

To clarify, use of `EnumValues()` is illustrated in the following script. This script lists the names and types of all values in `HKLM\SOFTWARE\Microsoft\Windows NT\CurrentVersion\Winlogon`; as many Registry hackers will remember, this key is a fond favorite of the system administrators, because it holds the values used to configure such delights as automatic logon and legal notices; the security conscious may even know it as the place where GINAs are selected. The numeric values returned in the type array are converted to their mnemonic equivalents by a simple `Select Case` statement.

```
'listvalues.vbs - list value names and type of Winlogon reg key
Option Explicit

Dim refRegObject
Dim arrValueNames
Dim arrValueTypes
Dim strKeyPath
Dim strType
Dim i

Const HKLM = &H80000002
strKeyPath = "Software\Microsoft\Windows NT\CurrentVersion\Winlogon"

Set refRegObject=GetObject("Winmgmts:root\default:StdRegProv")

If refREgObject.EnumValues(HKLM,strKeyPath,arrValueNames,arrValueTypes) = 0 Then
    For i = 0 to UBound(arrValueNames)
        Select Case arrValueTypes(i)
            Case 1 : strType = "REG_SZ"
            Case 2 : strType = "REG_EXPAND_SZ"
            Case 3 : strType = "REG_BINARY"
            Case 4 : strType = "REG_DWORD"
            Case 7 : strType = "REG_MULTI_SZ"
        End Select
        WScript.Echo arrValueNames(i) & ":" & strType
    Next
```

```
End If

Set refRegObject = Nothing
```

This script could be improved by the addition of error handling, and by replacing the hardwired strKeyPath with a set of command-line parameters. We leave this alteration as an exercise for the interested reader. If you are feeling really enthusiastic, you could combine this script with calls to the GetValue* methods discussed earlier, to create a tool that displays the name, type, and value of each Registry value in a key. If you want to do this, you could modify the Select Case block so that it calls the GetValue* method appropriate for each data type.

Creating Keys

StdRegProv provides a CreateKey() method to create new keys; there is no equivalent method for value creation, because this task is handled by the SetValue* methods already discussed.

CreateKey() is an extremely simple method. It takes two parameters: the numeric value corresponding to the root key, and a string corresponding to the path of the value to create. In common with all the other StdRegProv methods, it returns 0 if operation is successful or an error value if not.

Use of CreateKey(), in conjunction with SetStringValue(), for value creation, is illustrated in the following script fragment. The fragment creates a key called WMIBook under HKLM\SOFTWARE and a then creates a value of ChapterNums under the new key. The fragment assumes that refRegistry holds a valid reference to StdRegProv and that HKEY_LOCAL_MACHINE has been declared.

```
'first create the key
strKey = "SOFTWARE\WMIBook"
If refRegistry.CreateKey(HKEY_LOCAL_MACHINE,strKey) = 0 Then
    'good - success! Announce the fact and create the value
    WScript.Echo "Key successfully created"
    If refRegistry.SetStringValue( _
          HKEY_LOCAL_MACHINE,strKey,"NumChapters","eleven") = 0 Then
        'good - it worked
        WScript.Echo "Value created"
    Else
        'oops - value creation failed
        WScript.Echo "Value not created"
    End If
Else
    'oops - key creation failed
    WScript.Echo "Key not created"
End If
```

If an attempt is made to create a key that already exists, `CreateKey()` returns 0 and does nothing; if an attempt is made to create a subkey in a key that does not yet exist (for instance, `HKEY_LOCAL_MACHINE\cheese\cheddar` when `HKEY_LOCAL_MACHINE\cheese` does not exist), the entire key hierarchy is created in one operation.

Deleting Keys and Values

Just as keys and values can be created, `StdRegProv` offers facilities to delete them. Keys are deleted with `DeleteKey()` and values with `DeleteValue()`. `DeleteKey()` takes two parameters: a numeric value representing the relevant root key, and a string corresponding to the key that should be deleted. When a key is deleted, all of its values are also deleted. `DeleteKey()` is exemplified by the following code fragment, which deletes a fictitious key `"HKLM\SOFTWARE\WMIBook"`:

```
If refRegObject.DeleteKey( _
        HKEY_LOCAL_MACHINE,"Software\WMIBook") = 0 Then
    WScript.Echo "Key deleted"
Else
    WScript.Echo "Key could not be deleted"
End If
```

An attempt to delete a key will fail if the specified key does not exist, returning an error code of 2. Likewise, it will fail if the specified key contains subkeys, returning error code 5. Whereas all values are automatically deleted if a key is removed, subkeys are not. If you need a tool that recursively deletes Registry keys, you could write a script that combines the recursive key enumeration technique discussed in the preceding section with calls to `DeleteKey()`. Unfortunately, we have no space here to present such a script; but if you would like to write one, here's how:

1. Write a function that takes two parameters: the name of a key to delete, and a reference to `StdRegProv`. The function should enumerate the subkeys of the key name and then *recursively call itself* for each subkey, passing the complete path to the subkey as the first parameter. Then it should call `DeleteKey()`. The effect of such a function would be to recursively enumerate and delete all subkeys of the key with whose name it was first called, before deleting the key itself.
2. Write a script that connects to the WMI service of a machine, retrieves a reference to `StdRegProv`, and then calls the function you have written, passing it the name of the key you want to delete and a reference to `StdRegProv`.

As you may have already guessed, deleting a value is extremely simple: `DeleteValue()` takes three parameters, namely a root key, key name, and value name; presuming the value exists, it will be deleted.

Note About Registry Security

None of the actions described in any of the previous sections will work unless the user attempting to carry them out has the relevant permissions. If you are writing your Registry hacking scripts conscientiously, therefore, you will want to check that the user running them has the relevant permissions before carrying out any Registry operations. This can be accomplished with `StdRegProv`'s `CheckAccess()` method. This method takes four parameters, two of which are the familiar root and key specifications, the third of which is a number representing the permissions to check, and the fourth of which is a Boolean `out` value. The method returns 0 if it executes successfully or some other number if an error occurs. The third and fourth parameters merit further discussion.

The third value is a bit mask (see Chapter 5, "WMI Security," for a discussion on bit masks) that represents the set of permissions whose presence or absence should be checked. This value is created by OR'ing or adding any combination of the Windows 2000 Registry security values, which are listed in Table 7.5.

Table 7.5 Registry Security Values

Value	Description
1	Query value. (That is, use `GetValue*` methods)
2	Set value. (That is, use `SetValue*` methods.)
4	Create subkey. (That is, use `CreateKey()` method.)
8	Enumerate subkeys. (That is, use `EnumKey()` method.)
16	Receive change notification. (This cannot be done via `StdRegProv`.)
32	Create a link. (This cannot be done via `StdRegProv`.)
65536	Delete key. (That is, use `DeleteKey()` method.)
131072	Read access control information. (That is, use `CheckAccess()` method.)
262144	Write access control information. (This cannot be done via `StdRegProv`.)
524288	Write owner information. (This cannot be done via StdRegProv.)

The final value receives the result of the call to `CheckAccess()`: if the user making the call has the permissions specified in the third parameter, this value is set to true; otherwise, it is set to false. This is exemplified in the following code fragment, which checks the key `HKLM\SOFTWARE\Microsoft` for delete key and create subkey permissions:

```
Set refRegistry = GetObject("winMgmts:root\default:StdRegProv")
Const HKEY_LOCAL_MACHINE = &H80000002
numAccessMask = 4 OR 65536
If refRegistry.CheckAccess( _
   HKEY_LOCAL_MACHINE, "SOFTWARE\Microsoft", numAccessMask, boolAllowed _
   ) = 0 Then
    If boolAllowed Then
        WScript.Echo "Access allowed"
    Else
        WScript.Echo "Access denied"
    End If
Else
    WScript.Echo "Some error has occurred"
End If
```

Despite the apparent simplicity, we think we should warn you about one small idiosyncrasy surrounding `CheckAccess()`. According to the WMI Software Development Kit documentation, the preceding code fragment is exactly what is required to check permissions on a Registry key and discriminate between error conditions and access denial. The documentation even includes a Visual Basic code example that is not completely dissimilar from the one shown here. We can tell you, however, that all is not what it seems: In the preceding example, the words `"Access denied"` will never actually display, whatever permissions the user running the script happens to have on the `HKLM\SOFTWARE\Microsoft` key. The reason is that, contrary to what the documentation implies, if `CheckAccess()` discovers that the user does not have the permissions specified in the access mask, it returns a nonzero error code. This can be most confusing if you write a script that attempts to discriminate between errors and denials! Arguably, the preceding code example above should be rewritten to read as follows:

```
Set refRegistry = GetObject("winMgmts:root\default:StdRegProv")
Const HKEY_LOCAL_MACHINE = &H80000002
numAccessMask = 4 OR 65536
If refRegistry.CheckAccess( _
   HKEY_LOCAL_MACHINE, "SOFTWARE\Microsoft", numAccessMask, boolAllowed _
   ) = 0 Then
    WScript.Echo "Access permitted"
Else
    WScript.Echo "Access denied or some error has occurred"
End If
```

The problem with making this change, and writing a script that does follow the advice in the WMI Software Development Kit documentation, is that a future version of WMI may well alter this behavior; if it does, your script will stop working. Be warned!

Summary

This chapter has been concerned with using WMI to carry out system administration tasks. The first part of the chapter focused on services, demonstrating how WMI objects can be used to retrieve information and control the Win32 Services on a computer. It then moved on to a discussion of the Windows Registry, and demonstrated how WMI can be used to read and manipulate it.

8

Proactive Troubleshooting with WMI Events

By the time you have read this far, you will have realized that WMI can be an invaluable part of any system administration armory. After all, not many tools out there enable you to write scripts that can check, report on, and configure an entire fleet of Windows workstations and servers, all without even leaving your desk! Despite all this, you may be a little surprised at the title of this chapter. WMI, as we have described it, may be powerful, but it is surely of somewhat limited use as a troubleshooting tool because its operation requires too much administrative intervention. It might not be hard to write scripts using WMI that report on the health of your computers and even solve specific kinds of problems remotely whenever they are found, but for a problem to be found in the first place, somebody has to be running the right script at the right time. This hardly constitutes proactive troubleshooting.

Consider, for example, a really simple script that checks to ensure that hard disks on your important servers are not becoming full. If it finds that they are, it pops up a message reporting the name of the suspect server. Such a script, if run regularly, could form part of a solid server maintenance regime. You could even use the Windows Scheduler to automate its execution regularly throughout a day, thus maximizing the likelihood that a problem would be detected before causing chaos. There is, however, one small snag. What happens if you forget to run the script one day, or if something goes spectacularly wrong and fills up your hard disk *between* two scheduled script executions? Theoretically you could schedule script execution so frequently that a problem would invariably be caught, but this "solution" could have other unpleasant side effects, such as putting an unreasonable amount of additional load on servers and your workstation. The basic problem cannot be avoided: A script is far too retroactive to be really useful for proactive troubleshooting.

Imagine, by contrast, a world in which your script can detect a problem *at the very moment* it occurs, regardless of whether it happens to be executing at the time. Imagine if you could write code that responds to virtually any event on a local or remote computer and takes action without your intervention. In this chapter, we introduce WMI Event Notification, a system designed to accomplish exactly this kind of task with much more ease than one might otherwise expect. We start by presenting the basics of WMI events, explaining what they are, where they fit into the WMI world and how they can be controlled from VBScript. Then, in the later parts, we investigate more sophisticated techniques that enable you to write event-driven scripts that constantly monitor your network.

WMI Event Basics

The principle behind WMI Event Notification is extremely simple. It relies on the observation that whenever components of a computer system represented by instances of WMI classes change in some meaningful way, this change will be reflected in the Repository. Whenever an application is launched, for example, a new `Win32_Process` object is created to represent it. Whenever a file is modified, the `LastModified` property of the `CIM_DataFile` representing it changes too. Whenever a file is deleted or a process dies, the object representing it is deleted. WMI can detect all of these changes to its world and model them as events.

Just as a program or script can ask WMI for a collection of objects that fulfil certain criteria merely by passing a WQL query to the WMI service on a machine, it also can ask WMI for notification of certain kinds of events. There is an important difference, however: Whereas a request for a collection of WMI objects results in those objects being returned to the script as soon as WMI can retrieve them, an event notification request results in WMI events being "delivered" to the script *if and when they occur*. We will worry about what "delivered" actually means in this context later in this chapter. First, however, we turn to the concept of events themselves.

The WMI Event Zoo

In literal terms, a WMI event is just a WMI object descended from the *abstract* `__Event` class. The class is *abstract* because no objects can be instantiated directly from it. Instances are created only from subclasses of `__Event`. The rather peculiar pair of underscore characters prefixing the class name indicate that `__Event` is a *system class*. Instances of its subclasses do not represent part of the external managed world but are internal to the operation of WMI itself. `__Event` is derived from an `__IndicationRelated` class, which is in turn derived from `__SystemClass`. None of these classes define any properties or methods. The `__Event` class, therefore, represents a type of thing, namely a WMI event, but does not specify any particular behavior. That task is left to a range of more specific subclasses. These subclasses are arranged in a hierarchy that provides a neat taxonomy of the event-based world, splitting it into various types and subtypes in the same way that a naturalist splits species. It is this taxonomy that has provoked as into thinking of the range of `__Event` subclasses as a "zoo."

Classes representing specific types of events do not inherit directly from `__Event` itself, but from one of five immediate subclasses, each of which describes a broad category of noteworthy happenings in the managed world. This layer of the zoo is described in the following bulleted list and are illustrated graphically in Figure 8.1:

- **`__NamespaceOperationEvent`.** This abstract class represents all events that occur as a result of changes to the namespaces managed by WMI, such as the creation of a new namespace or deletion of an old one. Currently, three different subclasses of `__NamespaceOperationEvent` are defined:

  `__NamespaceCreationEvent`

  `__NamespaceModificationEvent`

  `__NamespaceDeletionEvent`

  Instances of these classes are instantiated, as their names imply, in response to namespace creation, modification, or deletion, respectively.

- **`__ClassOperationEvent`.** This abstract class represents events that occur as a result of changes to class definitions within WMI, such as the creation of a new class within the Repository, the deletion of an old one, or modification to the specification of an existing class. Currently, three different subclasses of `__ClassOperationEvent` are defined:

  `__ClassCreationEvent`

  `__ClassModificationEvent`

  `__ClassDeletionEvent`

  Instances of these classes are created in response to class creation, modification, or deletion, respectively.

- **`__InstanceOperationEvent`.** This abstract class represents all events that occur as a result of changes to instances of WMI classes (that is, WMI objects). Events of this type represent most happenings in the managed world, such as the launching of applications and modification of files. These managed-world events are represented by one of three subclasses of `__InstanceOperationEvent`:

  `__InstanceCreationEvent`

  `__InstanceModificationEvent`

  `__InstanceDeletionEvent`

We leave you to guess what types of happening instances of each of these classes represent.

- **__ExtrinsicEvent.** Subclasses of this abstract class can be used to represent happenings in the managed world that do not correspond directly to any changes within the Repository. WMI itself defines no generic subclasses of `__ExtrinsicEvent`, but providers are free to do so if they want to implement event notification that does not fit comfortably into any of the other categories. A good example is the Registry provider: Although the Windows system Registry itself is represented within WMI as a `Win32_Registry` object, none of the keys and values inside the Registry are represented directly. As you saw in Chapter 7, "System Configuration," there is no `Win32_RegistryKey` or `Win32_RegistryValue` class, so creation, modification, or deletion of a Registry key or value does not provoke a change inside the Repository. Activity in the Registry, therefore, cannot evoke `__InstanceOperationEvents`. As the team who wrote the WMI Registry Provider clearly thought that it would be useful if changes to the Registry could spark WMI events, they have overcome this difficulty by implementing three subclasses of `__ExtrinsicEvent`:

  `RegistryTreeChangeEvent`

  `RegistryKeyChangeEvent`

  `RegistryValueChangeEvent`

  These are instantiated in response to changes to the Registry key structure, changes within a key, and changes to values, respectively.

- **__TimerEvent.** As the name implies, this class represents some time having elapsed or having been reached. A program or script can ask WMI to fire a `__TimerEvent` once at a specified time (an absolute timer) or to fire `__TimerEvents` regularly at a specified interval (an interval timer).

From a system administration perspective, the most interesting group of events are those derived from `__InstanceOperationEvent`, and this chapter focuses almost exclusively on this category. The principles, however, are the same for all `__Events`, so knowledge gleaned here will be equally applicable throughout the WMI event model.

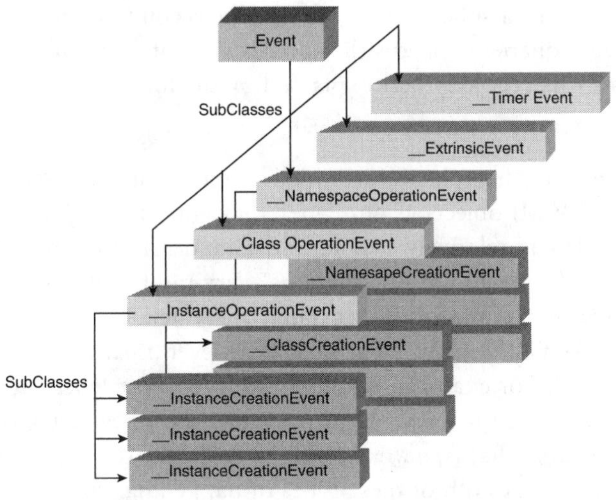

Figure 8.1 *The hierarchy of WMI event classes.*

Although this array of event classes might at first seem a little bewildering, there are really only two important things to note at this stage. First, WMI events are represented by subclasses of `__Event`. Second, a hierarchy of different subclasses is defined to represent the various types of happening that WMI can model. With these facts in mind, we can now begin to investigate how events are "delivered" to a script.

Event Query Basics

The first stage in preparing for event notification is the construction of a WQL query that specifies the range of events that a program or script is interested in knowing about. The basic form of such a query is extremely similar to the standard data queries that have appeared throughout this book:

```
SELECT * FROM <classname>
```

Or, in cases where further discrimination is required:

```
SELECT * FROM <classname> WHERE <property> <operator> <value>
```

There are only two major differences between the semantics of event queries and the data queries with which we are now so familiar. The first is that whereas in a data query `SELECT * FROM <classname>` means "find me all WMI objects whose class is `<classname>`," the equivalent event query means "deliver me all events of type `<classname>` as and when they occur." A `<classname>` in a data query is usually the name of a WMI class representing part of the managed world; in an event query, however, it is the name of an event class (that is, a subclass of __Event). The second difference between data and event queries concerns the specification of scope and the use of the WHERE clause. It is probably best explained by the following example:

```
SELECT * FROM __InstanceCreationEvent
```

This query means "from henceforth, deliver me events corresponding to all newly created WMI objects as and when they enter the Repository." The query is simple and relatively easy to understand. Unfortunately, however, it is not particular useful in most situations. Very rarely will you want to be notified every single time any WMI object is created. In practice, you are much more likely to want to be notified whenever a *particular type* of WMI object is created. For example, you may want to know when an application starts (that is, a Win32_Process object is created) or a new entry is written to the NT Event Log (that is, a Win32_NTLogEvent object is created). Even if you want to know about both of these types of happening, you will almost certainly want to be able to differentiate between them. Contrary to what might be expected, these various types of events are not represented by a zoo of __InstanceCreationEvent subclasses. For instance, there is no such thing as a __Win32ProcessCreationEvent or a __Win32NTLogEventCreationEvent. Given this fact, an obvious question to ask is how on earth can these various types of events be differentiated in a WQL query.

A clue to answering this question can be found by considering the equivalent question for data queries, namely how can a query retrieve only a limited subset of the instances of a given WMI class. The answer, of course, lies in judicious use of the WQL WHERE clause, stipulating that only objects whose properties have a certain range of values should be retrieved. Examples of this abound throughout the book. If __InstanceCreationEvent has suitable properties, perhaps these could be used to fulfil the same goals. To investigate this, we turn to an examination of the structure of an __InstanceCreationEvent object.

__InstanceOperationEvent, the superclass of __InstanceCreationEvent, defines just a single property, TargetInstance. This one property does indeed contain all the information required to uniquely identify the source of an event. It contains a reference to the WMI object that caused the __InstanceOperationEvent to be sparked in the first place. For example, the TargetInstance of an __InstanceCreationEvent sparked as a result of an application being launched would contain a reference to the newly created Win32_Process object. The __InstanceDeletionEvent sparked as a result of a process dying would contain a reference to the Win32_Process object that has just been removed from the Repository. All we need to do to narrow the scope of a WQL event query, therefore, is to specify a value for

`TargetInstance` that corresponds to the event sources that we are interested in knowing about.

There is one slight complication, however, which becomes immediately obvious if you actually try to formulate such a query. In a data query, `WHERE` is used to restrict the scope to a specific set of *instances* of a given class. In an event query, it is used to restrict the scope to a specific set of *classes*. Although superficially similar, these two circumstances require quite different treatment because in this latter context, the familiar operators `=`, `<`, and `>`, normally used in the `WHERE` clause do not make any sense at all. If you cannot see the difficulty, look at the following query, which has its operator missing, and try to work out which operator is needed so that the query reads "notify me of all `__InstanceCreationEvents` that occur as the result of a new process starting":

```
SELECT * FROM __InstanceCreationEvent
WHERE TargetInstance <operator>
```

At first glance you may think `=` is appropriate, but it is not. The `TargetInstances` that we are interested are certainly of the `Win32_Process` class, but they do not "equal" it. What is needed here is an operator which means "X is of the class Y." Thankfully, such an operator does exist and, unsurprisingly, is ubiquitous in the world of WQL event queries. It is the `ISA` operator. Therefore, the solution to the puzzle is as follows:

```
SELECT * FROM __InstanceCreationEvent
WHERE TargetInstance ISA 'Win32_Process'
```

The meaning of this query is gratifyingly transparent. It is the prevalence of this `ISA` operator and the comparison of *class* rather than *instance* that constitutes the second major difference between event queries and data queries. In practice, this query, although syntactically correct, will fail miserably in its current form. The reason, which has nothing to do with the `ISA` operator, is revealed slightly later on in this chapter.

Often, a script written to make use of WMI events will not want to receive notification of *all* events corresponding to *all* `TargetInstances` of a particular class. Instead they may well want to receive only a very limited subset. For example, a script may not want to know about creation of *all* `Win32_Process` objects but only about creation of `Win32_Process` objects corresponding to, say, the launch of Internet Explorer. This can be accomplished by specifying properties of the `TargetInstance` as part of the query:

```
SELECT * FROM __InstanceCreationEvent
WHERE TargetInstance ISA 'Win32_Process' AND
                TargetInstance.Name = 'iexplore.exe'
```

Although use of this facility is often unnecessary, because a script can trivially check once an event has been delivered whether any action is needed, this facility can be invaluable in situations in which a class definition alone would result in a huge number of events being delivered.

Subscribing for Deliveries

So far, our discussion of WMI Event Notification has been entirely theoretical. We have discussed the zoo of classes that make up the WMI event system and how to write simple event queries. Now we are finally ready to consider the notion of event "delivery" and to put our knowledge into practice.

Conceptually, the notion that events can be delivered to a script seems somewhat counter-intuitive. After all, scripts as we have seen them so far are little more than sequences of commands. They *do* things; they do not have things delivered to them. The flow of script execution is predetermined by a programmer who issues commands to retrieve WMI objects, to read their properties, and to execute their methods. Conditional execution gives the programmer flexibility, enabling her to specify alternative courses of action whose execution depends on the contingencies of a specific situation. Although this model has worked very well for us so far, it seems to allow little scope for an `__Event` object to soar toward a running script, announce its presence, and change the course of that script's execution! Such a scenario, surely, requires a complete paradigm shift in which flow of execution is controlled not so much by the predetermined wishes of a programmer, but by the vagaries of an ever-changing world.

Note: Windows is an Event-Driven World

This conceptual difficulty is not unique to WMI scripts, but is ubiquitous within the world of Windows programming, where almost all interaction is based on the concept of events. Whenever you click a button or drag an icon on the Windows desktop, Windows notices the event and "delivers" it to the program that must take the appropriate actions. ◆

WMI provides two fundamentally different mechanisms for resolving this apparent dichotomy, both of which are examples of more general programming principles. One is really a bluff: WMI *pretends* to "deliver" events as and when they occur while actually allowing a script to maintain a conventional flow of execution. The other is a genuine implementation of the so-called *inversion of control* principle, where external events really do determine script behavior. The remainder of this section is devoted to a discussion of the first of these mechanisms, which has the advantage of being easy to understand and trivial to use. Later on in the chapter, we consider the limitations of this mechanism and turn our attention to the second, which may be more complicated than the first but is significantly more powerful.

A Blocking Method Call

The first mechanism exploits something known as a *blocking* method call. A script that wants to have an event delivered calls a method that literally *blocks* (that is, does not return control to the caller) until it is ready to return an instance of `__Event`. Once a script calls such a method, it effectively freezes, coming back to life if and when a WMI event occurs. The moment that the blocking call returns is the moment when the event is "delivered." Setting up such a scenario with a script involves performing three steps:

1. Connect to the WMI service on the machine whose events should be delivered. This is accomplished in exactly the same way as it has been throughout the book, namely with a call to `GetObject()`.
2. Register that you want to have events delivered. This is accomplished by constructing a WQL event query and passing it to the `ExecNotificationQuery()` method of `SWbemServices`. Assuming that registration is successful, the method returns an `SWbemEventSource` object.
3. `SWbemEventSource` has a single method, `NextEvent()`; this is the *blocking* method. When called, execution will block until an event of the registered type occurs. When it does, the `__Event` object representing that event will be "delivered" in the return value of the method call.

The following script example illustrates how all of this works in practice. It connects to WMI and registers to be notified of all `__InstanceCreationEvents` whose `TargetInstance` is a `Win32_NTLogEvent`. In other words, it registers an interest in new entries written to the NT Event Log. It then blocks with `NextEvent()` until an event of the requisite type is delivered. When woken by a delivery, the script displays a brief description of the log entry, with data gleaned from the `SourceName` and `Message` properties of the `Win32_NTLogEvent` returned in the `TargetInstance` property of the `__InstanceCreationEvent`. For the sake of brevity, error handling has been omitted from this example.

```
'logeventdelivery.vbs - register to receive notification
'of new entries in the Event Log. Report the first entry
'that occurs
Option Explicit
Dim refWMI
Dim refEventSource
Dim strQuery
Dim refEvent
```

```
'connect to WMI with privileges needed to get events
'from the Security Event Log
Set refWMI = GetObject("winMgmts:{(security)}")

'prepare WQL event query
strQuery = "SELECT * FROM __InstanceCreationEvent "  & _
            "WHERE TargetInstance ISA 'Win32_NTLogEvent'"

'pass the query to ExecNotificationQuery to get a reference
'to an SWbemEventSource
Set refEventSource = refWMI.ExecNotificationQuery(strQuery)

'make the blocking call to NextEvent.
'This line will remain blocked until WMI can return
'an __InstanceCreationEvent matching our criteria
Set refEvent = refEventSource.NextEvent()

'if we get here, an entry must have been written in the
'Event Log. Display the source name and Message
WScript.Echo refEvent.TargetInstance.SourceName & _
     " has just registered an Event. Details: "  & _
       refEvent.TargetInstance.Message

'clean up
Set refEvent = Nothing
Set refEventSource = Nothing
Set refWMI = Nothing
```

Run this script and watch it freeze, waiting for an event to occur. As soon as something is written to the NT Event Log, it will spring back to life and report the source and message of the log entry. Note that the properties of the `Win32_NTLogEvent` object embedded within `TargetInstance` are directly addressable. There is no need to extract the embedded object before interacting with it. To clarify this point, examine the following two code fragments, which are functionally identical. Assuming that `refEvent` is a valid `__Event` object that has been returned by `NextEvent()` as a result of an event notification query, they both display the `SourceName` property of the embedded `Win32_NTLogEvent`:

```
'fragment one
WScript.Echo refEvent.TargetInstance.SourceName

'fragment two
set refLogEntry = refEvent.TargetInstance

WScript.Echo refLogEntry.SourceName
```

A major limitation of the preceding script is that it receives only one event before quitting. In most real-world situations, you would probably want to register for event notification and then continue to receive every event of the relevant type until execution is explicitly halted. This behavior can be achieved trivially by taking advantage of the fact that the `NextEvent()` method of `SWbemEventSource` objects can be called multiple times. With every call, the method will obediently block and wait for the next event to be delivered. If we want to receive every event of the type specified by our query, from the moment the query is executed until the moment the script is forcefully halted by user intervention, all we need to do is ensure that each time `refEvent.NextMethod()` returns, we carry out any operations that we want to accomplish in response to the delivery, and then call the method again. The simplest way to achieve this is to place the code inside a loop that never ends (that is, a loop whose test condition always evaluates to *true*).

This suggestion is demonstrated in the following modified script. The code here is identical to the one earlier, except that the call to `refEventSource.NextEvent()` is placed within a never-ending loop. For the purposes of brevity, most comments have been removed from this listing:

```
'logmanydeliveries.vbs - register to receive notification
'of new entries in the Event Log.
'Report each entry that occurs
Option Explicit
Dim refWMI
Dim refEventSource
Dim strQuery
Dim refEvent

Set refWMI = GetObject("winMgmts:{(security)}")
strQuery = "SELECT * FROM __InstanceCreationEvent "  & _
           "WHERE TargetInstance ISA 'Win32_NTLogEvent'"

Set refEventSource = refWMI.ExecNotificationQuery(strQuery)

'loop forever, waiting for events and announcing them
While True
    Set refEvent = refEventSource.NextEvent()
    WScript.Echo refEvent.TargetInstance.SourceName & _

           " has just registered an Event. Details: " & _
           refEvent.TargetInstance.Message
Wend

'this will never get called, but never mind...
Set refEvent = Nothing
Set refEventSource = Nothing
Set refWMI = Nothing
```

Note that the never-ending behavior here is accomplished using a `While...Wend` loop, whose condition is the value *true*; by definition, *true* always evaluates to *true*, which is why this loop never ends. If the script is run using cscript.exe (the command-line scripting interface that we have suggested using throughout this book), script execution can be halted by pressing Ctrl+C in the script's console window. If it is run using wscript.exe, the easiest way to halt it is to kill it using the Windows Task Manager.

Tip: Running the Monitoring Script with Wscript.exe

The main reason why we have recommended the use of cscript.exe as the default scripting host throughout the book is that many of our scripts produce extensive textual output that is far more conveniently displayed in a console window (cscript.exe's behavior) than in a series of pop-up dialog boxes (wscript.exe's behavior). A minor disadvantage of cscript.exe, however, is that each script requires an open console window to run, which takes up valuable screen real estate. A script such as the one described here would be a suitable contender for running with wscript.exe. When run with wscript.exe, it will sit unnoticed in the background, but each time a new entry is written to the NT Event Log, it will pop up a dialog box containing a summary of the entry. In other words, it becomes a neat little watchdog, alerting you to potential problems on your workstation without you having to constantly monitor the Event Viewer. To start the script using wscript.exe, either type ***wscript logmanydeliveries.vbs*** *at the command-line, or if wscript.exe is your default scripting host (see Chapter 3, "Examining the Filesystem with WMI") double-click the script file's icon in Explorer.* ◆

Event Providers and Event Polling

As you may remember from Chapter 1, "Introduction to WMI," instances of classes such as `Win32_NTLogEvent`, `CIM_DataFile`, and the like do not actually live inside the Repository. If they did, WMI and the rest of Windows 2000 would be constantly grinding to a halt. Every entry posted to the Event Log, every change to the status of a file or some other component of the managed world would involve writing a change to a rather overstretched Repository. Instead, although the *class* definitions for each type of object WMI knows about are stored in the Repository, most *instances* are created on demand by providers. In response to a query such as `SELECT * FROM Win32_Directory`, WMI contacts the relevant provider (the Win32 Provider in this case) and asks it to create the desired objects. Given this state of affairs, however, you might be wondering how on earth event notification can work. How can WMI inform a script every time, say, a `Win32_NTLogEvent` object is "created" when the objects don't really exist unless explicitly requested? The answer, as you might have already guessed, is that just as there are instance, property, and method providers to service WMI's object creation and manipulation needs, there also are *event providers*. Their task is to inform WMI whenever any changes occur in their part of the managed world. When we executed the event notification query in the previous script, WMI informed the Event Log event provider of our interest in Win32_NTLogEvent objects. From that moment on, this event provider took responsibility for noticing new entries in the Event Log and informing WMI. WMI, in its turn, could then inform our script.

Although this mechanism provides a reliable, efficient way for WMI to find out and inform scripts about changes that occur within the managed world, it can work only for WMI classes supported by event providers. Many of the core classes discussed in this book, such as CIM_DataFile, Win32_Process, and Win32_Service, are not in this position. If you are not sure what the significance of this might be, consider the following query, which performs the function of requesting notification whenever a new process starts on a machine:

```
SELECT * FROM __InstanceCreationEvent WHERE
              TargetInstance ISA 'Win32_Process'
```

Because there is no event provider registered to keep track of Win32_Process objects, the query will fail.

If there were no way at all to receive notification of changes to objects of these types, the scope of event notification would be severely limited. Therefore WMI provides a second mechanism for tracking changes to objects that are neither within the repository itself or supported by event providers: the event *polling* mechanism. The principle of polling is simple. It involves taking a snapshot of all instances of the classes we are interested in monitoring, and then repeatedly checks to see whether further such snapshots produce different results. This could be accomplished manually, albeit in a slightly cumbersome manner, by writing a script that repeatedly executes a standard data query to retrieve all objects of the specified class and comparing each collection with the preceding one. Thankfully, such an approach is not required, because the WMI polling mechanism does this for us.

Activating polling for event notification requires augmenting a WQL event query with a WITHIN clause. Such a clause, placed between the FROM and the WHERE clauses tells WMI to use polling and specifies the number of seconds that should elapse between polls. For example, the following query tells WMI to use the polling mechanism to check every 30 seconds for the creation of new Win32_Process objects:

```
SELECT * FROM __InstanceCreationEvent WITHIN 30
              WHERE TargetInstance ISA 'Win32_Process'
```

This explanation raises two obvious questions. The first of which is how on earth we find out whether the classes whose creation, modification, or deletion we want to receive events for in any given context require a WITHIN clause or whether they are supported by event providers is to trawl through the WMI documentation hoping that the class developers have provided the relevant information. A somewhat faster approach, however, is usually to try it and see. An attempt to call `ExecNotificationQuery()` without a `WITHIN` clause when no event provider for the relevant `TargetInstance` exists results in `SWbemServices` raising an error whose description is completely unambiguous:

```
"WITHIN clause must be used in this query due to lack of event providers"
```

If you encounter such an error, use a `WITHIN` clause. Because this test is one that you will probably want to perform on a regular basis if you make serious use of WMI event notification, we present a simple script that wraps it up neatly. The script takes a single command-line parameter, the name of a WMI class, and reports whether an event provider exists to support the class or whether a `WITHIN` clause is required. It works by building a query that attempts to register for `__InstanceCreationEvents` with a `TargetInstance` of the named class, and passing it to `ExecNotificationQuery()`. The value of `Err.Number` is checked immediately after this call, and the results of the check reported with `WScript.Echo`. The full code listing is as follows:

```
'checkprovider.vbs - check whether an Event Provider
'exists for a cmd-line specified target
Option Explicit
On Error Resume Next
Dim strQuery
Dim refWMI
Dim refEventSource

'first check cmd-line args for sanity
If WScript.Arguments.Count <> 1 Then
    WScript.Echo "Usage: checkprovider.vbs <classname>"
    WScript.Quit
End If

'now build query that registers for all creations of
'the specified TargetInstance

strQuery = "SELECT * FROM __InstanceCreationEvent WHERE " & _
          "TargetInstance ISA '" & WScript.Arguments(0) & "'"

'now connect to WMI and test the query
'enable Security privelege for Event Log and the like
set refWMI = GetObject("winMgmts:{(security)}")
set refEventSource = refWMI.ExecNotificationQuery(strQuery)

'check the error and report accordingly
'-2147213310 corresponds to 0x40082002, the error code for
'the missing event provider error
Select Case Err.Number
    Case -2147213310: WScript.Echo "WITHIN clause required."
    Case 0: WScript.Echo "Event provider exists."
    Case Else: WScript.Echo "Oops. An error occurred. "
```

```
End Select

Set refWMI = Nothing
Set refEventSource = Nothing
```

The runtime behavior of this script should be obvious. Calling it with `Win32_NTLogEvent` as a parameter would result in the output `Event provider exists.` Calling it with `Win32_Process` would result in `WITHIN clause required.` Calling it with `Win32_U(*&(^` would result in `Oops. An error occurred.` There is a small limitation of which you need to be aware if you are intending to make regular use of the script to check for the existence of event providers: It checks only for `__InstanceCreationEvent` scenarios. In the vast majority of cases, the presence of a provider capable of detecting creation for a given `TargetInstance` implies the capability to detect modification and deletion, but this is not *necessarily* the case because the WMI Provider framework permits a developer to support only a subset of possible event types. After all, sometimes it makes no sense to support all types. For example, `Win32_NTLogEvent` objects can never be modified, so it would be ridiculous for the Event Log Provider to claim to be able to produce `__InstanceModificationEvents`. To be really sure that the script produces accurate information, therefore, it should be modified to attempt to register a notification query for `__InstanceCreationEvent`, `__InstanceModificationEvent`, and `__InstanceDeletionEvent` objects. We leave this task as an exercise for the interested reader.

Note: A Peculiar Contradiction

The WMI Software Development Kit documentation for provider developers strongly encourages the writing of event providers for all classes, to avoid the inefficiency of polling. Unfortunately, Microsoft appears to have ignored their own guidelines here, as a vast proportion of the standard Win32 classes are not supported by an event provider. ◆

The second question raised by our discussion of `WITHIN` clauses concerns how often to ask WMI to poll for events. Our earlier query example that queried for creation of `Win32_Process` objects polled once every 30 seconds. What was the rationale for that frequency? Unfortunately, there is no easy answer to that question, because it all depends on the specifics of any given situation. We can, however, make two observations that suggest an approach to answering it:

- The more frequently WMI polls for changes in the managed world, the sooner a script can be notified of this change and the sooner it can carry out any actions. Therefore, the more frequent the polling, the more responsive the script.
- Polling is a very inefficient process because it requires WMI constantly to interrogate parts of the managed world and compare changes with previous snapshots. Therefore, the more frequent the polling, the more resources WMI needs to operate, and the slower both WMI and quite possibly the rest of the computer works.

Taken together, these observations suggest that the optimal polling frequency in any situation is the slowest that you can use without compromising the usefulness of a script's behavior. If the purpose of a script is to log to a file every time a new application is launched for the purposes of compiling statistics, for example, a frequency of 60 seconds is probably ample because the vast majority of programs are likely to remain open for at least 60 seconds, allowing WMI to detect the change between to poll attempts. On the other hand, a script intended to monitor open file handles on a file server could well find even a 1-second frequency too slow. At the other end of the spectrum, a script whose job is to keep a daily journal of changes to files in a filesystem would not need a polling frequency of faster than once per day. Often, it is easy to guess the load that polling for particular `TargetInstances` will place on a system. If WMI has to detect changes to all `CIM_DataFile` objects within a huge filesystem, for example, the load is likely to be huge. If it has to check only for changes to the state of `Win32_Service` objects, the load will be negligible. Note that in reality, filesystem polling excepted, it usually takes a *lot* of polling to slow a system dramatically. Perhaps the best advice we can give is this: Work out your requirements, try the query, and see how WMI reacts.

Responding to More Than One Event Type

By now, you should have a reasonably good understanding of how to write scripts that detect creation, modification, or deletion of WMI objects. In essence, these three variants are identical. The only difference lies within the `FROM` clause of a WQL query. Things become slightly more complicated, however, when we need to be able to detect more than one type of event within the same script and we do not know in advance the order in which the events will occur. The problem is that a single WQL query can only specify a single `FROM` clause, and we can block only on one `SWbemEventSource` at a time. In short, it is not possible to write a WQL query that asks for, say, `__InstanceCreationEvent` objects *and* `__InstanceDeletionEvent` objects.

The solution is to make use of the __Event inheritance hierarchy. Instead of attempting to register for notification of all __InstanceCreationEvent objects and __InstanceDeletionEvent objects, we can register to receive all __InstanceOperationEvent objects and work out the specific subclass to which each event belongs at the time it is delivered. The following query, for example, tells WMI to poll every 30 seconds for the creation, modification, or deletion of Win32_Process objects:

```
SELECT * FROM __InstanceOperationEvent WITHIN 30
                        WHERE TargetInstance ISA 'Win32_Process'
```

Assuming that this query is registered with WMI and a corresponding SWbemEventSource object is held in the variable refEventSource, the following fragment will wake up each time a process is created, modified, of deleted and output the name of the process involved:

```
While True
    Set refEvent = refEventSource.NextEvent()
     WScript.Echo refEvent.TargetInstance.Name

Wend
```

Since TargetInstance is a property of __InstanceOperationEvent that is inherited by the subclasses and, given the preceding query, we know that all TargetInstances will be Win32_Process objects, we can be sure that the second line of code will always be valid and produce sane results. If, as is frequently the case, we want to know what type of event has been delivered (that is, which subclass of __InstanceOperationEvent), we can call on the services of the SWbemObject representing the __InstanceOperationEvent and ask it for the textual representation of the class to which it belongs. This is accomplished by calling the Path_() method of SWbemObject and reading the Class property of the SWbemObjectPath that is returned. The details of SWbemObjectPaths will be discussed in more detail in Chapter 11, "WMI Internals"; for now, take it on trust that if refObject is a reference to any WMI object, the following code fragment evaluates to the name of the object's class:

```
refObject.Path_.Class
```

To clarify, look at the following simple script, which uses an __InstanceOperationEvent query in conjunction with Path_().Class to report each time a process is created or destroyed:

```
'monitorprocs.vbs - report each time a process starts or stops
Option Explicit
Dim refWMI
Dim refEventSource
Dim refEvent
Dim strQuery
```

```
'connect to WMI
Set refWMI = GetObject("winMgmts:")

'register to receive the relevant events
strQuery = "SELECT * FROM __InstanceOperationEvent " & _
           "WITHIN 2 WHERE TargetInstance ISA 'Win32_Process'"

Set refEventSource = refWMI.ExecNotificationQuery(strQuery)

'start the endless loop
While True
    'make the blocking call
    Set refEvent = refEventSource.NextEvent()

    'check the classname of the event and perform relevant action
    If refEvent.Path_.Class = "__InstanceCreationEvent" Then
        WScript.Echo "The program " & _
             refEvent.TargetInstance.Name & " has just been launched"

    Else
        If refEvent.Path_.Class = "__InstanceDeletionEvent" Then
            WScript.Echo "The program " & _
                              refEvent.TargetInstance.Name & " has been terminated"
        End If
    End If
Wend

'this code below will never run. Oh well...
Set refWMI = Nothing
Set refEventSource = Nothing
Set refEvent = Nothing
```

As you can see from the `GetObject()` call, this script monitors processes on a local machine. It can easily be modified, however, so that it connects to a remote machine and monitors remote processes. As with many things in WMI, event notification queries work just as well remotely as locally.

Responding to More Than One *TargetInstance*

In addition to detecting different subclasses of `__InstanceOperationEvent` objects, there may be circumstances in which a single script needs to be able to respond to events relating to more than one type of `TargetInstance`. For example, a script that monitors `Win32_Process` creation may also need to monitor the status of `Win32_Service` objects. Setting up a query to detect changes to multiple WMI classes for situations such as this is utterly trivial; it merely involves adding relevant information to the `WHERE` clause of a WQL event query. All `__InstanceOperationEvent` objects relating to `Win32_Processes` and `Win32_Services` can be detected with the following query:

```
SELECT * FROM __InstanceOperationEvent WHERE
                      TargetInstance ISA 'Win32_Process'
                          OR TargetInstance ISA 'Win32_Service'
```

Registering this query with `EventNotificationQuery()`returns a `SWbemEventSource` whose `NextEvent()` method returns events relating to either of the specified `TargetInstances`. There is, however, one small complication: Each time an event is returned, the `TargetInstance` could be either a `Win32_Process` or a `Win32_Service`; any code that addresses the properties or methods of the `TargetInstance` must be able to work with either type. Consider, for example, the following code fragment, which assumes that `refEventSource` is a valid `SWbemEventSource` created with the preceding query:

```
While True
    Set refEvent = refEventSource.NextEvent()
    WScript.Echo refEvent.TargetInstance.Name
Wend
```

Each time an event is delivered, this fragment attempts to display the `Name` property of `refEvent.TargetInstance`. When the event in question happens to involve a `Win32_Process` `TargetInstance`, everything works happily. On the other hand, if `TargetInstance` contains a `Win32_Service`, the fragment crashes miserably because `Win32_Service` does not have a property called `Name`. In short, the fragment is requesting the impossible. Fortunately, this problem has a simple solution. Whenever an `SWbemEventSource` delivers events for more than one type of `TargetInstance`, check which type has been delivered before making any assumptions about it. This can be accomplished using the same technique as described in the preceding section "Responding to More Than One Event Type," namely, by reading the `Class` property of the `TargetInstance`'s object path. This is illustrated by the following script fragment:

```
While True
    Set refEvent = refEventSource.NextEvent()
    If refEvent.TargetIntance.Path_.Class = "Win32_Process" Then
        '... (do stuff with Win32_Process objects)
    Else
        '... (do stuff with Win32_Service)
    End If
Wend
```

Before we leave this part of the chapter, we should admit that none of the script examples presented so far have in themselves been particularly useful in real-world scripting situations. Their purpose has been to illustrate the basics of the WMI event model. We do not want to confuse the issue with lots of peripheral coding. A vitally important thing to remember, however, is that once an event has been delivered to a script, its `TargetInstance` property contains an ordinary WMI object that is no different from any other discussed in this book. Any of the techniques discussed in previous chapters can be used to interact with these objects. The fact that they have been delivered by events imposes no additional restrictions. The possibilities of event delivery for system administration are limited only by the imagination of the administrator.

Asynchronous Event Notification

The mechanism for event delivery described earlier provides a simple, convenient facility for interacting with WMI events from VBScript. Despite its convenience, however, it has one serious limitation: At any given time, a script using this mechanism can respond only to events emanating from a single `SWbemEventSource` object. In practice, this imposes two irritating restrictions. First, a single script cannot respond to different types of event simultaneously unless they can all be specified in a single query. Second, a single script can receive events from only one machine at a time. One of the most exciting promises of WMI Event Notification is its capability to constantly monitor the state of machines across a network, so this second restriction is somewhat fatal! In this section, therefore, we introduce *asynchronous event notification*, a mechanism that removes both of these restrictions.

Principles of Asynchronous Notification

We start this discussion about asynchronous notification by considering why the *blocking method call* mechanism that we have been using so far imposes these limitations. An understanding of the restrictions of a blocking mechanism should make the concept of asynchronous notification a little easier to understand.

The whole point of a blocking method call mechanism is that it allows events to be delivered to scripts at the time they occur *while still allowing VBScript to retain a conventional flow of code execution*. Ironically, the mechanism's limitations stem from this very point: A conventional flow of code execution involves things happening sequentially, predictably, one after the other; WMI events emanating at unpredictable times in an unpredictable order from a variety of sources on a variety of machines do not lend themselves at all well to this model! In fact, the situation described here calls for something quite *unlike* a conventional flow of code execution. It calls for a situation in which any event from any source on any machine can be delivered to a script and relevant code executed *regardless of what that script happens to be doing at the moment the event is delivered*. In other words, it calls for *asynchronous notification*.

The principle behind asynchronous event notification is simple. Instead of passing a WQL event query to the `ExecNotificationQuery()` method on an `SWbemServices` object and then perpetually polling `NextEvent()` on the returned SWbemEventSource, asynchronous event notification frees a script to register any number of queries with any number of SWbemServices objects. Each time an event occurs matching any one of the registered queries, WMI calls a subroutine in the script and passes it a reference to the __Event object.

You might be wondering at this stage how on earth WMI can "call" a subroutine in a script. If you are, you may find the answer somewhat surprising: WMI can "call" subroutines of a script in exactly the same way that a script can "call" methods of a WMI object. Throughout this book we have been connecting to WMI, retrieving references to objects, and then calling methods on those objects. Each time we call a method of a WMI, we are, in reality, commanding the execution of some code hidden somewhere deep within a WMI provider. We always know which methods are available to be called because they are specified in the documentation. If we want WMI to be able to call subroutines in a script that we write, all we need to do is turn the tables around. Instead of retrieving references to a WMI object and executing its methods, we *give* WMI a reference to an object that *we have created* and allow *WMI* to call *our* methods whenever it has an event that it wants to deliver to us. In other words, we pass WMI an object whose methods it can call as required. The method that we write contains all the code we want to execute on event delivery. This is an example of a more general programming concept known as a *callback*; the reason for the name should be self-explanatory.

How does WMI know which methods of our object it should call when it wants to "deliver" an event? Part of the deal is that when we give WMI the reference to an object, we give it an object whose class is known to WMI. Specifically, we give it an object that implements a COM interface known as IWbemObjectSink. WMI knows that all IWbemObjectSink objects have two methods, Indicate() and SetStatus(), which it can call with impunity whenever it feels the need.

To use asynchronous event notification, therefore, all we need to do is create a class that implements IWbemObjectSink, write whatever code we like for the Indicate() and SetStatus() methods, and finally pass an instance of our new class to WMI, using the ExecNotificationQueryAsync() method of WbemServices. As you might have guessed, this method takes two parameters: a WQL event notification query and a reference to an object that implements IWbemObjectSink. How do we know under what circumstances WMI will call Indicate() and SetStatus() on our object? We read the SDK documentation, and discover that Indicate() will be called to deliver an event. Hence, our implementation of Indicate() should contain the event-handling code.

The principle, therefore, is clear enough. Sadly, however, life for the VBScript programmer is not so simple in practice. Creating and implementing a COM object in VBScript, although not impossible, is certainly no trivial feat. Describing how to do it is certainly well beyond the scope of this book. Furthermore, if you are the sort of person who knows enough to be able to successfully implement `IWbemSinkObject` from within VBScript, you would probably choose to do it a different way. Thankfully, the designers of the WMI scripting interface appear to be well aware the difficulty and have provided a solution in the form of `SWbemSink`, a COM object whose purpose is to implement `IWbemSinkObject` on a script's behalf. An `SWbemSink` object can be instantiated using VBScript's `CreateObject()` function (see Chapter 4 "Remote Administration") and a reference to it passed on to WMI. Whenever an event occurs for which notification has been requested, WMI calls the `SWbemSink`'s `Indicate()`method.

At this point you might be wondering how `SWbemSink` solves any problems at all. By implementing `IWbemObjectSink` it may keep WMI's `ExecNotificationQueryAsync()` method happy, but this is not enough for successful asynchronous event notification to arrive at our script. Surely the question has merely shifted from "how does WMI call a subroutine in a script" to "how does `SWbemSink` call a subroutine in a script?" Although this is certainly true, this new problem is much easier to solve, thanks to the combination of a specific feature of COM and some Windows Scripting Host magic.

This feature of COM is something known as a *connection point*, a COM-specific event notification mechanism. Details of its operation are not particularly relevant to this book. One thing you do need to know about it is that it allows one COM object to *connect* with another and deliver events of a *named type*. Further, every delivery can be accompanied with some arbitrary data (for instance, a COM object). As you might have guessed, delivery is accomplished using a callback mechanism. Despite the similarity of implementation and of terminology, it is important to note that COM events are *not the same* as WMI events. WMI events are WMI objects of a specific class which can be "delivered" to a script through specially designed mechanisms. Each `__Event` object encapsulates a unique happening in a managed world. By contrast, COM events are not objects at all. They are just a mechanism whereby one object can tell another via a callback that a named type of happening has occurred, and pass some data that may be of relevance to the announcement.

The "magic" in the Windows Scripting Host is just that it knows how to act as a host for COM connection points. (That is, it can expose the relevant COM interfaces for callback.) To receive event notifications from a COM object that implements connection points, a script *connects* the object to the currently running Windows Scripting Host using WScript's `ConnectObject()` method. This method takes a reference to the COM object and a text string. Once connected, each time a COM event is fired, WScript translates the event into a subroutine call whose name matches a concatenation of text string passed to `ConnectObject()` and the name of the event type. Any data packaged with the COM event is passed to the subroutine as a parameter.

By now, you have probably guessed the relevance of COM connection points and WScript's support for them to `SWbemSink` objects: As well as implementing the `IWbemObjectSink` interface, `SWbemSink` objects are COM connection points. Whenever WMI delivers an event to a `SWbemSink` by calling its `Indicate()` method, the `SWbemSink` object fires a COM event. Specifically, it fires the `OnObjectReady` event. WScript translates this event into a call to a subroutine named `<prefix>OnObjectReady()`, where `<prefix>` is the arbitrary text string assigned to the connection point when it was connected. The WMI `__Event` object itself is passed as a parameter to `SWbemSink`'s `Indicate()` and thence as a parameter to the subroutine in our script. Therefore, the `<prefix>OnObjectReady()` subroutine should contain the code we want to execute whenever a WMI event is delivered.

Note: SWbemSink *Object Shorthand*

In the text that follows, we will be referring to `SWbemSink` *objects frequently. For the sake of brevity, we use the term sink to mean an* `SWbemSink` *object.*◆

In short, `SWbemSink` acts as a gateway between the world of WMI events and the world of Windows Scripting Host in which our script resides (see Figure 8.2). Thanks to `SWbemSink`, we can easily write VBScript code that responds to WMI events of any type we choose, delivered from any machine across a network.

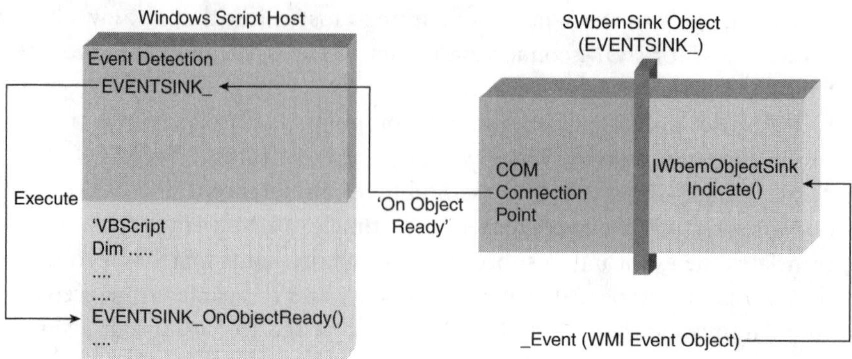

Figure 8.2 `SWbemSink`—*a gateway between WMI and the Windows Scripting Host.*

Scripting Asynchronous Notification

Having considered the theory, we are now ready to write VBScript that puts asynchronous event notification into practice. We begin by writing code that creates and connects a `SWbemSink` object and registers with WMI for asynchronous event notification. We also write a simple subroutine for callback. The first stage in our script is to create an `SWbemSink` object. `SWbemSink` is a *creatable* COM object, which means that it can be instantiated with VBScript's `CreateObject()` function. The full registered `ProgID` is `WbemScripting.SWbemSink`, so we can create an instance with a code fragment looking something like this:

```
Set refSink = CreateObject("WbemScripting.SWbemSink")
```

Having created the sink, we use WScript's `ConnectObject()` method to connect it to the Windows Scripting Host and associate it with a subroutine-naming prefix. Assuming that we choose the prefix `"EVENTSINK_"`, the following code performs the connection:

```
WScript.ConnectObject refSink ,"EVENTSINK_"
```

Alternatively, both of these operations can be accomplished in one step using a shortcut provided by WScript for this very purpose:

```
Set refSink = _
    WScript.CreateObject("WbemScripting.SWbemSink","EVENTSINK_")
```

After the `SWbemSink` has been created and connected with WScript, every event that it fires will be translated into a call to a subroutine in our script named `EVENTSINK_<eventname>`, where `<eventname>` is the type name of the COM event fired. `SWbemSink` is capable of firing four different events because it is designed for use in several different situations. Only `OnObjectReady` is of concern to us here, however, because `SWbemSink` fires this event each time WMI delivers an `__Event` to it. To get the script to respond to WMI events, therefore, we must ensure that we have implemented an `EVENTSINK_OnObjectReady()` subroutine. `SWbemSink` specifies that the callback for `OnObjectReady`, which in this case is `EVENTSINK_OnObjectReady()`, must take two parameters. When the subroutine is called, the first parameter receives a reference to the WMI `__Event` object that caused it to be called in the first place. The second parameter is not used for event notification, but must be defined nonetheless. A sample implementation of `EVENTSINK_OnObjectReady()`is presented here. Each time it is executed, it uses `WScript.Echo` to display the class name of the `__Event` that is passed to it:

```
Sub EVENTSINK_OnObjectReady(refEvent,refContext)
    WScript.Echo refEvent.Path_.Class
End Sub
```

Back in the main script, we are now ready to construct a WQL event query and register with WMI to receive event notifications. The illustration here registers to receive all `__InstanceCreationEvents` whose `TargetInstance` is a `Win32_NTLogEvent`. First, we connect to WMI, with the "security" privilege, which is required to receive information about the security Event Log. Then to register the query, we call `ExecNotificationQueryAsync()`, passing it a reference to the `sink` and the query:

```
Set refWMI = GetObject("winMgmts:{(security)}")
strQuery = "SELECT * FROM __InstanceCreationEvent " & _
           "WHERE TargetInstance ISA 'Win32_NTLogEvent'"
refWMI.ExecNotificationQueryAsync refSink, strQuery
```

If all these steps execute successfully, we should have fully operational asynchronous event notification. An `SWbemSink` has been created and connected to WScript. The sink has also been registered with WMI to receive events of a specified type, and we have written a subroutine to be called asynchronously on event delivery. To make sure that these steps are absolutely clear, the code is presented again here in one coherent block:

```
'asynchronousRegistration.vbs - connect to WMI and
'register for asynchronous event notification
Option Explicit
Dim refWMI
Dim refSink
Dim strQuery

'connect to WMI and create a sink object
Set refWMI = GetObject("winMgmts:{(security)}")
Set refSink = CreateObject("WBemScripting.SWbemSink")

WScript.ConnectObject refSink ,"EVENTSINK_"
```

```
'execute an async notification query
strQuery = "SELECT * FROM __InstanceCreationEvent " & _
           "WHERE TargetInstance ISA 'Win32_NTLogEvent'"

refWMI.ExecNotificationQueryAsync refSink, strQuery

set refWMI = Nothing

'callback for Event Notification
Sub EVENTSINK_OnObjectReady(refEvent,refContext)
    WScript.Echo refEvent.Path_.Class
End Sub
```

In one sense, this code is a fully working script. It is syntactically correct and really will perform the actions that it purports to do. Unfortunately, there is a major snag: It will not actually do anything useful! Sure, it will create an `SWbemSink`, connect this `sink` with WScript and even register with WMI to receive asynchronous event notifications. The problem is just that `EVENTSINK_OnObjectReady()` will never get called. By the time WMI has an event to deliver, the script will have stopped running. It will have reached the end of its flow of execution and stopped. Every script presented in this book has carried out a sequence of actions and, once those actions are complete, ceased execution. There is absolutely no reason for the script here to be any different. The fact that it happens to have registered its interest in event subscriptions with WMI is of no relevance at all to VBScript. As far as it is concerned, once the line `Set refWMI = Nothing` has been executed, its job is complete.

If we are to ensure that this script ever receives event notification, we must prevent it from reaching the end of its flow of execution. Probably the easiest way to accomplish this is to pop a message box on the screen. When such a box is displayed, script execution blocks until someone clicks it away. When running a script using wscript.exe, a message box is popped up every time `WScript.Echo()` is invoked. Therefore, when using wscript.exe, the following line of code is enough to prevent a script from ceasing execution:

```
WScript.Echo "Click here to stop script execution"
```

When using cscript.exe to run the code, `WScript.Echo()` does not block but merely prints a line to standard output. To ensure that a script blocks when running under either scripting host, we can use VBScript's `MsgBox()` function, which pops up a message box on screen and blocks until OK is clicked:

```
MsgBox "Click here to stop script execution"
```

Invoking this command as the final line ensures that the script can hang around long enough to receive notifications of WMI events.

Although inserting a call to `MsgBox()` will make the preceding script work as planned, one more problem still remains outstanding. After

ExecNotificationQueryAsync() has been called on an SWbemServices object, WMI will perpetually attempt to deliver events to the registered sink until *explicitly* told not to do so. If you tried running the script presented here, it might not have worked for reasons that are now evident, but WMI will still be sitting on your machine delivered events to the SWbemSink object that you created. The SWbemSink object will, in its turn, be firing COM OnObjectReady events event although there is no Windows Scripting Host to listen.

Tip: Stopping Event Delivery

If you have run asynchronous registration.vbs and are worried about having a random SWbemSink *firing COM events randomly into the ether for eternity, you can stop them with a reboot. An attempt to avoid a reboot by restarting the WMI service on your machine is unlikely to work because the WMI Driver Extensions service, which is likely to be running and which depends on the WMI service, cannot be stopped once it has started* ◆

To prevent a large collection of useless event sinks building up on a system as the days go by, you must explicitly cancel event subscriptions when you no longer want to receive notification. SWbemSink makes this task extremely simple. It has a cancel() method that performs all the operations necessary to inform WMI that event notification is no longer required. Thanks to the blocking MsgBox() function, ensuring that cancel() gets called when you no longer want to receive notifications is simple. You merely call cancel() immediately after MsgBox() returns, ensuring that when the user clicks away the message box, registration is cancelled. This is illustrated here, in a script that modifies the one presented earlier so that it actually works and behaves correctly. Error handling has not been included for the sake of brevity:

```
'asynchronousNotification.vbs - connect to WMI and
'register for asynchronous event notification
'block until user clicks "OK" and then cancel notification
Option Explicit
Dim refWMI
Dim refSink
Dim strQuery

'connect to WMI and create a sink object
Set refWMI = GetObject("winMgmts:{(security)}")
Set refSink = CreateObject("WBemScripting.SWbemSink")

WScript.ConnectObject refSink ,"EVENTSINK_"

'execute an async notification query
strQuery = "SELECT * FROM __InstanceCreationEvent " & _
         "WHERE TargetInstance ISA 'Win32_NTLogEvent'"
```

```
refWMI.ExecNotificationQueryAsync refSink, strQuery


'block until user clicks ok - at this stage we are able
'to receive asynchronous event notifications because
'WScript can call EVENTSINK_OnObjectReady() whenever it wants
MsgBox "Click here to stop receiving event notifications"

'when we reach here, "OK" must have been clicked
'so cancel event notification
refSink.Cancel()

'now we can disconnect the sink from WScript and lose
'a reference to it. This step is not necessary, as it
'will happen anyway when the script quits, but it's
'aesthetically pleasing :)
WScript.DisconnectObject(refSink)
Set refSink = Nothing
set refWMI = Nothing

'--end of script

'callback for Event Notification
Sub EVENTSINK_OnObjectReady(refEvent,refContext)
    WScript.Echo refEvent.Path_.Class
End Sub
```

Run this script either using wscript.exe or cscript.exe, and you will receive notification every time a new entry is written to the Event Log. If you are trying to run it but are struggling to trick your machine into writing a new event into the log, try adding a new printer. Although the script's payload is not exactly useful, the crucial thing to note is that you can substitute *any* code to accomplish *anything* inside the `EVENTSINK_OnObjectReady()` subroutine. The only difference between code placed in this subroutine and any code presented anywhere else in this book is that this code is executed in response to a WMI event. Inside the subroutine, you have access to the `__Event` object and, of course, you can always call on the services of `refWMI`.

Asynchronous Notification Across a Network

The discussion so far has focussed on receiving event notification from single queries on single machines, but it is perfectly possible to write scripts that can receive events from any number of queries registered on any number of machines. If the same code should be executed regardless of the event source, you just register the same `sink` with each source. On the other hand, if you require different code to be executed, you create a new `sink` for each different bit of code. As the `cancel()` method of an `SWbemSink` cancels notification on *all* sources with which it is registered, managing asynchronous event notification from multiple sources is hardly more complex than doing so from a single source.

There is only one minor complication when handling events from multiple sources: When a callback such as `EVENTSINK_OnObjectReady()` is called, you may want to know the name of the machine whose WMI event caused the call. Imagine, for example, a script whose task is to warn a system administrator when the disks become too full on a server. The script could register a query on each server using the same `SWbemSink` so that a single callback handles all events. On a large network, however, the script would be utterly useless without a way of working out which of the server sparked each event. As it happens, the script idea described here would probably have received events whose `TargetInstance` contain `Win32_LogicalDisc` objects. These have a `SystemName` property, which would solve the problem. For the more general case, however, the solution lies within the WMI `__Event` object itself. All WMI objects possess a system property called `__SYSTEM` that contains the name of the computer on which they reside. Although this property cannot be accessed directly from VBScript (see Chapter 11), it can be extracted from the object's `SWbemObjectPath`. This is demonstrated in the following code fragment, which displays the machine name of an `__Event` object referenced in `refEvent`:

```
WScript.Echo refEvent.Path_.System
```

To illustrate the use of asynchronous event notification across a network and to end the discussion of notification in general, we present a script that carries out the task suggested in the preceding example. It raises the alarm whenever the disks on a machine become too full. It works by reading a list of machine names from the command line and attempting to connect to the WMI service on each. If connection is successful, it registers to receive the event notification based on the `Win32_LogicalDisk` class, which has a `FreeSpace` property that holds the number of bytes remaining on the disk. As we are not interested in receiving notification of *all* changes to `Win32_LogicalDisk` objects but only those that correspond to a fall of `FreeSpace` below an acceptable limit, we construct a query that asks for notification of `__InstanceModificationEvents` whose `TargetInstance` properties hold a `Win32_LogicalDisk` and whose `TargetInstance.FreeSpace` is lower than a command-line-specified number of bytes. Each time such an event occurs, it emails the administrator using the scripting capabilities of Microsoft Outlook.

Before we present the script itself, there is one more general technique we want to introduce that can improve the cosmetics of scripts such as this that are intended to run constantly in the background. It concerns an inconvenience associated with running lots of scripts on a workstation, all of which use asynchronous event notification: The desktop becomes cluttered with lots of little dialog boxes, all of which say "click here to stop receiving event notifications." If the scripts are running on a dedicated scripting machine, this may not matter, but for those of us who run our WMI scripts from our own desktops, it certainly does. To solve this problem, we need to find a way to prevent a script from exiting without using `MsgBox()`.

One way to achieve this goal is to follow event registration with an endless loop within which nothing happens:

```
While True
Wend
```

Although this code is certainly endless, it also has a rather nasty side effect that makes it unusable: Any machine that attempts to run it will grind to a halt as the processor furiously whirrs round and round, looping round and round the loop as fast as it can. To prevent this, you can make a small modification:

```
While True
    WScript.Sleep 5
Wend
```

Much better! Now, thanks to the `WScript.Sleep()` method (first introduced in Chapter 4), the code gracefully loops once every 5 seconds *ad infinitum* at a cost of virtually no processor power. Sadly, the problem is still not quite solved, because you now need to find a way to break out of the loop and end the scripts. Logging off of the workstation or rebooting is not an acceptable solution because of the need to `cancel()` event notifications first. There are potentially several ways to solve the problem, but our preferred trick is to do it with WMI event notification itself, using the following technique.

First, instead of testing `True` in an endless loop, we test the value of some Boolean variable, say `boolKeepLooping`. The preceding code is modified as follows:

```
boolKeepLooping = True
While boolKeepLooping
    WScript.Sleep 5
Wend
```

In the absence of any external interference, this code will loop forever.

Next, in addition to any events our script is interested in monitoring, we register for notification of every `__InstanceCreationEvent` whose `TargetInstance` is a `Win32_Process` and whose `TargetInstance.Name` is stopscript.exe. The callback for this event sets `boolKeepLooping` to false, thus causing the loop to exit. Code following the loop can deal with all the event cancellations.

When this mechanism in this place, all we need to do if we want to stop our scripts gracefully is to start up a program called stopscript.exe and leave it running long enough for WMI to pick it up and pass the event off to our script. On this book's web site, you can download a small program called stopscript.exe that was written with exactly this purpose in mind. It does nothing except pop up a dialog box that you can dismiss at your leisure as soon as all scripts you are trying to stop have noticed the running program and quit.

Note: Replacing stopscript.exe

There is nothing magic about stopscript.exe. You can write a script that detects any process you like or, in fact, any WMI event that you can easily cause to fire. The reason why we use stopscript.exe is that its use is utterly unambiguous; we will never be running it unless we want to stop asynchronous event notifications. ◆

Finally, we are ready to present the remote disk-monitoring script that, as you will probably not be surprised to hear, uses a combination of a loop and `Win32_Process` event checking to decided when it should stop executing. In addition to demonstrating the block-without-`MsgBox()` trick, the script has been written deliberately to consolidate many of the concepts covered so far in the chapter. First, it provides a demonstration of using a single `SWbemSink` to register for notification on multiple machines. Second, it illustrates the use of two separate `SWbemSinks` for executing different callbacks within one script. Third, it uses embedded `TargetInstance` subcriteria in a WQL event query. Fourth, it shows how to read an `SWbemObjectPath`'s `System` property to detect the name of a machine that raised an event. Finally, it illustrates how to use Outlook's automation objects to send email. Although we do not discuss this in detail, as a discussion of MS Office automation is well beyond the scope of this book, the code itself should be self-explanatory.

The script requires at least two command-line options: first, the threshold (in bytes) below which a `"DISK FULL!!"` alarm will be set off; and second, the name of a machine whose disks are to be monitored. Any further command-line options are taken to be the name of other machines to monitor. If any of the named machines cannot be contacted or a problem occurs while attempting to register a notification query, that machine is ignored and a message displayed with `WScript.Echo()`.

```
'diskspace.vbs - email administrator when hard disks
'on monitored machines become too full
Option Explicit
On Error Resume Next
Dim refWMI
Dim refDiskSink
Dim refProcSink
Dim numLimit
```

```
Dim strQuery
Dim boolKeepLooping
Dim refOutlook
Dim i

'change this to point to the right email address
Const ADMINISTRATOR = "w2kadmin@someorganization.com"

'check command line for sanity and save first one into numLimit
If WScript.Arguments.Count < 2 Then
    WScript.Echo "Usage: diskspace.vbs <free> <machine> [machines...]"
    WScript.Quit
End If
numLimit = WScript.Arguments(0)
If Not IsNumeric(numLimit) Then
    WScript.Echo "free space must be specified as a number of bytes."
    WScript.Quit
End If

'create a Microsoft Outlook scripting object
Set refOutlook = CreateObject("Outlook.Application")
If Err <> 0 Then
    WScript.Echo "Unable to create Outlook object. Oh dear."
    WScript.Quit
End If

'create two sinks (one for disk space notification and
'one to detect Win32_Processes) and connect them to WScript
Set refDiskSink = _
    WScript.CreateObject("WBemScripting.SWbemSink", "DISKSINK_")
Set refProcSink = _
    WScript.CreateObject("WBemScripting.SWbemSink", "PROCSINK_")
If Err <> 0 Then
    WScript.Echo "Unable to create SWbemSink objects. Oh dear."
    WScript.Quit
End If

'connect to WMI on local machine and attempt to register
'Win32_Process Query for 1 minute poll or quit
strQuery = "SELECT * FROM __InstanceCreationEvent " & _
           "WITHIN 60 WHERE TargetInstance ISA 'Win32_Process' " & _
           "AND TargetInstance.Name = 'stopscript.exe'"
Set refWMI = GetObject("winMgmts:")
refWMI.ExecNotificationQueryAsync refProcSink, strQuery
If Err <> 0 Then
    WScript.Echo "Could not register with local WMI. Sorry."
    WScript.Quit
End If

'construct WQL event query for disk monitoring every 2 mins
strQuery = "SELECT * FROM __InstanceModificationEvent " & _
           "WITHIN 120 WHERE TargetInstance ISA " & _
           "'Win32_LogicalDisk' AND TargetInstance.FreeSpace < " & _
           numLimit
```

```
'loop through each cmd-line specified machine and
'attempt to connect to WMI on each one and register
'the query. Report failure to WScript.Echo()
For i = 1 To WScript.Arguments.Count - 1
    Set refWMI = GetObject("winMgmts:\\" & WScript.Arguments(i))
    If Err <> 0 Then
        WScript.Echo "Could not connect to " & WScript.Arguments(i)
    Else
        refWMI.ExecNotificationQueryAsync refDiskSink, strQuery
        If Err <> 0 Then WScript.Echo _
             "Could not register query on " & WScript.Arguments(i)
    End If
Next
Set refWMI = Nothing

'start loop that continues until boolKeepLooping is toggled
boolKeepLooping = true
While boolKeepLooping
    WScript.Sleep 5
Wend

'when we reach here, a stopscript.exe Win32_Process must
'have been started so cancel event notification
refDiskSink.Cancel()
refProcSink.Cancel()

'tidy up
WScript.DisconnectObject(refDiskSink)
WScript.DisconnectObject(refProcSink)
Set refDiskSink = Nothing
Set refProcSink = Nothing

'--end of script

'callback for Disk Monitoring
Sub DISKSINK_OnObjectReady(refEvent,refContext)
    Dim refMailItem
    Set refMailItem = refOutlook.CreateItem(0)
    refMailItem.To = ADMINISTRATOR
    refMailItem.Subject = "DISK FULL!!"
    refMailItem.Body = "The disk is full on " & _
        refEvent.Path_.Server & chr(13) & chr(13) & _
        "Only " & refEvent.TargetInstance.FreeSpace & _
        " bytes remain."
    refMailItem.Send
End Sub

'callback for Process monitoring
Sub PROCSINK_OnObjectReady(refEvent,refContext)
    boolKeepLooping = false
End Sub
```

Before you run this script, change the `ADMINISTRATOR` string constant to contain the email address of the person in your organization who should be informed of `"DISK FULL!!"` errors. The workstation and account on which you intend to run it needs a fully configured MS Outlook installation.

Permanent Event Subscription

All the event notifications described in the preceding section are examples of *temporary event subscription*. A script connects to WMI, registers (a.k.a. subscribes) to receive notification of a specified set of events and, provided that the script continues to run and notification is not explicitly cancelled, events will continue to be delivered each time they occur. As soon as a script quits, however, notification ceases. Likewise, unless a script is explicitly started, no events will ever be delivered. In short, the event delivery is *temporary*.

In many circumstances, this behavior is absolutely fine. If you need to ensure that particular types of events never go unnoticed, just make sure that the script written to respond to them is always running. On occasion, however, this level of reliability is quite simply not good enough. Imagine, for example, that you are using WMI event notification to monitor important subsystems on a mission-critical server. The possibility that a script that is meant to warn you of impending trouble is not actually running constitutes far too great a risk. To cater for situations such as this, WMI provides another mechanism known as *permanent event subscription*. If you are prepared to accept either a vast increase in complexity or a small reduction in flexibility, you can configure WMI to perform an action whenever events of a specified type occur, regardless of whether one of your management scripts happens to be running. In fact, permanent event subscription does not necessarily involve any scripts at all! In this, the final section of the chapter, we introduce the basics of Permanent Event Subscription and illustrate some situations in which it is useful.

Permanent Event Subscription Basics

Whereas a temporary subscription is set up when a script retrieves a reference to an `SWbemServices` object representing WMI on a machine and calls its `ExecNotificationQuery()` or `ExecNotificationQueryAsync()` method, permanent subscription does not involve `SWbemServices` at all. Instead, permanent subscriptions are initiated when two objects in the Repository, an `__EventConsumer` and an `__EventFilter`, are bound together with a

__FilterToConsumerBinding. Permanent subscriptions exist not as callbacks to scripts but as static objects within the Repository itself. Setting up a permanent subscription involves creating the relevant objects and joining them together in an appropriate way. Removing one involves deleting the objects or severing associations between them. Because permanent event subscriptions are actually written to the Repository, once they are created, they really are permanent, even through reboots. The only way that they can disappear is if they are explicitly deleted.

The permanent event subscription architecture is a model involving two completely separate components: an __EventFilter and an instance of a subclass of __EventConsumer. An __EventFilter specifies a set of events, thereby fulfilling a role similar to that of a WQL query in the temporary subscription model. An __EventConsumer is responsible for receiving WMI events and taking action when they arrive. __EventConsumer is an abstract class. Therefore, the specifics of any action taken by an __EventConsumer object depends on an event consumer provider that provides implementation code for the subclass of which the object is an instance. It is important to note that these __EventFilters and __EventConsumers are *completely independent* of each other. An __EventFilter *only* specifies that a set of events should be delivered, and has no regard whatsoever for what actions might be taken in response, or even to whom they should be delivered. By contrast, an __EventConsumer receives events and acts upon them, but has absolutely no interest in specifying criteria under which events should be delivered to it. This design makes the permanent subscription model quite different from its temporary counterpart, where specification of event-delivery criteria and response to events that ensue are both handled by the same program or script.

The only link between a stream of events defined by an __EventFilter and a set of actions defined by an __EventConsumer is the __FilterToConsumerBinding associator that connects them together. Once connected, any events defined by the __EventFilter will be delivered to its associated __EventConsumer. Although this may seem to be a rather convoluted system, the decoupling between filters and consumers has one huge advantage over a more monolithic model: A single __EventFilter can deliver events to a vast number of __EventConsumers; likewise, a single __EventConsumer can receive events from a vast number of __EventFilters. This architecture enables us to define filters and consumers as isolated components, and plug them together in any way we choose, as and when the need arises.

As you have probably deduced by now, setting up a permanent event subscription involves creating an `__EventFilter` and an `__EventConsumer`, and linking them together with a `__FilterToConsumerBinding`. In the sections that follow, we consider each of these topics in turn. Before we do, however, we should briefly consider how event notification with permanent subscriptions works in practice. When an `__EventFilter` enters the Repository, WMI reads its query and notifies relevant event providers. From then on, each time an event provider fires an event, the following sequence of operations ensues:

1. WMI, or more specifically, the CIM Object Manager checks to see whether any existing `__EventFilters` match the event that has been fired. If they do, it determines whether the relevant `__EventFilter` (or `__EventFilters`) are involved in any `__FilterToConsumerBindings`.
2. For each `__FilterToConsumerBinding`, WMI locates the associated `__EventConsumer` object and determines whether the provider responsible for servicing that object (that is, the actual code behind the `__EventConsumer` in question) is running. If it is not, WMI reads the provider registration information (see Chapter 11) and starts it.

WMI delivers both the `__Event` object and the `__EventConsumer` instance data to the event consumer provider, using a special COM interface that all event consumer providers must implement.

The event consumer provider carries out whatever activities it wants in response to the event.

This sequence of events is illustrated in Figure 8.3. The figure has two sections. The first depicts the process of creating a permanent event subscription, the second shows the event firing sequence.

With this general architecture in mind, we now move on to the specifics of creating the various components of the permanent event subscription system.

Creating an *__EventFilter*

`__EventFilter`, therefore, is the first piece in the permanent event subscription jigsaw. It is a WMI system class which, like `__Event`, is derived from `__IndicationRelated` and thence from `__SystemClass`. Its purpose, as already noted, is to represent a filtered subset of all the WMI events that could theoretically occur in a system. An `__EventFilter` is to the permanent event subscriber mechanism what a `SWbemEventSource` is to a synchronous temporary subscription. It is a source of events selected according to specific criteria.

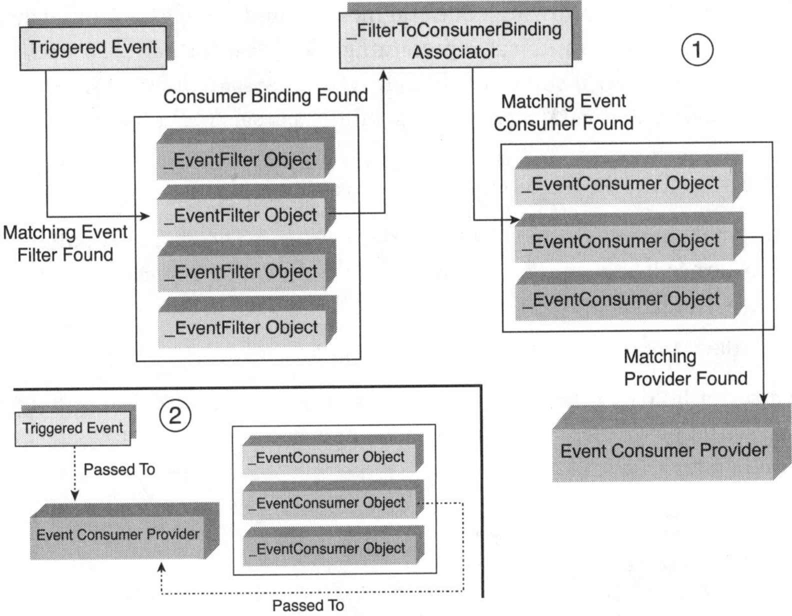

Figure 8.3 *Permanent subscriber event delivery.*

`_EventFilter` objects have four properties: `Name`, `CreatorSID`, `Query`, and `QueryLanguage`. `Name` is the primary key and is used uniquely to identify each instance within the Repository. `CreatorSID` holds the SID of the user who created the instance in the first place; although this information is used by WMI to restrict certain aspects of event behavior, it is of little interest to us here and will not be discussed further in this chapter. The most interesting property by far is `Query`, which is the very heart of an `_EventFilter`. It holds a query string that specifies the actual set of events that the object receives (filters). `QueryLanguage` is a related property. As the name implies, it specifies the query language used in the `Query` string. In the present version of WMI, the value of this property must always be `"WQL"`.

The first step in setting up permanent event subscription is to create an instance of `_EventFilter` and configure it to filter events that you are interested in knowing about. As the principles involved in accomplishing this should by now be rather familiar, we will proceed directly with an example, and create an `_EventFilter` that filters all events corresponding to changes to `Win32_Service` objects.

WMI provides several different mechanisms for creating new objects of an existing class, but in keeping with the general theme of this book, our discussion here focuses on doing so with VBScript, using the `SpawnInstance_()` method of `SWbemServices` first discussed in Chapter 5,

"WMI Security." The following code fragment should serve as a reminder. It retrieves a reference to an object representing the `__EventFilter` class itself, and then creates a new instance of that class using `SpawnInstance_()`. (The fragment assumes that `refWMI` points to a valid `SWbemServices` object.)

```
Set refEventFilterClass = refWMI.Get("__EventFilter")
Set refNewFilter = refEventFilterClass.SpawnInstance_()
```

Assuming that the `refEventFilterClass` reference is not needed again after the new instance has been created, the same result can be achieved more concisely, with the following single line of code:

```
Set refNewFilter = refWMI.Get("__EventFilter").SpawnInstance_()
```

When a script holds a reference to a new instance of `__EventFilter`, we are ready to set its properties. This can be accomplished with the following code fragment:

```
With refNewFilter
    .Name = "ServiceChangeFilter"
    .QueryLanguage = "WQL"
    .Query = "SELECT * FROM __InstanceModificationEvent " & _
             "WITHIN 120 WHERE TargetInstance ISA 'Win32_Service'"
End With
```

The `__EventFilter` is now configured to filter for changes to `Win32_Service` objects, requesting that WMI should poll for changes once every two minutes. We have named the new filter `ServiceChangeFilter`. This was an arbitrary choice, but seems to be a befitting name for the query. Note that we have not set `CreatorSID`; this will be done on our behalf by the provider responsible for servicing the `__EventFilter` class when we save our object in the Repository.

Tip: With...End *With Reminder*

The `With...End With` *VBScript seen in the code example here has not been used since Chapter 5. Its purpose is to provide a way of accessing a whole load of properties of a single object without having to specify the full variable name on every line.* ◆

Having completed configuration of the new `__EventFilter`, you can attempt to save it in the Repository, using `SWbemObject`'s `Put_()` method:

```
refNewFilter.Put_()
```

At this stage, WMI will raise an error if either it or the provider responsible for `__EventFilter` is unhappy. If no error is raised, the new object has been saved successfully.

All these steps are presented, along with basic error handling, in the following miniature script. As it is only a few lines long, we only check errors once at the end. If the attempt to connect to WMI fails, the remaining steps will each fail in turn until the error is finally detected:

```
'makeEventFilter.vbs - create an __EventFilter, configure it
'to receive notification to changes to Win32_Service objects
'and save it in the repository
Option Explicit
On Error Resume Next
Dim refWMI
Dim refNewFilter
Set refWMI = GetObject("winMgmts:")
Set refNewFilter = refWMI.Get("__EventFilter").SpawnInstance_()
With refNewFilter
    .Name = "ServiceChangeFilter"
    .QueryLanguage = "WQL"
    .Query = "SELECT * FROM __InstanceModificationEvent " & _
             "WITHIN 120 WHERE TargetInstance ISA 'Win32_Service'"
End With
refNewFilter.Put_()
If Err = 0 Then
    WScript.Echo refNewFilter.Name & _
         " successfully written to repository"
Else
    WScript.Echo "Oh dear. I could not create a new __EventFilter"
End If
```

If you run this script, your WMI Repository will find itself with a new inhabitant. Modify the code to connect to WMI on a remote machine, and the remote machine will find its Repository inhabited by a new member too. If you need convincing, open the object browser, search for instances of `__EventFilter` and see for yourself!

After an `__EventFilter` object has been created and saved to the Repository, it can later be retrieved just like any other WMI object with a WQL query or a `GetObject()` call such as this:

```
Set refFilter = _
       GetObject("winMgmts:__EventFilter.Name="ServiceChangeFilter")
```

Modifications to an existing filter can be made either by retrieving a reference, making the changes and invoking `Put_()`, or by modifying the preceding script and rerunning it. An attempt to save a new WMI object to the Repository, which has the same key as an existing object, just results in the original being overwritten. To delete an `__EventFilter` from the Repository, retrieve a reference to it and call `the SWbemObject Delete_()` method.

Tip: Modifying __EventFilters *Without Scripts*

A very quick way to modify an existing `__EventFilter` *without any scripting is to change its properties using the WMI object browser.* ◆

Creating an *__EventConsumer*

The second step in setting up a permanent event subscription is to create an `__EventConsumer`, an object that determines what actions should be taken when an event matching an associated `__EventFilter` is delivered. Unfortunately, this is where things start to get rather tricky! All we had to do to create an `__EventFilter` was instantiate a new object of a preexisting class, set a few properties, and save it to the Repository. Creating an `__EventConsumer`, on the other hand, involves defining and implementing a new WMI class. The reason for this difference is simple. No matter what WQL query an `__EventFilter` encapsulates, the actual code needed to run it is identical because all `__EventFilter` objects essentially do exactly the same thing. They filter events. By contrast, the function that any particular `__EventConsumer` needs to fulfil depends on the specific purpose for which it was created. Just as this book is full of different scripts, each written to carry out a specific task, every `__EventConsumer` must be implemented with unique code if it is to carry out a unique task.

The process of creating an `__EventConsumer` involves creating and implementing a subclass of `__EventConsumer`. This requires four steps:

1. A class definition must be defined, using MOF syntax (see Chapter 11). This definition specifies names and types of any properties that the subclass may possess, and also contains the information needed by WMI to locate the provider responsible for implementing the new class.
2. An event consumer provider must be created. This is a COM object containing the code that actually implements the new class. Whenever WMI delivers an event to an `__EventConsumer`, it is really delivered to the provider responsible for implementing the specific subclass to which any particular `__EventConsumer` object happens to belong. The provider uses information from the `__Event` object and from the properties of the `__EventConsumer` instance to perform whatever actions are required of it.
3. The new subclass must be registered with WMI. This is accomplished by compiling the MOF file into a namespace (see Chapter 11).
4. Finally, instances of the new subclass can be created to represent specific actions to be taken on event deliveries. Just like any other WMI class, instances are differentiated by their primary key. A provider that has implemented extra properties can use information contained within them to mediate the activities it performs. This enables the writing of

__EventConsumers that can carry out a range of actions, depending on the configuration of a given instance.

We provided this description of the steps involved in creating an __EventConsumer because to do so is in line with the book's philosophy of explaining the concepts behind WMI features that we use. However, at this point, our discussion must abruptly stop, because an explanation of MOF at the level required to define a new WMI class and accomplish step 1 would take at least a chapter all on its own. Furthermore, writing a WMI Provider (step 2) is something that can be recommended only to an experienced C++ programmer well versed in COM. The task cannot be accomplished at all using VBScript. In other words, we fall down at the first two hurdles. Defining __EventConsumer subclasses is not something that even the most accomplished system administrators want to be spending their time doing!

If you were beginning to get excited by the prospect of configuring permanent event subscriptions on all your servers, you will be delighted to hear that despite the difficulty of subclassing __EventConsumer, all is not lost. Lurking deep within WMI is a set of useful __EventConsumer subclasses that have already been written for you by the WMI team: A LogFileEventConsumer class writes information to a file each time an event is delivered, an SMTPEventConsumer sends email, an ActiveScriptEventConsumer runs scripts, a CommandLineEventConsumer runs programs, and a NTEventLogEventConsumer writes entries into the NT Event Log. Using these classes, you can set up permanent event subscriptions that carry out a whole range of actions without writing a single line of code.

Note: EventConsumer *Subclass Shorthand*

From this point on in the chapter, objects that are instantiated from subclasses of __EventConsumer *will be referred to as "consumers."* ◆

Currently, all these consumers are in beta; although they were distributed with the Windows 2000 WMI installation, they are not registered with WMI by default. The first step involved in using each, therefore, is to make WMI aware of its existence. When this is accomplished, instances can be created in exactly the same way as for __EventFilters—namely, by spawning, setting properties, and saving to the Repository. The sections that follow demonstrate the use of the event consumer that we find the most useful, namely the SMTPEventConsumer, and give a brief description of the ActiveScriptEvenConsumer. For information on the others, check out the "Beta Release" section of the WMI Software Development Kit documentation. Although usage details vary from consumer to consumer, the principles are the same for all. Therefore, information in the following sections is relevant to any consumer.

Using the *SMTPEventConsumer*

The `SMTPEventConsumer` class is defined in a file called smtpcons.mof, which can be found in %SYSTEMROOT%\system32\wbem on any Windows 2000 system. For the purposes of the present discussion, we are not particularly interested in the file's contents. If you are curious, however, feel free to browse with your favorite text editor; MOF files are human-readable. To inform WMI about the consumer's existence, we "compile" the file into the WMI Repository using mofcomp.exe, a command-line tool designed for the purpose. The tool's operation is discussed in slightly more detail in Chapter 11. For now, however, just execute the following at the command line:

```
c:>mofcomp -N:root\cimv2 %SYSTEMROOT%\system32\wbem\smtpcons.mof
```

This command, which must be executed by a user with WMI schema modification permissions (for instance, an administrator), loads the contents of the MOF file into the root\cimv2 namespace of the WMI Repository. If execution is successful, you should see the following output:

```
Microsoft (R) 32-bit MOF Compiler Version 1.50.1085.0001
Copyright (c) Microsoft Corp. 1997-1999. All rights reserved.

Parsing MOF file: C:\WINNT\system32\wbem\smtpcons.mof
MOF file has been successfully parsed
Storing data in the repository...
Done!
```

WMI now knows about the `SMTPEventConsumer` class and the provider that services it. This operation only ever has to be executed once on each machine on which the `SMTPEventConsumer` is to be used. Once registered, a WMI class remains in the Repository until explicitly deleted. Removing a consumer, once installed, is no different from removing any other WMI object or class. It can be done programmatically or, perhaps more easily, using the CIM Studio (see Chapter 11).

Note: Choosing a Namespace

The `SMTPEventConsumer` *class does not necessarily have to be loaded into the root\cimv2 namespace. The mofcomp.exe* `"-N"` *option can be used to specify any existing namespace. In fact, it is perfectly acceptable to load the same class into several namespaces. However, an* `__EventConsumer` must *live in the same namespace as the* `__Events` *that are to be delivered to it. Because most of the* `__Events` *we are interested in this book concern parts of the managed world represented by WMI objects within the root\cimv2 namespace, this seems to be the most appropriate home for the* `SMTPEventConsumer` *class and any instances that we create.* ◆

Once the consumer is successfully, registered, you can start creating instances of it to encapsulate specific email actions. This process is no different from creating an __EventFilter. You spawn a new instance of SMTPEventConsumer, set its properties, and Put_() the new object in the Repository.

SMTPEventFilter defines several properties which, between them, control the provider's operation on event delivery. A complete list of properties, excluding those inherited from __EventConsumer, are listed in Table 8.1.

Table 8.1 SMTPEventFilter *Properties*

Name	Description
BccLine	The email address of a recipient who should receive a blind carbon-copy of the mail.
CcLine	The email address of a recipient who should receive a carbon-copy of the mail.
FromLine	The email address that should appear in the From: header of sent mail.
HeaderFields	An array of strings, each of which will be placed verbatim into the headers of all sent mail.
Message	The text of the email itself.
Name	A name by which a particular instance of an SMTPEventConsumer can be uniquely identified. Name is the primary key.
ReplyToLine	The email address that should appear in the Reply to: header of sent mail.
SMTPServer	The DNS name or IP address of the SMTP server through which mail delivery should be attempted.
Subject	The subject line of the mail.
ToLine	The email address of the message's primary recipient.

The following VBScript fragment demonstrates the creation of an SMTPEventConsumer which will send w2k@myorganization.com an email with the subject line "Hello" and the message body "An event has been delivered" every time it receives a WMI event. The fragment assumes that refWMI points to a valid SWbemServices object:

```
Set refConsumer = refWMI.Get("SMTPEventConsumer").SpawnInstance_()
With refConsumer
    .Name = "MailW2KAdmin"
    .SMTPServer = "smtp.myorganization.com"
    .FromLine = "nobody@myorganization.com"
    .ToLine = "w2k@myorganization.com"
    .Subject = "Hello"
    .Message = "An event has been delivered"
End With
refConsumer.Put_()
```

If any events ever reach this consumer, a mail will be sent using the SMTP server `"smtp.myorganization.com"` as if from the user `nobody@myorganization.com`.

As we have described it so far, the `SMTPEventConsumer` class is already pretty useful. When associated with an appropriate `__EventFilter`, it can be used to mail a concerned administrator whenever something happens in the managed world. To be of serious use, however, the email needs to contain some details of the event that caused it to be sent. In common with all the `__EventConsumer` subclasses included in the current WMI beta release, the `SMTPEventConsumer` enables this behavior through the use of *Standard String Templates*.

Standard String Templates, such as `EXPAND_SZ` Registry values and environment variables, allow the specification of strings whose values are not necessarily known to the person who writes them. Just as the familiar environment variable `%SYSTEMROOT%` enables us to specify paths within the Windows 2000 installation hierarchy when we do not necessarily know where Windows 2000 is actually installed on a particular system, Standard String Templates within WMI enable us to refer to properties of objects whose values we do not necessarily know when we write them. In the case of event consumers such as the `SMTPEventConsumer`, Standard String Templates enable us to refer to properties of a delivered `__Event` object when specifying the behavior of the consumer.

The syntax for using Standard String Templates is just `"%<propertyname>%"` where `<propertyname>` is the name of a property of the delivered `__Event` object. For example, `%__CLASS%` evaluates to the system property `"__CLASS"`, which holds the name of the specific subclass of which an `__Event` is an instance. `"%TargetInstance.Name%"` evaluates to the `Name` property of an `__Event`'s embedded `TargetInstance` property. This is probably best explained by a real example, so examine the following code fragment, which creates a modified version of the `"MailW2K"` `SMTPEventConsumer` presented earlier. Whereas the previous version just sent a bland email on every event delivery, this one sends an email whose From: header contains the name of the server on whose WMI system the event was delivered and whose message body gives information about the type of event that occurred and the name and type of the `TargetInstance`:

```
Set refConsumer = refWMI.Get("SMTPEventConsumer").SpawnInstance_()
With refConsumer
    .Name = "MailW2KAdmin"
    .SMTPServer = "smtp.myorganisation.com"
    .FromLine = "%__SERVER%@myorganisation.com"
    .ToLine = "w2k@myorganisation.com"
    .Subject = "Urgent warning"
```

```
        .Message = "An event concerning a " & _
                   "An %__CLASS% has been delivered whose " & _
          "TargetInstance is a %TargetInstance.__CLASS%" & _
                   "named %TargetInstance.Name%"
    End With
    refConsumer.Put_()
```

Remember that whenever an `__Event` is delivered that matches an `__EventFilter` associated with an `__EventConsumer`, the provider that services the `__EventConsumer` has access both to the `__Event` object and to the `__EventConsumer` subclass instance that caused it to be invoked. Therefore the provider is in a perfect position to be able to merge values from an `__Event` property with values from its `__EventConsumer` instances. It is thanks to this arrangement that the Standard String Templates can work, making the `SMTPEventConsumer` an extremely powerful tool in all sorts of management situations.

Note: Nonexistent Properties

If a Standard String Template is used erroneously to refer to a nonexistent property—for example, if `%TargetInstance%` *is specified for an instance of an* `__ExtrinsicEvent` *subclass—the string is just ignored. This means that templates can be used to provide detailed information that is highly specific to a particular class, without violating the principle that* `__EventConsumers` *are intrinsically separate from* `__EventFilters` *and cannot mind what sort of events are passed to them.* ◆

A Note About the *ActiveScriptEventConsumer*

Despite the usefulness of being able to send email in response to an event, you may have been surprised by our comment that the `SMTPEventConsumer` was, in our opinion, the most useful `__EventConsumer` subclass provided as part of the beta set, particularly when the `ActiveScriptEventConsumer` surely has so much more potential. In this section, we briefly describe the `ActiveScriptEventConsumer`, which is indeed a useful tool, and explain why we rarely use it.

As the name implies, the `ActiveScriptEventConsumer` runs a script when an event is delivered to it. Its definition is contained in a file called scrcons.mof in the %SYSTEMROOT%\system32\wbem directory on Windows 2000 and can be compiled into WMI in almost the same way as the `SMTPEventConsumer`. We say "almost" because to cajole this consumer into compiling into the root\cimv2 namespace, we have to make a small modification to the MOF file (see Chapter 11 for details). When installed, instances of `ActiveScriptEventConsumer` can be created in the usual way.

Instances can operate in one of two ways: Either they execute a small script fragment that is stored within a `ScriptText` property of the instance itself, or else they execute an external script pointed to in a `ScriptFileName` property. The following script fragment illustrates the creation of an `ActiveScriptEventConsumer` that executes a script called `"c:\scripts\hello.vbs"`. Note that only three properties need to be specified: the `ScriptFileName`, `ScriptingEngine` (which specifies which engine should be used to execute the script), and `Name` (which is the primary key):

```
Set refConsumer = refWMI.Get("ActiveScriptEventConsumer").SpawnInstance_()
With refConsumer
    .Name = "RunAScript"
    .ScriptFileName = "c:\scripts\hello.vbs"
    .ScriptEngine = "VBScript"
End With
refConsumer.Put_()
```

As you can see, the invocation of a script with the `ActiveScriptEventConsumer` is trivial to accomplish.

Although, in principle, there are few limits to what can be accomplished with a scripting engine and an imaginative mind, the `ActiveScriptEventConsumer` imposes several limitations worth listing here:

- Scripts that it runs do not execute under the auspices of the Windows Scripting Host; hence, there is no `WScript` object.

  Scripts must be noninteractive, so a function such as `MsgBox()` cannot be used in place of `WScript.Echo()`.

- Scripts run under the System account. They cannot use DCOM impersonation. Hence, a script can perform functions only that the System account is allowed to perform.

Scripts do not have direct access to the `__Event` object that caused their execution. They *can* use Standard String Templates to access an `__Event` object's methods. If they want an actual reference, however, they must use `GetObject()` in combination with information gleaned from the templates to retrieve it themselves.

These restrictions are all imposed for sensible reasons, namely efficiency and security. For the system administrator wanting to set up permanent event subscriptions, however, they can be very irritating. Given that dedicated `__EventConsumers` have been written to cater for sending email, logging to files and even launching programs, our advice is that unless you find yourself with highly idiosyncratic sets of requirements, you should avoid use of the `ActiveScriptEventConsumer`. If you want to respond to a WMI event in a fashion that requires complex scripting, use asynchronous event notification instead.

Binding an *__EventFilter* with an *__EventConsumer*

Having created instances of `__EventFilters` and `__EventConsumer`, the final piece in the permanent event subscription jigsaw is the creation of an association between these objects. You will, no doubt, be relieved to discover that this is the simplest step of all, and can be described in just a few sentences!

Instances of the `__FilterToConsumerBinding` associator are used to connect `__EventFilters` with `__EventConsumers`. In common with almost all associators, `__FilterToConsumerBinding` has two key properties: `Filter` and `Consumer`. The `Filter` property takes a string representing the *relative object path* of a filter. The `Consumer` property takes a string representing the *relative object path* of a consumer. A relative object path is just an object path name with the server name and namespace omitted (for instance, `"Win32_Process.Handle=0"`).

> **Note: __FilterToConsumerBindings *Properties***
>
> `__FilterToConsumerBindings` *have a few additional properties that control various details of their behavior, particularly relating to security boundaries between* `__EventFilters` *and* `__EventConsumers`. *A discussion of these, however, is beyond the scope of this chapter; for further details, turn to the WMI Software Development Kit documentation.* ◆

The following script fragment demonstrates the creation of a `__FilterToConsumerBinding` between the `__EventFilter` and `SMTPEventConsumers` whose creation we demonstrated earlier in the chapter. The fragment assumes that `refWMI` points to a valid `SWbemServices` object:

```
Set refBinding = _
      refWMI.Get("__FilterToConsumerBinding").SpawnInstance_()
refBinding.Filter = "__EventFilter.Name='ServiceChangeFilter'"
refBinding.Consumer = "SMTPEventConsumer.Name = 'MailW2KAdmin'"
refBinding.Put_()
```

As soon as the Repository contains a `__FilterToConsumerBinding` that joins an `__EventFilter` and an `__EventConsumer`, any events that match the filter will be delivered to the provider that services the consumer. Permanent event subscription is in operation!

> ***Note: When Permanent Subscription Fails***
>
> *If an* `__EventFilter` *contains an invalid query or one that specifies events that never occur, the result is simple:* `__EventConsumers` *associated with the* `__EventFilter` *never receive an event. The WMI Software Development Kit ships with a tool that can help detect this type of problem; this is discussed in Chapter 10, "Script Development and Deployment." If an* `__EventConsumer` *fails to carry*

continues ▶

▶ *continued*

out its activities, behavior depends on the provider implementation. Well-behaved providers should trigger a `__ConsumerFailureEvent`*, which, of course, can be detected and responded to using any of the techniques presented in this chapter. This behavior is not guaranteed, however, because a provider is perfectly entitled to fail silently.* ◆

A Fully Fledged Example

To end this discussion of permanent event subscription, we present a fully fledged example that puts all the components together. The example uses VBScript to create two `__EventFilters`, a single `SMTPEventConsumer`, and two `__FilterToConsumerBindings`. The result is a permanent event subscription that emails the administrator of a print server whenever a printer develops a fault or if ever the Print Spooler service changes its operational status. Because we wanted to demonstrate connecting two `__EventFilters` to a single `SMTPEventConsumer`, our instance contains only fairly generic information. It gives enough data so that the recipient can work out which of the filters caused the event delivery, but not enough to work out the details of why. If you intend you use this subscription in a production environment, you might like to make two separate consumer instances, more highly customized to suit each of the events for which it should act.

The code itself, presented in full below, should perhaps be considered more as a batch file than as a management script. It is designed to be run as a one-off, and does not contain any error-handling code. If you are intending to run it, ensure that you change the values of the `SMTPEventConsumer` properties to match the email setup of your organization, and that the `SMTPEventConsumer` is installed (as discussed earlier).

```
'monitorprintserver.vbs - set up permanent event subscription to monitor
'a print server and its printers
Option Explicit
Dim refWMI
Dim refFilterClass
Dim refFilter1
Dim refFilter2
Dim refConsumer
Dim refBindingClass
Dim refBinding1
Dim refBinding2

'connect to WMI
set refWMI = GetObject("winMgmts:")

'create filter objects and configure
'as we are making two instances, we may as well
'get a reference to the class first rather than
```

```
'doing it all in one step
set refFilterClass = refWMI.Get("__EventFilter")
set refFilter1 = refFilterClass.SpawnInstance_()
set refFilter2 = refFilterClass.SpawnInstance_()

'filter to monitor printer itself
'note the query that checks every 2 minutes
'and matches only where the Win32_Printer object detects
'an error state
With refFilter1
    .Name = "PrinterTroubleFilter"
    .QueryLanguage = "WQL"
    .Query = "SELECT * FROM __InstanceModificationEvent WITHIN 120 " & _
             "WHERE TargetInstance ISA 'Win32_Printer' AND " & _
             "TargetInstance.DetectedError <> 0"
End With
refFilter1.Put_()

'filter to detect changes to status of print spooler
'check is made once every two minutes on the print
'spooler service only
With refFilter2
    .Name = "SpoolerChangeFilter"
    .QueryLanguage = "WQL"
    .Query = "SELECT * FROM __InstanceModificationEvent WITHIN 120 " & _
             "WHERE TargetInstance ISA 'Win32_Service' AND " & _
             "TargetInstance.Name = 'spooler'"
End With
refFilter2.Put_()

'Now create and configure the consumer
'The message contains enough information to uniquely
'identify the type of event that occurred
'and the TargetInstance involved. This information comes
'from the __CLASS system property of the __Event
'and the __PATH system property of the TargetInstance
set refConsumer = refWMI.Get("SMTPEventConsumer").SpawnInstance_()
With refConsumer
    .Name = "MailW2KAdministrator"
    .SMTPServer = "smtp.myorganisation.com"
    .FromLine = "%TargetInstance.__SERVER%"
    .ToLine = "w2kadmin@myorganisation.com"
    .Subject = "PROBLEM WITH PRINT SERVER"
    .Message = "An %__CLASS% was delivered concerning " & _
               "%TargetInstance.__PATH%"
End With
refConsumer.Put_()

'create two __FilterToConsumerBinding instances
set refBindingClass = refWMI.Get("__FilterToConsumerBinding")
set refBinding1 = refBindingClass.SpawnInstance_()
set refBinding2 = refBindingClass.SpawnInstance_()
```

```
'bind the filters with consumers. Note that we use
'the RelPath property of SWbemObjectPath to ensure
'that a careless typo in specifying the names
'of __EventFilters and SMTPEventConsumer does not
'prevent the subscription from operating
With refBinding1
    .Filter = refFilter1.Path_.RelPath
    .Consumer = refConsumer.Path_.RelPath
End With
refBinding1.Put_()

With refBinding2
    .Filter = refFilter2.Path_.RelPath
    .Consumer = refConsumer.Path_.RelPath
End With
refBinding2.Put_()

'assuming all of this worked without raising an error,
'permanent event subscription is now set up. So let's
'tidy up and go home!
set refBinding1 = Nothing
set refBinding2 = Nothing
set refBindingClass = Nothing
set refFilter1 = Nothing
set refFilter2 = Nothing
set refFilterClass = Nothing
set refConsumer = Nothing
set refWMI = Nothing
```

Install this permanent event subscription on all of your print servers, and you will never need to worry again about a failed print job! Even better, after the initial installation, there are no scripts to go wrong and no maintenance tasks to worry about. A permanent event subscription, once set up, just exists as an internal part of WMI's world. The only time you need even be aware that it is there is when it sends you an email to warn you of a problem.

Tip: Setting Up a Permanent Event Subscription Remotely

If the `SMTPEventConsumer` *has been installed on all your machines, there is no need to visit all your print servers personally to set up permanent event subscription. Just change the call to* `GetObject()` *in the installation script so that it connects to WMI on each machine in turn, and set up the subscription remotely.* ◆

Before closing this chapter, we want to make a few final remarks about permanent event subscription. First, one of its most remarkable features in the context of this book is that it does not involve any scripting, except for the initial creation of `__EventFilters`, `__EventConsumers`, and `__FilterToConsumerBindings`. Even this does not actually *require* scripting, because all these steps can be accomplished via other means, such as with the WMI CIM Studio or with MOF (see Chapter 11). We happened to use scripts to create our WMI objects because it is in keeping with the spirit of the book. Furthermore, an always-open text editor and command-line window for writing small, error-handler-free, one-off scripts can often be quicker to use than any other tool.

Second, we want to address a nagging question that you may be asking yourself at this stage, namely, "if permanent event subscription is so easy to use and convenient, why should I ever bother with the other mechanisms?" There are several possible answers to this question, but most boil down to two points: flexibility and efficiency. Thanks to the array of `__EventConsumer` subclasses currently in beta, it is all too easy to forget that permanent event subscription is *not at all* easy or convenient. If you cannot find a prewritten provider to suit your needs, writing one is a really rather complex procedure. Although the *`ActiveScriptEventConsumer`* certainly alleviates this problem, it too has limitations (as previously discussed), and a scripting running under its control is certainly impoverished compared with many of the scripts presented elsewhere in the book. The `CommandLineEventConsumer` has similar limitations, imposed for very similar reasons.

As for efficiency, permanent event subscription, like its temporary counterpart, can place a significant load on WMI. particularly if an `__EventFilter` specifies a query likely to generate a frequent stream of events. It is not generally considered a good idea to have a transparent background process, such as the WMI service, generating significant load on an important system! The occasional event triggering an email to be sent to warn you of impending disaster is not going to harm anyone and could easily pay dividends very quickly. By contrast, a heavyweight script, compiling logs and statistics on your server's disk usage several times per minute, is not going to make anyone happy, least of all the poor server that has to run it. Our advice here is simple: For occasionally triggered light tasks, permanent event subscription offers a wonderfully reliable and robust mechanism. For anything more substantial, use one of the temporary subscription mechanisms so that you can keep tabs on what it is doing and easily stop when you need to do so.

Summary

This chapter presented a discussion of the WMI event model, a system for detecting happenings in a WMI-managed world as and when they occur. It opened with a demonstration of synchronous event delivery, a mechanism that allows a script to connect to the WMI service of a machine, register an interest in receiving notification of certain happenings, and then sit silently until a happening of the relevant type occurs. This was followed by a consideration of asynchronous event notification, a more sophisticated mechanism that allows a single script to respond to several different types of event, perhaps even emanating from several different computers, and to take appropriate action as each event is delivered. The final section of the chapter introduced permanent

9

WMI and Active Directory

If someone were to ask us the question, "What is the most important feature of the Windows 2000 management infrastructure?" we would probably answer "WMI." However, something else would come a very close second, something that for many administrators would undoubtedly be the uncontested victor: the Active Directory. The Active Directory is a hierarchically structured database that sits on domain controllers and acts as a central repository for information about the various users, computers, services, policies, and departmental structures that make up an organization's computing infrastructure. The ultimate goal of Active Directory is to be the single point of management for all things computer-related; and although it has not quite achieved that goal yet, it has at least made a start!

For many administrators, the term "Active Directory" may conjure up images of the graphical *Active Directory Users and Computers* (ADUC) tool, the MMC component used to define organizational units, manage user and computer accounts, and perform basic maintenance of the Active Directory itself. As you will probably not be surprised to learn, however, every operation that can be accomplished using the ADUC tool, and much more, can be accomplished through scripting. The Active Directory has a comprehensive scripting interface, ADSI, which allows the various components that make up a directory to be accessed as a series of COM objects. In other words, ADSI is to Active Directory what WMI is to a computer system: Where WMI presents a set of objects to model the various components that make up a computer system, ADSI presents a set of objects to model the various entities in an organization.

Note: Scope of ADSI

ADSI is a generic interface designed to provide a consistent programmatic interface to directory services, and is not specific to the Active Directory. Often people talk of ADSI as the programmatic interface to Active Directory, but in reality this

continues ▶

▶ *continued*

functionality is provided by the ADSI Lightweight Directory Access Protocol *(LDAP) provider. Throughout this chapter, references to ADSI are a shorthand for "ADSI in conjunction with the LDAP provider" except where stated to the contrary.* ◆

ADSI presents a very different style of scripting interface to WMI: Both are implemented as a set of COM objects, but here the similarity ends. ADSI has no equivalent of the repository or of `SWbemServices` to act as a central starting point for exploration. Instead, objects are referenced directly using LDAP path strings, or indirectly by traversing a hierarchy of containers; relationships between objects are defined not by associators, but by their relative locations within an LDAP namespace. The personality of the objects themselves differs greatly too. WMI defines a large number of classes, each of which contains a small number of properties and methods that focus on a specific theme. By contrast, ADSI has comparatively few different classes, some of which hold vast numbers of properties covering a range of disparate pieces of information.

Despite these differences, both ADSI and WMI ultimately fulfil the same purpose, namely to provide a programmatic interface for an aspect of IT management; therefore, anyone who does a lot of scripting is bound to find the occasional problem whose ideal solution would involve using a *combination* of ADSI and WMI. Thankfully, it would appear that the WMI programming team at Microsoft were well aware of the annoyances associated with ADSI and WMI presenting such different interfaces, because they have provided a facility specifically designed to alleviate the suffering. This facility is the *Directory Provider*, a WMI provider that wraps the entirety of ADSI in WMI classes; the Directory Provider allows a program or script to treat ADSI objects as though they were actually WMI objects.

This chapter is all about the Directory Provider. It explains how ADSI objects are "mapped" into the WMI namespace and shows how information in the Active Directory can be used to choose a set of machines in your organization on which to run WMI scripts; in other words, it picks up the mantle dropped at the end of Chapter 4, "Remote Administration." If you are now getting excited by the prospect of learning all about ADSI, however, we are going to have to disappoint you. A detailed discussion of ADSI, its classes, and its philosophy is not strictly relevant to WMI and would double the length of this book. Therefore, we focus only on the overall structure of the ADSI object hierarchy to the extent needed to understand how the Directory Provider translates this structure into WMI terms. To illustrate our discussion, we introduce a small number of ADSI objects and discuss some of their properties. If this chapter manages to whet your appetite for ADSI, you may want to supplement the material in this book with a book on ADSI or at least with the ADSI Software Development Kit documentation. This chapter assumes familiarity with Active Directory or at least with the basic concepts of a directory.

The Structure of ADSI and Its WMI Mapping

If you have been exploring the WMI world with the Object Browser tool, you may be somewhat surprised to learn that the Active Directory is mapped into WMI; after all, so far, you are unlikely to have met any objects there that look as though they represent anything in the Active Directory. The reason for this is that ADSI-mapped objects do not live in the root\cimv2 namespace; they are not part of the CIMv2 schema or Microsoft's extensions to it. Instead, all ADSI-mapped objects live in namespaces under root\directory; Active Directory objects live in a root\directory\LDAP namespace.

Tip: Object Browser Difficulties

Unless you have a machine with a massive amount of memory, do not try to browse the root\directory\LDAP namespace with the Object Browser. The most likely outcome from attempting to do so is a very long wait followed by an Out of Memory error. ◆

This section of the chapter looks at some of the classes within the root\directory\LDAP namespace and shows how they fit together to represent an Active Directory.

Mapping of ADSI Classes

ADSI provides classes to represent every type of object that appears in the Active Directory, both at *node* and *leaf* level. Node-level classes are those that represent containers, such as organizations and organizational units; leaf-level classes are those that represent noncontainer units such as users and computers. The Directory Provider maps every ADSI class on to a WMI class, and every instance of an ADSI class on to a WMI object. Therefore, for any object accessible through ADSI, there is an equivalent object accessible through WMI.

Note: Underlying COM Objects

ADSI objects are implemented differently from WMI objects. Underneath, every WMI object is actually a COM `SWbemObject` *(see Chapter 11, "WMI Internals"); hence all WMI objects have a core set of methods, such as* `Associators_()` *and* `InstancesOf_()`*. The difference between, say, a* `Win32_ComputerSystem` *object and a* `Win32_Directory` *object is a matter for WMI to worry about and is not noticed by COM. By contrast, ADSI objects are implemented directly as COM objects; for example, computers are implemented through an* `IADsComputer` *COM interface and organizational units through* `IADsOUs`*; in other words, the differences between the ADSI objects is apparent on a COM level. Functionality common to all ADSI objects is implemented through multiple interfaces: Every ADSI object implements a core interface, IADs, in addition to anything specific to its type.* ◆

Each ADSI class effectively has two names: first, there is the name of the COM interface that implements it; second, there is the name of the Active Directory unit type that it represents. For example, the `IADsOU` class represents an `organizationalUnit`; hence, `IADsOU` and `organizationalUnit` are two different names by which the class can be identified. To distinguish WMI objects from their ADSI counterparts, the WMI class representing this unit has a different name again. For all practical purposes, the WMI name of a mapped class can be deduced according to a simple rule: Take the Active Directory name of the represented ADSI class, and add the prefix `DS_`. For example, an organizational unit is represented in WMI as an instance of `DS_organizationalUnit`; a computer is represented as `DS_computer`. This systematic modification of names is sometimes known in computer programming parlance as *name mangling*.

In reality, the close correspondence between ADSI class names and their WMI equivalents is not there merely to make life easier for users; rather, it stems from something fundamental about WMI class definitions that make them different from all the classes that we have met so far in the book, namely that they are *dynamic*. The concept of a class with *dynamic instances* should by now be familiar, because you have already seen it several times. An example is the `Win32_NTLogEvent` class: Although the class definition is stored in the Repository, the instances are not; whenever we execute a query such as `SELECT * FROM Win32_NTLogEvent`, the NT Event Log Provider springs into action and dynamically creates objects on our behalf. The Directory Provider takes this idea a stage further: not only the instances, but even the class definitions themselves are dynamic, created by the provider on demand. This gives the Directory Provider a marvelous future-proofing mechanism: It does not need to know about all the ADSI classes that exist or that may exist in the future; all it needs to know is that if it is asked about any class in the root\directory\LDAP namespace, it should look for an ADSI class whose name it can deduce.

Note: Class Mapping in Practice

For all practical purposes, the heuristic that allows a WMI class name to be deduced from its ADSI equivalent by prefixing the Active Directory name with `DS_` *works fine. However, it is a simplification of the real name mangling system. In practice, the "Active Directory" name used is the* `LDAP-Display-Name` *property of the ADSI class in question, and most classes are actually mapped to abstract WMI classes with an* `ADS_` *prefix from which the nonabstract* `DS_`*-prefixed classes are derived. For further details, and rationale for this system, refer to the Directory Provider documentation in the MSDN documentation.* ◆

Of course there is more to mapping a class than inventing a system of class names; properties and methods need mapping too. If you understand the class naming system, you will find property names a breeze: Every property in a WMI ADSI-mapped class is given the same name as its ADSI equivalent, but it is prefixed with `DS_`. For example, the `cn` (common name) property common to user and computer ADSI objects is mapped in WMI as `DS_cn`. No equivalent mapping is needed for methods, however. In ADSI, changes to objects are handled exclusively by writing to property values; where methods do appear, they handle more generic activities, such as creating new ADSI objects, deleting old ones, and enumerating the contents of container objects. In WMI, activities such as object creation, deletion, and enumeration are handled through a totally different mechanism, such as through methods of `SWbemServices` and `SWbemObject` and through WQL. Therefore, ADSI methods are not mapped into the WMI namespace.

Locating WMI-Mapped ADSI Objects

An understanding of class mapping between WMI and ADSI might be interesting, but it is certainly not sufficient knowledge if you intend to make use of the Directory Provider. After all, in most real-world scripting situations, you will not want to retrieve ADSI classes from the Repository, but *objects* representing particular users, particular computers and so on. The next topic we need to consider, therefore, is how to locate an object in ADSI and how this translates into WMI terms.

ADSI objects can be retrieved in VBScript in exactly the same way as WMI objects, namely through a call to the `GetObject()` function. Just like WMI, ADSI has its own format for moniker strings. A moniker string for connecting to an object within the Active Directory object looks something like this:

```
LDAP://<server or domain>/<path>
```

The `LDAP:` prefix tells `GetObject()` that the remainder of the moniker string should be interpreted by the LDAP service. Using `<server or domain>` fulfills the same role as the machine portion of a WMI moniker string. If a machine name is specified here, an attempt is made to connect directly to the LDAP service on the named machine; if a domain is specified, an attempt is made to connect to the LDAP service of any domain controller in the domain. If no server or domain is specified, an attempt is made to connect to the LDAP service of a domain controller in the same domain as the machine on which the script is running. The interesting part of the moniker string is `<path>`, which must uniquely specify the name of the object to be retrieved. This is specified as a standard LDAP path string, or more specifically, as the *distinguished name* of the object in question. Distinguished name is LDAP-speak for a string that uniquely identifies the object by fully specifying the path to its position within a directory hierarchy. Sadly, there is no space here to go into the details of LDAP naming systems, but the following two moniker strings, both of which specify fictitious objects on a fictitious system, should be sufficient to give you an idea:

```
LDAP://OU=IT,OU=Departments,DC=someorganization,DC=com
LDAP://CN=Peter Icraces,OU=IT,OU=Departments, DC=someorganization,DC=com
```

The first of these retrieves an object representing the *organizational unit* (OU) called IT that lives in another organizational unit called `Departments` in an Internet domain called `someorganization` within the top-level domain com. The second retrieves an object representing someone whose common name is Peter Icraces and whose object resides in the aforementioned `OU`. The important thing to note about these LDAP paths is that there can be only one Peter Icraces in the `IT` OU, and there can only be one IT in the `Departments OU`, and so on; the system works because every name is guaranteed to be unique within the context of the parent container. Neither of these examples specifies a server or domain, so the LDAP request is assumed to be destined for an LDAP server in the local domain.

Note: LDAP

LDAP is an acronym for the Lightweight Directory Access Protocol, *an Internet standard for querying and retrieving information from directory services. It is specified in a range of RFCs. The format of an LDAP URL string is specified in RFC2255.* ◆

The following short script demonstrates how to retrieve a user object using ADSI (that is, not WMI) and display some basic information by reading a few of its properties. For the sake of brevity, error handling has been omitted. If you want to try out the script yourself, change the LDAP moniker string to point to a valid distinguished name in your organization.

```
'aboutpeter.vbs - use ADSI to provide reader with a little
'information about fictitious user Peter Icraces
Option Explicit
Dim strPath
Dim refPeter
strPath = "LDAP://CN=Peter Icraces,OU=IT,OU=Departments," & _
          "DC=intranet,DC=someorganization,DC=com"
Set refPeter = GetObject(strPath)
WScript.Echo "Here is a little information about Peter:"
WScript.Echo "(Information courtesy of ADSI)"
WScript.Echo " Common name is " & refPeter.cn
WScript.Echo " Home directory is at " & refPeter.homeDirectory
WScript.Echo " Email address is " & refPeter.mail
WScript.Echo " Logon name is " & refPeter.samAccountName
Set refMe = Nothing
```

Translating this script into WMI terms is for the most part simple. You merely have to retrieve the relevant `DS_user` object and read the equivalent `DS_`-prefixed properties. There is only minor difficulty: retrieving the object in the first place. As you have no doubt noticed, the hierarchical LDAP paths used to specify objects within ADSI look nothing like WMI object paths, so there is no obvious way to correlate the two. The Directory Provider's designers have solved this problem in a foolproof, if perhaps inelegant way: Every object created by the Directory Provider, in addition to all the properties mapped from ADSI, possesses an `ADSIPath` property, which acts as the primary key for the object. This `ADSIPath` property contains the string `LDAP://` followed by the distinguished name of the entity represented by the object. In other words, the `ADSIPath` of the `DS_user` object representing Peter Icraces is exactly the same as the moniker string used in the preceding example to retrieve the ADSI object, as follows:

```
LDAP://CN=Peter Icraces,OU=IT,OU=Departments,
                          DC=Intranet,DC=someorganization,DC=com
```

The following script demonstrates the use of `ADSIPath` to retrieve a `DS_user` object and display the same information as the earlier example. Note that you connect to the root\directory\LDAP namespace on the local machine to retrieve the information; the WMI service on any machine can be used to retrieve objects representing the contents of the Active Directory in their own domain.

```
'aboutpeteragain.vbs - use WMI to provide reader with a little
'information about the fictitious user Peter Icraces
Option Explicit
Dim strPath
Dim refPeter
strPath = "LDAP://CN=Peter Icraces,OU=IT,OU=Departments," & _
          "DC=intranet,DC=someorganization,DC=com"
Set refPeter = GetObject _
```

```
    ("winMgmts:root\directory\LDAP:DS_User.ADSIPath='" & _
      strPath & "'")
WScript.Echo "Here is a little information about Peter:"
WScript.Echo "(Information courtesy of WMI)"
WScript.Echo " My common name is " & refPeter.DS_cn
WScript.Echo " My home directory is at " & refPeter.DS_homeDirectory
WScript.Echo " My email address is " & refPeter.DS_mail
WScript.Echo " My logon name is " & _
             refPeter.Properties_.item("DS_sAMAccountName")
Set refPeter = Nothing
```

Once `refPeter` points to a valid WMI object, the script looks almost identical to the ADSI version, except for the prevalence of `DS_` prefixes! One peculiar difference of note concerns `DS_sAMAccountName`, whose value is retrieved using a completely different mechanism from the other properties. Instead of using *direct access* as we have done almost exclusively throughout the book, `DS_sAMAccountName` is here accessed through the `SWbemObject`'s `Properties_` collection. This mechanism, which is available for all WMI properties, is described more fully in Chapter 11; for now the important thing to note is that a line of code such as this

```
WScript.Echo refSomeWMIObject.SomeProperty
```

should behave identically to

```
WScript.Echo refSomeWMIObject.Properties_.Item("SomeProperty")
```

The emphasis here is on the word "should"; the reason why our script example uses indirect access for `DS_sAMAccountName` is that an attempt to invoke this property directly causes a runtime error. We have noticed this phenomenon for quite a few mapped ADSI properties; we can assume only that it is due to a problem with the Directory Provider that will hopefully be solved in a future release. Meanwhile, we suggest that if ever you encounter an Invalid Index error while attempting to read a mapped property, try using indirect access.

This minor peculiarity notwithstanding, accessing Active Directory objects courtesy of the Directory Provider is not a difficult task. A slightly more difficult task is working out what properties are actually available on a mapped object. The difficulty lies in the fact that the ADSI class documentation is not the best piece of literature to have emanated from Microsoft headquarters; although most of the information can be found within the ADSI Software Development Kit documentation, specifically in the "LDAP ADSI Provider" section, the layout is not very scripter-friendly. If you are prepared to use a little guesswork, to read through a very large list of properties and accept that some properties that exist in theory are not necessarily implemented by the LDAP ADSI provider in practice, there is an alternative, quick way to retrieve a complete list of properties: Write a script that iterates through the `WMI Properties_` collection. Assuming that `refMe` points to a valid `DS_user` object, the following code fragment will display the name of every `DS_user` property. Be warned: The list is long! You will want to redirect the script's output to a file (that is, type something like **script.vbs > file.txt**):

```
For Each refProperty in refMe.Properties_
    WScript.Echo refProperty.Name
Next
```

If you are unsure about how or why this little script works, do not worry for now; all will be revealed in Chapter 11.

Mapping Containers

For ADSI objects that present leaves in the Active Directory, such as users and computers, there is no more to WMI mapping than that already described. For ADSI objects that represent *nodes* such as organizational units, however, there is an additional concern. To the extent that an organizational unit is just another object with a unique distinguished name and a set of properties, it can be mapped in WMI in the normal way as a `DS_organizationalUnit` with a unique `ADSIPath` and a set of `DS_`-prefixed properties. The additional concern is that an organization unit in ADSI is more than just an object; it is also a *container*, within which other objects reside. If the Directory Provider is truly to represent the hierarchical organization of the Active Directory, it must map the idea of containment.

Within ADSI itself, container objects are presented to languages such as VBScript as standard *collections*. Hence, a script that displays the name property of every item within a specified OU can be written trivially. The following example demonstrates this for a fictitious OU in the someorganization.com Active Directory. Error checking is omitted for the sake of brevity:

```
'membersofanOU.vbs - display the name of every
'object that resides in Peter Icraces's OU
Option Explicit
Dim strPath
Dim colOU
Dim refItem

strPath = "LDAP://OU=IT,OU=Departments, " & _
          "DC=intranet,DC=someorganization,DC=com"
Set colOU = GetObject(strPath)
For Each refItem in colOU
    wscript.echo refItem.name
Next
colOU = Nothing
```

The general look of this script should be very familiar; iterating through the contents of an organizational unit is no different from iterating through a collection of WMI objects as returned by `ExecQuery()`; a standard collection mechanism is used in both cases.

Active Directories are hierarchical structures, so it is highly likely that an organizational unit would contain all sorts of different objects, some of which are leaves and some of which are nodes. The IT organizational unit whose contents were queried in the previous script contains several user objects, a few computers, and several further organizational units. The ADSI design team must have realized that the ability to list the members of a container differentially by type (that is, list all users, or all computers, or all organizational units) would be a common requirement. This requirement is fulfilled by a `Filter` property, common to all container objects, which can be set to an array of type names. When a `Filter` is set, the collection representing the container yields only objects of the specified type. This is illustrated in the following script, which modifies the earlier code to list the names only of *users* within the IT organizational unit. It should be noted that the script will also output the names of every computer in the unit as well as human users, because computer is a subclass of user in ADSI-speak.

```
'usersinanOU.vbs - display the name of every
'user that resides in Peter Icraces's OU
Option Explicit
Dim strPath
Dim colOU
Dim refUser

strPath = "LDAP://OU=IT,OU=Departments, " & _
          "DC=intranet,DC=someorganization,DC=com"
Set colOU = GetObject(strPath)
colOU.Filter = Array("user")
For Each refUser in colOU
    wscript.echo refUser.name
Next
colOU = Nothing
```

Theoretically, there is no reason why the Directory Provider developers could not have mapped these ADSI features directly into WMI. After all, WMI makes extensive use of collections, so the concept is hardly alien; although the `Filter` property is not a particularly WMI-like concept, the Directory Provider could always have added it as a special case. Despite the possibility, however, the Directory Provider does *not* map container objects and filters in this way, probably because the ADSI mechanisms as described here do not fit at all well with the WMI ethos. To be sure, WMI has collections, but these are for the most part convenience groupings; they are not used to define relationships between objects. By contrast, in the ADSI world as described earlier, collections are considerably more than convenience classes; they define relationships between Active Directory objects.

In WMI, relationships between disparate objects are represented by associator classes. Therefore, to better map ADSI concepts into the WMI world, the Directory Provider replaces container collections with associators. Specifically, relationships between containers and their contents are modeled by instances of the `DS_LDAP_Instance_Containment` associator. This associator joins ADSI-mapped objects through its `ParentInstance` and `ChildInstance` properties. Therefore, to list the contents of a given OU using WMI, you connect to the root\directory\LDAP namespace of the WMI service on a machine in the relevant domain and execute an associator query. This is illustrated in the following script, which performs the same task as the first one presented in this section, namely to display the names of all objects in a specified OU. This script looks significantly more complex than its ADSI equivalent, but this is only because the WQL query string is rather verbose. Note that the query specifies a `ResultRole`; if it did not, the result set returned would include the parent OU as well as the children; the relationship between an OU and its parent is also defined by an `DS_LDAP_Instance_Containment`.

```
'membersofanOUagain.vbs - display the name of every object
'that resides in Peter's OU
Option Explicit
Dim strPath
Dim colOU
Dim refItem

Set refWMI = GetObject("winMgmts:root\directory\LDAP")
strPath = "LDAP://OU=IT,OU=Departments, " & _
          "DC=intranet,DC=someorganization,DC=com"
strQuery = "ASSOCIATORS OF {DS_OrganizationalUnit.ADSIPath='" & _
           strPath & "'} WHERE " & _
           "AssocClass=DS_LDAP_Instance_Containment " & _
           "ResultRole=ChildInstance"
Set colOU = refWMI.ExecQuery(strQuery)
For Each refItem in colOU
    WScript.Echo refItem.DS_name
Next
Set colOU = Nothing
Set refWMI = Nothing
```

We hope you agree that despite the verbosity of the query, this script is very transparent, and not dramatically different from many others presented in the book. In short, the Directory Provider does an excellent job of mapping ADSI hierarchical structures on to the conventions of the WMI world.

Modifying this script so that it displays only the users within the IT organizational unit is extremely simple; in fact, in our opinion, the WMI interface allows this to be accomplished much more easily than with ADSI. In WMI, we have no need of `Filter` properties or cumbersome arrays because the ability to discriminate between types is built in to associator queries. All you need to do is add a `ResultClass` qualifier to the query, as illustrated in the following modified script:

```
'usersinanOUagain.vbs - display the name of every user
'that resides in Peter's  OU
Option Explicit
Dim strPath
Dim colOU
Dim refUser

Set refWMI = GetObject("winMgmts:root\directory\LDAP")
strPath = "LDAP://OU=IT,OU=Departments, " & _
          "DC=intranet,DC=someorganization,DC=com"
strQuery = "ASSOCIATORS OF {DS_OrganizationalUnit.ADSIPath='" & _
           strPath & "'} WHERE " & _
           "AssocClass=DS_LDAP_Instance_Containment " & _
           "ResultRole=ChildInstance " & _
           "ResultClass=DS_user"
Set colOU = refWMI.ExecQuery(strQuery)
For Each refUser in colOU
    WScript.Echo refUser.DS_name
Next
Set colOU = Nothing
Set refWMI = Nothing
```

In fact, you could make the query slightly shorter: If you specify `DS_user` as a `ResultClass`, `ResultRole` can be safely omitted; after all, a `DS_user` can only *ever* be the `ChildInstance` of a container.

Context-Independent Searches

You have now seen how ADSI classes, objects, and the relationships between them are mapped into the WMI root\directory\LDAP namespace. Armed with this information and some ADSI documentation, you can now write scripts that retrieve information from Active Directory using the familiar WMI mechanisms and idioms. Before we leave the topic altogether, however, there is one more aspect to consider: *deep searching*. So far in this chapter, we have assumed that a script wants to retrieve a specific object within the Active Directory or to iterate the contents of a specific container object, and that in either case, the distinguished name of the object in question is known. This assumption is reasonable in many circumstances: The whole point in a directory structure is that it presents an organized hierarchical structure; if you are intending to write scripts that access your directory, you should probably know the directory is structured first! At times, however, you may want to access objects representing parts of an Active

Directory without necessarily knowing the distinguished name of the objects in advance. For example, you may want to list *all* the users in a directory regardless of where they sit in the organizational hierarchy, or search for an object whose location—and therefore distinguished name—is unknown. In these cases, what you really want is to perform a *deep search*.

If you are a C or C++ programmer, ADSI provides a simple, elegant directory searching mechanism in the form of an `IDirectorySearch` COM interface. Unfortunately, however, `IDirectorySearch` is not an *automation* interface, which means that it does not expose `IDispatch`, the COM interface used by VBScript to invoke method calls and property operations. In short, it means that it is not available to a VBScript programmer. The only way to search directories with ADSI from VBScript is via *ActiveX database objects* (ADOs), a set of COM objects that provide a backend-independent facility for interacting with databases. In common with the WMI and ADSI models, ADO isolates programs that want to use its facilities from the details of a particular database system through a provider interface. A database makes itself ADO compliant by presenting a COM API conforming to the ADO provider specifications; a client can access the database through ADO without worrying about whether the backend is MS Access, a huge mainframe database system, or an Active Directory.

Although ADO is a very powerful tool that makes life a dream for programmers who need to write database front ends, using it from VBScript just to enumerate a set of objects of a given type or to find an object within the Active Directory is a little bit like using a sledge-hammer to crack a nut, or a nuclear warhead to kill a fly! To give you some indication of the overkill, describing ADO in enough detail to present a fully explained example here would take a chapter in its own right; entire books have been written exclusively on the subject of ADO.

To be fair to ADSI, it is possible to enumerate objects without using ADO, provided you are prepared to indulge in a little bit of creative scripting. This is illustrated in the following script, which displays the common name of all users in the Active Directory in `someorganization.com`. It works by using a recursive subroutine call: first, it retrieves a reference to the ADSI object representing our intranet domain, and then it calls the subroutine `displayUsers()`, passing it a reference to the ADSI domain object. The `displayUsers()` subroutine takes a container as a parameter; each time it is called, it performs the following set of operations:

- It sets the container's `Filter` property to `users` and then iterates through the container's contents, displaying the common name of all users.
- It changes the `Filter` to `container` and `organizationalUnit`. Again it iterates through the contents, but this time each retrieved object is a

container or organizational unit rather than a user. For each element, it recursively calls `displayUsers()`, passing the element in question as a parameter.

The result is a complete listing of every user object in every container in the entire domain.

For a reminder of recursive calls, turn back to Chapter 3, "Examining the Filesystem with WMI." In common with the other scripts presented so far in this chapter, error handling is omitted.

```
'allcommonnames.vbs - display the names of all users in an
'Active Directory
Option Explicit
Dim strPath
Dim colDomain
strPath = "LDAP://DC=intranet,DC=someorganization,DC=com"
Set colDomain = GetObject(strPath)
displayUsers(colDomain)
Set colDomain = Nothing

Sub displayUsers(colOU)
    Dim refOU
    colOU.Filter = Array("user")
    For Each refUser in colOU
        WScript.Echo refUser.cn
    Next
    colOU.Filter = Array("container","organizationalUnit")
    For Each refOU in colOU
        displayUsers(refOU)
    Next
    colOU.Filter = Empty
End Sub
```

Now we have an enumeration solution that does not rely on ADO. Performing a similar trick for a more discriminating search, however, would be extremely difficult, if not impossible. Of course it would always be possible to check every single object in the directory to see whether it matches a set of search criteria, but that would be absurdly inefficient.

If you have been wondering up until now whether there is any point in using the Directory Provider given that ADSI seems to offer a perfectly good interface for most purposes, here is the moment to be convinced. When it comes to searching a directory, the WMI interface shows effortless superiority! Searches may require the heavy machinery of ADO for ADSI, but not so for WMI, because search-and-retrieval functionality lies at the very core of WMI's design. Retrieving an object representing every user in the Active Directory from within WMI is just a matter of executing an `InstancesOf()` method call for `DS_user` objects, or executing the following trivial WQL query:

```
SELECT * FROM DS_user
```

A WMI version of this script needs no recursive subroutine calls or cumbersome filtering; it just connects to the root\directory\LDAP namespace of a machine in the domain, executes the query, and iterates through the returned collection in the usual WMI way. This is illustrated, without error handling, here:

```
'grab ALL users on a system with WMI
'allcommonnamesagain.vbs - display the names of all
'users in an Active Directory, using WMI
Option Explicit
Dim refWMI
Dim colEveryone
Dim refUser
set refWMI = GetObject("winMgmts:root\directory\LDAP")
set colEveryone = refWMI.ExecQuery("SELECT * FROM DS_User")
For Each refUser in colEveryone
    WScript.Echo refUser.DS_cn
Next
Set colEveryone = Nothing
Set refWMI = Nothing
```

If you agree with us that this solution is more convenient than the ADSI approach, the best is yet to come! As already noted, a more discriminating enumeration or a directory search in ADSI requires the use of ADO; by contrast, we can change the scope of objects returned by the preceding WMI script merely by adding a trivial `WHERE` clause to the query. To end this section of the chapter, we provide a fully fledged script example that demonstrates the use of WMI to search for objects in the Active Directory. The purpose of the script is to find the name and logon identifier of a user whose location within the directory is not known but whose email address is. The script takes a single command-line parameter, namely, an email address, which it uses to perform a WQL query.

```
'finduserfrommail.vbs - find a user within the Active Directory
'based on command-line specified email address
Option Explicit
On Error Resume Next
Dim refWMI
Dim colEveryone
Dim refUser
Dim strQuery

'check cmd-line argument
If WScript.Arguments.Count <> 1 Then
    WScript.Echo "Usage: finduserfrommail.vbs <email address>"
    WScript.Quit
End If

'attempt to connect to WMI
set refWMI = GetObject("winMgmts:root\directory\LDAP")
```

```
If Err <> 0 Then
    WScript.Echo "Oh dear. Could not connect to LDAP namespace"
    WScript.Quit
End If

'build and execute query
strQuery = "SELECT * FROM DS_user WHERE DS_mail = '" & _
           WScript.Arguments(0) & "'"
set colEveryone = refWMI.ExecQuery(strQuery)

'display users' common name and logon
'logon uses Properties_() to avoid weird DS Provider bug
For Each refUser in colEveryone
    WScript.Echo refUser.DS_cn & " - " & _
                 refUser.Properties_("DS_sAMAccountName")
Next

Set colEveryone = Nothing
Set refWMI = Nothing
```

This script could, of course, be modified to perform a search based on any properties of `DS_user`, or even on a different ADSI-mapped class altogether. Thanks to the Directory Provider, scripts can operate on Active Directory objects as though they were just another part of WMI that happens to be mapped into the root\directory\LDAP namespace.

Note: Object Creation and Deletion

This chapter is concerned exclusively with retrieving information from the Active Directory. A very common use of ADSI, however, is to write management scripts that create and delete user objects. Because this book focuses squarely on computer systems rather than user management, we do not discuss this aspect of ADSI. Note, however, that the Directory Provider supports object creation and deletion through the usual WMI mechanisms, namely `SpawnInstance_()` *and* `Delete_()`. *For more information on these methods, see Chapter 5, "WMI Security," and Chapter 11, "WMI Internals"; for information about ADSI user management, see the ADSI Software Development Kit documentation.* ◆

Selecting Computers to Manage with Active Directory

So far in this chapter, we have considered how the Directory Provider maps an Active Directory into a WMI namespace, and have suggested circumstances in which the flexibility of the WMI interface makes it preferable to ADSI for management scripting. If you intend to take this further and undertake any serious Active Directory scripting either through WMI and the Directory Provider or directly via ADSI, you should refer to ADSI documentation for information about classes that exist and the properties that they expose.

This part of the chapter demonstrates a specific use of the Directory Provider and Active Directory that has direct relevance to the core theme of the book, namely, computer selection. Much of the latter part of Chapter 4, "Remote Administration," was devoted to a discussion of various ways in which scripts could perform operations in bulk, connecting to the WMI service of a number of machines chosen according to command-line arguments, IP address ranges, or the contents of a text file. Here we present a more sophisticated selection approach that connects to the WMI service of machines chosen according the Active Directory search criteria. Specifically, we demonstrate how to connect to the WMI service on all computers in a domain, all servers in a domain, or all domain controllers to run targeted WMI operations in bulk.

Connecting to the WMI service on a series of machines in turn involves constructing a moniker string for each one and passing it as a parameter to VBScript's `GetObject()` function. Assuming that the moniker string is built correctly, the client and server machines are both networked, WMI is working correctly, and the security clearance adequate, this method works regardless of the source of the information from which the moniker strings are built. Connecting to the WMI service on a series of machines chosen according to an Active Directory search, therefore, just involves retrieving ADSI-mapped objects corresponding to the machines in question and finding some data in each that can be used to build the moniker string. Every computer in a Windows 2000 domain is registered somewhere in the Active Directory, either in the "computers" container, or in a well-structured directory, somewhere within an organizational unit hierarchy. Within WMI, Active Directory computer objects are represented by instances of `DS_computer`, a subclass of `DS_user`. As will be revealed shortly, `DS_computer` objects have several properties that can be used to build a moniker string. Before we worry about these, however, we need to consider how to retrieve a set of `DS_computer` objects in the first place. This is accomplished in exactly the same way as in the user examples in the preceding section, as is illustrated by the suggestions later in this chapter.

Selecting Computer Objects

A very common requirement for administrators making regular use of scripts to manage remote workstations and servers is to be able to run a script on every machine on the network or, in Active Directory terms, on every machine in the domain. Retrieving a collection of `DS_computer` objects representing every machine in a domain via WMI is utterly trivial. As you have probably already guessed, it can be accomplished with two lines of VBScript, illustrated in the following code fragment:

```
'connect to WMI and retrieve a collection of DS_computers
Set refWMI = GetObject("winMgmts:root\directory\LDAP")
Set colComputers = refWMI.ExecQuery("SELECT * FROM DS_Computer")
```

Just as with any other WMI query, the scope can be narrowed by the introduction of a `WHERE` clause. For example, workstations can be targeted with a query such as this:

```
SELECT * From DS_computer WHERE
                    DS_OperatingSystem='Windows 2000 Professional'
```

Likewise, servers can be targeted with this:

```
SELECT * From DS_computer WHERE DS_OperatingSystem='Windows 2000 Server'
```

If you examine the huge number of properties presented by the `DS_computer` class, either by reading the ADSI documentation or by using the property iteration trick described earlier in the chapter, there is virtually no limit to the criteria that can be invented for selecting computers.

Note: ADSI Objects Impinge on WMI

Examination of the `DS_computer` *class reveals significant overlap between properties that it exposes and information made available by the* `Win32_ComputerSystem` *class under the root\cimv2 namespace with which you are rather more familiar. In fact, ADSI presents several entire classes that model components well covered by WMI classes, such as services and print queues.* ◆

A criterion that does deserve special mention here is the isolation of domain controllers. At first glance, it seems that querying for domain controllers might be a rather difficult task because `DS_computer` does not obviously yield information in any of its properties that can be used to distinguish a domain controller from a normal, humble server. We can overcome this difficulty by observing that computer objects representing domain controllers all live in a special organizational unit called *domain controllers* just below the domain root of an Active Directory; to retrieve the `DS_computer` objects, you can use an `ASSOCIATORS OF` query, as illustrated here:

```
ASSOCIATORS OF {
        DS_OrganizationalUnit.ADSIPath=
        'LDAP://OU=Domain Controllers,DC=intranet,DC=someorganization,DC=com'
        } WHERE AssocClass=DS_LDAP_Instance_Containment
                ResultClass=DS_computer
```

The query may be look somewhat different from the other examples, but the principle is the same: We use WQL to specify criteria for retrieving `DS_computer` objects from the Active Directory.

Building a Moniker String

Having retrieved a collection of DS_computer objects representing each machine on which we would like a script to run, the next stage in connecting to WMI is to build a set of moniker strings to pass to GetObject(). DS_computer has several properties that can potentially be used to construct a moniker; the two most useful ones are DS_cn and DS_dNSHostName.

DS_cn is inherited from DS_user and, as you have already seen, contains the LDAP common name of the object. In Microsoft networking terms, this corresponds to the machine name. Therefore, assuming that refComputer holds a valid reference to a computer object, the following line of VBScript constructs a moniker string suitable for connecting to the default namespace of the WMI service on the machine represented by that object:

```
strMoniker = "winMgmts:\\" & refComputer.DS_cn
```

Theoretically, as far as LDAP is concerned, there could be several computer objects in a domain whose common name is identical, provided that they reside in different organizational units; therefore, from an LDAP perspective, the preceding line of code is ambiguous. Because Microsoft networking dictates that all machine names on a network must be uniquely named, however, you can be confident that a moniker string constructed in this way does actually point unambiguously to the WMI service of the machine represented by refComputer.

If you want to be absolutely sure that any moniker string you construct points to a machine whose name is unique Internet-wide, the solution is to read DS_computer's DS_dNSHostName property. As the name implies, this property stores the fully qualified host name of the machine as registered with DNS. The following fragment of code creates a WMI moniker string using DS_dNSHostName:

```
strMoniker = "winMgmts:\\" & refComputer.DS_dNSHostName
```

When refComputer points to the machine on which I am currently writing, the above line of code yields a moniker string of

```
"winMgmts:\\albatross.intranet.someorganization.com".
```

Before we leave the somewhat uninteresting topic of DS_computer properties that can be used as part of WMI moniker strings, one final property deserves a mention: the rather tantalizingly named DS_wbemPath. One might be forgiven for thinking that this property might actually contain a fully formed moniker string suitable for connecting to the default namespace of the represented machine; sadly, however, it does not. At the time of writing, the current version of the LDAP ADSI provider does not use this property at all; its value is null.

Note: IWMIADSIExtension

When using ADSI to retrieve a collection of computer objects, the need to construct a moniker string can be bypassed altogether, thanks to `IWMIADSIExtension`*, an extension that adds three methods to the ADSI computer object. One of these,* `GetWMIServices()`*, returns a* `SWbemServices` *object representing the WMI service on the machine in question. This method uses the standard connection mechanisms under the hood; it merely wraps them. Therefore, it is subject to all the same constraints and susceptible to the same errors as a manual connection attempt. We do not consider* `IWMIADSIExtension` *to be a particularly useful addition to the WMI programmer's arsenal!* ◆

The final stage in connecting to the WMI service on a machine represented by a `DS_computer` object is to pass the newly created moniker string to `GetObject()`. This procedure needs no discussion here because it is exemplified by virtually every script in the entire book.

To consolidate this and the preceding section, we present below the following fully fledged script example that attempts to connect to the default namespace of the WMI service on every machine in the domain in which it is run. The script is presented complete with error handling: If it fails to connect to a machine, it outputs an error message and tries the next one; if connection is successful, it outputs a message to that effect and calls a `CarryOutActions()` subroutine, passing a reference to the WMI service to which it has connected. In the following implementation, `CarryOutActions()` just outputs a message; to use this script in a real-world situation, replace the subroutine body with something useful.

```
'bulkoperate.vbs - connect to the WMI service of
'each machine in a domain in turn, so that WMI
'operations may be performed
Option Explicit
On Error Resume Next
Dim refWMI
Dim colComputers
Dim refComputer
Dim refHostWMI
Dim strMoniker


'first connect to LDAP namespace on local machine
Set refWMI = GetObject("winMgmts:root\directory\LDAP")
If Err <> 0 Then
    WScript.Echo "Oh dear. I cannot connect to the LDAP namespace"
    WScript.Quit
End If

'retrieve all DS_computer objects. Attempt to connect to WMI
'on each, using DS_dNSHostName
```

```
Set colComputers = refWMI.ExecQuery("SELECT * FROM DS_computer")
For Each refComputer in colComputers
    strMoniker = "winMgmts:\\" & refComputer.DS_dNSHostName
    Set refHostWMI = GetObject(strMoniker)
    If Err <> 0 Then
         WScript.Echo "Could not connect to " & refComputer.DS_cn
         Err.Clear
    Else
      WScript.Echo "Connected to " & refComputer.DS_cn
      CarryOutActions refWMI
    End If
Next

'tidy up
Set refWMI = Nothing

'fill in the body of this subroutine with
'useful code. It is called once for every machine in the domain.
Sub CarryOutActions(refWMI)
    WScript.Echo "Doing useful things..."
End Sub
```

This script framework, therefore, in conjunction with any of the script bodies presented anywhere else in this book, provides a simple yet powerful way of controlling or retrieving information about all the machines on your network. Of course, the script could be altered so that `CarryOutActions()` is executed only on domain controllers, on servers, or on machines based on any other criteria; we leave any such modifications as an exercise to the reader.

Summary

This chapter demonstrated the use of WMI to retrieve information from an Active Directory, thus providing a single, coherent programmatic interface for managing both directories and computers. It explained how ADSI objects modeling the components of a directory service are mapped by the Directory Provider into WMI terms, and illustrated situations in which the WMI interface has advantages over its ADSI counterpart. Finally, it showed how to run scripts that connect to the WMI service of machines in a domain based on information stored in the domain's Active Directory.

10

Script Development and Deployment

We have now almost arrived at the end of our WMI tour. Hopefully, you are now inspired to start writing scripts that make use of WMI objects to keep you informed about the state of your computer systems and to keep those systems running smoothly. In this, the penultimate chapter of the book, we take a break from WMI itself and pause to consider some tools and techniques that can help you develop reusable, robust scripting solutions and deploy them across an organization.

Making Use of the Windows Scripting Host

Every script presented so far in this book has used the Windows Scripting Host (WSH) in two ways. First, each has quite literally been run *by* WSH. WSH has opened a file containing VBScript code and passed the data on to the VBScript runtime engine. Second, we have made use of several COM objects provided at runtime by WSH, the most obvious being `WScript`, whose `Echo()` method has appeared in literally every one of our scripts. In this light, the section title "Making Use of the Windows Scripting Host" may seem rather strange. After all, we have being doing just that all along! However, there is rather more to WSH than first meets the eye. Not only can its runtime behavior be usefully modified with a number of command-line options, but it also has an entire mode of operation that we have not even discussed yet! The section presents the most useful command-line parameters and introduces this new mode of operation.

Useful Command-Line Options

As noted before, there are two executable files associated with WSH: WScript.exe and cscript.exe. When the former runs a script, caused by an invocation such as wscript c:\temp\myscript.vbs, WSH executes in Windows mode, in which all user interaction is handled by pop-up dialog boxes. With the notable exception of the asynchronous event subscriber scripts presented in Chapter 8, "Proactive Troubleshooting with WMI Events," we have recommended the use of the other alternative, cscript.exe. A command such as cscript c:\temp\myscript.vbs causes WSH to run in Command-Line mode, in which user interaction is handled by the console. As mentioned briefly in Chapter 3, "Examining the Filesystem with WMI," VBS files under Windows 2000 are *associated* with the Windows Scripting Host, which means that an invocation such as myscript.vbs at the command-line is enough to spark execution without any explicit mention of wscript.exe or cscript.exe. By default, a WSH session sparked by file association runs using wscript.exe. As noted in Chapter 3, you can change this default behavior by running cscript.exe or wscript.exe once with the `//H:<host>` command-line option. Typing the following at the command-line causes cscript.exe to be the default host from that moment on:

```
c:>cscript //H:cscript
```

The following complementary invocation causes the default to revert to wscript.exe:

```
c:>cscript //H:wscript
```

`//H:<host>` is the only command-line option discussed so far in this book. However, it is by no means the only option offered by wscript.exe and cscript.exe. Many of the other options are useful only in rare circumstances. After all, we have got through almost an entire book without mentioning them. Three, however, deserve a mention here:

- First, something cosmetic. When running scripts in Command-Line mode, as you have probably been doing throughout this book, you might have been irritated by the two-line Microsoft copyright notice that appears before any script output. You can suppress this notice with `//nologo`. For example, cscript //nologo myscript.vbs launches myscript.vbs without displaying the copyright message.
- When running a script unattended, it would be reassuring to know that a WMI query does not take all day to execute, or that a programming error does not result in an unattended script running wild. For circumstances such as this, you can use the `//T:<sec>` option to provide a hard timeout. For example, cscript //T:20 myscript.vbs runs myscript.vbs in the usual way, but forcibly halts execution after the script has been running for 20 seconds. By default, script execution is never timed-out, which is the equivalent of specifying `//T:0`. Ideally, scripts should be self-monitoring, and it would certainly be rather bad programming practice to rely on WSH timeouts for flow control. However, the facility can occasionally be useful and is there if you want it.

- A command-line option such as `//nologo` may well be something that you would want to specify every single time any script is run. In which case, the `//S` option is your friend. This option "saves" any other specified options for future default use. In other words, a one-off invocation of `cscript //nologo //S` would ensure that all further scripts are run with an implicit `//nologo` option.

For information on other command-line options offered by cscript.exe and wscript.exe, check out the Windows Scripting Host documentation on the MSDN web site (`http://msdn.microsoft.com`).

Note: Why Double Slashes in Command-Line Parameters?

There is a convention for programs written on Microsoft platforms which states that command-line options are preceded by a single slash (for instance, `dir /p`*). However, all options for cscript.exe and wscript.exe must be preceded by a double slash (for instance,* `cscript //H:cscript`*). There is a very good reason for this break with convention: It allows WSH to discriminate between command-line options for WSH itself and command-line options for the script that it is running. In an invocation such as the following, there is no real room for confusion:*

```
c:>cscript //nologo myscript.vbs /goose
```

The option following `cscript` *is clearly destined for WSH, and the option following* `myscript.vbs` *is destined for the script. (The example, of course, assumes that* `myscript.vbs` *is expecting* `/goose` *as a parameter.) Ambiguity does arise, however, when cscript.exe is being invoked implicitly owing to file associations. Without the double-slash convention, there would be no way of distinguishing whether an option was intended for WSH or for a script. Thanks to the convention, wscript.exe or cscript.exe can interpret anything beginning with a double slash as an option for itself, and anything else as a parameter for the script. Hence, the following invocation:*

```
c:>cscript //nologo myscript.vbs /goose
```

can be replaced with this:

```
c:>myscript.vbs //nologo /goose
```

Both will have exactly the same effect. If you are using this sort of thing, however, note one small caveat: Do not write a script that expects to receive a parameter beginning with two slashes; it will not work! ◆

WSH 2.0 and WSF Files

The command-line options described in the preceding section add a few minor conveniences, but are hardly revelatory. There is another feature of the Windows Scripting Host that we have yet to discuss, however, that can make a dramatic difference to the ease with which scripts can be developed and reused: the WSF file.

So far in this book, whenever we have wanted to create a script, we have typed the relevant VBScript syntax into an editor, saved it with a .vbs extension, and then run it. By doing this, we have actually been running the Windows Scripting Host in version 1 Compatibility mode. Since the launch of WSH 2.0, which ships with Windows 2000, there has been another possibility, namely to write WSF files. These files can contain code written in VBScript, JScript, or any other WSH-compliant language, but the code is wrapped in XML tags. A typical WSF file looks something like this:

```
<?xml version="1.0"?>
<job id="hellojob">
    <script language="vbscript">
    <![CDATA[
      'script data goes here
      WScript.Echo "Hello. I am your script"
      WScript.Quit
    ]]>
    </script>
</job>
```

The first line is an XML directive that should appear at the top of every XML document. It merely asserts that the file contains an XML document and specifies the XML version being used. Next is a `<job>` tag, demarking the start of a scripting job. Optionally, a job can have an `id` string, a textual name by which it can be identified. WSF files could contain code written in one of several languages, so the next line, `<script language="vbscript">`, asserts that script code is about to appear and that it should be parsed by the VBScript scripting engine. Even if you are unfamiliar with XML, you may have guessed the meaning of every tag mentioned so far; by contrast, `<![CDATA[` probably needs an explanation. In XML, certain characters, notably < and > take on a special meaning; yet, such characters may also appear within a script as part of the VBScript code (for instance, `If numChapter > 9 Then ...`). The `<![CDATA[` tag is a special XML directive that tells the XML parser to ignore any special characters and treat all ensuing text as raw data. To continue our journey through the WSF file, the `]]>` tag closes the `<![CDATA[` block, `</script>` closes the script block, and `</job>` closes the `<job>` block. A golden rule in XML is that every tag *must* be accompanied by a complementary closing tag. A closing tag, just like in HTML, contains the name of the opening tag preceded by a slash.

If you type the preceding example into a text editor, save it with a .wsf extension, and execute it with `wscript` or `cscript`, you should find `Hello. I am your script` appearing on your screen.

Note: Packages

A single WSF files can include several `<job>` `</job>` *pairs, all enclosed in a* `<package>` `</package>` *pair. By default, WSH executes the first job in a WSF file; another job can be specified with the* `//j:<jobname>` *command-line option.* ◆

From the description of WSF files given so far, you might be wondering what on earth their point might be. We have had to sandwich our script with several lines of XML gobbledy-gook for no apparent gain! For a script as trivial as the preceding one, this assessment would almost certainly be fair. There would be very little point in writing such as script in this format. For the minor inconvenience of writing a little XML around our scripts, however, WSF does in fact offer some extremely useful facilities. Perhaps the most useful of these, and the one we will focus on here, is the ability to automatically include code written in other files.

At various points throughout this book, we have presented small utility functions that carry out tasks that could be useful in a number of WMI scripting situations. For example, Chapter 3 presented conversion functions that turn WMI date strings into VB dates and vice versa. In Chapter 4, "Remote Administration" a pair of functions converted between a string and numeric representation of an IP address. If you write scripts on a regular basis, it is highly likely that you will build quite a library of such functions as the need for various routines arises. One of the main points in writing standalone functions or subroutines for scripting is that once written, they can be used again and again in future scripts.

If all your scripts are written in .vbs files, however, reusing code in this way is a rather cumbersome process; it involves either retyping the function code every time you want to use it, or else extensive use of cut-and-paste. Both of these solutions are inconvenient, and both can easily introduce annoying errors. WSF files present a simple and elegant solution to this problem: It allows functions and subroutines to be referenced from external libraries.

Referencing external VBScript code within a script job is just a matter of including an invocation, such as the following, inside the `<job>` tag:

```
<script language="vbscript" src="c:\scripts\library.vbs"/>
```

This means "start a script block, and take the code from c:\scripts\library.vbs." Note that the closing bracket is preceded by a slash. This is the XML syntax for a tag that does not have a matching close tag. Once an invocation such as this has been made, other code in the job can use any functions or subroutines in c:\scripts\library.vbs as though they had been typed directly into the WSF file itself.

Note: Including Code from Other Languages

A WSF file can reference code written in any language registered with the Windows Scripting Host of a machine. The language attribute merely needs setting appropriately. For example, a code library written in JScript can be included (and then used from VBScript) with an invocation such as this:

```
<script language="jscript" src="c:\scripts\library.js"/> ◆
```

By way of illustration, consider the following two scripts, the first of which defines a function, `getHelloText()`, and the second, which uses that function:

```
'sillyfunc.vbs - a vbs file containing a silly function
Function getHelloText()
    getHelloText = "Hello. I am hello text"
End Function
```

Second file:

```
<?xml version="1.0"?>
<!-- usefunction.wsf: a WSF file that uses getHelloText() —>
<job>
    <script language="vbscript" src="c:\scripts\sillyfunc.vbs"/>
    <script language="vbscript">
    <![CDATA[
        'calling external function...
        WScript.Echo getHelloText()
    ]]>
    </script>
</job>
```

Assuming that the first script is saved to a file called c:\scripts\sillyfunc.vbs, the second can call `getHelloText()` as though the function had been implemented locally. Running the second script causes the text `"Hello. I am hello text"` to display.

Tip: XML Comments

In XML, comments are demarked by `<!--` *and* `—>` *tags.* ◆

Thanks to the WSF facility for including source code from other files, you can build a large library of useful functions, store them all in a single file, and reference them in any scripts when you need them. If you do a lot of scripting for system administration, the usefulness of this facility easily outweighs the minor inconvenience of having to enclose scripts within XML tags.

The idea of writing reusable code components can be taken a step further with Windows script components, sets of script functions that appear to the outside world as COM objects. The `WMIBook.SimpleReport` object introduced in Chapter 6, "Logs and Reports," is an example of such a beast.

Unfortunately, an explanation of how to write such components, although not particularly complicated, is beyond the scope of this book. Therefore, if you want to write such components yourself, or want to find out more about the WSF files and the facilities they offer, check out Parts I and II of Tim Hill's excellent book, *Windows 2000 Windows Script Host.*

Debugging Tools and Techniques

In an ideal world, no scripts would ever have bugs. There would be no typing errors, no conceptual misunderstandings, and everything would work seamlessly all the time. Sadly, such a picture is rarely reality. Inevitably, complex scripts do not work immediately as intended, either owing to an error on the part of the scripter or, occasionally, because the system being scripted is itself problematic or badly documented. This section considers some of the common bugs that recur when writing scripts that use WMI and suggest some tools and techniques that can be used to combat them. Many bugs, particularly those involving syntax errors and typing mistakes, are not WMI-specific but crop up generally when programming VBScript. This section, however, concentrates mainly on matters specific to WMI. The section ends with a few more general observations.

WQL Queries

In our experience, the single most common cause of script misbehavior is an incorrect WQL query. One of three things can, and regularly does, go wrong with queries:

- They can be syntactically incorrect.
- They can refer to nonexistent (a.k.a. misspelled) classes or properties.
- They can be seeking nonexistent instances.

All three types of errors should be completely avoidable. Regrettably, however, even people like ourselves who are using WMI virtually every working day of our lives commit all three on an all-too-regular basis. For the curious, the most common errors that we have encountered, both in our own and other people's scripts, are `WHERE` clauses in `ASSOCIATORS OF` queries. For some reason, everyone seems to forget that independent parts of these clauses should not be conjoined with `AND`. This mistake is made over and over again, even by people who should and do know better!

Most WQL errors, although ubiquitous, are easy to spot. They prevent a script from working correctly and, unless disguised by devious error-handling techniques, they show up at runtime as VBScript fatal errors. Sadly, fixing them is not always as trivial as finding them, especially in sophisticated scripts where WQL query strings are built up programmatically. Thankfully, two invaluable tools can help in the debugging task.

The first of these is a rather unassuming tool that we have met many times before: `WScript.Echo()`. You might think that this method is merely a way of displaying script output, but it is much, much more. It is probably the single most useful debugging tool available to the VBScript programmer. The power of `WScript.Echo()` lies in its simplicity. It allows you to display the value of a string or numeric variable at any time during code execution. If you are building a WQL query programmatically, display the result with `WScript.Echo()` before you pass it to WMI, and you will be amazed at how many times the problem leaps out from the display. Perhaps an apostrophe is missing, or two keywords are unintentionally joined because of a missing space. Perhaps you used an `AND` to conjoin two terms in the `WHERE` clause of an `ASSOCIATORS OF` query.

If you encounter a WQL error whose cause cannot be deduced by examining the query visually, a more sophisticated tool can help: the *Windows Management Instrumentation Tester*. This tool, as the name implies, is a general-purpose program for testing WMI systems. Most of the tool's functionality, such as the capability to display classes and instances and to examine MOF definitions, is better handled by the more modern and user-friendly Object Browser and CIM Studio (see Chapter 6, "Logs and Reports" and Chapter 11, "WMI Internals" respectively); however, it has one feature that is not duplicated elsewhere, namely the capability to execute queries passed to it directly in WQL syntax. Here, we concentrate only on this use.

To start the Windows Management Instrumentation Tester, type **wbemtest.exe** into the Run dialog box on the Start menu and click OK. A dialog appears on the screen containing many buttons, each of whose legends corresponds to a WMI activity (see Figure 10.1).

Most of these buttons are initially disabled, because before the tool can be used, you must log on to a namespace. This is accomplished by clicking Connect, which displays the logon dialog box (see Figure 10.2). In this dialog box, you can select a namespace to which to connect, choose a number of connection options such as the DCOM impersonation and delegation levels, and, if connecting to a remote machine, supply a username and password. Almost all of these options are self-explanatory and need no specific discussion here. Two options, however, need further explanation:

- A rather strange pair of radio buttons allows you to select whether an empty password should be interpreted as NULL or Blank. If NULL is chosen, an attempt is made to connect to WMI without a password. If Blank is chosen, a zero-length password string is sent.

- Beneath the User and Password fields is an Authority field. This is used to specify whether a connection to a remote machine should be attempted using NTLM or Kerberos authentication (see Chapters 5, "WMI Security" and Chapter 6).

Because the most useful function of wbemtest.exe is to test WQL queries, a task that can almost invariably be accomplished using WMI on a local machine, both of these options are largely irrelevant in most situations.

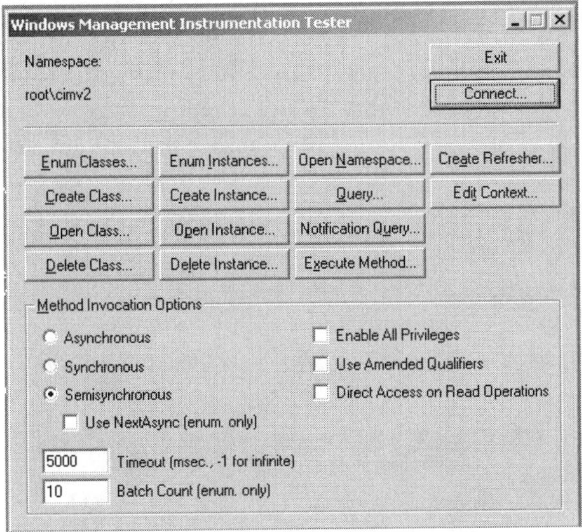

Figure 10.1 *The Windows Management Instrumentation Tester.*

Figure 10.2 *wbemtest logon dialog.*

After wbemtest has connected to a namespace, all the options in the main dialog box become available. We will look at two of these: Query and Notification Query.

Clicking on Query results in a simple dialog box appearing into which a WQL query may be typed. Type in your suspect query and click Apply. If it is syntactically invalid, you will be informed of this fact with an Invalid Query error. If you are attempting to query against a nonexistent class, this also will be revealed. Where wbemtest really comes into its own is when a query is syntactically correct but does not return the result set you are expecting; because when a query successfully executes, its results display in a pop-up dialog box (see Figure 10.3). Often, seeing the result set returned by a query without any of the VBScript trappings surrounding it gives enough of a clue to allow you to isolating what has gone wrong and what needs to be changed.

Tip: Object Details in wbemtest

If you double-click any of the objects in a wbemtest results list, a second dialog box appears giving details of the object. The format is so ugly that we do not consider this to be a useful feature; the Object Browser is a better tool for this job. ◆

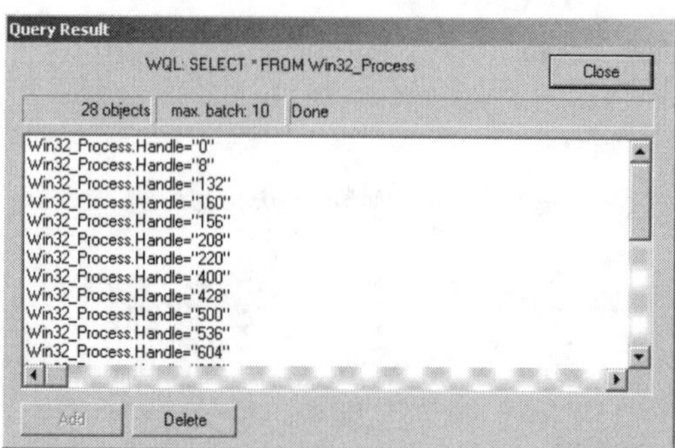

Figure 10.3 `SELECT * FROM Win32_Process.`

The Notification Query button on the wbemtest main dialog box fulfils the equivalent role for notification queries. Typing a query such as `SELECT * FROM __InstanceCreationEvent WITHIN 10 WHERE TargetInstance ISA 'Win32_Process'` and executing it with wbemtest results in a dialog box appearing into which events are "delivered" within 10 seconds of a new process being created.

Note: Event Viewer

For debugging permanent event subscription queries, WMI provides a rather useful Event Viewer tool. This is an `EventConsumer` *that responds to each event it receives by displaying the event details in a dialog box. For information about the* `EventConsumer` *architecture, refer to Chapter 8, "Proactive Troubleshooting with WMI Events". For details on how to use the Event Viewer tool, see the WMI Software Development Kit documentation.* ◆

The Windows Management Instrumentation Tester is clunky and unpleasant to use, but it is an extremely convenient tool for those times when you want to test WQL queries alone, without any surrounding VBScript code. This functionality, sadly, is not duplicated in any of the more aesthetically pleasing WMI tools. If you are about to use the tool to test a problematic `ASSOCIATORS OF` query, check it with `WScript.Echo()` first. You will probably find that the query works just fine as long as you remove those conjunctions!

Errors

Perhaps the most common cause of runtime errors within WMI scripts involves attempts to connect to remote machines. Difficulties can arise either through an incorrectly formatted moniker string or, more usually, because the remote machine is nonexistent or temporarily unavailable. Throughout the book, we have been dealing with such errors using standard error-handling techniques, specifically by invoking `On Error Resume Next` and checking the value of `Err.Number` immediately after a connection attempt. In a production environment, this is exactly what you want; runtime errors should be quietly dealt with and suppressed. During script development, however, you probably want to see all errors as they occur. Error codes are among the most useful tools at a script programmer's disposal, because they can give many useful clues as to what is going wrong and why.

When error handling is switched off, VBScript responds to an error by halting script execution and outputting the error code, a description, and the script line at which the error was raised. Often, the error description is somewhat unhelpful. For a sensible explanation of what a specific WMI error actually means, it is always advisable to turn to the WMI Software Development Kit documentation, where every error raised by WMI is listed under the "Return Codes" book. Table 10.1 lists a few of the most commonly found error codes and their meanings.

Table 10.1 Common WMI Error Codes

Code	Meaning
`0x80041002`	A requested object could not be found. This error is frequently caused by a `Get()` request on a nonexistent object path. Note that this error is *not* raised in response to a machine being unavailable, because this condition causes a DCOM error (specifically, error 462) rather than a WMI one.
`0x80041008`	A requested resource is unavailable. This error normally occurs when communication with a remote computer is hindered by network trouble.
`0x80041010`	An invalid class has been specified. This error occurs when an attempt is made to retrieve an object or class definition of a nonexistent class.
`0x80041017`	An attempt has been made to execute an invalid WQL query. Have you checked those `AND`'s in `ASSOCIATORS OF` queries?
`0x80041024`	A provider is not capable of accomplishing an operation requested of it. This can occur if an attempt is made to write to properties of an object whose provider does not support writing, if a query is too complex for the provider to cope with, or if an attempt is made, say, to create or delete an instance when a provider does not support such operations.
`0x80041023`	An attempt has been made to modify a read-only property.
`0x8004103A`	An invalid object path has been specified.
`0x80041033`	A requested operation could not be accomplished because the WMI service is shutting down. You might think that this error should occur only rarely, but if you are running a lot of scripts remotely on a large network, it can happen all the time.

As can be seen even from the small sample presented in the preceding table, WMI errors are generally raised for one of two reasons: either a script has bugs in it and therefore needs fixing, or an unanticipated runtime condition has occurred. In the first case, the error should be picked up when you are developing your script, and can be fixed as soon as it is found. The second case, however, is slightly more problematic.

As previously noted, in many real-world scripting scenarios, judicious placement of `Err.Number` checks is sufficient to keep a script running smoothly. In some cases, however, it is helpful not only to suppress an error, but also to behave differentially depending on what error actually occurred. Consider, for example, a script designed to gather statistics about programs running on your computers. You might want to silently ignore failed connection attempts but warn the script's operator (non-fatally) when any other error occurs. In these cases, you need to check the value of `Err.Number` against a list of possibilities that you want to handle within the script itself.

In terms of program flow, this scenario can be handled with a standard conditional execution block, such as in the following script fragment, which assumes that numAnErrorToIgnore holds the numeric value of a specific error whose occurrence should be ignored:

```
refWMI = GetObject("winMgmts")
If Err <> 0 AND Not Err = numAnErrorToIgnore Then
    'alarm bells - we want to notify someone
    'about this error!
Else
    'ignore error and continue
End If
```

An alternative, for more sophisticated control, is to respond to errors with a Select Case block:

```
refWMI = GetObject("winMgmts")
Select Case Err.Number
Case numSomeError:
    'respond to some error
Case numSomeOtherError:
    'respond to some other error
Case 0
    'no error has occurred
Case Else
    'unanticipated error has occurred
End Select
```

Blocks of code such as this, particularly when placed neatly into an error-handling function, allow a script to react gracefully to various different types of errors. When dealing with WMI-raised errors, there is one small complication to consider, however: The error numbers reported by VBScript in response to WMI-raised errors bear no obvious relation to the numbers as listed in the WMI Software Development Kit documentation. If you don't believe us, try running the following code fragment on your machine. The script connects to WMI and attempts to retrieve a reference to an object whose class does not exist. Therefore, we should expect error 0x80041010 to occur. In practice, the script outputs -2147217392, even though the correct value displays when error handling is disabled and the error causes script execution to halt.

```
On Error Resume Next
Set refGoose = GetObject("winMgmts:Win45_Goose='gander'")
WScript.Echo Err.Number
```

The problem is that the error codes as listed in the Software Development Kit documentation and displayed by VBScript on halt are hexadecimal numbers. The 0x prefix denotes them as such. Unfortunately, VBScript interprets them as signed integers. The solution is to use the built-in VBScript Hex()

function, which converts an integer into its hexadecimal representation. The following script fragment displays the output `80041010`, which can be directly compared with the officially documented error numbers:

```
On Error Resume Next
Set refGoose = GetObject("winMgmts:Win45_Goose='gander'")
WScript.Echo Hex(Err.Number)
```

To clarify this, the following short script attempts to connect to the WMI service on a machine called STYX and retrieve a nonexistent object. If no errors occur or if the connection attempt fails, the script outputs the message `"I could not find anything wrong with the request"`. In response to error `0x80041010`, however, it displays `"you have made a ridiculous request. Please be more careful"`:

```
Option Explicit
On Error Resume Next
Dim refGoose
Set refGoose = GetObject("winMgmts:\\syzx:Win45_goose='gander'")
If Hex(Err.Number) = 8001010 Then
    WScript.Echo "I could not find anything wrong with the request"
Else
    WScript.Echo "you have made a ridiculous request."
    WScript.Echo "Please be more careful"
End If
Set refGoose = Nothing
```

Techniques such as this provide an excellent way of making scripts handle errors flexibly. If you are writing scripts for other people to use, handling errors selectively in this way also allows you to provide more friendly or organization-specific error messages.

Note: VBScript and Numeric Types

VBScript's dynamic type system can often be rather irritating when it deals with numeric data passed to it from other languages. As you might remember from Chapter 6, unsigned integers are particularly problematic, in extreme cases leading to ridiculous results such as negatively sized files. ◆

WMI Log Files

No matter how carefully you write scripts, and no matter how fine-grained your selective error handling something unexpected is always going to happen. WMI is a large, complicated system, and it is perfectly possible that you will encounter a bug or a documentation inconsistency. In cases such as this, just knowing the error code associated with a problem might not be enough. You might need to find out more about what WMI is doing to raise the error. In cases such as this, you can sometimes find clues hidden within the WMI logs.

WMI keeps a number of log files, some of which are specific to particular providers and some of which are more general. Their purposes are all documented in the "Development Environment" book in the WMI Software Development Kit documentation, and the interested reader is strongly advised at least to browse this documentation. Instead of repeating information found in the documentation, we will make a few general points about the logs:

- By default, all the WMI logs are found in the %SYSTEMROOT%\system32\wbem\logs directory on Windows 2000. However, this location, and the maximum log file size, can be set on the Logging page of the WMI MMC snap-in property sheet. (See Chapter 5 for information about how to open the WMI MMC snap-in.)
- Information contained within each log varies considerably. Because many entries are written by individual providers, the extent and format of the information provided depends on the developers of each specific provider. Some entries are very terse, others are quite verbose and informative.
- WMI defines two levels of logging: the WMI MMC snap-in Logging page provides radio buttons that can be used to select between Verbose, Errors Only, or No Logging levels. The default of Errors Only is sufficient for most purposes.
- The two most useful logs for general troubleshooting are framework.log and wbemcore.log. Although many of the entries in them are of interest only to provider writers, they also can help diagnose script problems, particularly those related to networking and authentication problems.

For those of you who are not provider writers, and use WMI to manage and monitor computers, the logs contain more information about the inner workings of WMI than is really desirably to know. If you encounter a strange error whose cause you just cannot work out, however, you might find the answer lurking within one of them.

General Tips and Tricks

An entire book could quite easily be filled with programming tips aimed at minimizing the chances of bugs creeping into code and handling problem neatly when they do occur. We certainly do not presume to be able to give you thorough insight into this in just a few paragraphs. Having said this, because this chapter focuses on script development issues, it seems appropriate to take the opportunity to make a few suggestions that might help you with the development process.

First, we want to reiterate a point first made in Chapter 4. When you are developing a script, *do not use error handling*. Just to make this absolutely clear, *never* include the phrase `On Error Resume Next` anywhere in your script until you have reached the point where you are convinced that the code actually works. When you are writing new scripts, you *want* errors to occur; at least, you want to see them clearly when they do. Only after all obvious problems are ironed out should you include and activate error-handling code.

When writing general-purpose subroutines or functions to put in a library for later use, getting the error handling right is even more important than it is when writing standalone scripts. Nothing is more frustrating than spending ages trying to diagnose a script problem that ends up being not a problem with your script at all, but with a function that you have written earlier but whose idiosyncrasies you have forgotten. As a general rule, the internal operations of a function or subroutine should be invisible to its user. Therefore, any problems should be suppressed entirely or else made known to the user in a controlled and consistent way. Short of hiding problems from the user entirely, you can take three fundamentally different approaches when writing a function that needs to handle errors:

- One approach is not to handle the error at all, and leave the job to the function's user. If a function does not include the invocation `On Error Resume Next`, errors raised during its execution are passed on to the caller.
- A neater solution in many circumstances is to handle errors internally, and inform the user of problems via a return value. For example, a function designed to find the size of a file could return `-1` as an indication of error; because a file can never be –1 bytes long, such a "code" could be used unambiguously to inform the caller of a problem. The following code shows the basic framework of a function that returns `-1` if any errors were raised internally during its execution:

```
Function someFunction()
    On Error Resume Next
    'function code goes here

    'check if an error has been raised anywhere
    If Err.Number <> 0 Then
        someFunction = -1
    Else
        someFunction = someValue
    End If
End Function
```

You can implement a more sophisticated interface that returns, for example, different negative numbers depending on what error occurred in very much the same way as a WMI method calls return error values. Of course, a function can return an error code for any reason. This behavior is not restricted to moments when actual VBScript errors are raised internally.

- A third possibility is for a function to raise its own error in response to a problem. This can be accomplished with the `Raise()` method of the VBScript `Err` object. `Raise()` can take up to five parameters, three of which are of relevance here. The first is an error number, which should uniquely identify the error type. You are free to choose any number you want for the error provided that it falls outside the range of numbers reserved for VBScript errors, namely 0-999. The second parameter is a string that identifies the error source, and the third is a description of the error that occurs. These three parameters correspond to `Err.Number`, `Err.Source`, and `Err.Description` of the raised error (see Chapter 4). The following script fragment demonstrates raising an error from within a function:

```
Function willRaise()
    'oh dear - something has gone wrong
    Err.Raise 1001, "willRaise", "something has gone wrong"
End Function
```

  The error can be handled in the usual way by any calling code. Provided that descriptions are carefully worded and that errors are raised judiciously, this approach can provide the basis of an excellent, reusable function library.

Which of these methods is best? It all depends on the circumstances and your preferred style. All have their strong and weak points. Return values are perhaps the most elegant approach, but a function that chooses to inform users of errors in a return value must do so judiciously to ensure that error values are not confused with real return values. Passing errors straight through is ugly because it exposes the function's implementation. However, it does provide the user with more detailed information about what actually went wrong. Raising your own errors is perhaps a good compromise between the two, but it requires the user to handle potential errors explicitly, which can sometimes be annoying. In short, there is no one correct way.

If you are building a library of functions, all of which are intended to be used together, you should settle on a convention and stick to it religiously. This allows other scripters to use your handiwork more easily, because they become used to your interface style.

Tip: Functions Can Be Better Than Subroutines

Because subroutines do not return values, scope for reporting problems to a caller are rather more limited. In fact, the only possibility is to allow internal errors to escape to the caller or, where appropriate, to raise your own errors. If, like us, you do not particularly like having to deal with VBScript's error-handling system any more than you have to, you can always write functions rather than subroutines. Even though you may not need *to return a value, you can always return a success value of zero, or an error code if something goes wrong.* ◆

We have talked enough about error handling. To finish this section, therefore, we make three brief comments about error avoidance and code maintenance.

First, keep code lines short. In common with almost all languages that support complex structures or object-oriented programming principles, VBScript allows several implicit operations to be carried out using a single line of code. For example, the following three lines of code:

```
Set refWMI = GetObject("winMgmts")
Set refFile = refWMI.Get("CIM_DataFile.Name='c:\boot.ini'")
numSize = refFile.FileSize
```

can be written in a single statement, like this:

```
numSize = GetObject( _
           "winMgmts:").Get("CIM_DataFile.Name='c:\boot.ini'").FileSize
```

Encoded within this single statement are two method calls and a property read operation. Cool? No! Although in some circumstances this sort of coding is perfectly acceptable and can even be clearer than multilined equivalents, it is normally best resisted at all costs. There are two problems with multiple-concept single-line extravaganzas: They can be difficult to read; and, if an error occurs, it is never immediately obvious which of the many operations actually caused the problem. Short-term amusement can lead to much lost time.

Our second tip focuses on a VBScript incantation that has appeared at the start of every complete script presented in this book, namely `Option Explicit`. As you know by now, this incantation forces VBScript to complain whenever an attempt is made to refer to a variable that has not been explicitly declared with a `Dim` statement. At first glance, `Option Explicit` appears to be a pedantic and unnecessary addition to a script, doing little more than causing irritation by making VBScript refuse to run perfectly good scripts that just happens not to declare their variables. The minor inconvenience of having to declare variables explicitly, however, is easily compensated by the power of `Option Explicit` to prevent insidious and sometimes virtually undetectable errors. Consider, for example, the following short script (which does not use `Option Explicit`):

```
'oops.vbs
someNumber = 3
anotherNumber = somNumber + 5
WScript.Echo anotherNumber
```

Due to a minor typographic error, the output of this fragment will not be `8` as one might expect, but `5`.

In a script this short, of course, the error is easy to spot and correct. If embedded within a larger body of code, however, it could easily go undetected, perhaps even permanently. Imagine if the code were part of the calculation for a bank transaction or, more likely in a WMI context, a calculation about the amount of free space on the disks of a critical server. You will never even notice the problem until the bank balance seems noticeably lower than expected or the server crashes through lack of disk space. With `Option Explicit`, insidious errors such as this can never occur. It is to avoid such errors that we use `Option Explicit` in all of our code. We strongly recommend that you do likewise.

The final point we want to raise concerns a rather mundane issue, namely documentation. Very few inalienable truths apply in the world of programming. If there is one, however, it is this: That which is obvious today will appear strange indeed in six months time. The hack you included to overcome a limitation you encountered, the clever little trick you used to speed up some process, or the weird and wonderful flags passed to the strangely implemented WMI method all seem quite clear the minute after you write them. When you return to your script in the future, however, perhaps to fix a problem that seemed unimportant at the time or to modify its behavior in some way, you will look bemusedly at the weird symbols and only wish that *you had commented your code.* Every function, every constant, and absolutely everything out of the ordinary should be accompanied by a short comment explaining its purpose. It takes very little time to do, and the benefits are incalculably great. If you believe nothing else in this entire book, believe this or suffer the consequences.

If you are writing code that others will have to modify in the future, or a library of functions that other scripters may want to use, fastidious code commenting is even more important. In addition, a library should be accompanied by documentation explaining the interface of each function (its parameters and return values), its behavior under duress, and any known limitations. We do not pretend that such tasks are not tedious and superficially unrewarding compared with writing new scripts. In the long term, however, even the best code in the world is useless without adequate documentation.

Notes on Script Deployment

Back in 1999, we wrote a book about Windows NT maintenance and configuration using Perl. An entire chapter focused on ways to deploy scripts so that they would run on workstations across a network. With the advent of WMI, that entire discussion has become somewhat less crucial because "deploying" a script across a network is just a matter of running the script on your own workstation and making it connect to the WMI service of remote machines. Sometimes, of course, you will want to distribute scripts, for reasons of security, network reliability, or performance. For the most part, however, the logistical difficulties of ensuring that potentially thousands of machines are all running the latest version of your management script vanish completely in the WMI world.

Despite this massive improvement, making extensive use of scripts to manage remote machines does involve some consideration of deployment issues. After all, if a script is to do anything useful, someone or something has to run it, possibly at regular intervals, possibly in a consistent fashion. Therefore in this, the final section of the chapter, we make a few suggestions to aid in the smooth running of networkwide scripting solutions. This section does not attempt to present an exhaustive list of deployment possibilities. Doing so would be an impossible task. Instead, this section gives you some ideas that you can employ when devising deployment solutions appropriate to your environment.

Running WMI Scripts at User Logon

A script that performs housekeeping duties, such as clearing workstation temporary directories, does not normally need to provide a system administrator with any immediate feedback, but may well need to retrieve and manipulate a large number of WMI objects. To carry out its job, such a script does not require any network resources. If run remotely, however, it would use quite a lot of them. Every single object retrieval, method call, or property read would result in unwanted network traffic. In an ideal world, such a script would run locally on each machine rather than over the network. The downside of running scripts locally is that it introduces all the deployment problems that WMI usually avoids. Unless you want to start inventing elaborate security procedures or using guest-mountable network shares, you have to ensure that an up-to-date script is available to each machine that has to run it.

A solution to this difficulty is to run such scripts when a user logs on. Logon scripts can be assigned to a user, an organizational unit, or even an entire domain using group policies, using the Active Directory Users and Computers tool. Once assigned, the script will run every time a user logs on to a computer. A particularly useful feature of logon scripts is that the script code itself is stored on a domain controller; so although scripts run locally, complex deployment issues are completely avoided. Another rather significant feature is that the scripts run as the logged on user. Therefore, if they do need to access network resources, they can do so provided that the user in question has the relevant permissions.

The use of logon scripts does entail a downside: If the user logging on does not have permission to perform any WMI operations that the script needs to carry out, execution fails miserably. Another potential pitfall is that in an environment in which users stay logged on for extended periods, such as months at a time, a logon script is hardly ever run. We think they are worthy of mention, however, because many administrators think of logon scripts as tools to help set up a user's environment. Although this is certainly true, they should not be ruled out as a mechanism for deploying workstation maintenance scripts.

Tip: Run Logon Scripts Asynchronously

If you write scripts that take more than a few seconds to execute, and you set them up as logon scripts, they should be set in the Active Directory for asynchronous operation so that users do not have to wait for them to complete before they can start working. ◆

Running Scripts from a Scheduler

If you have scripts that take a long time to execute, are processor-intensive, or need to traverse a network to connect to a large number of machines, it can often be desirable to run them overnight. This is particularly appropriate for large report-generating scripts that do not need immediate interaction with a system administrator. If running such scripts on a regular basis, you might want to consider using the Windows Scheduler, which can run arbitrary commands at an arbitrary time.

A scheduled job can be registered with the Scheduler using the command-line program at.exe. This program has a number of options that allow specification of the name of a command to execute, an execution time, and a date in a number of different formats. For a full description of the tool, check out the Windows 2000 online help. To give a brief indication of its operation, we present an example here. This invocation tells the Scheduler to run the script c:\scripts\myscript.vbs on the local machine at 10 p.m. every Friday.

```
c:>at 10pm /every:friday "cscript.exe c:\scripts\myscript.vbs"
```

Scripts run in this way execute with the permissions of the Scheduler service.

Scheduled jobs are not particularly convenient for running maintenance scripts on large numbers of computers, because of the difficulty of deployment, ensuring the relevant permissions, and the like. They are extremely convenient, however, for running time-consuming scripts on small numbers of machines at antisocial hours.

Running Scripts in a Web Browser

The vast majority of scripts presented in this book and, in fact, the vast majority of scripts that we have ever written to make use of WMI, are intended to be run interactively by a system administrator sitting at his own workstation. Throughout the book, we have tacitly implied that such scripts are always run using the Windows Scripting Host. In reality, however, there are other hosts available on most Windows 2000 machines within which scripts can be run. The most useful of these is Internet Explorer.

Running a script from within Internet Explorer involves embedding it within a set of `<SCRIPT></SCRIPT>` tags within an HTML document. This can provide a neat alternative to the reporting solutions presented in Chapter 6, by allowing output from WMI scripts to be embedded directly within an HTML document. From a WMI perspective, writing a script to run within Internet Explorer does not dramatically differ from writing it for the Windows Scripting Host. Bear in mind just two major important factors: There is no `WScript` object, and there is no `GetObject()` function.

There is no `WScript` object when a script runs under Internet Explorer because `WScript` is a COM object exclusive to the Windows Scripting Host. An equivalent of the `Echo()` method, arguably `WScript`'s single most useful feature, is IE's `Document.Write()` method. Whereas `WScript.Echo()` displays output in a dialog box or on the console, `Document.Write()` displays it in the current web page. Therefore, anything displayed with `Document.Write()` appears as if the text were actually part of the HTML document in which the script is embedded.

The lack of `GetObject()` under Internet Explorer is slightly more of a nuisance. As you have probably noticed, this function has been a crucial component of every script presented in this book. Thankfully, the WMI scripting interface designers have given us a solution to a potentially devastating bootstrapping problem in the form of the `SWbemLocator` object. `SWbemLocator` is a creatable object, part of the `WbemScripting` package. Instances of it can be created with `CreateObject()`, a method that *is* available under Internet Explorer. The object has a single method, `ConnectServer()`, which returns an `SWbemServices` object. In other words, a combination of `CreateObject()` and `SWbemLocator.ConnectServer()` replace all the functionality that we needed from `GetObject()`.

`ConnectServer()` has several optional parameters that allow specification of a machine to which to connect, a set of credentials, and security flags. In its simplest form, however, it can be executed with no parameters at all. The effect, as you might have guessed, is to connect to the WMI service on the local machine with the credentials of the logged on user and no special privileges. The VBScript code needed to accomplish this is illustrated in the following fragment:

```
Set refLocator = CreateObject("WbemScript.SWbemLocator")
Set refWMI = refLocator.ConnectServer()
```

After a reference to an `SWbemServices` object has been retrieved, it can be used in exactly the same way as under the Windows Scripting Host.

To briefly illustrate the running a WMI script within Internet Explorer, we present a simple HTML page that uses an embedded script and WMI to display a list of services running on the machine on which the page is viewed. Type the script into a text editor, save it with an .html extension, and open it with Internet Explorer. Depending on your browser's security settings, you might be asked whether you want to allow an ActiveX object to be opened. Click Yes and, after a few moments, the dynamically created page will display.

```
<HTML>
  <HEAD>
    <TITLE>Services running on my machine</TITLE>
  </HEAD>
  <BODY>
    <H1>Services running on my machine</H1>
    <UL>
    <SCRIPT language="vbscript">
      Option Explicit
      Dim refLocator
      Dim refWMI
      Dim colServices
      Dim refService

      'connect to WMI with an SWbemLocator
      Set refLocator = CreateObject("WbemScripting.SWbemLocator")
      Set refWMI = refLocator.ConnectServer()

      'retrieve a collection of running services in the usual way
      Set colServices = refWMI.ExecQuery( _
              "SELECT * FROM Win32_Service WHERE started='true'")

      'print the name of each service preceded by an <li> tag
      For Each refService in colServices
          Document.Write "<LI>" & refService.Name
      Next
```

```
        Set colServices = Nothing
        Set refWMI = Nothing
        Set refLocator = Nothing
      </SCRIPT>
      </UL>
</HTML>
```

With a little imagination and lots of time, it is possible to build entire scripting solutions around web pages; theoretically, you could build an entire management scripting infrastructure around your own personal set of web pages. The decision as to whether this is appropriate for your environment, or whether the time taken to build smart looking web pages might be better spent on writing further management scripts or reusable components is, of course, entirely up to you. Our job at this stage is merely to offer you possibilities.

Running Scripts in Perpetuity

One final method of deployment that deserves special mention is the "perpetual operation" method, in which a script runs in perpetuity on a dedicated scripting workstation. A dedicated workstation with a dedicated scripting account with domain admin privileges is the ideal platform for running scripts that use asynchronous event notification or the like to constantly monitor a fleet of machines for signs of trouble. This might seem like a rather dull approach to script deployment, but sometimes the simplest solutions are the best.

Summary

This chapter has reviewed techniques and tools that can aid in the development and deployment of WMI scripts. It opened with a discussion of Windows Scripting Host facilities that can help in writing robust, reusable scripts. It then moved on to consider some common bugs that beset WMI scripters, and suggested how some of these can be avoided or fixed. Within this discussion, a special section was devoted to techniques for handling errors in function libraries. This chapter ended by suggesting various tricks and techniques that you can use to deploy and execute scripts on a fleet of Windows 2000 machines in a real-world environment.

11

WMI Internals

We have now covered all the concepts and techniques that are required to understand and use WMI as a system administration tool. The script examples presented in this book, in conjunction with the WMI Software Development Kit reference documentation, should give you all the information and advice you need to start writing custom WMI scripts for your own Windows 2000 environment. In this, the final chapter of the book, we take a slightly different course, and look around some of WMI's internals. We begin by examining the Repository, asking what it means for objects to "live" there, and consider how class definitions come to exist in the first place. In the second, rather longer section of the chapter, we look more formally at the WMI scripting API. This is a set of COM objects that we have been using consistently throughout the book but that have not yet been discussed directly in their own right.

If you are keen to start writing WMI scripts immediately and do not care too much about WMI internals, you can safely avoid reading this chapter. If, on the other hand, you would like a better understanding of how the WMI infrastructure works, or if you are a software developer who has read this book as a quick introduction to the WMI world, we strongly encourage you to read on.

Inside the Repository

Throughout this book we have referred time and time again to a rather ethereal concept known as the *Repository*. Within this central hub of WMI reside namespaces, classes, and objects, all ready to be retrieved at the whim of a script. This section discusses the Repository in more concrete terms.

In reality, the repository is just a database. It is a file with a .REP extension that normally resides in the %SYSTEMROOT%\System32\WBEM\Repository directory on a Windows 2000 machine. Delete this file and there is no more Repository; WMI effectively ceases to exist on the machine. If you open the WMI MMC snap-in (see Chapter 5, "WMI Security"), you will notice that one of its property sheets is labeled Backup/Restore. Turn to this sheet and you will find options to make a backup copy of the Repository, restore it from previous backups, and set up a periodic automatic backup regime (see Figure 11.1). On a fresh installation of Windows 2000, automatic backup is pre-configured to run every 30 minutes. As far as the WMI programming team is concerned, the Repository is clearly a database worth protecting. Inside this database are records that hold all the class and object definitions that make up WMI.

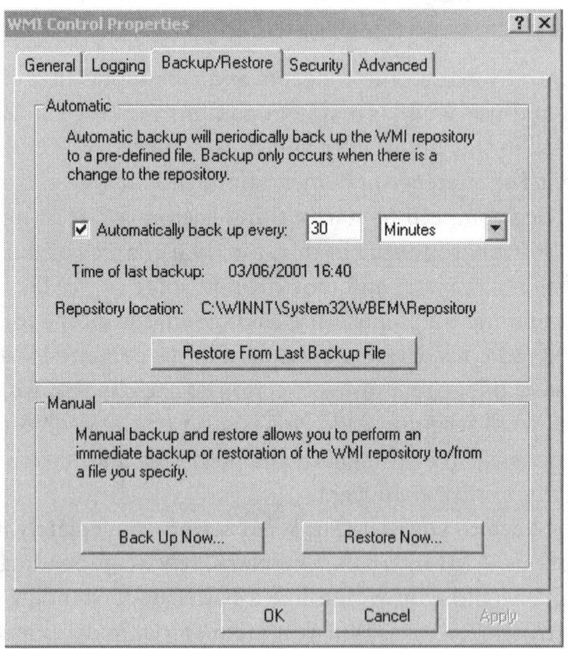

Figure 11.1 *WMI Control Backup/Restore sheet.*

As previously discussed, classes and objects broadly fall into two categories: static and dynamic. These are represented quite differently within the repository, as follows:

- *Static instances* of *static classes* are the simplest of all. Here, both the class definitions and the instances (that is, sets of values for properties of each instance) are stored. If all WMI classes and objects were static, the Repository would be no different from any conventional database; it would just hold structured data. Static instances tend to be those that represent parts of a system that are persistent and rarely change. A typical example is a __FilterToConsumerBinding (see Chapter 8, "Proactive Troubleshooting with WMI Events").

- *Dynamic instances* of *static classes* present a slightly more complex picture. Here, the class definitions are stored as static data in the Repository, but instances are supplied on demand by providers. Almost all the WMI objects discussed in this book fall into this category, because it is well suited to many aspects of computer systems (in which *types* of things tend to change rarely, but *instances* frequently do). An obvious example is CIM_DataFile.
- *Dynamic instances* of *dynamic classes* are not stored in the Repository at all. Instead, both class definitions and instance data are provided dynamically on demand. The notion of dynamic classes is rather odd, and is not often used. The only examples discussed in this book are the Active Directory classes (see Chapter 9, "WMI and Active Directory").

When a script requests an object that happens to be a static instance of a static class, the role of the Repository is utterly straightforward: the CIM Object Manager (a.k.a. the WMI service or SWbemServices) merely reads the relevant data from the database and passes it back to the script. The chain of events is not so clear, however, for dynamic instances or dynamic classes. After all, if data is not held directly in the Repository, there must be some mechanism to trigger the providers. Furthermore, there must be some mechanism to work out which provider needs to be triggered in response to any given client request.

The solution to this difficulty is quite just that providers are registered as static instances within the Repository. Every provider is represented by an instance of the __Win32Provider system class and by a subclass of the __ProviderRegistration class. The properties of __Win32Provider contain information about the provider's implementation, such as the CLSID referencing the actual COM object that holds the provider code. The various subclasses of __ProviderRegistration have properties that determine the scope of a provider's power, such as the types of queries it can accept. When a script requests an object that is a dynamic instance of a static class, the CIM Object Manager first retrieves the class definition from the Repository. Part of this class definition will be *qualifiers* declaring instances to be dynamic and specifying the name of the provider that creates them. The CIM Object Manager can read this information, look up the provider registration and call the appropriate code. When a script requests an object whose *class* definition is dynamic, the procedure is slightly different because there is no obvious initial starting point for the CIM Object Manager's search. This difficulty is solved by __ClassProviderRegistration, the class used to register dynamic class providers. Among its properties are WQL queries that describe the scope of objects for which the represented class is responsible. The CIM Object Manager can use these as filters to work out whether to pass any particular query to a class provider for processing. If this sounds rather inefficient, that is because it is! Microsoft recommends that dynamic classes should be used only when absolutely necessary because of the huge burden they put on the entire WMI system.

In short, the Repository is a massive database of definitions, not only of classes and objects, but also of providers. Even in cases when our interaction with WMI is restricted to dynamic instances of dynamically defined classes, the repository plays a concrete and crucial part. Given its importance, it is perhaps appropriate to consider how definitions get there in the first place. We turn to this topic in the following section.

The Repository and Managed Object Format Files

There are two primary mechanisms by which namespace, class, and object definitions are created, modified, or deleted from the Repository. The first mechanism is by programmatic access. The `SWbemObject` `Put_()` method, mentioned in several earlier chapters, is perhaps the most ubiquitous and simplest example of this mechanism. We retrieve a reference to a WMI object and use `Put_()` to write changes. Alternatively, we use `SpawnInstance_()` to create a new WMI object, and use `Put_()` to deposit the object in the Repository. Although we have not discussed them in this book, `SWbemObject` in fact provides several more methods that allow class and object definitions to the Repository. The C++ COM API, which has significantly more functionality than the scripting API that we have been using throughout this book, provides everything required to make any modifications to the Repository. So-called *push* providers, those that are responsible for the creation of static instances, use these methods to update the Repository when the objects for which they are responsible need to be altered.

Despite the rich programmatic interface, almost all additions and modifications to the Repository are carried out with a program called mofcomp.exe, that compiles *Managed Object Format* (MOF) files and writes their contents directly into the Repository. MOF is a language invented by the DMTF as part of WBEM (see Chapter 1, "Introduction to WMI"). It is derived from *Interface Definition Language*, a language designed for specifying objects, and looks a bit like C with strange appendages. If you are a provider writer, MOF provides the primary means of specifying what your provider is capable of doing and registering your class and instance definitions in the repository. On the other hand, if you are a system administrator, the closest you will ever probably get to MOF is to invoke mofcomp.exe on a prewritten MOF file. You might need to do this as part of the installation process for a new provider.

Note: Using MOF for Permanent Event Subscription

Some people advocate using MOF in a system administration context to create static instances of predefined static classes. A typical example would be to create an instance of `SMTPEventConsumer` *and a* `__FilterToConsumerBinding`. *Our feeling on this, however, is that VBScript provides a perfectly good interface for such simple activities, as indeed does the CIM Studio (as discussed later); grappling with MOF for these tasks is just unnecessary.* ◆

Even a cursory explanation of the MOF language and the concepts required to fully understand it would make this a very long chapter. In fact, in a book on WMI Provider development, it would almost certainly be worthy of a chapter in its own right. Despite this, for the sake of completeness, we present a sample MOF file and provide a brief description of its various components. The intention is not necessarily that you go and attempt to write MOF files, but just so that if you do encounter one, you will recognize it and know in principle what its components mean.

The MOF file we present contains two definitions: one class and one instance of that class. The class is a fictitious one called `Book`, which we declare in a fictitious namespace called root\random. The `Book` class defines five properties, which contain information about the title, author, publisher, and number of chapters. The primary key consists of a single property, `Title`. In addition, the class defines a single `Read()` method, which takes a chapter number as a parameter. Our instance, unsurprisingly, represents this book. If this instance really were in the repository, it could be retrieved with the following line of VBScript:

```
Set refWMIBook = GetObject("winMgmts:root\random:Book.Title='WMI'")
```

Here, then, is the MOF file itself. The structure is fairly self-explanatory. The keyword `class` introduces the class definition and `instance of` introduces the instance definition. Definitions are enclosed within pairs of braces (`{}`). Semantically complete lines end in semicolons (`;`). Comments, which are ignored by the compiler, are denoted by a pair of slashes (`//`).

```
//wmibook.mof - a MOF file defining the Book class and an instance
//write all definitions that follow into root\random
#pragma namespace ("\\\\.\\root\\random")

//declaration of Book class
//the class is serviced by the BookProvider (not defined here)
[Provider ("BookProvider")]
class Book
```

```
{
    //properties
    [key] string Title;
    string Author1;
    string Author2;
    string Publisher;
    uint32 NumChapters;

    //method declaration
    [Implemented] void Read ([in] uint32 Chapter);
};

//declaration of a Book instance
instance of Book
{
    Title = "WMI";
    Author1 = "Matthew Lavy";
    Author2 = "Ashley Meggitt";
    Publisher = "NewRiders"
    NumChapter = "11";
};
```

An attempt to compile this MOF file with mofcomp.exe would fail miserably, not least because the namespace root\random does not actually exist. In addition, the class would be utterly useless because we have neither defined nor implemented a provider capable of supporting the `Read()` method. In principle, however, there is nothing wrong with our definitions. If the namespace and method provider both existed, the file would be compiled and written into the Repository without a hitch.

Although the details of MOF look somewhat strange when compared with VBScript, the structure maps clearly on to the WMI concepts, which are by now very familiar. The simplest part of the file is the instance definition. It lists each property in turn and assigns a value. Most of the interest lies within the class definition. This consists of a list of properties and methods each of which is given a *type* and optionally a *qualifier*. The class definition itself also is marked with a *qualifier*. Only one line of code is part of neither the class or instance definitions. This is the *preprocessor directive* that tells mofcomp.exe to compile the definition into the root\random namespace.

For further information on the Managed Object Format, its syntax, and uses, we refer you to the WMI Software Development Kit "Development Environment" section. To end our discussion here, we talk briefly about types, qualifiers, and preprocessor directives and illustrate how mofcomp.exe can be used to compile a MOF file into the Repository.

Types

In WMI, just as with most modern object-based programming systems, properties are *typed*. In our MOF example, the class definition did not just define five variables. It defined four string variables and one `uint32` variable. The keywords `string` and `uint32` prefixing the variable names are what is known in the programming world as *type declarations*.

By this stage in the book, it should be very clear why types are important. A property's type determines how values should be interpreted and limits the actions that can be performed on it. For example, attempting to perform an arithmetic subtraction on two values that are strings is clearly ridiculous.

VBScript is rather liberal in its typing rules. Wherever possible, it will attempt to coerce a value into a type that is appropriate for the context (see Chapter 2, "Using VBScript"). Furthermore, it does not visibly discriminate between different types of numeric value. WMI, which is a C++-based invention, is much more discriminating. For example, a number is not just a number; it can be a signed integer of 8, 16, 32, or 64 bits (`uint8`, `uint16`, `uint32`, or `uint16`), a signed integer in the same range (`sint8`, `sint16`, `sint32`, or `sint64`), or a floating-point number (`real32` or `real64`). Properties that are not numeric may hold strings (`string`), dates (`datetime`), Booleans (`boolean`), objects (`object`) or references (`ref`). In addition, of course, a property may hold an array, adding an extra layer for diversity. For a full description of the various types that can be used in a WMI class definition, refer to the WMI Software Development Kit documentation.

Note: Variant Data Types

In reality, all VBScript variables are of a single special type, namely the variant. *Variants are structures that hold both the data itself and a special value (from an enumeration) that denotes the data's type. Because both parts of the structure can be changed dynamically, it is easy to "convert" the data between different types. Variants are at the heart of VBScript's internal operations.* ◆

Qualifiers

The text inside square brackets in our MOF example, appearing as part of the class definition and method declaration, specifies WMI *qualifiers* that apply to the class and method, respectively. Qualifiers define some behavioral aspect of the qualified item. A qualifier can be Boolean, in which case its presence equates to a value of true, or else it can hold a value.

In our example, there are three qualifiers. The simplest ones are `Key` and `Implemented`, which are Boolean. They take no parameters. Their presence just implies true. The `Key` qualifier, placed before the definition of the `Title` property, indicates that the property is part of the class's primary key. The `Implemented` qualifier, placed before the `Read()` method declaration, indicates that the method in this class has been implemented by some provider. Any method declaration that does not include this qualifier is assumed to be abstract. The third qualifier in our example is `Provider`, placed just before the class definition. This qualifier, which takes a value, specifies the name of the provider responsible for implementing the class's methods. Had the `Provider` qualifier been accompanied by `Dynamic`, as in the following MOF fragment, the provider would also be deemed responsible for creating instances of the class:

```
[Dynamic, Provider ("BookProvider")] class Book {...};
```

There is a huge number of standard DMTF- and WMI-defined qualifiers, most of which are of interest only to provider writers and WMI itself. In addition, MOF includes a syntax for defining new qualifiers, so there is no limit to their potential scope and uses. If you are interested in finding out about some of the standard qualifiers, we refer you once more to the WMI Software Development Kit. Alternatively, the qualifiers associated with a particular object, property, or method can be viewed using the Object Browser tool (see Chapter 6, "Logs and Reports").

A small extra twist connected with qualifiers is that qualifiers themselves can be qualified through a mechanism known as *flavors*. Whereas a class, method, or property qualifier specifies aspect's of the class, method, or property behavior that it qualifies, a flavor specifies the scope and influence of the qualifier it flavors! A standard set of flavors specifies whether a given qualifier propagates to subclasses of the defined class, whether it affects instances, and whether it can be overridden. Further details are given later on in this chapter.

Pragmas

Perhaps the most peculiar looking line in our entire MOF example is the `#pragma` directive, which specifies the namespace into which our class and instance should be written:

```
#pragma namespace ("\\\\.\\root\\random")
```

The string representing the namespace itself is straightforward enough. It just looks slightly alien because MOF requires backslashes to be escaped with a second backslash (that is, `\` becomes `\\`) and the string uses the period (`.`) shorthand (which means "current machine").

The peculiar part is the `#pragma`, an incantation that is known to the C programmer as a *preprocessor directive*. Such directives are not strictly part of the MOF definition itself, but are instructions to the compiler. In this case, the `#pragma namepace` directive tells the compiler to create the objects in a specific namespace within the Repository. Another commonly found `#pragma` MOF directives is `#pragma deleteclass`, which tells the compiler not to create the specified class or object from the Repository, but to delete it.

At first glance, it seems odd that a namespace specification should be a preprocessor directive rather than part of a class definition. The reason why it is not an integral part of the definition is that the same class or instance can be compiled into more than one namespace. By convention, all WMI classes representing components of a computer system live in the root\cimv2 namespace, all ADSI-mapped objects live in subnamespaces of the root\directory namespace, and WMI system classes live in root\WMI. However, this is only a convention. As discussed in Chapter 8, "Proactive Troubleshooting with WMI Events," there are classes, such as `SMTPEventConsumer`, which logically belong to many namespaces. There is one other, more fundamental reason for the distinction: A class definition is normally created by a provider writer; a Repository's namespace should be under the control of the system administrator running the computer on which it resides.

Mofcomp.exe

The most common thing a system administrator will want to do with a MOF file is compile it. Although the core WMI providers and classes are precompiled when WMI is first installed on a system, extra providers may need to be compiled manually. As you saw in Chapter 8, the `EventConsumer` subclasses provided as part of the current WMI beta need to be manually compiled into a namespace before they can be used. The tool to accomplish this is mofcomp.exe

At its simplest, compiling a MOF file just involves invoking mofcomp.exe with the filename as a parameter, as illustrated here:

```
c:>mofcomp wmibook.mof
```

This process should be executed by a user with permissions to write to the repository. Alternatively, the `-U` and `-P` option allows a username and password pair to be entered on the command line. In addition to `-U` and `-P`, a number of command-line options control the compiler's behavior. A full description of these may be found in the WMI Software Development Kit documentation. For now, we will consider only one of these, namely `-N`. This option allows specification of a namespace into which the MOF file should be compiled. It takes the following form:

```
c:>mofcomp -N:<namespacepath> <moffile>
```

Therefore, to specify that wmibook.mof should be compiled into the root\random namespace, the following command should be invoked:

```
c:>mofcomp -N:root\random wmibook.mof
```

This is equivalent to the `#pragma` namespace directive described earlier. Note that a `#pragma` namespace directive, if present in a MOF file, always takes precedence over the `-N` option. If you want to guarantee that a class or instance will be compiled into the namespace of your choice, the safest solution is to edit or insert such a directive in the file instead of relying on the command-line options.

WMI System Properties

Notably absent from the sample MOF file was any definition of the WMI system properties. These are not defined in MOF, because they are created automatically by WMI as part of the object creation process.

WMI system properties provide information about an object's essential statistics, such as location within the repository, the class hierarchy from which it is derived and the number of properties it possesses. Although we have referred to several of these properties at many points in the book, we have not yet discussed them directly. Later on in this chapter, we demonstrate how the scripting API can be used to find out the values of an object's system properties. In Table 11.1, we list these properties, in alphabetic order, and give a brief description of their purpose.

Table 11.1 WMI System Properties

Property	Purpose
`__CLASS`	The object's class name (for instance, `Win32_Process`).
`__DERIVATION`	An array listing a class inheritance hierarchy (for instance `CIM Process, CIM LogicalElement, CIM ManagedSystemElement`).
`__DYNASTY`	The ultimate base class from which a class derives (for instance, `CIM ManagedSystemElement`).
`__GENUS`	A numeric value indicating whether the object is a class (`1`) or an instance (`2`).
`__NAMESPACE`	The namespace in which the object resides (for instance, root\cimv2).
`__PATH`	The full path to the object (for instance, `\\STYX\root\cimv2:` `➥Win 32 Process. Handle="0"`).
`__PROPERTY COUNT`	The number of properties presented by the class.
`__RELPATH`	The path relative to the namespace (for instance, `win32 Process.Handle="0"`)__
`__SERVER`	The machine on which the object resides (for instance, STYX).
`__SUPERCLASS`	The immediate superclass (for instance, `CIM_Process`)

Navigating the Repository

A discussion of the repository and its contents would hardly be complete without at least a mention of the ways in which namespaces can be traversed and the Repository's inhabitants examined. On the other hand, this entire book is about exactly that issue. For at least the past eight chapters, we have been demonstrating ways in which WMI objects (a.k.a. inhabitants of the Repository) can be retrieved and manipulated. Furthermore, the second half of this chapter, which concentrates on the WMI scripting API, is devoted to a discussion of how VBScript can be used to examine the structure of WMI classes and objects at a more mechanical level than considered so far. In light of these observations, a section labeled "Navigating the Repository" seems somewhat redundant. However, we take this opportunity to present two tools, both provided as part of the WMI Software Development Kit. These tools are explicitly designed to examine the contents of the Repository, not in terms of WMI objects and the associators that bind them, but in terms of WMI's hierarchical class structure and the Repository. The first of these tools is the graphical CIM Studio; the second is a command-line alternative, wbemdump.exe.

CIM Studio

In terms of both look and operation, CIM Studio is a very similar tool to the Object Browser discussed at length in Chapter 6. In common with the Object Browser, its purpose is to browse through the WMI world. The fundamental difference between the two tools is that whereas the Object Browser shows this world as a hierarchy of WMI *objects*, connected to each other through association, the CIM Studio shows it as a hierarchy of WMI *classes*. At the root of the Object Browser's tree pane is an instance of `Win32_ComputerSystem` representing the computer system to whose WMI service it is connected. By contrast, the equivalent tree in the CIM Studio has no single root. Instead, at the top level, it has all the base classes from which the WMI class hierarchy descends (see Figure 11.2).

The selected class in the figure is `Win32_Process`. In the tree, we can see its relationship not to a computer or to files, but to the parent class, `CIM_Process`. The object pane on the right hand looks virtually identical to its Object Browser equivalent. It is showing the Properties pane, which lists all the `Win32_Process` properties. Notice, however, that the value of each property is marked as `<empty>`; it is a class, not an object, that we are seeing in the figure. If you want instead to see an instance, you can click the Instances button in the toolbar about the Property pane (see Figure 11.3). This produces a list of all instances of the selected class in exactly the same format as the instance lists produced by Object Browser. Double-clicking an entry in the list brings the corresponding instance's properties to the fore. In this mode, the CIM Studio yields the same information in the same format as the Object Browser.

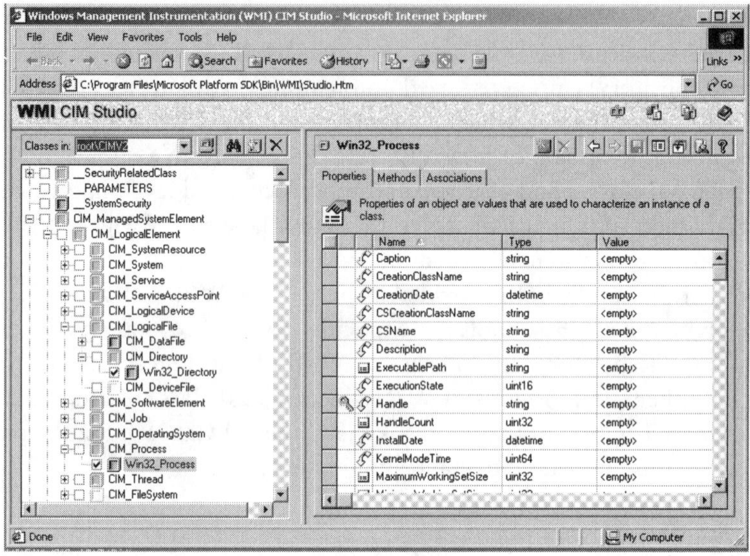

Figure 11.2 *The WMI CIM Studio.*

Figure 11.3 *Instances button.*

As well as providing a class-hierarchy view of WMI, the CIM Studio has a few extra features to excite the WMI enthusiast. First is the ability to create and delete instances, with the Create Instance and Delete Instance buttons respectively (see Figure 11.4). Once a new instance is created, values can be assigned to the properties and then saved to the repository in the same way as modification is carried out using the Object Browser. Deleting an instance, a one-click operation, does exactly what you might expect to the currently selected instance. It removes it from the Repository. Although not particularly useful in most system administration contexts, this pair of features provides an alternative to scripting for setting up permanent event subscription.

Figure 11.4 *Create Instance and Delete Instance buttons.*

The other features are the MOF wizards, accessed from three icons at the upper-right corner of the title bar (see Figure 11.5). One of these wizards, the MOF Compiler Wizard is effectively a graphical front end to mofcomp.exe. It allows selection of a MOF file from the filesystem, and guides the user through the compilation process. The other two are really only of interest to provider writers and operate on classes whose definitions are already stored in the Repository. One generates skeleton provider code for the class's implementation, and the other is an MOF definition. To use either of these wizards, at least one class definition must be "selected" in the tree pane. This is accomplished by marking the check box next to the class whose definition is selected. In Figure 11.1, `Win32_Process` is selected in this way. Although of very little use to the system administrators, these wizards are great fun for the curious.

Figure 11.5 *The MOF wizards.*

Wbemdump.exe

Wbemdump.exe is essentially a version of CIM Studio for people who love command lines. As the name implies, its primary purpose is to "dump" information from WMI to a standard output. When given a namespace and class name as parameters, it outputs a list of every instance of the class including the name, type, and values of all properties. Alternatively, if given a namespace and an object path, it outputs the name, type, and values of each of the object's properties. The following invocation would list information about all `Win32_Process` objects:

```
c:>wbemdump root\cimv2 Win32_Process
```

This one provides information only about the idle process:

```
c:>wbemdump root\cimv2 Win32_Process.Handle='0'
```

For more sophisticated operation, the `/Q <querylanguage> <query>` option instructs wbemdump.exe to dump objects based on the results of a query.

This is illustrated in the following simple example, which produces the same output as our first invocation:

```
c:>wbemdump root\cimv2 /Q WQL "SELECT * FROM Win32_Process"
```

Note: Namespace Selection

wbemdump.exe does not read the default namespace from a system's WMI configuration information. Therefore, all invocations of the command must *specify a namespace in which to work.* ◆

In addition to this basic mode of operation, wbemdump.exe boasts a vast number of command-line options that allow it to output MOF syntax, show system properties, and dump its output to file rather than to the console. For the more adventurous, there are options to control the underlying mechanisms used to retrieve information, to calculate query execution time and set various security parameters.

We rarely use wbemdump.exe in practice, because it is usually more convenient to use one of the graphical tools for browsing, or to write a script to handle more sophisticated requirements. However, it is a powerful tool for those who do want to use it. Thorough documentation may be found in the "WMI Reference" section of the WMI Software Development Kit.

The WMI Scripting API

As noted earlier, WMI classes and objects exist only within the world of WMI itself. Within this world, `Win32_Process`, `CIM_DataFile`, and `DS_Computer` objects are all completely different. They all have different properties and methods, and they all represent very different parts of a computer system. As far as the scripting API is concerned, however, every single WMI object is essentially the same. Each is an instance of `SWbemObject`. Each has a common set of properties and methods exposed by the `SWbemObject interface`. Only through `SWbemObject's` methods can we discover what each instance represents in WMI terms.

Note: WMI Objects in COM

It is not only the scripting interface that sees all WMI objects as instances of the same class. In COM itself, the architecture underlying WMI, each WMI object is just a COM object that exposes an `IWbemClassObject` *interface.* ◆

When we write a script that reads a property of `CIM_DataFile` or calls a method of `Win32_Process`, VBScript is carrying out some magic on our behalf. It *seems* as though we really are dealing with an object known to have a FileSize property or a Terminate() method; in reality, however, VBScript is having to ask the SWbemObject "do you have a property called filesize?" or "do you have a method called Terminate?" The reply is either no, in which case a runtime error occurs and we return to reading the WMI documentation more carefully, or else it is yes. In this case, a flurry of behind-the-scenes COM activity occurs, and the property is accessed or the method called through a mechanism called a *function pointer*. VBScript and COM handle the entire transaction without our intervention. Thanks to all this magic, generally known as *COM automation*, the link between VBScript and the WMI world is totally transparent.

Occasionally, however, the link goes wrong, as we saw in Chapter 9, "WMI and Active Directory"; in these cases, we can use special properties and methods of SWbemObject itself to find out about and control WMI objects. In fact, even when things do not go wrong, it can sometimes be useful to consider a WMI object not as an instance of, say Win32_Process, but just as an SWbemObject. When we think of a WMI object as an instance of SWbemObject, we know that it possesses a set of properties and methods that are always guaranteed to be available, no matter what the WMI concept that the object represents. We can use these to explore the WMI representation manually at our leisure, and to interact in a more finely tuned way with the WMI world.

It is not just WMI objects themselves that are represented by COM objects within the scripting API. Instead, every time we connect to the WMI service on a machine, retrieve a collection of objects, or even just read a property, we are interacting with one of the scripting API's COM objects. Some of these objects, such as SWbemServices, will by now be very familiar from earlier chapters; others, such as SWbemProperty, we have not discussed explicitly at all. In this section of the chapter, we return for a final time to some WMI basics. We consider how to connect to WMI, execute a query, read properties, and execute methods. This time, however, we consider each of these activities from the perspective of the scripting API objects that are involved. Our journey begins with SWbemServices, the COM object that represents the WMI service on a machine.

SWbemServices

SWbemServices is the first port of call for almost all our interactions with WMI. An instance of SWbemServices is returned by a line of code such as this:

```
Set refWMI = GetObject("winMgmts:")
```

Many of SWbemServices' methods, such as ExecQuery(), are by now familiar, having been used at several places throughout the book. A few more obscure but occasionally useful ones have not yet been mentioned, however. Without exception, these methods are concerned with performing simple operations against the Repository. They either retrieve objects, register for event notification, or delete objects. In all, nine different operations can be carried out with SWbemServices. Each of these is represented by two methods: one *synchronous* and one *asynchronous*.

Throughout this book, we have been mainly concerned with synchronous methods. When executed, these methods perform some operation against the Repository and, after they have finished, almost all return either an object or a collection. More specifically, they return either an SWbemObject or an SWbemObjectSet. An example of such a method that returns an SWbemObject is Get(). The most familiar method that returns an SWbemObjectSet is probably ExecQuery(). For most purposes, synchronous methods provide the simplest, cleanest way of interacting with SWbemServices from scripts. Hence we have used them whenever possible throughout the book.

There are occasions when fast user-interface response of the ability to carry out multiple operations simultaneously are more important than simplicity. For these circumstances, asynchronous methods are ideal. These methods do not return objects or collections directly. Instead, when called, they immediately pass control back to the calling, and use an SWbemSink callback to inform it of progress. We have discussed only one asynchronous method in the book so far, namely ExecNotificationQueryAsync() (see Chapter 8, "Proactive Troubleshooting with WMI"). However, every one of the synchronous methods has an asynchronous equivalent for programs or scripts that want to use it. Asynchronous methods have exactly the same name as their synchronous counterparts, with the suffix Async added (for instance, ExecQuery() becomes ExecQueryAsync()). Asynchronous method calls all take the same parameters as their synchronous counterparts, except that an SWbemSink must always be passed as the first parameter.

A complete list of the SWbemServices synchronous method calls, along with a brief explanation of their function, is given in Table 11.2. For reasons of space, we do not provide details of the method parameters here. However, many of them have been discussed elsewhere in the book, and in any event, all are well documented in the WMI Software Development Kit documentation.

Table 11. 2 SWbemServices *Synchronous Methods*

Method	Purpose
`Get()`	Retrieves an `SWbemObject` representing a WMI object or class, based on an object path.
`ExecQuery()`	Retrieves an `SWbemObjectSet` containing the results of executing a WQL query.
`InstancesOf()`	Retrieves an `SWbemObjectSet` containing all instances of a named WMI class. This method is equivalent to calling `ExecQuery()` with a `SELECT` query and no `WHERE` clauses (for instance, `SELECT * FROM Win32_Process`).
`AssociatorsOf()`	Retrieves an `SWbemObjectSet` containing all WMI objects that are connected to a named object via associators. This method is equivalent to calling `ExecQuery()` with an `ASSOCIATORS OF` query.
`ExecNotificationQuery()`	Registers a notification query on the basis of a WQL event query, and returns an `SWbemEventSource` that can be polled for events.
`ReferencesTo()`	Returns an `SWbemObjectSet` containing all WMI objects that hold references to a named object. Typically, this might include associators. Whereas `AssociatorsOf()` returns objects that are connected via associator objects, `ReferencesTo()` can return the associators themselves. This method is the equivalent to calling `ExecQuery()` with a `REFERENCES TO` query. This book does not contain any examples of this method in use.
`SubclassesOf()`	Returns an `SWbemObjectSet` containing `SWbemObjects` that represent WMI class objects. Specifically, they represent all subclasses of a named class. This book does not contain any examples of this method in use.
`Delete()`	Deletes an object based on an object path. This book does not contain any examples of this method in use.
`ExecMethod()`	Executes a named method against a named object. With this method, a script can execute a WMI object's methods without first retrieving a reference to the object in question. This method is of almost no value for VBScript users, and is not discussed anywhere in this book.

Between them, these `SWbemServices` methods and their asynchronous counterparts provide a script with all the functionality it needs to interact with WMI.

In addition to the 18 properties (9 in the preceding table and their 9 asynchronous counterparts), `SWbemServices` has a single property, namely `Security_`. This holds an `SWbemSecurity` object representing the `AuthenticationLevel`, `ImpersonationLevel` and `Privileges` associated with an instance of SWbemServices. So far in this book, we have set security options in the moniker string used to retrieve a reference to SWbemServices in the first place. As will be demonstrated later in this chapter, however, the SWbemSecurity object stored in the Security_ property can be changed to modify these settings after the initial connection has been made.

SWbemObjectSet

Many of the SWbemServices methods return collections of WMI objects. The capability to retrieve and iterate through such collections lies at the heart of many of the scripts presented throughout the book. Although we have not referred to them by name before, whenever we have encountered such collections, they have in fact been SWbemObjectSets.

In common with all collections, SWbemObjectSet has a Count property and an Item() method. Count contains the number of elements in the collection, and Item() returns an individual element, based on a key. We have not needed to use Item() or Count during the course of this book, because we have invariably wanted to operate on all items within the collection, something which can be accomplished with standard collection iteration syntax, as illustrated in the following code fragment:

```
Set colProcesses = refWMI.ExecQuery("SELECT * FROM Win32_Process")
'now we have a collection and can iterate through it
For Each refProcess In colProcesses
    'do something useful here
Next
```

There is no need to check that the Count property is greater than 0 before using a For Each...Next loop, because iterating through a 0-length collection is a perfectly acceptable thing to do. Count can be useful occasionally, however—for example, in circumstances when you want to give users feedback as to the progress of a script. This usage is illustrated in the following code fragment, a modified version of the preceding example:

```
Set colProcesses = refWMI.ExecQuery("SELECT * FROM Win32_Process")[sr]

WScript.Echo "About to operate on " & colProcesses.Count & " processes"
numCount = 1 'an increment variable
For Each refProcess In colProcesses
    WScript.Echo "Operating on process " & numCount & " of " & _
                 colProcesses.Count
    'do something useful here
    numCount = numCount + 1
Next
```

This code uses a combination of colProcesses.Count and an increment variable to report its progress every time it moves through the For Each...Next loop.

Tip: To Save Time, Do Not Read Count

Sometimes, a call to `ExecQuery()` *may return a huge number of objects, perhaps many more than you were expecting. It may be tempting to read the* `Count` *property before attempting to iterate through the elements of an* `SWbemObjectSet`*, perhaps to warn the user of the number of elements and give him the opportunity to abort execution. If you are thinking of doing this, be warned: The first time* `Count` *is invoked, WMI must iterate through the entire collection itself to perform the count; this, in itself, may be a rather time-consuming operation.* ◆

Elements within an `SWbemObjectSet` are indexed according to *relative object paths* (that is, the object path without computer or namespace components, such as `Win32_Directory.Name="c:\temp"`). Individual elements can be retrieved directly from the collection, therefore, via the `Item()` method. If `colFiles` is a collection containing all `CIM_DataFiles` on a computer, for example, the following line of code will retrieve the element representing `c:\boot.ini`:

```
refBootFile = colFiles.Item("CIM_DataFile.Name='c:\boot.ini'")
```

This facility is rarely needed; after all, WMI provides plenty of mechanisms for retrieving individual objects directly from the Repository. If you want to use it, however, the facility is there. An attempt to call `Item()` with a relative object path to an object that does not exist within the collection causes error `0x80041002` to be raised.

In addition to the standard collections interface, `SWbemObjectSet` has one additional property, namely `Security_`. This serves the same function as its `SWbemServices` counterpart.

SWbemObject

`SWbemObject` is arguably the single most important COM object in the WMI scripting API. It is the scripting API's representation of a WMI object or class. An `SWbemObject` is returned after each successful call to the `SWbemServices Get()` method. Every element of an `SWbemObjectSet` is also an `SWbemObject`.

As previously noted, the magic of COM automation enables us to access and manipulate methods and properties of WMI objects directly, without worrying about the underlying `SWbemObject` layer. As also noted, however, `SWbemObject` itself has several methods and properties of its own. These are completely independent from the WMI layer, and are available on all `SWbemObjects`, irrespective of the specific WMI class that each represents. Their purpose is to perform operations against the Repository that are relevant to the object on which they are called, to provide access to WMI system properties, and to supply information that identifies the object's identify and location within the Repository.

All `SWbemObject` methods and properties have names that are suffixed with an underscore character (_). This makes them clearly distinguishable from any methods or properties that belong to the represented WMI class.

SWbemObject Methods

`SWbemObject` presents 19 methods that allow interaction with and manipulation of a WMI object independent of the specific WMI class that the object represents. Seven of these are just asynchronous versions of standard synchronous methods. Twelve of them are just convenience methods; they duplicate functionality provided by `SWbemServices`, but operate specifically on the object against which they are called. For example, `Associators_()` and its asynchronous colleague `AssociatorsAsync_()` perform the same function as `SWbemServices AssociatorsOf()` and `AssociatorsOfAsync()`; the difference is that the `SWbemServices` methods operate on a named object whose path is provided as a parameter, whereas the `SWbemObject` versions operate on the class represented by the `SWbemObject` in question. To clarify, consider the following two code fragments, both of which return an `SWbemObjectSet` containing all associators of the WMI object representing the file C:\boot.ini:

```
'fragment 1
Set refWMI = GetObject("winMgmts:")
Set colAssocs = refWMI.AssociatorsOf("CIM_DataFile.Name='c:\boot.ini'")

'fragment 2
Set refWMI = GetObject("winMgmts:")
Set refBootIni = refWMI.Get("CIM_DataFile.Name='c:\boot.ini'")
Set colAssocs = refBootIni.Associators_()
```

In this particular example, the first fragment presents a rather more concise approach; in a more sophisticated script, however, where a need arises to find the associators of a class that has already been retrieved from the Repository, the `SWbemObject` method can be much more convenient.

All the synchronous `SWbemObject` convenience methods that duplicate `SWbemServices` functionality are listed in Table 11.3.

Table 11.3 SWbemObject *Synchronous Convenience Methods*

Method	Purpose
`Associators_()`	Equivalent to `SWbemServices AssociatorsOf()`, but finds the associators of the WMI object or class represented by the `SWbemObject` against which it is called.
`Instances_()`	Equivalent to `SWbemServices InstancesOf()`, but finds instances of the WMI class represented by the `SWbemObject` against which it is called. This method may be called only against an `SWbemObject` representing a WMI class.
`References_()`	Equivalent to `SWbemServices ReferencesTo()`, but finds references to the WMI object or class represented by the `SWbemObject` against which it is called.
`Subclasses_()`	Equivalent to `SWbemServices SubclassesOf()`, but finds subclasses of the WMI class represented by the `SWbemObject` against which it is called. This method may be called only against an `SWbemObject` representing a WMI class.
`Delete_()`	Equivalent to `SWbemServices Delete()`, but deletes the WMI object or class represented by the `SWbemObject` against which it is called. Deleting an object or class removes it permanently from the Repository. A script that deletes an object using `delete_()` does not lose a reference to the `SWbemObject` even if the `delete_()` operation is successful. Therefore, until the reference is actually lost (for instance, the variable holding it is set to `Nothing`), a call to `Put_()` can reinstate it (as discussed later).
`ExecMethod_()`	Equivalent to `SWbemServices ExecMethod()`, but executes a method of the WMI class or object represented by the `SWbemObject` against which it is called. `ExecMethod_()` presents a cumbersome, difficult way of executing a WMI method. In VBScript, it is never required, and we do not recommend its use

The remaining `SWbemObject` methods provide functionality not obviously duplicated elsewhere. These methods fall into two categories: those that present information about the WMI object or class represented by the `SWbemObject` against which they are called; and those that perform an ontological operation, such as cloning an object or writing to the Repository. In the first category are two methods, both of which operate synchronously. They are described in the Table 11.4.

Table 11.4 SWbemObject *Information-Retrieval Methods*

Method	Purpose
`CompareTo_()`	Compares the `SWbemObject` against which it is called with another `SWbemObject` passed to it as a parameter. If both `SWbemObjects` represent the same WMI class or object, the comparison returns true. The scope of the test performed can be controlled by a second optional parameter (see the WMI SDK documentation).
`GetObjectText_()`	Returns the MOF representation of the WMI class or object represented by the `SWbemObject` against which it is called.

A final set of four methods, two of which we have already met at several points during the course of this book, are concerned with the creation of new WMI objects. These are presented in Table 11.5.

Table 11.5 SWbemObject *Creation Methods*

Method	Purpose
`SpawnInstance_()`	Returns an `SWbemObject` representing a new instance of the WMI class represented by the `SWbemObject` against which it is called. As you first saw in Chapter 3, "Examining the Filesystem with WMI," the object returned by this method does not live anywhere in the Repository. It is brand new instance, all of whose fields are blank. Calling this method is normally the first step in creating a new WMI object from a script.
`Put_()`	Writes the WMI object or class represented by the `SWbemObject` against which it is called into the Repository. If the object's primary key corresponds to something that already exists within the Repository, the old definition is overwritten with the new data (presuming that the calling script has relevant permissions). If the primary key does not correspond to an existing object, a new instance is written to the Repository. A call to this method, which we have used several times throughout the book, is usually the final step in creating a new WMI object from a script.
`Clone_()`	Returns an `SWbemObject` representing a clone of the WMI object or class represented by the `SWbemObject` against which it is called. This method provides a quicker mechanism for creating a large number of new objects than `SpawnInstance_()` in cases where almost all the fields of each object are to be identical. One template object can be created first with `SpawnInstance_()`, the common fields can be filled in, and then the new customized template can be `Clone_()`d as many times as necessary. Only the unique fields (such as the key fields) need be filled individually on each clone.

Method	Purpose
SpawnDerivedClass_()	This method, which is appropriate only to SWbemObjects representing WMI classes, returns an SWbemObject representing a new subclass of the class against which it is called. This is one of a number of methods and properties available within the scripting API that allow new class definitions to be created. For such a definition to be useful, however, a provider supporting any subclassed operations must be created. Such a task is beyond the scope of this book, and beyond the needs of most system administrators using WMI.

SWbemObject Properties

In our opinion, by far the most interesting part of SWbemObject is the properties that it exposes. These present information about the represented object's place within the WMI world, yield information about the object's definition, and even allow access to the object's properties. Of the six properties exposed, only one holds data directly. The others hold references to other COM objects presented by the WMI scripting API.

The property that holds data directly is Derivation_. As the name implies, it provides access to the system property __DERIVATION on the WMI class or object that it represents. Specifically, it is an array of strings, each of which holds the class name of a superclass from which the represented object is derived. The lowest index in the array holds the most immediate superclass and the highest the most distant. For example, an attempt to read each element of this array in turn from an SWbemObject representing the Win32_Process class (or an instance of that class) would yield CIM_Process, followed by CIM_LogicalElement, followed by CIM_ManagedSystemElement. The VBScript code required to produce this output is presented in the following fragment:

```
Set refProcess = GetObject("winMgmts:Win32_Process")
For Each strDerived In refProcess.Derivation_
    WScript.Echo strDerived
Next
```

Because Derivation_ is an array rather than an automation collection, the following code is equally valid:

```
Set refProcess = GetObject("winMgmts:Win32_Process")
For i = LBound(refProcess.Derivation_) To UBound(refProcess.Derivation_)
    WScript.Echo refProcess.Derivation_(i)
Next
```

Note: Accessibility of WMI System Properties

As you might remember from Chapter 8, WMI system properties are not directly accessible via the scripting API. Therefore, the only means of access is indirectly through properties of `SWbemObject`. ◆

The `Derivation_` property of `SWbemObject` is unlikely to be very useful in a production script, but it can be extremely helpful during the development process. Often, it is useful to know the derivation of a class, particularly when constructing queries that rely on common supertypes. Writing a quick one-off script, such as the ones presented earlier in this chapter, can often be considerably quicker than firing up a tool such as the Object Browser or CIM Studio, searching for the class in question, and reading its `__DERIVATION` property!

The five other `SWbemObject` properties are discussed in detail later on in this chapter, because each holds a COM object to which a section of text is devoted. In the interests of providing a coherent picture of the API from a scripter's perspective, however, a brief description of each of these properties is given in Table 11.6.

Table 11.6 SWbemObject *Properties Holding COM Objects*

Property	Purpose
`Properties`	This hold an `SWbemPropertytSet` containing all the properties of the represented WMI object or class. By iterating through this collection, we can discover the name, type, and value of each property that the WMI object or class presents.
`Path`	This holds an `SWbemObjectPath`, which contains all the information encoded by the WMI system properties. With the exception of`_DERIVATION`, which is duplicated by `Derivation`, system properties of a WMI object are only available through this `Path` property.
`Methods`	`Methods` is to WMI methods what `Properties_` is to WMI properties. It holds an `SWbemMethodSet` containing information about all the methods exposed by a WMI object or class.
`Qualifiers_`	This holds an `SWbemQualifierSet` containing the list of WMI object qualifiers that apply to the represented object or class.
`Security_`	This serves the same function as its equivalent in all the other scripting API objects we have seen so far. It holds an `SWbemSecurity` object encapsulating the DCOM security settings associated with the instance.

An `SWbemProperty` object, therefore, is the scripting API's representation of a WMI object or class. Its methods and properties stand independent of the specific WMI object being represented. As such, they stand as constant hooks that allow a script to interact not so much with the WMI world of

Win32_ComputerSystems and CIM_DataFiles, but with the mechanisms through which that world exists.

SWbemProperty and *SWbemPropertySet*

An SWbemPropertySet is a collection of SWbemProperty objects. An SWbemProperty is the scripting interface's representation of a WMI property. As you have seen, every SWbemObject has an SWbemPropertySet stored in its Properties_ property. As discussed in Chapter 9, the SWbemPropertySet can be used to access property values as an alternative to the *direct access* method. This is illustrated in the following three code fragments, all of which are functionally identical:

```
'fragment 1
Set refBootIni = GetObject("winMgmts:CIM_DataFile.Name='c:\boot.ini'")
WScript.Echo refBootIni.FileSize

'fragment 2
Set refBootIni = GetObject("winMgmts:CIM_DataFile.Name='c:\boot.ini'")
WScript.Echo refBootIni.Properties_.Item("FileSize")

'fragment 3
Set refBootIni = GetObject("winMgmts:CIM_DataFile.Name='c:\boot.ini'")
WScript.Echo refBootIni.Properties_("FileSize")
```

The difference between these fragments is that whereas the first used COM automation magic to access the FileSize property of a WMI object (see earlier in this chapter), the second reads the value from an item in an SWbemPropertySet. The second fragment works because the items in an SWbemPropertySet are indexed by property names, and the default property of an SWbemProperty is its value. The third fragment is essentially the same as the second, except that it takes advantage of the fact that Item() is a default method of Properties_ and is therefore assumed if omitted.

If you have decided that the first fragment is by far the tidiest, and are currently wondering why on earth anyone would ever bother reading values from an SWbemPropertySet, the answer is threefold:

- When using a language that does not support COM automation (and hence does not support direct access to WMI properties and methods), retrieving elements from an SWbemPropertySet is the only way to access them.
- Very occasionally, direct access does not work, as we discussed in Chapter 9. In these cases, SWbemPropertySet constitutes an alternative mechanism to try.
- The individual SWbemProperty objects stored in an SWbemPropertySet tell far more about the properties than their value. We can use this information to explore a WMI object without recourse to a tool such as the Object Browser.

In the context of this book, we can dismiss the first reason. VBScript (the language used throughout) and JScript and Perl (discussed in Appendix B, "Accessing WMI from Other Languages") can all use direct access. They never *need* to resort to the more cumbersome `Properties_` approach. Likewise, although the second reason is valid in that it helped us out in Chapter 9, it is not exactly compelling in the general case. The third reason, however, is far more interesting, so it is to this that we now turn.

`SWbemPropertySets` are similar to all the other collections that discussed in this book in that they have an `Item()` method, used to retrieve individual elements, a `Count` property that yields the number of elements in the collection, and can be iterated over with a `For Each...Next` loop. This may sound thoroughly unremarkable, but it gives us an extremely useful facility, namely the ability to list all the properties defined by a WMI class. To discover the names of all available methods, all we do is iterate through the `SWbemPropertySet` held in the `Properties_` property of the `SWbemObject` representing that class. This technique has already been demonstrated in Chapter 9, but because an example takes a mere four lines of code, we present one again here. This code fragment lists all properties of `CIM_DataFile`:

```
Set refCIMDataFile = GetObject("winMgmts:CIM_DataFile")
For Each refProperty In refCIMDataFile.Properties_
    WScript.Echo refProperty.Name
Next
```

The code could equally be called on an `SWbemObject` representing a specific instance of a `CIM_DataFile`. If you have tried running a script containing this code, you might have noticed that none of the WMI system properties (for instance, `__DERIVATION`) are listed. An `SWbemPropertySet` contains only properties that are specifically part of the class's or a superclass's definition.

Note: Add() and Remove()

`SWbemPropertySets` are mutable. In other words, elements can be added to and removed from them with `Add()` and `Remove()` methods, respectively. However, we put this feature in the same category as the `SWbemObjectSpawnDerivedClass_()` method. It is great for provider writers who want to generate class definitions without using MOF, but not of much interest to the average system administrator. ◆

Listing an object's property names is only the beginning, because `SWbemProperty` holds much more information about a property than its name and value. It holds the property's type (where in a class hierarchy, a property was originally declared) and what its qualifiers are. The complete list of `SWbemProperty` properties is presented in Table 11.7.

Table 11.7 SWbemProperty *Properties*

Property	Purpose
`Value`	This default property holds the actual value of the represented WMI property. For example, if representing `FileSize`, this property holds the actual size.
`Name`	Holds the name of the represented property (for instance, `FileSize`).
`Origin`	Holds the name of the class within which the represented property was defined. For example, the `Origin` of an `SWbemProperty` representing `CIM_DataFile.FileSize` would be `CIM_LogicalFile`, because this is the class from which the property is inherited.
`IsLocal`	A convenience property that holds whether the represented property was defined in the local class rather than a superclass. It holds no information that cannot be gleaned from `Origin`.
`CIMType`	A numeric value indicating the CIMType of the property represented. A complete list of types may be found in the WMI Software Development Kit documentation. Among the most commonly found are 3 (32-bit signed integer), 8 (string), 11 (Boolean), 13 (object), 19 (32-bit unsigned integer), 101 (datetime) and 102 (reference).
`IsArray`	A Boolean value stating whether the property being represented is actually an array rather than an individual value. This information is not stored in CIMType. Both must be read to be sure about a property's true type. For example, a `CIMType` of 8 and `IsArray` of false means the property contains a string. However, a CIMType of 8 and IsArray of true means the property is an array of strings.
`Qualifiers_`	Holds an `SWbemQualifierSet`, which contains a list of `SWbemQualifiers` representing the WMI qualifiers that apply to the represented property. `SWbemQualifiers` are discussed later in the chapter.

Between them, the properties exposed by `SWbemProperty` enable us to find out much about a WMI object's properties by writing a quick script. Although not often useful in a production environment, this facility can be a valuable tool in the WMI user's armory. As a quick demonstration of `SWbemProperty` as a tool in action, we present the following short script, which displays the name and value of every property of a WMI object whose object path is specified as a command-line parameter. If the property is an array, each item within the array displays. In essence, this script is no different from many of the ones presented in earlier chapters. It connects to WMI, retrieves an object reference, and operates on that object. The difference is that it does not directly read properties exposed by the WMI object. Instead, all interaction with the WMI object is mediated by properties of `SWbemObject`.

```
'showproperties.vbs - display the names and values
'of all the properties of an object whose object path
'is given as a command-line parameter. Warning: this
'script does not like objects some of whose properties
'contain embedded objects!
Option Explicit
On Error Resume Next
Dim refWMI
Dim refObject
Dim refProperty
Dim theValue 'for property values (type is unknown)

'first check cmd-line for sanity
If WScript.Arguments.Count <> 1 Then
    WScript.Echo "Usage: showproperties.vbs <objpath>"
    WScript.Quit
End If

'connect to WMI
Set refWMI = GetObject("winMgmts:")
If Err <> 0 Then
    WScript.Echo "Could not connect to WMI"
    WScript.Quit
End If

'attempt to retrieve specified object
Set refObject = refWMI.Get(WScript.Arguments(0))
If Err <> 0 Then
    WScript.Echo "Could not retrieve object."
    WScript.Quit
End If

'iterate through property collection
'for arrays, print the name and value list
'for nonarrays, print "name: value"
For Each refProperty in refObject.Properties_
    If refProperty.IsArray Then
        WScript.Echo refProperty.Name & ":-"
        For Each theValue In refProperty.Value
            WScript.Echo " " & theValue
        Next
    Else
        WScript.Echo refProperty.Name & ": " & _
                     refProperty.Value
    End If
Next

Set refObject = Nothing
Set refWMI = Nothing
```

To use this script to read all the properties of the WMI object representing the file c:\boot.ini, type the following at the command prompt:

```
c:>showproperties.vbs CIM_DataFile.Name='c:\boot.ini'
```

Note that this script is far from perfect, and could be improved dramatically by using the `CIMType` property to spark conditional execution. For example, it could convert a date into a human-readable format and resolve an object reference by displaying properties of the embedded object and the like. The current version cannot handle embedded objects or references at all. We leave these improvements as an exercise for the interested reader.

SWbemMethod and *SWbemMethodSet*

As you have probably already guessed, `SWbemMethod` is the scripting API's representation of a WMI method; `SWbemMethodSet` is a collection of `SWbemMethods`. The `Methods_` property of `SWbemObject` holds an `SWbemMethodSet` containing one `SWbemMethod` for each method that the represented WMI object exposes. Just as you can use an `SWbemPropertySet` to find out programmatically about a WMI object's properties, you can use an `SWbemMethodSet` to find out about its methods. Contrary to what you might expect, however, `SWbemMethod` does not provide a facility for executing the method it represents. This is the task of `SWbemObject`'s `ExecMethod_()` method.

An `SWbemMethodSet` is a simple collection. It supports an `Item()` method which, when given a method name, returns the `SWbemMethod` representing the named method, and a `Count` property, which returns the number of methods in the collection. Unlike its `SWbemPropertySet` counterpart, `SWbemMethodSet` does not have facilities for adding and removing members. This is likely to be rectified in a future release of WMI.

`SWbemMethod` itself has five properties. Three of which, namely `Name`, `Origin` and `Qualifiers_`, have the same purpose as their `SWbemProperty` equivalents. The other two, `InParameters` and `OutParameters`, hold details of the input and output parameters that the method uses. If you expected these values to be arrays of values or something similar, prepare to be surprised! The `InParameters` and `OutParameters` properties in fact hold embedded instances of `SWbemObject`.

Although `SWbemObject` might seem a strange choice for holding details of method parameters, it does make a degree of sense because `SWbemObject`, or at least `SWbemObject`'s `SWbemPropertySet`, is capable of holding exactly the information needed to define method parameters, namely a set of names, values, and types. Each input parameter is represented by an `SWbemProperty` in the `InParameters` `SWbemObject`; each output parameter is represented by a single `SWbemProperty` of the `OutParameter` `SWbemObject`. Information about the return value is also stored here, in a property called `ReturnValue`.

To clarify all this, examine the following extended code fragment, which prints the names, input parameters, and output parameters of all methods of `Win32_Process`. It works by looping through each `SWbemMethod` in the

SWbemMethodSet, outputting the name, and then looping through the SWbemPropertySet of the embedded SWbemObjects stored in the InParameters and OutParameters properties. There is one slight complication to note: When a method has no input parameters, its InParameters is null and contains no SWbemObject. Unfortunately, VBScript seems incapable of recognizing null values returned from WMI and therefore crashes when an attempt is made to loop through a null collection. To solve this problem, we precede the loop with an invocation of On Error Resume Next. Therefore, when a method has no input parameters, the problem is safely ignored. An invocation of On Error Goto 0 switches error handling back on once the looping is complete.

```
Set refProcess = GetObject("winMgmts:Win32_Process")
'loop through each method
For Each refMethod In refProcess.Methods_
    WScript.Echo "Method " & refMethod.Name & "()"

    'now list the in parameters by iterating
    'the SWbemPropertySet of the embedded SWbemObject
    'first turn on error handling to avoid problems when
    'a method has no input parameters
    On Error Resume Next
    Set refParams = refMethod.InParameters
    WScript.Echo " Input Parameters:-"
    For Each refParam In refParams.Properties_
        WScript.Echo "  " & refParam.Name
    Next

    'error handling off
    On Error Goto 0

    'now use the same technique to list outparams
    'no need for error handling here, as ALL methods
    'have at least one out parameter, namely the
    'return value
    Set refParams = refMethod.OutParameters
    WScript.Echo " Output Parameters:-"
    For Each refParam In refParams.Properties_
        WScript.Echo "  " & refParam.Name
    Next
Next
```

If you incorporate this code into the showproperties.vbs script presented in the preceding section, you will have a comprehensive command-line class-inspection script.

Note: Calling Methods with ExecMethod_()

We have noted that from the perspective of a VBScript programmer, `SWbemObject`*'s* `ExecMethod_()` *is a cumbersome alternative to the direct access approach to executing WMI methods. For the curious, if you* did *want to use it, here are the details:*

First, retrieve the object stored in the `InParameters` *property of the* `SWbemMethod` *that you want to execute. Then call its* `SpawnInstance_()` *or* `Clone_ ()` *method to make a fresh* `SWbemObject` *representing the input parameters of the method you want to call. Specify each input parameter value in turn by setting values of the relevant properties in the* `Properties_` *collection. You will then have an* `SWbemObject` *representing the input parameters that you would like to pass to the method.*

Finally, call `ExecMethod_()` *on the WMI class or object that you want to invoke it against, passing your newly created* `SWbemObject` *as a parameter. Assuming execution is successful,* `ExecMethod_()` *will return an* `SWbemObject` *representing the output parameters (and return value). You can read the values of all* `SWbemProperties` *in its* `Properties_` *to find out what the method call has done.*

This is not as complicated as it may sound but, as we warned, it is very, very cumbersome. ◆

SWbemQualifier and *SWbemQualifierSet*

`SWbemQualifierSet` appears in the `Qualifiers_` property of `SWbemObject`, `SWbemProperty` and `SWbemMethod`. It is a mutable collection, containing `Add()` and `Remove()` methods, as well as the standard `Item()` method and `Count` property. As the name suggests, an `SWbemQualifierSet` holds a collection of `SWbemQualifier` objects, each of which represents a WMI qualifier that mediates the behavior of a class, object, property, or method (as discussed earlier in this chapter).

`SWbemQualifier` has seven properties, each of which encodes some aspect of the qualifier it represents. Predictably, two of these are `Name` and `Value`, whose purpose is self-explanatory. The other five Boolean properties encode the qualifier's scope and origin. Table 11.8 describes them.

Table 11.8 SWbemQualifier *Scope and Origin Properties*

Property	Meaning
`PropagatesToInstance`	This qualifier propagates to instances.
`PropagatesToSubclass`	This qualifier is inherited by subclasses.
`IsAmended`	This qualifier has been altered in the local class or object.
`IsLocal`	This qualifier has been defined in the local class or object.
`IsOverridable`	This qualifier can be overridden by subclasses or instances.

The following code fragment illustrates how the contents of an SWbemObject's SWbemQualifierSet can be used to list the WMI qualifiers associated with the Win32_Directory class. The output here, which gives an indication as to the qualifier's propagation and origin, is intended to mimic the information displayed by the Object Browser's Object Qualifier window (see Chapter 6).

```
Set refObject = GetObject("winMgmts:Win32_Directory")
For Each refQual in refObject.Qualifiers_
    strInfo = refQual.Name & " [ "
    If refQual.PropagatesToInstance Then _
        strInfo = strInfo & "I "
    If refQual.PropagatesToSubclass Then _
        strInfo = strInfo & "C "
    If refQual.IsOverridable Then _
        strInfo = strInfo & "O "
    If refQual.IsAmended Then _
        strInfo = strInfo & "A "
    strInfo = strInfo & "]"
    WScript.Echo strInfo
Next
```

With a few minor modifications, the script fragment could of course be used to list the qualifiers of Win32_Directory's properties and methods.

SWbemObjectPath

An SWbemObjectPath, as the name implies, is the WMI scripting API's representation of an object path. In other words, it is the object path component of a moniker string (that is, everything after the winMgmts: prefix) presented in a structured format. An SWbemObjectPath is stored in the Path_ property of an SWbemObject.

SWbemObjectPath has 13 properties, which fall broadly into two categories. One set contains parts of the object path that are represented by WMI system properties; because system properties cannot be accessed directly from the scripting API, these SWbemObjectPath properties provide an alternative way to access them. The other set contains path-related information that is not represented by WMI system properties. A single property that falls into neither category is Security_; this fulfils the same purpose as it does in SWbemServices, SWbemObjectand, and so on.

We have used SWbemObjectPath explicitly very few times in this book. Whenever we have done so, such as in Chapter 8, we have been interested in those properties that hold information that would theoretically be available through WMI system properties were they accessible through the scripting API. The mapping between SWbemObject properties and WMI system properties is shown in Table 11.9.

Table 11.9 SWbemObjectPath *to WMI System Property Mapping*

SWbemObjectPath Property	WMI System Property
`Class`	__CLASS
`IsClass`	__GENUS
`Namespace`	__NAMESPACE
`Path`	__PATH
`Relpath`	__RELPATH
`Server`	__SERVER

With the exception of `IsClass` and __GENUS, the mapping between the two domains is completely clear and the data types of the properties correspond. The only difference between `IsClass` and __GENUS is that the former is a Boolean value whereas __GENUS is numeric. When `IsClass` is true, __GENUS is 1; when `IsClass` is false, __GENUS is 2.

Several of the WMI system properties are notable by their absence from the preceding list. Specifically, `__DERIVATION`, __DYNASTY, __PROPERTY_COUNT and __SUPERCLASS do not have equivalents in `SWbemObjectPath`. The reason, of course, is that the information that they hold can easily be gleaned by other means:

- Information held by `__DERIVATION` is available from `SWbemObject's` `Derivation_` property.
- Information held by __PROPERTY_COUNT can be retrieved from an `SWbemPropertySet`'s `Count` property.
- __DYNASTY *and* __SUPERCLASS *contain no information that cannot be gleaned indirectly from* `__DERIVATION`.

Hardly any of the second set of `SWbemObjectPath` properties are useful in a system administration scripting environment; but for the sake of completeness, all are presented in Table 11.10. Properties are presented in order of decreasing usefulness.

Table 11.10 SWbemObjectCount *Properties Not Related to WMI System Properties*

Property	Purpose
`DisplayName`	Holds a fully formed moniker string that, if passed to `GetObject()`, would retrieve the object to which the `SWbemObjectPath` refers. This can be a useful debugging tool, because the string includes DCOM security information and a fully specified namespace and object path.

continues ▶

Table 11.10 Continued

Property	Purpose
Keys	Holds an SWbemNamedValueSet (see below) representing the names and values of all properties of the object referenced by the SWbemObjectPath that are part of the primary key. It can be used as a quick way of determining the primary key components from within a script.
Authority	When a connection to WMI includes an Authority component, this value holds the authority string used for the connection (see Chapter 6). This is occasionally useful as a debugging tool.
IsSingleton	Reports whether the object referenced by the SWbemObjectPath is a singleton.
Locale	Holds a string value representing the locale used in the current WMI connection.
ParentNamespace	Holds a string value representing the parent of the namespace in which the object referred to by the SWbemObjectPath resides (for instance, for any object in the root\cimv2 namespace, this value would be root).

In addition to these properties, SWbemObjectPath has two methods, SetAsClass() and SetAsSingleton(). SetAsClass() changes an SWbemObjectPath rerefencing an instance into one representing a class. SetAsSingleton() changes an SWbemObjectPath referencing an instance so that it refers to a singleton. Of course, invoking either of these methods on an SWbemObjectPath stored in the Path_ property of a SWbemObject would make no sense at all, because a successful invocation would invalidate the path. In fact, an attempt to do this fails with error 0x80041001 (unspecified error). The reason for the existence of these methods is that SWbemObjectPath is a creatable object as demonstrated by the following valid code fragment, which creates an SWbemObjectPath representing the Win32_Directory class on a machine called STYX:

```
Set refNewPath = CreateObject("WbemScripting.SWbemObjectPath")
With refPath
    .Server = "STYX"
    .Class = "Win32_Directory"
End With
```

We have not managed to think of any reason why you might conceivably want to do this; however, if you do, the facility is there!

SWbemSecurity, SWbemPrivilege and *SWbemPrivilegeSet*

Almost every COM object in the WMI scripting API that we have examined so far in this chapter has a Security_ property. This property holds an SWbemSecurity object, which encapsulates the DCOM security settings associated with the object. So far in this book, we have handled all security issues at the time of our initial connection to a WMI service. We have specified any impersonation level, authentication level, or privileges we required as part of the initial moniker string. Once specified, these security settings persist for the entirety of a connection, and apply to any WMI objects retrieved from the repository via the initial `SWbemServices` object. If you require more fine-grained control over the security settings (for example, to enable a privilege just for the `SWbemObject` that needs it, or enable delegation just to carry out a few operations), you can change the settings associated with an individual `SWbemObject` or even `SWbemServices` itself, via its `Security_` property.

`SWbemSecurity` has three properties: `ImpersonationLevel`, `AuthenticationLevel`, and `Privileges`. `ImpersonationLevel` holds a numeric value representing the DCOM impersonation level associated with an object. This value is both readable and writeable, as demonstrated by the following script fragment:

```
'connect to WMI
Set refWMI = GetObject("winMgmts:")

'display the current impersonation level.
'by default on W2K, this will be 3 (impersonate)
WScript.Echo "DCOM impersonation level is " & _
             refWMI.Security_.ImpersonationLevel

'set level to "Delegate"
refWMI.Security_.ImpersonationLevel = 2

'prove that it has changed
WScript.Echo "DCOM impersonation level is " & _
             refWMI.Security_.ImpersonationLevel
```

For a full discussion of the various impersonation levels and the numeric values that represent them, refer to Chapter 5.

The `AuthenticationLevel` property also holds a numeric value, namely the DCOM authentication level associated with the object whose security settings are represented by a particular instance of `SWbemSecurity`. Like `ImpersonationLevel`, this property may be read or written at any time.

The third and perhaps most interesting `SWbemSecurity` properties is `Privileges`. This holds an `SWbemPrivilegeSet`, a mutable collection containing `SWbemPrivilege` objects. By adding and removing privileges from an `SWbemPrivilegeSet`, the effective privileges for an `SWbemServices` object or even an `SWbemObject` representing a specific instance of a specific WMI class can be changed. `SWbemPrivilegeSet` has four methods that can be used to change the privilege set. Table 11.11 describes these.

Table 11.11 SWbemPrivilegeSet *Mutator Method*

Method	Purpose and Usage
`Add()`	This method, which takes an integer value, creates an `SWbemPrivilege` object corresponding to the integer passed to it, and adds this `SWbemPrivilege` to the collection.
`AddAsString()`	This method, which takes a privilege string as a parameter, creates an `SWbemPrivilege` object corresponding to the string passed to it, and adds this `SWbemPrivilege` to the collection. Privileges must be specified in their full form, namely the string `Se` followed by the privilege name, followed by the string `Privilege` (for instance, `SeBackupPrivilege`).
`Remove()`	This method, which takes an integer value, removes the `SWbemPrivilege` object corresponding to the value from the collection.
`DeleteAll()`	This method, which takes no parameters, removes all privileges from the collection.

`SWbemPrivilegeSet` is different from most other collections in that its `Add()` and `Remove()` method does not take an `SWbemPrivilege` object as a parameter even though each privilege is represented as such objects inside the collection itself. The reason for this decision, presumably, was to ensure that WMI's treatment of privileges was similar to other programming contexts in which privileges are used. For a list of privilege names and their corresponding numeric values, refer to the Win32 Software Development Kit documentation or, for a brief summary, to the `WbemPrivilegeEnum` page in the "WMI Scripting API Constants" section of the WMI Software Development Kit.

Note: Only on Windows 2000

Changing the `SWbemPrivilegeSet` *after an initial call to* `GetObject()` *works only with Windows 2000.* ◆

The `SWbemPrivilege` object itself has four properties that encapsulate information about each privilege in an `SWbemPrivilegeSet`. Table 11.12 describes these.

Table 11.12 SWbemPrivilege *Properties*

Property	Purpose
`Name`	Holds the textual name of the represented privilege (for instance, `SeSecurityPrivilege`).
`Identifier`	Holds the numeric value of the represented privilege (for instance, `SeSecurityPrivilege` corresponds to a value of `7`).

Property	Purpose
IsEnabled	Reports whether the represented privilege is enabled. Given that SWbemPrivilegeSets hold only those privileges that are specifically requested, it seems that the only reason why this value should ever be false is if an attempt to enable a privilege failed.
DisplayName	Holds a textual description of the privilege as displayed by the Windows 2000 GUI. (For instance, SeSecurityPrivilege corresponds to "manage auditing and security logs.")

Odds and Ends

We have almost reached the end of our tour of WMI from the scripting API's perspective. You have seen explicitly how the WMI objects and collections that we have been using throughout the book map on to SWbemObject and its colleagues. Although we have covered all the scripting API objects that relate to core WMI functionality, there are six more objects that we have not discussed. Three of these—SWbemSink, SwbemEventSource, and SwbemLocator—have already be considered in Chapter 8 and Chapter 10, and will not be considered further here. The other three—SWbemNamedValue, SWbemNamedValueSet, and SWbemLastError—deserve brief explanation.

SWbemNamedValue and *SWbemNamedValueSet*

SWbemNamedValueSet is, of course, a collection of SWbemNamedValue objects. Its Item() method allows an individual SWbemNamedValue to be retrieved via its Name property. The Count property, in common with that of all collections, holds the number of items currently in the collection. The collection is mutable. It provides Add() and Remove() methods and also a DeleteAll(). One final method, Clone(), returns a clone of the SWbemNamedValueSet against which it is called. SWbemNamedValue objects themselves are possibly the simplest objects in the entire WMI world, let alone the scripting interface. They have just two properties: Name and Value.

SWbemNamedValueSets are intended for situations in which there is need to hold arbitrary data that can be referenced by name. As discussed earlier in this chapter, an SWbemObjectPath uses an SWbemNamedValueSet to store the names and values of a WMI object's primary key properties. Its use here is somewhat unusual, however. Usually, SWbemNamedValueSets are created to pass provider-specific information as method parameters. Microsoft strongly recommends that providers do not require the use of SWbemNamedValueSets because their very nature is contrary to the entire philosophy of WMI. WMI's strength lies in the rigid separation it places between providers and clients; the very fact that SWbemNamedValueSets hold arbitrary, provider-specific information violates this separation. Despite the warnings, the facility is there for providers that want to use it. occasionally, therefore, you will be forced use it in management scripts. Hence, we mention it here.

SWbemLastError

`SWbemLastError` is a creatable object that, as the name implies, represents the last WMI error that occurred before the object was created. Under usual circumstances, the error information received in the return value of methods or a VBScript error raised by a failed WMI operation gives sufficient information to work out what has gone wrong. When this is not the case, as discussed in Chapter 10, a combination of tools such as wbemtest.exe, examination of the WMI logs, and common sense usually prevail. If you are extremely persistent or naturally curious, however, you might want to investigate `SWbemLastError`. You might create an `SWbemLastError` object immediately after a WMI method call has failed. An attempt to create one under any other circumstances will itself fail, raising an error of its own! `SWbemLastError` has exactly the same properties and methods as `SWbemObject`, but instead of representing a WMI object, they represent a WMI error. We should admit at this point that we have never found information yielded from an `SWbemLastError` to be remotely useful. However, we feel honor bound to tell you about its existence. If we have raised your curiosity, for further information, you are directed to the WMI Software Development Kit.

Summary

This chapter opened by considering how classes and objects come to "live" in the Repository. It discussed MOF, the language used to create class and instance definitions, and introduced two tools designed to examine them. It also discussed system properties and qualifiers, features common to all WMI objects. Finally, it investigated in more detail the various COM objects that make up the WMI scripting API and showed how they fit together into a coherent framework.

Currently, Windows XP, the successor to Windows 2000, is in public beta. The WMI system in this new operating system does not look dramatically different from that of Windows 2000. All the information contained within this book in general, and this chapter in particular, will continue to apply. The new release does look as though it will contain several enhancements and improvements, including some extensions to the scripting API. Because these are still in beta and subject to change, however, we do not think it expedient to discuss them here. We await the final release with eager anticipation....

WMI on Other Microsoft Platforms

Throughout this book, we have talked about WMI almost exclusively in the context of Windows 2000. However, WMI is also available on Windows 95 OSR2, Windows 98, Windows Me, and Windows NT 4 (with Service Pack 4 or greater), so many of the techniques discussed in this book can be used across platforms if you are running a heterogeneous Microsoft network, albeit with some loss of functionality. The new Windows XP platform, soon due for release, also ships with WMI as a core component. Functionality here will be almost identical to Windows 2000 and even promises a number of enhancements and extensions.

This appendix is devoted to a brief discussion of the installation and configuration of WMI on Windows NT and Windows 9*x* platforms. In addition, it addresses some of the limitations that you are likely to encounter when you use them.

Download and Installation

Windows Me and Windows 98 Second Edition include WMI as a core component of the operating system. Running WMI on these systems, therefore, requires no special installation process. In contrast, the other platforms do not come with WMI by default; to use it, you need to download the latest version (v1.5) from Microsoft's web site. Currently, the relevant files can be found under the Windows Development section of the MSDN downloads web site. Because the specific location on the site might change from time to time, the safest plan is to go to `http://msdn.microsoft.com/downloads/➥default.asp` and search for "WMI." Find the WMI "core components" (v1.5) and download them. A single self-extracting executable contains the WMI installer for Windows 95 OSR2, Windows 98, and Windows NT 4.0. The installation process is trivial. Just run the executable, agree to the licensing terms when prompted, and watch the system install itself.

Behind the scenes, the installer performs a number of actions. It installs the files needed to run and monitor WMI—namely, binaries, log files, and the all-important Repository. It also makes some changes to the Registry to configure COM. The WMI files are installed to a WBEM directory under %WINDIR%/system on Windows 95 and Windows 98, or to %SYSTEM-ROOT%/system32 on Windows NT 4. Finally, it builds the Repository by registering all the providers with COM and running mofcomp.exe on the standard MOF files (see Chapter 11, "WMI Internals"). If you are curious to know exactly what the installer does, you can browse a detailed log of its actions, which can be found in the Instcore.log file in the new WBEM directory.

Note: Naming Confusion

Microsoft appears to be having a bit of an identity crisis over the naming of WMI. Although it is usually called Windows Management Instrumentation (WMI), the older, generic name, Web-Based Enterprise Management (WBEM), still appears from time to time. Although most recent documentation uses WMI, WBEM is still used for the name of the WMI directory. Furthermore, the underlying COM interfaces are all named with an `IWBem` *prefix. As an extra twist, there seems to be some dispute over the initials WMI, too. Whereas most documentation refers to it as Windows Management Instrumentation, a couple of Microsoft dialogs call it Windows Management Infrastructure. Oh well...* ◆

Running WMI on Windows 95, 98, and Me

Windows 95, 98, and Me do not have the concept of services, so WMI must run as a standard executable. To test an installation, start winmgmt.exe and write a simple script that interrogates the local machine through WMI. Hopefully, everything will work just fine! VBScript and the Windows Scripting Host are installed as part of the WMI installation on those platforms, which do not include these components as standard.

If you want to do more than just run scripts locally on Windows 95, 98, and Me boxes, and actually integrate these platforms into your remote management regime, installation and testing are sadly not the end of the story. Unfortunately, WMI is *not* configured to allow remote access on these platforms by default. Even more unfortunately, the procedure for enabling remote access is not at all obvious, and no information about it is given during the installation process. Thankfully, the WMI SDK documentation does outline the procedure, which can be distilled into the following steps:

1. Open the Windows Registry, and find the key HKEY_LOCAL_MACHINE\Software\Microsoft\OLE.

2. Within this key, find a value called `EnableRemoteConnect`. By default, this is set to `N`; change it to `Y`. The meaning of this change, which affects not just WMI but the whole of DCOM, should be self-explanatory.
3. Within the same key, there is also a value called `EnableDCOM`. Ensure that this is also set to `Y`; on most systems, it will be.
4. Configure WMI security. This can be accomplished with wbemcntl.exe, a tool that fulfills the same purpose as the Windows 2000 MMC snap-in (see Chapter 5, "WMI Security"). This tool can be found in the %WINDIR%/system/wbem directory. Because Windows 95, 98, and Me do not have fully-fledged security subsystems, you can take two approaches to setting up WMI security. Start wbemcntl.exe, and follow one of the following procedures:

   - Assuming that users are set up on the machine in question or you have configured it to authenticate using a domain controller, permissions can be assigned to namespaces as described in Chapter 5. The difference is that because these platforms have no concept of groups, access must be assigned to users on an individual basis. To accomplish the configuration, open the Security property page in wbemcntl.exe, select the root\CIMv2 namespace, and add permissions for each user as required.
   - Alternatively, a less-secure approach that might be acceptable in some environments is to enable anonymous share-level access to WMI. As the phrase implies, this allows any user to connect to any WMI namespace without authentication. To enable this option, go to the Advanced property page in wbemctrl.exe and check the checkbox granting anonymous permission, as shown in Figure A.1.

5. The only other setting that must be configured before WMI can be used remotely on Windows 9x platforms concerns the startup behavior of winmgmt.exe. On Windows 2000 and Windows NT, winmgmt.exe runs as a service, and by default it starts in automatic mode each time the computer boots. If configured to run in manual mode, it starts whenever a local or remote machine attempts to connect to WMI. Achieving the same level of convenience on Windows 9x machines, however, requires explicit configuration. If you look again at the Advanced property page in wbemcntl.exe (see Figure A.1), you will see three startup options. To ensure that WMI is always running when you need it, select the `Always auto restart` option, which will start winmgmt.exe each time the computer boots. Two other start modes are available if you want them. In manual mode, WMI becomes operable only when winmgmt.exe is explicitly executed from the command line. Do not be seduced by the `Auto restart if Event Subsystem needs it` mode, whose purpose is to start WMI whenever a local program

attempts to access it. Due to DCOM limitations, winmgmt.exe will not start even if needed in response to a remote connection attempt!

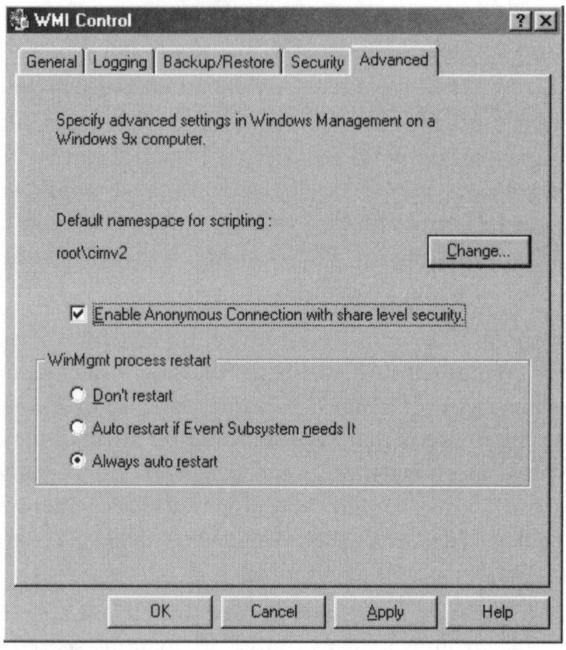

Figure A.1 *Setting WMI startup mode with wbemcntl.exe.*

6. After you have made your changes to the Registry and the security settings, you must restart the service (the service will be running if you have run the WMI control application) in order for these changes to take effect. The `/kill` command-line option for winmgmt.exe shuts down the service sensibly, allowing the process to write information to the log file winmgmt.log. As the name implies, this option kills the process but does not restart it. You have to do this manually.

Note: Versions of WMI Prior to 1.5

If your system has an early version of WMI, you might find that wbemcntl.exe looks slightly different from Figure A.1. Notably, the v1.1 program is a single dialog (without property pages) and has no facility to configure permissions. Instead, this task is carried out by a separate program, wbemperm.exe. Despite the visual differences, the same options are available. If you are running a version prior to WMI, however, we strongly recommend that you install an upgrade, because the later versions include several new features and some important bug fixes. ◆

Running WMI on Windows NT 4.0

On the surface, the installation process for Windows NT 4.0 is very similar to that for Windows *9x*. After it's installed, however, the WMI system and its behavior are much more akin to Windows 2000 than to the other platforms; this makes configuration considerably simpler and more convenient. After the initial installation and mandatory post-installation reboot, WMI is already configured to run as an automatically-starting service. Furthermore, because Windows NT 4.0 supports a sane notion of authentication, it supports remote connections and is set with default security settings that are adequate for most purposes.

For the most part, WMI security on Windows NT 4.0 works like its Windows 2000 equivalent. There is, however, one important difference between the two platforms: Whereas both support NTLM authentication, only Windows 2000 supports Kerberos. Although this does not impose serious limitations under most circumstances, it does have ramifications for any scripts that require DCOM delegation. Delegation requires Kerberos, so under Windows NT 4.0, it quite simply cannot work. If you are not sure why and where this matters, this limitation probably will not bother you too much. If you would like a reminder of a scripting situation in which delegation is essential, turn back to Chapter 6, "Logs and Reports."

Caveats and Crevices

Although WMI can be installed and basically made to work on all Microsoft platforms, attempts to use it in earnest on platforms other than Windows 2000 and Windows NT 4.0 very quickly encounter limitations. The problem is simple: WMI relies on the underlying functionality of the operating system. The Windows *9x* range of operating systems, Windows Me included, does not have nearly the functionality of Windows NT 4.0 or Windows 2000. For example, Windows *9x* platforms do not have Event Logs, services, or system performance monitors, so an attempt to control these things from a script will obviously fail. Another major limitation, as has been suggested already in this appendix, is that these platforms do not have the fully-fledged security system of a filesystem that has the capabilities of NTFS. Several WMI classes that represent these missing features do not appear at all except on Windows NT and Windows 2000; some of the classes that are available on all platforms lose part of their functionality, depending on the specific platform on which they are running.

The list of cross-platform differences is far too great for us to list here; it permeates a huge range of classes, and sometimes even specific properties and methods. If you intend to do any serious scripting in a mixed environment, we strongly recommend that you check platform requirements for each WMI class you use before implementing a solution. Differences are for the most part clearly documented in the WMI Software Development Kit documentation.

A final suggestion we would make for multiplatform system administrators is that life is a lot easier if you use Windows 2000 as a main control workstation from which remote scripts can be run. At least if the scripts are running on Windows 2000, you know that they are running in a reasonably stable, fully operational environment! Certainly, we strongly advise that you do not attempt to develop scripts on Windows *9x* platforms. If you do, you will very quickly come up against a major problem: Although WMI itself might be installed even on Windows 95 OSR2, the Software Development Kit, which includes all the useful tools such as the Object Browser, is available only on Windows NT 4.0 SP5 or greater. These tools also require Internet Explorer 5.0 to be installed.

B

Accessing WMI from Other Languages

This book has investigated WMI from a VBScript perspective. We chose this language because it is relatively easy to learn, an interpreter for it ships with Windows 2000 as standard under the auspices of the Windows Scripting Host, and there is a good chance that it will be reasonably familiar to you. Apart from the minority of discussions that specifically focused on using the VBScript language itself, the concepts and techniques covered in this book stand independent of any particular language. After all, the whole point of WMI is that it presents a unified interface to computer management that stands independent of any particular language or even platform.

This appendix, therefore, is devoted to a brief demonstration of how WMI objects can be accessed from three languages commonly used for scripting or building quick solutions. Specifically, it demonstrates the use of WMI from within JScript, Perl, and Visual Basic. The demonstration focuses on two short scripts that contain an example of connecting the WMI service on a machine, retrieving a collection of objects, iterating through that collection, reading a property, and responding to an event. We are emphatically *not* providing a tutorial on how to program in JScript, Perl, or VB, or even a full tutorial on programming WMI from these languages. Instead, the intention is to give anyone already familiar with one of these languages a quick start in writing WMI-savvy code.

The first example is a script that lists all the services installed on the local machine and states whether each of them is running. In VBScript, the code looks like this:

```
'services.vbs - list services and report whether
'or not they are running.
Option Explicit

Dim refWMI
```

```
Dim colServices
Dim refService

'connect to WMI and retrieve a collection of
'Win32_Service objects
Set refWMI = GetObject("winMgmts:")
Set colServices = refWMI.InstancesOf("Win32_Service")

'loop through collection and report whether each
'service is running
For Each refService In colServices
    If refService.Started Then
        WScript.Echo refService.Name & " is running"
    Else
        WScript.Echo refService.Name & " is not running"
    End If
Next
Set colServices = Nothing
Set refWMI = Nothing
```

As you can see, this code connects to the WMI service with a call to `GetObject()`, retrieves a collection of `Win32_Service` objects with an `InstancesOf()` method call, and then loops through each object, using the `Name` and `Started` properties of `Win32_Service` to supply its output.

The second example demonstrates the use of an event notification query to announce whenever the status of a service has changed. In VBScript, it looks like this:

```
'service-events.vbs - go ping within 10 seconds of a service
'starting or stopping
'run this script with wscript!
Option Explicit

Dim refWMI
Dim refSink
Dim strQuery

'connect to WMI and create a sink object
Set refWMI = GetObject("winMgmts:")
Set refSink = WScript.CreateObject("WBemScripting.SWbemSink","EVENTSINK_")

'execute an async notification query and block with a msgbox
strQuery = "SELECT * FROM __instancemodificationevent " & _
           "WITHIN 10 WHERE TargetInstance ISA 'Win32_Service'"
refWMI.ExecNotificationQueryAsync refSink, strQuery
WScript.Echo "Now blocked and waiting..."

'cancel event notification
refSink.Cancel
Set refSink = Nothing
Set refWMI = Nothing
```

```
'callback for Event Notification
Sub EVENTSINK_OnObjectReady(refEvent,refContext)
    If refEvent.TargetInstance.Started Then
      WScript.Echo refEvent.TargetInstance.Name  & " has started"
    Else
      WScript.Echo refEvent.TargetInstance.Name & " has stopped"
    End If
End Sub
```

The script starts by connecting to WMI and creating an `SWbemSink` object, for which the `EVENTSINK_ObjectRead()` subroutine is implemented. It then uses `ExecNotificationQueryAsync()` to post an event query and uses the `WScript.Echo()` trick to prevent premature script termination. In order for this trick to work, the code must be run with wscript.exe rather than cscript.exe. (See Chapter 8, "Proactive Troubleshooting with WMI Events.")

Translating into JScript

If you account for the fact that JScript as a language looks rather different from VBScript, an attempt to translate the two examples into JScript for execution within the Windows Scripting Host yields code that is largely identical. JScript has excellent COM support and has a built-in `GetObject()` function that works in the same way as its VBScript counterpart. The most noticeable difference concerns collections: JScript does not have a language equivalent of the VBScript `for...next` loop, so WMI collections need to be wrapped in JScript Enumerator objects in order for their elements to be accessed. This is illustrated in the following JScript version of the earlier service-listing script:

```
/* services.js - list services and report whether
 * or not they are running. JScript translation of
 * the first VBScript script.
 */
var refWMI;
var colServices;
var refService;

//connect to WMI and retrieve a collection of
//WMI Services objects, wrapped in an Enumerator
refWMI = GetObject("winMgmts:");
colServices = new Enumerator(
    refWMI.InstancesOf("Win32_Service")
);

//enumerate objects and report whether each
//service is running
for (;!colServices.atEnd();colServices.moveNext()){
    refService = colServices.item();
    WScript.Echo(refService.Name + " is "
       + (refService.Started ? "not ":"")
```

```
            + "running"
        );
    }

    colServices = null;
    refWMI = null;
```

Note the similarity of layout and program flow between this version and the VBScript version. Apart from the collection, which is painlessly wrapped in a standard JScript Enumeration, the only difference in flow is the lack of a conditional execution block inside the collection loop. Thanks to the elegance of JScript's ternary operator, you have no need for its cumbersome presence!

A translation of the second script also yields something strikingly similar to the original. Given that the callback mechanism is handled by WScript's event handling capabilities, responding to WMI events in JScript is as trivial as in VBScript:

```
/* service-events.js - go ping within 10 seconds of
 * a service starting or stopping
 */

var refWMI;
var refSink;
var strQuery;

//connect to WMI and create a sink object
refWMI = GetObject("winMgmts:");
refSink = WScript.CreateObject("WBemScripting.SWbemSink","EVENTSINK_");

//execute an async notification query and block with a msgbox
strQuery = "SELECT * FROM __instancemodificationevent " +
           "WITHIN 10 WHERE TargetInstance ISA 'Win32_Service'"
refWMI.ExecNotificationQueryAsync(refSink, strQuery);
WScript.Echo("Now blocked and waiting...");

//cancel event notification
refSink.Cancel();
refSink = null;
refWMI = null;

//callback for Event Notification
function EVENTSINK_OnObjectReady(refEvent,refContext)
{
    WScript.Echo(refEvent.TargetInstance.Name
        + " has "
        + (refEvent.TargetInstance.Started ? "started" : "stopped")
    );
}
```

Like its VBScript counterpart, this script works only if it's executed with wscript.exe, because it uses the `WScript.Echo()` trick to prevent the script from terminating before any events have been received.

As should be abundantly clear from these examples, translating any of the VBScript code presented in this book would be a trivial task. COM support in the two languages is very well matched.

Translating into Perl

Although Microsoft's evident support for VBScript and JScript mean that Perl might not be quite as prevalent in the world of Windows 2000 as it was under NT 4.0, the language remains a powerful scripting tool, and it certainly deserves a mention here! If you are a Perl aficionado, you will be delighted to hear that the language allows you to access COM objects through the `Win32::OLE` module that ships as standard with ActiveState's Perl distributions. This module provides a `GetObject()` function, the equivalent of a `CreateObject()`, elegant collection handling, and even support for event handling. A translation of our original VBScript, the service-listing script, looks something like this:

```
#services.pl - list services and report whether
#or not they are running
use Win32::OLE;

#connect to WMI and retrieve a collection of
#WMI Services objects
my $refWMI = Win32::OLE->GetObject("winMgmts:");
my $colServices = $refWMI->InstancesOf("Win32_Service");

#loop through collection using Win32::OLE's in
#function and report whether each service is running
foreach $refService(in $colServices){
      print $refService->{Name}
            . " is "
            . ($refService->{Started} ? "not " : "")
            . "running\n";
}

undef $colServices;
undef $refWMI;
```

Note that you can get a reference to WMI trivially using `Win32::OLE->GetObject()` and then call any of the `SWBemServices` methods using the standard Perl semantics. The most notable feature of this Perl translation is the wonderfully elegant collection provision that `Win32::OLE` provides for looping through the elements of a collection. The thing that looks like an `in` keyword is in fact a function within the `Win32::OLE` package that returns all elements of a COM collection object as an array. Thanks to this function, you can loop using the standard Perl `foreach` syntax.

The second script is slightly more complex, because the `Win32::OLE` module's support for event handling cannot match the simplicity of its VBScript and JScript counterparts. Also, the documentation stresses that support for event handling should be considered alpha code. You have been warned! Writing code to respond to WMI events is a three-stage process. First, you create `SWBemSink` using the `Win32::OLE->new()` method. Next, you register this sink as an event provider using `Win32::OLE->WithEvents()`, which takes as parameters your newly created object reference and a reference to a callback function. Finally, you write the callback function. Unlike the VBScript and JScript examples, the same callback is used regardless of the `SWBemSink` method that WMI invokes. In other words, there is no specific `OnObjectReady()` function. This is not a problem, however, because the callback function is passed a reference to the object that has raised the event and the name of the method being called as parameters. The `Win32::OLE` manual does provide a method of invoking different callbacks depending on the specific event being raised, but we find this unnecessarily cumbersome and do not use it here.

Before presenting the script, we should comment on one other small difficulty: Perl does not normally have a message loop, so unless you do something to remedy this, no events will ever be delivered to your script. Luckily, the difficult part is handled for you by `Win32::OLE` through its `spinMessageLoop()` function. Having set yourself up as an event consumer, you continually call this function until a key on the keyboard is pressed.

One final thing to note is that the `use` directive for `Win32::OLE` here quotes `EVENTS`; this is required to tell the module to use the single-threaded apartment, the only threading model under which its event support works at the moment. If you don't understand what single-threaded apartment means, don't worry; just trust us—use the directive! Herewith is the script:

```
# service-events.pl - go ping within 10 seconds of
# a service starting or stopping

#declare use of OLE module and init console
use Win32::OLE qw(EVENTS);
use Win32::Console;

my $console = Win32::Console->new(STD_INPUT_HANDLE);

#connect to WMI and create a sink object
my $refWMI = Win32::OLE->GetObject("winMgmts:");
my $refSink = Win32::OLE->new ('WBemScripting.SWbemSink');

#register $refSink as an event provider
Win32::OLE->WithEvents($refSink,\&eventCallback);
```

```
#execute an async notification query and block with a msgbox
my $strQuery = "SELECT * FROM __instancemodificationevent "
            . "WITHIN 10 WHERE TargetInstance ISA 'Win32_Service'";
$refWMI->ExecNotificationQueryAsync($refSink, $strQuery);

#spin message loop
print "Waiting for events...\n";
my $continueLooping = 1;
while ($continueLooping){
    #if a key has been pressed, quit
    if ($console->GetEvents() != 0){
        my @cons = $console->Input();
        if ($cons[1] != 0){
            undef $continueLooping;
        }
    }
    Win32::OLE->SpinMessageLoop();
    Win32::Sleep(500);
}

#cancel event notification
$refSink->Cancel();
Win32::OLE->WithEvents($refSink);
undef $refSink;
undef $refWMI;
undef $console;
print "Finished.\n";

# callback forEvent Notification
#note we are not discriminating between the various
#IWbemObjectSink methods here
sub eventCallback()
{
    my ($refSource,$refEventName,$refEvent,$refContext) = @_;
    if ($refEventName eq "OnObjectReady") {
        print $refEvent->TargetInstance->{Name}
            . " has "
            . ($refEvent->TargetInstance->{Started}
            ? "started" : "stopped")
            . "\n";
        }
}
```

It can hardly be denied that this is significantly more verbose and complex than the VBScript or JScript version, but that is the price of excellent regular-expression support and the other marvels of Perl! It should be noted that we have been slightly unfair here, because there is an easier way. ActiveState's Perl distribution can now run Perl from within the Windows Scripting Host. In this context, the WScript object is made available in a global `$WScript` variable. This means that event handling can be accomplished using an invocation such as this:

```
$WScript->CreateObject($refSink,"EVENTSINK_")
```

and then writing the appropriate callbacks. The reasons why we decided not to illustrate this technique are twofold. First, if you take this approach, WScript effectively handles all the difficult bits; you can work out how to accomplish it yourself by examining the JScript example. Second, and more importantly, if you are a Perl programmer, you might find yourself wanting to run scripts independently of the Windows Scripting Host; we felt that we should show you how this is done.

If you intend to write serious WMI scripts in Perl, we strongly recommend that you read the `Win32::OLE` documentation very carefully. Have fun!

Translating into Visual Basic

Visual Basic is not exactly a scripting language, but if you ever find yourself craving graphical front ends for your scripts or if you want to write a more substantial WMI application, it is a very useful tool. Hence, we thought it deserved a mention here. You will probably not be at all surprised to hear that accessing WMI from Visual Basic is very similar to accessing it from VBScript. Converting a VBScript application into a Visual Basic application can involve as little as adding some type information and writing the user interface.

So what type do various WMI objects have? (In other words, when the object variables are declared, what should they be declared *as?*) It will probably not surprise you to learn that VB itself neither knows nor can find out anything about, say, `Win32_ComputerSystem` objects. Instead, as you have probably guessed from reading Chapter 11, "WMI Internals," all such objects are instead declared as `SWBemObject`. This typing allows properties and methods to be accessed either via the `Properties_` property and `ExecMethod_()` method or directly thanks to the magic of COM. Following this pattern, collections should be declared as `SWBemObjectSet`, the WMI service itself as a `SWBemServices`, and so on.

The following program, then, is a translation of the service listing script. It prints its output to the Debug window to save you from having to make any assumptions about the forms you might or might not have defined in a project. Note that it is practically identical to the VBScript script except for the typing and the fact that the whole thing is wrapped in `Sub Main()`. One small point to note if you intend to try out this program or do any WMI development in Visual Basic is that you should make sure that your project references the Microsoft WMI Scripting library. Otherwise, the environment will know nothing about `SWBemObjects` or any of their friends.

```
'services.bas - list services and report whether
'or not they are running.
Option Explicit
```

```
Sub Main()
      Dim refWMI As SWBemServices
      Dim colServices As SWbemObjectSet
      Dim refService As SWbemObject

      'connect to WMI and retrieve a collection of
      'Win32_Service objects
      Set refWMI = GetObject("winMgmts:")
      Set colServices = refWMI.InstancesOf("Win32_Service")

      'loop through collection and report whether each
      'service is running
      For Each refService In colServices
        If refService.Started Then
          Debug.Print refService.Name & " is running"
        Else
          Debug.Print refService.Name & " is not running"
        End If
      Next
      Set colServices = Nothing
      Set refWMI = Nothing
End Sub
```

The second VBScript script, responding to changes in a service's status, also lends itself well to Visual Basic conversion. The only difference here (apart from the types, of course) is that events are handled slightly differently to fit in with the standard Visual Basic event model. Significantly, they can only be handled within a form. Assuming that this requirement is met, all that is required is for an event source to be declared as such at a form level (that is, using the `WithEvents` keyword outside of a sub or function), for it to be created, and for an event handler sub to be written. Of course, you also have to inform WMI of your wish to receive events of a certain kind, but the procedure for doing this does not vary between languages, as should now be clear. Creation of an `SWBemSink` object to act as the event source does not, of course, require a `CreateObject()` function, because Visual Basic understands the concept of COM object creation natively; it is accomplished with the keyword `new`.

The code listing for the form is presented next. This code assumes that it is attached to a form containing a label called `lblOutput` and a button called `btnStop`. `btnStop` provides a mechanism for stopping the program after gracefully canceling the event registration.

```
'service-events.frm - go ping within 10 seconds of a service
'starting or stopping
'This code listing assumes that you have created a form with
'a label called lblOutput and a button called btnStop
Option Explicit

Dim WithEvents refSink As SWbemSink
```

```
Private Sub Form_Load()
      Dim strQuery
      Dim refWMI As SWBemServices
      'connect to WMI and create a sink object
      Set refWMI = GetObject("winMgmts:")
      Set refSink = New SWbemSink

      'execute an async notification query and block with a msgbox
      strQuery = "SELECT * FROM __instancemodificationevent " & _
           "WITHIN 10 WHERE TargetInstance ISA 'Win32_Service'"
      refWMI.ExecNotificationQueryAsync refSink, strQuery

      'deference WMI
      Set refWMI = Nothing
End Sub

'callback for Event Notification
Private Sub refSink_OnObjectReady( _
          ByVal refEvent As WbemScripting.ISWbemObject, _
          ByVal refContext As WbemScripting.ISWbemNamedValueSet)
      If refEvent.TargetInstance.Started Then
            lblOutput.Caption = refEvent.TargetInstance.Name & " has started"
      Else
            lblOutput.Caption = refEvent.TargetInstance.Name & " has stopped"
      End If
End Sub

'
Private Sub btnStop_Click()
      refSink.Cancel
      Set refSink = Nothing
      End
End Sub
```

And that really is all there is to it.

Tip: Graphical COM Components

If you intend to use VB to write WMI-based programs, you might be interested to know that Microsoft has written a number of graphical components that can be used in your project. They are all documented in the WMI SDK. Sadly, discussion of them is beyond the scope of this appendix. ◆

A Note About C/C++

It goes without saying that WMI can be accessed from C and C++. In fact, some WMI facilities cannot reasonably be accessed *except* through these languages. Unfortunately, however, a translation of these script examples into C++ and the accompanying explanation would quintuple the size of this appendix. If you are a C/C++ programmer, however, we offer you these few notes. First, WMI is a COM-based technology, so it is accessed using standard COM techniques. Each of the `SWbem` scripting components mentioned in this book has a standard COM equivalent. Their names are for the most part obvious, such as `IWbemServices`, `IWbemObjectSink`, `IWbemObjectSet`, and so on. Slightly counterintuitively if you are used to the scripting interface, WMI objects themselves present an `IWbemClassObject` interface. Properties and methods can be accessed indirectly using, for example, the `Properties_` and `ExecMethod_` members of `IWbemClassObject`. Alternatively, you can always pretend to be a Microsoft scripting language and use `IDispatch` for "direct" access! A few utility classes help with building object paths and manipulating strings, but in general, our advice to C or C++ programmers is simple: Make sure you really understand COM, and then read the SDK documentation. Most of the useful WMI documentation uses C++ for its examples, so there is no shortage of help there.

Index

Symbols

A

B

C

D

E

H

I

J-K-L

M

N

O

Q-R

S

T

U-V

W-X-Y-Z

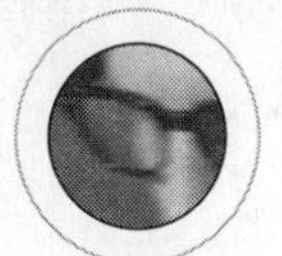

HOW TO CONTACT US

VISIT OUR WEB SITE

WWW.NEWRIDERS.COM

On our web site, you'll find information about our other books, authors, tables of contents, and book errata. You will also find information about book registration and how to purchase our books, both domestically and internationally.

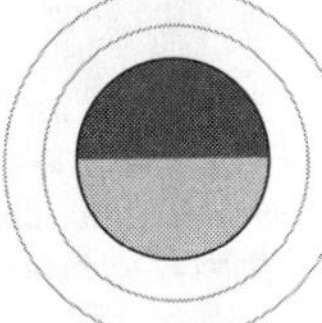

EMAIL US

Contact us at: **nrfeedback@newriders.com**

- If you have comments or questions about this book
- To report errors that you have found in this book
- If you have a book proposal to submit or are interested in writing for New Riders
- If you are an expert in a computer topic or technology and are interested in being a technical editor who reviews manuscripts for technical accuracy

Contact us at: **nreducation@newriders.com**

- If you are an instructor from an educational institution who wants to preview New Riders books for classroom use. Email should include your name, title, school, department, address, phone number, office days/hours, text in use, and enrollment, along with your request for desk/examination copies and/or additional information.

Contact us at: **nrmedia@newriders.com**

- If you are a member of the media who is interested in reviewing copies of New Riders books. Send your name, mailing address, and email address, along with the name of the publication or web site you work for.

BULK PURCHASES/CORPORATE SALES

If you are interested in buying 10 or more copies of a title or want to set up an account for your company to purchase directly from the publisher at a substantial discount, contact us at 800-382-3419 or email your contact information to `corpsales@pearsontechgroup.com`. A sales representative will contact you with more information.

WRITE TO US

New Riders Publishing
201 W. 103rd St.
Indianapolis, IN 46290-1097

CALL/FAX US

Toll-free (800) 571-5840
If outside U.S. (317) 581-3500
Ask for New Riders
FAX: (317) 581-4663

WWW.NEWRIDERS.COM

VOICES THAT MATTER

RELATED NEW RIDERS TITLES

ISBN: 1562059297
1450 pages
US $49.99

Inside Windows 2000 Server

William Boswell

"*I can't believe how many great books these people publish.* Inside Windows 2000 *is an extremely thorough reference for anyone deploying or supporting Windows 2000. Don't try to read it cover to cover. It is much too exhaustive for that. It is my primary reference for Windows 2000 issues.*"

—An online reviewer

ISBN: 1578700477
380 pages
US $32.00

Windows NT Shell Scripting

Tim Hill

A complete reference for Windows NT scripting, this book guides you through a high-level introduction to the shell language itself and the shell commands that are useful for controlling or managing different components of a network.

ISBN: 1578701392
448 pages
US $35.00

Windows Script Host

Tim Hill

"*This book is an excellent reference and tutorial on WSH and VBScript. It seems to be somewhat geared toward system administrators, but any Windows user seeking to utilize WSH would benefit from this book. I was pleased with the thorough coverage of VBScript. Since I could find no other book on the subject, this was a gold mine to me.*"

—An online reviewer

ISBN: 1578702194
700 pages
US $45.00

Windows NT/2000 ADSI Scripting for System Administration

Thomas Eck

Active Directory Scripting Interfaces (ADSI) allow administrators to automate administrative tasks across their Windows networks. This title fills a gap in the current ADSI documentation by including coverage of its interaction with LDAP and provides administrators with proven code samples that they can adopt to effectively configure and manage user accounts and other time-consuming tasks.

Colophon

The year is 1935; the place is Bangkok city, Siam. It is Tuesday morning at 10 a.m. The sun swelters in the sky, the city goes about its business quietly; in fact, everything signifies peaceful normality. Yet, somehow you know that this is going to be a really bad day. As a senior civil servant with the municipal authorities, your task over the coming months is to instigate an audit of all metal cooking utensils on sale in the city. The question you are attempting to answer is—did the construction of the railroad seven years ago exhaust the local supply of high quality iron?—a daunting task. You and your colleagues will have to traverse the city, find every utensil salesman (see picture), buy a sample utensil and bring it to the lab for analysis.

This scenario might seem a far cry from the high-tech world of computing in the 21st century but, in reality, it is not as far as you might think. Imagine now that you are a systems administrator responsible for a large Windows 2000-based network; your task is to perform an audit of all your machines, checking (and perhaps altering) driver configurations. This could be every bit as daunting as the iron audit: you have to go round to every single machine, log in, check its drivers... Alternatively, you could let WMI take care of the task for you, something that would not have been possible in 1935! So our imaginary scene in Bangkok, just like the photo on the cover of the book, has absolute relevance even here in a book about Windows Management Instrumentation...

—Matthew Lavy

The book was laid out in QuarkXpress. The fonts used for the body text are Bembo and MCP Digital. It was printed on 50# Husky Offset Vellum paper at VonHoffman Graphics in Owensville, Missouri. Prepress consisted of PostScript computer-to-plate technology (filmless process). The cover was printed at Moore Langen Printing in Terre Haute, Indiana on Husky Offset Vellum, coated on one side.